# CULTURE WARS

*Culture Wars* investigates the relationship between the media and politics in Britain today. It focusses on how significant sections of the national press have represented and distorted the policies of the Labour Party, and particularly its left, from the Thatcher era up to and including Ed Miliband's and Jeremy Corbyn's leaderships.

Revised and updated, including five brand new chapters, this second edition shows how press hostility to the left, particularly newspaper coverage of its policies on race, gender and sexuality, has morphed into a more generalised campaign against 'political correctness', the 'liberal elite' and the so-called 'enemies of the people'. Combining fine-grained case studies with authoritative overviews of recent British political and media history, *Culture Wars* demonstrates how much of the press have routinely attacked Labour and, in so doing, have abused their political power, distorted public debate, and negatively impacted the news agendas of public service broadcasters. The book also raises the intriguing question of whether the rise of social media, and the success of its initial exploitation by Corbyn supporters, followed by Labour as a whole in the 2017 General Election, represent a major shift in the balance of power between Labour and the media, and in particular the right-wing press.

*Culture Wars* will be of considerable interest to students and researchers in the fields of media, politics and contemporary British history, and will also attract those with a more general interest in current affairs in the UK.

**James Curran** is Professor of Communications at Goldsmiths, University of London, UK. He is the author or editor of over twenty books about the media, including (with Jean Seaton) *Power Without Responsibility*, 8th edition (2018).

**Ivor Gaber** is Professor of Political Journalism at the University of Sussex, UK. He has published widely in the field of political communications and is a former producer and programme editor for BBC TV and Radio, ITV News, Channel Four and Sky News.

**Julian Petley** is Professor of Journalism at Brunel University London, UK. He is the editor of *Media and Public Shaming* (2013), a member of the editorial board of the *British Journalism Review* and is a principal editor of the *Journal of British Cinema and Television*.

# PRAISE FOR FIRST EDITION

'Admirable book', *Times Higher*

'Deftly illustrates how the audience can be influenced on some occasions and not others', *Guardian*

'Useful and accessible text for teaching about media power and influence', *Journalism*

'The strength ... of the book as a whole lies in the way it highlights, in an easily digestible fashion, the complex and two-way relationship between politics and the media', *Media, Culture and Society*

'An excellent history and analysis', *Free Press*

# PRAISE FOR SECOND EDITION

'I read this book with mounting enthusiasm as it documented and analysed the roller coaster journey of what in the 1980s was ridiculed and repressed as the "Loony Left", with its roots in the counter-culture of the 1960s, through the defeats of the Blair era to its "resurrection from the undead" in the leadership of Corbyn and McDonnell.

Careful and revealing in its empirical analysis, *Culture Wars* provides an original and convincing perspective from which to understand the media's changing relation to Labour politics, including the new Labour leadership's ability to establish its own rapport with a new generation of voters.'

*Hilary Wainwright, Co-editor of* Red Pepper

'We may be living through a media revolution but this brilliantly forensic book shows that one constant factor still applies – the relentless anti-Labour bias in most newspapers and their continuing influence. *Culture Wars* is a must-read for all those seeking to make sense of UK politics. Indeed, it is impossible to make sense of what is happening and what has happened without reading it.'

*Steve Richards, Political columnist and broadcaster*

'This outstanding new edition of the classic text *Culture Wars* revisits and analyses the complex relationships between the media, journalism and politics in the UK. The authors' focus is on press (mis)representations of the Labour left in the context of radical changes in the Labour leadership, the diminished influence of print media and the growth of social media and fake news. They address provocative and significant questions concerning the shifting influence of politicians, citizens and media in public debates about gender, sexuality, race and environmental policy in an age of digital journalism and media.

James Curran, Ivor Gaber and Julian Petley's eloquent, authoritative and for-ward-looking *Culture Wars* is essential reading for everyone interested in the signifi-cant role of news journalism in democracies.'

*Bob Franklin, Foundation Chair in Journalism Studies*
*at the University of Cardiff*

'To understand the left of the Labour Party is, today, essential to understanding the future of contemporary British politics. This book shines a really valuable light on one of the culture wars now raging in Britain.'

*Tony Travers, Professor in the Department of Government,*
*London School of Economics*

'It is not only generals who fight the next war as if it was the last. The British media, and especially its national press, is unable to escape its past as it eviscerates history. This is why the new edition of *Culture Wars* is not just important and gripping – it is essential reading as its authors start to account for the renewed strengths of the left in the UK, whose tap-roots they examine with unique authority.'

*Anthony Barnett, founder of* openDemocracy

# COMMUNICATION AND SOCIETY

## Series Editor: James Curran

This series encompasses the broad field of media and cultural studies. Its main concerns are the media and the public sphere: on whether the media empower or fail to empower popular forces in society; media organisations and public policy; the political and social consequences of media campaigns; and the role of media entertainment, ranging from potboilers and the human-interest story to rock music and TV sport.

For a complete list of titles in this series, please see: https://www.routledge.com/series/SE0130

**Africa's Media Image in the 21st Century**
From the 'Heart of Darkness' to 'Africa Rising'
*Edited by Mel Bunce, Suzanne Franks and Chris Paterson*

**Comparing Political Journalism**
*Edited by Claes de Vreese, Frank Esser, and David Nicolas Hopmann*

**Media Ownership and Agenda Control**
The Hidden Limits of the Information Age
*Justin Schlosberg*

**An Introduction to Political Communication, Sixth edition**
*Brian McNair*

**Misunderstanding News Audiences**
Seven Myths of the Social Media Era
*Eiri Elvestad and Angela Phillips*

**Culture Wars, Second edition**
The Media and the British Left
*James Curran, Ivor Gaber and Julian Petley*

# CULTURE WARS

## The Media and the British Left

Second edition

*James Curran, Ivor Gaber and Julian Petley*

Routledge
Taylor & Francis Group

LONDON AND NEW YORK

First published 2019
by Routledge
2 Park Square, Milton Park, Abingdon, Oxon OX14 4RN

and by Routledge
711 Third Avenue, New York, NY 10017

*Routledge is an imprint of the Taylor & Francis Group, an informa business*

*British Library Cataloguing-in-Publication Data*
A catalogue record for this book is available from the British Library

*Library of Congress Cataloging-in-Publication Data*
Names: Curran, James, author. | Gaber, Ivor. | Petley, Julian.
Title: Culture wars: the media and the left in Britain/James Curran, Ivor Gaber and Julian Petley.
Description: Second edition. | Abingdon, Oxon; New York, NY: Routledge, 2018. | Series: Communication and society | Includes bibliographical references and index.
Identifiers: LCCN 2018010457| ISBN 9781138223028 (hardback: alk. paper) | ISBN 9781138223035 (pbk.: alk. paper) | ISBN 9781315406183 (ebook: alk. paper)
Subjects: LCSH: Social change–Great Britain–History. | Political culture–Great Britain–History. | Social values–Great Britain–History. | Conflict of generations–Political aspects–Great Britain. | Mass media–Political aspects–Great Britain. | New Left–Great Britain–History. | New Left–Press coverage–Great Britain. | Right and left (Political science)
Classification: LCC HN385.5 .C86 2018 | DDC 306.0941–dc23
LC record available at https://lccn.loc.gov/2018010457

ISBN: 978-1-138-22302-8 (hbk)
ISBN: 978-1-138-22303-5 (pbk)
ISBN: 978-1-315-40618-3 (ebk)

Typeset in Bembo
by Deanta Global Publishing Services, Chennai, India

Printed and bound in Great Britain by
TJ International Ltd, Padstow, Cornwall

# CONTENTS

# FIGURES

# TABLES

# 1

# INTRODUCTION

## Resurrection of the undead

*James Curran*

Labour's current triumvirate – Leader Jeremy Corbyn, Shadow Chancellor of the Exchequer John McDonnell and Shadow Home Secretary Diane Abbott – were leading members of the 'loony left', the pejorative label deployed by the popular press to delegitimise the 1980s new urban left.[1] Jeremy Corbyn was a councillor on 'loony' Haringey Council before becoming a Labour MP in 1983. Diane Abbott was a press officer at the 'loony' Greater London Council (GLC), and then head of PR at the 'loony' Lambeth Council, before being elected to Parliament in 1987. John McDonnell was Deputy Leader of the GLC, and later Head of the Policy Unit at 'loony' Camden Council, before being elected an MP in 1997.

In a more general sense, Labour's triumvirate also have a shared pedigree. They are baby boomers: they were born between 1949 and 1953. They all represent London constituencies. Above all, they are representative of the main constitutive strands of the 1980s new urban left. Jeremy Corbyn belongs to its mainstream: informally dressed, iconoclastic, with a long record of involvement in peace, anti-racist, environmental and human rights politics. Diane Abbott is a pioneer of Labour's black section, a key component of the new urban left, who became the first black woman to be elected to parliament. John McDonnell – who once had a vocation for the priesthood[2] and is usually formally dressed – and has tended to focus on economic and class issues. But he was strongly influenced by 1980s social radicalism, and is representative of the old left of his generation who were recruited into the ranks of London's new municipal left.

The municipal left gained prominence for a brief time during the 1980s. However, it was demonised by the tabloid press, disowned by Labour's leadership, shunned by much of the Labour movement and replaced by the 'managerialist left' on local councils. It had a brief renaissance when Ken Livingstone, former leader of the GLC (1981–6), became Mayor of London (2000–8). But he was defeated by the Conservative populist, Boris Johnson, and subsequently fell into disfavour.

Corbyn, McDonnell and Abbott were marginalised in Parliament as members of an insignificant awkward squad. While Diane Abbott had a short-lived career as an opposition spokeswoman,[3] Corbyn and McDonnell remained backbenchers. All three were judged by many of their colleagues (and lobby correspondents) to be 1970s dinosaurs: people who had not adjusted to a changed world, and who had failed to make their mark in Parliament.

The 'loony left' – the people who were at the centre of the first edition of this book – thus seemed set to become minor footnotes in the history of a terminally defeated left. That is, until 2015, when Jeremy Corbyn, a backbencher for over thirty years, was elected Leader of the Labour Party. This resurrection of the political undead makes the study of their ideas, and of the political soil they spring from, of renewed interest.

## Generational outriders

Corbyn's election as Labour Leader was viewed by most of the media-political class as a tsunami coming from nowhere. When he was re-elected in 2016 with an increased majority, many journalists were dumbfounded. Eighty per cent of Labour MPs had previously passed a motion of no confidence in him. Britain's only two pro-Labour dailies had both called for his resignation.[4] The received elite wisdom, after his re-election, remained that Corbyn was 'unelectable' on a national stage, a view that perhaps encouraged Theresa May to call a snap election. *Guardian* columnist, Jonathan Freedland, declared that Theresa May's election gamble was 'about the surest bet any politician could ever place',[5] while the *Sun* (19 April 2017) predicted that 'PM's Snap Poll Will Kill Off Labour'.

The political rise of Corbyn and his close allies is now widely attributed to a backlash against neo-liberalism. Their rejection of austerity politics, and their insistence that the state should have an activist role in creating jobs, fostering greater equality and promoting security, appealed to many with precarious work, stagnant wages, soaring rents and, in some cases, enormous student debt. But this only captures one aspect of their politics, and the reasons for their rise.

Jeremy Corbyn and his 'loony' allies were social radicals who were the outriders of generational cultural change. Although their views provoked derision in 1980s tabloids, these views gained much greater acceptance in the subsequent period. Support for feminism, gay rights, environmentalism and anti-racism became part of mainstream opinion among young people, even if it still repelled some among the older generation. Corbyn and his allies were in touch with the changing currents of feeling in the wider population. Losers in the culture war of the 1980s, the 'loony left' were ultimately the victors.

This overall assessment was a central theme of the first edition, published in 2005. It needs to be updated and revised in the light of subsequent developments, not simply in the success of Corbyn and his allies, but because the social radical tradition of which they are a part made further cultural gains in the period after 2005 (notably in relation to sexuality, gender relations and attitudes towards the environment). But this tradition also lost ground in relation to race, and was confronted by resurgent social conservatism in the 2016 European Union referendum.

## Battle for the soul of the Labour Party

A sustained press campaign against the 'loony left' in the 1980s rendered the Labour left electorally toxic in the country (if not in London). New Labour was constructed as a successful electoral brand in the 1990s based in part on the reassuring claim that it had slayed the dragons of the hard and loony left. A virulent press campaign against the left assisted Labour's centre-right coalition to consolidate their control over the party, and eventually make a successful electoral pitch to the country.

But the Labour Party is now led by the left, and dire warnings about the left's un-electability were called into question by Labour's relative success in the 2017 general election. One element of this change (though how much has changed remains to be seen) is, as already mentioned, both a revolt against the politics of neo-liberalism and a shift towards social liberalism among young people.

Another is a reduction in the power of the press. The ancient bazookas of the tabloid press were trained on Corbyn, McDonnell and Abbot during the 2017 general election campaign, portraying them as 'APOLOGISTS FOR TERROR'[6] and fantasists forever shaking a magic money tree. But this relentless bombardment failed to prevent a Corbyn-led Labour Party from winning 3.5 million more votes (compared with the 2015 general election), and making a major breakthrough among younger people. The role of the press that loomed large in the first edition has diminished in the era of the internet.

So, the rationale for this new edition is that the new urban left of the 1980s – once seemingly eclipsed and irrelevant – warrants closer attention because it now leads the Labour Party. The new urban left was an outrider of cultural change in the political realm, but in a way that needs to be re-examined. The part played by the press in the internal affairs and political direction of the Labour Party has also changed. This, too, needs to be looked at afresh.

This second edition has had to be kept at roughly the same length as the first. So, old content has been deleted or compressed (sometimes through rewriting) in order to make way for the new. Inevitably, revisiting old content has generated temptations difficult to resist. The chapter on the left and sexuality in the 1980s has been substantially rewritten in order to focus more closely on the active role of the right-wing press in promoting repressive legislation, whilst the focus of the chapter on 'loony' myths has been broadened in order to show how such stories exemplify a more general process of myth-making in the press. However, most of the new material – including five new chapters – relates primarily to the more recent period.

## Notes

1 The new urban left is sometimes referred to in the academic literature as the new municipal left or, more simply, the urban left.
2 As he commented to the author (9 December 2017): 'Coming from a Liverpool Irish family, there had to be at least one priest in the family somewhere!'
3 She was appointed by Ed Miliband to an opposition shadow post in 2010 and sacked in 2013.
4 J. Schlosberg, 'Should he stay or should he go? Television and online news coverage of the Labour Party in crisis', Media Reform Coalition, p. 4, available at: www.media-reform.org.uk/wp-content/uploads/2016/07/Corbynresearch.pdfmedia (accessed in June 20, 2017).
5 Cited in A. Nunns, *The Candidate*, 2nd edition (London: OR Books, 2018), p. 2.
6 *Daily Mail* 7 June 2017.

# 2

# RISE OF THE 'LOONY LEFT'

*James Curran*

To understand the political significance of the new urban left, it is necessary first to grasp the depth of the Labour Party's crisis in the early 1980s. Even before Margaret Thatcher's first general election in 1979, perceptive commentators warned that the new right were connecting to dynamic social currents in British society, whereas Labour was locked into a downward spiral of decline.[1] Labour's core constituency of manual workers was shrinking. Growing individualism and market consumerism posed a threat to collectivist politics. Resentment against state bureaucracy allegedly weakened support for the welfare state. Above all, it was argued, the liberal corporatist system of government – the way that Britain had been run for the last forty years – no longer worked. Governments experienced growing difficulty in delivering full employment, while business and labour were increasingly unwilling to participate in a social contract brokered by the state. The crisis-ridden record of the Wilson/Callaghan government (1974–9) – its IMF bailout, public spending cuts, rising inflation and growing industrial conflict – seemed to indicate that social democracy delivered through corporatist conciliation had run its course.

If the currents of change were seemingly flowing against Labour, the party greatly added to its problems by tearing itself apart. After the 1979 election defeat, activists pressed for greater grassroots influence on the grounds that they had been let down by their right-wing leaders. The response of one part of the Labour right (and centre) was to form in 1981 the breakaway Social Democratic Party, which merged with the Liberal Party in 1988. This had the effect of splitting the progressive vote, and deepening Labour's woes. In the 1983 general election, Labour's share of the vote dropped to 28%, its lowest since 1918.[2]

In an atmosphere of growing crisis and demoralisation, a new social movement within the party led mainly by youngish people proposed themselves as saviours. From their local council base, they were resisting, they claimed, the ravages of Thatcherism in a more effective way than Labour MPs. They were doing politics in a new way by involving people in decision-making. And they were building a new social coalition of support through progressive politics that connected to a society that had become less class-centred and more fragmented. This siren call grabbed the attention of people looking for a new political road-map, a new way out of Labour's crisis. 'And Now for the Good News' was how the new urban left was hailed in a New Socialist anthology of essays.[3] 'Renewal is under way, and the GLC [Greater London Council] is very much part of it', concurred *Marxism Today*.[4]

However, the new urban left was viewed with suspicion by traditionalists on both Labour's right and left. The traditionalist left, in particular, viewed the new urban left as middle class 'trendies' preoccupied with issues that were a diversion from class politics. Thus, David Blunkett, the young firebrand leader of Sheffield Council, objected to the new urban left's feminism on the grounds that it made an unhelpful distinction between the interests of working men and women, and threatened to 'sap the energy of the class struggle'.[5] Similarly, leading figures on Liverpool Council – then dominated by the Trotskyist Militant Tendency – complained that the new urban left's positive action policies, designed to assist disadvantaged ethnic minorities, were setting workers against workers.[6]

What was the urban left doing to provoke such antagonism but also, in some quarters, optimism and hope? And why was London the cockpit of a municipal experiment in contrast to the staid world of local government in many other parts of the country?

## Product of transition

The urban left in London gained increased influence partly in response to rapid economic change. Between 1964 and 1974, Greater London lost 40% of its man-ufacturing jobs.[7] In the subsequent period 1973–83, manufacturing jobs in the capital again almost halved.[8] This was offset by a rapid growth of the service sector, which gave rise to an increase in the proportion of left-leaning, middle-class members within the London Labour Party. Their increasing influence was reinforced by a critical grassroots response to the rightward drift of the Wilson/Callaghan government (1974–9). In 1977, the left gained control of the London Labour Party Executive – a victory that symbolised an historic shift in the met-ropolitan Labour Party long dominated by the centre-right.[9]

The changing social composition of the London Labour Party also had a direct impact on local government. From the late 1960s onwards, a growing number of middle-class people moved into poverty-stricken inner-city areas, attracted by their central location and cheap housing. In some cases, they joined inactive branches of local Labour parties, with small memberships, and rapidly acquired positions of influence.[10] Many of these confident, new recruits – in areas like Islington, Camden, Southwark and Lambeth – set out to make councils more effective agencies of change by extending their role in the local community.

By contrast, areas untouched by gentrification, such as Barking, tended to stand aloof from local socialist experiment throughout the 1980s.

If one key influence shaping the London Labour Party was a change in its social composition, a second formative influence was the rise of the women's movement. The shift from industrial production to the service sector resulted in a growing proportion of married women gaining full-time paid employment, especially in the period after 1970. Increasing economic independence was reinforced by the 'second wave' of feminism. London became the forcing ground for change. It was where the historic Women's Liberation Workshop was founded in 1968, followed by the launch of *Spare Rib* in 1972, the Virago publishing house in 1973 and the National Women's Aid Federation in 1975. While some feminists settled for creating women-only enclaves of mutual support, others sought to change society through a more interventionist approach. Both approaches were adopted by Labour feminists who transformed a number of almost moribund women's sections, traditionally concerned with social events and fund-raising, into feminist caucuses.[11] These maintained a steady broadside of criticism against the male domination of contemporary politics in which women accounted for only twenty-eight out of 650 MPs in 1983,[12] and only 22% of London councillors in 1986.[13] Labour feminism exerted strong pressure on radical councils to change, and become more women-friendly.

A third influence reshaping the London Labour Party in the 1980s was immigration. A large number of migrants, from the West Indies, India and Pakistan, arrived in London in the 1950s and early 1960s. The rate of immigration declined in the next two decades, following the restrictive 1962 Commonwealth Act, and still more restrictive legislation in 1968, 1971 and 1981. Even so, enough immigrants settled in London to change significantly its ethnic mix. By 1981, one in five people living in inner London, and one in ten in outer London, were of Asian or Afro-Caribbean descent.[14]

However, it took some time before immigration affected left politics. The first generation of Afro-Caribbean and Asian migrants (like their Irish and Jewish predecessors) tended to keep their heads down, partly in order to avoid trouble in a city where racism was both widespread and open. Their communities were still fragmented in the 1950s by allegiances to their places of origin, sometimes reinforced by different religious affiliations. Many immigrant newspapers in Britain reported extensively during this period on what was happening in the countries where their readers came from.[15] However, the second generation was more integrated into the wider community, and less willing to put up with racial prejudice. During the late 1960s and 1970s, Londoners of Afro-Caribbean descent developed in particular a more unified subculture, radicalised by the American civil rights campaign, black pride movement and the bruising contradictions of a complex, 'refused' British identity.[16] Out of this grew a new mood of militancy, especially during the 1980s when rising unemployment affected disproportionately ethnic minority groups. Anger erupted into major riots in south London (Brixton) in 1981, and in north

London (Broadwater Farm) in 1985. This increased militancy, combined with black lobbying inside the Labour party and the mushrooming of ethnic minority organisations, led to a belated political adjustment. Black representation in London town halls doubled in 1982, rising to seventy-seven black councillors (4% of the total).[17] By 1987, three black councillors – Bernie Grant, Linda Bellos and Merle Amory – led London local authorities.

The emergence of ethnic minority protest coincided with the rise of gay liberation. Successive generations of gay men had kept a low profile during the period when it was a criminal offence for them to make love in private. When gay sex over twenty-one was legalised in 1967, it was widely held that tolerance was conditional upon discretion. This attitude often concealed latent hostility, and could give rise to casual, violent assaults on gay men who were judged to be flaunting their sexuality. This combination of prejudice and intimidation was challenged by a group of gays and lesbians in London who set up the Gay Liberation Front in 1970. Its three main objectives were to assert the validity of homosexuality ('Gay is Good'), to be open ('Coming Out') and to organise for reform and mutual support.[18]

London became the main centre of this more combative approach, and acquired a network of organised gay groups, telephone help-lines, community services, gay theatre, cinema, newspapers and journals. The gay liberation movement also set out to influence public attitudes, cultivating successfully the word 'gay' in place of the then oppressive label 'queer'.[19] In the more liberal climate of the 1970s, gays and lesbians came to be portrayed more sympathetically on television, at least in comparison to the past.[20]

With a new sense of confidence, gay campaigners demanded freedom from discrimination in employment, and called upon progressive councils to join them in openly fighting sexual prejudice. A section of the gay community thus engaged in a new kind of public politics very different from the cautious lobbying for reform of the pre-1967 era.

In short, the late 1970s and early 1980s marked a time when a number of groups who were discriminated against or marginalised entered politics with growing effectiveness. The Labour Party in the capital was in process of transition, responding to economic change and the social recomposition of its membership. The coming together of these different influences produced a new kind of local politics.

Something rather similar happened in Manchester, and elsewhere, in the mid-1980s[21] in response to a broadly comparable conjunction of influences. But the London-centred national press focused on the new urban left in the capital, and this was consequently where public attention was directed. Indeed, left-wing London councils were regularly in the national news throughout the period 1981–7. They were the cynosure for a new politics, the context where public and internal party reactions to anti-racist, feminist and 'pro-gay' policies would be put to the test.

## Product of a generation

If the radical politics of the London left was partly a response to a change in the political environment, it also expressed the values and concerns of a new political generation. Many of the leading figures of the new urban left in London during the early 1980s were in their thirties or, at most, early forties. This was most noticeably the case in relation to the left's flagship authorities, the Greater London Council (GLC) and Inner London Education Authority (ILEA). Its leading figures, such as Ken Livingstone, Frances Morrell, Tony Banks, John McDonnell, Michael Ward and John Carr, all gained their majority in the 1960s. Many of the people they appointed to influential policy and advisory positions – such as Reg Race, Hilary Wainwright and Sheila Rowbotham – belonged to the same age cohort. The cultural revolution of the 1960s (extending into the early 1970s) provided the formative political experience of this group.

The great political and social causes of the left during the 1960s were peace (Vietnam War), anti-racism (US civil rights movement), personal freedom and, to a lesser degree, feminism and environmentalism. It was also a time of cultural experiment, in which deference to authority and class power was explicitly repudiated in music, fashion, film and literature. Infusing this new cultural politics were also values that fitted uneasily within the left tradition: growing individualism and distrust of the state.[22] Youth cultures of the 1960s shaped the politics of the new urban left. It predisposed them to respond sympathetically to the rise of ethnic minority, gay and feminist lobbies. It also encouraged them to attempt to manage local government in a non-hierarchical way that involved local people. Out of the 1960s' revolt grew the urban radicalism of the 1980s.

Thus, one common thread linking the concerns of 1960s' protest and 1980s' municipal politics was anti-racism. Growing concern about racism gave rise to pioneer anti-racist legislation in 1965 and 1968, which was strongly supported by the young left (some of whom attacked their parents' assumption of racial superiority inherited from the days of empire). The new urban left were heavily involved in the Anti-Nazi League, a broad left movement founded in 1977 that successfully campaigned against the advance of the far-right National Front. By deploying a new style of campaigning that involved spectacle, pop music, celebrity and agitprop, people mostly in their twenties and thirties set about persuading teenagers that racism was uncool – with striking success.

Some people involved in the Anti-Nazi League also turned their attention to municipal politics in the late 1970s. In particular, a group of Labour activists in Lambeth argued that anti-racism should entail more than confronting the overt racism of the far right. There was a problem in Labour's own backyard, they argued, which the standard left rhetoric of 'we are committed to colour-blind socialism' and 'there is no race problem here', failed to acknowledge. While about 30% of the Lambeth population consisted of people from ethnic minorities (mostly Afro-Caribbean), there were in 1974 no black Lambeth councillors and senior officers, and only a small minority of black staff in the council workforce. Activists' vocal criticism resulted in Lambeth Council establishing in 1978 an ethnic minorities' working party. This became the forerunner of the ethnic minorities unit established in the GLC in 1982, and similar bodies, in nine radical councils in London, created between 1978 and 1986.[23]

Their creation led to more members of ethnic minorities being employed in local government. A number of radical London councils initiated ethnic monitoring of their workforce, partly as a way of demonstrating the need for change. They established or strengthened equal opportunities procedures that made appointments open and fair, and took positive steps to increase ethnic minority employment by, for example, including advertisements in ethnic minority publications. Some councils introduced race training to discourage subtle forms of racial discrimination (sometimes in an aggressive form that could be counterproductive). The Greater London Council (GLC) also carried a 'positive action' approach one stage further by adopting the 'contract compliance' strategy used to combat anti-Catholic employment practices in Northern Ireland. The GLC refused to buy any product or service from a private company that did not adhere to equal opportunities procedures.

Left-wing councils in London, and elsewhere, adopted other measures to aid ethnic minorities. Some modified the rules governing council house allocations in response to growing awareness that, for a variety of reasons, ethnic minorities had by far the worst council accommodation. Information about council services was translated into the relevant foreign languages, in areas where there was a large number of Asian migrants with imperfect English. Pressure was also exerted on the police to take racial harassment more seriously in places where 'Paki-bashing' was a recurring problem. Ethnic minority organisations (including the black arts movement that flourished under GLC patronage) were funded partly in order to assist the expression of ethnic minority concerns.

In addition, members of ethnic minorities were co-opted on to council bodies in order to increase their influence on council policy. A conscious policy was pursued of promoting multiculturalism in schools: through the recruitment of more ethnic minority teachers and governors, and through additions to the curriculum that connected pupils to ethnic minority cultures and histories. The GLC also sought to promote a positive view of London as a multiethnic, multicultural, cosmopolitan city through free concerts, festivals and public events, in which different types of music were played, different kinds of ethnic cuisine were often available, GLC sideshows conveyed appropriate messages and above all the large crowds drawn from different ethnic and social groups in London embodied the plural, inclusive understanding of community that the council was seeking to foster.[24]

In short, the new urban left set out to offset the disadvantages of ethnic minorities in terms of jobs, housing, education and social esteem, and to support their collective organisation and political inclusion. While these policies were the natural culmination of radical sixties anti-racism, the municipal championship of women occurred in a more pressured way. The 1960s and early 1970s had modified gendered behaviour and attitudes among young people, in subtle ways that were reflected in contemporary films, magazines and fashion.[25] Young Labour activists were especially disposed to recognise – at least in principle – that arrangements between men and women were in general unfair and needed changing. This made young male councillors distinctly uncomfortable when they were subjected to a barrage of questions from feminist party members. Why did so many housing estates lack adequate play areas, lighting and security? Why did the council have no crèche facilities? Why was daycare for children so inadequate throughout the capital? The answer, councillors were told, was because they were overwhelmingly men with little insight into the practical needs of women. In this, they were no different from the senior council officers and leaders of community organisations they regularly dealt with. Women, it was argued, were the main consumers of council services, yet they were not part of the decision-making process.[26]

Feminist pressure led Lewisham Council to pioneer in 1979 a women's rights working party. This became the model for the women's committee established at the GLC in 1982, and for similar committees or units introduced in eleven London councils between 1981 and 1987.[27] These became channels through which women's groups in the community exerted influence on local government policy. Their main effect was to redirect expenditure in support of a large expansion of day-care provision for the under-fives in London during the 1980s. They also helped to funnel money into a variety of women's projects, facilities, groups and training schemes. More generally, they led to improved equal opportunity procedures, staff training (to assist women up the ladder), and provision for maternity and paternity leave. Feminist criticism also contributed to the adoption of a more user-oriented approach, in which during the mid- and later 1980s[28] a number of left-wing authorities in London commissioned surveys into what people wanted.

The London left's championing of lesbians and gays also had its roots in the 1960s' cultural revolution. The 1960s were a time when large numbers of young people were drawn towards youth subcultures that celebrated freedom from social conformity, and affirmed the importance of individual self-realisation and human empathy. This shift was part of a more general process of liberalisation, registered in shifting attitudes towards sex, illegitimacy, divorce, marriage and homosexuality that gave rise to a series of landmark legal reforms during the 1960s.[29] The urban left's support for gays and lesbians was merely a continuation of this trend, though in a form that was new to mainstream politics. When Ken Livingstone, in his third month as leader of the GLC, spoke at a Harrow Gay Unity meeting, and said that men had both male and female characteristics in their make-up, there was a collective raising of eyebrows in Fleet Street.[30] It was a break from convention for a heterosexual politician to attend a gay liberation meeting at all, let alone speak in this unguarded fashion. It signalled the arrival of 1960s' cultural values in the traditionalist sphere of local government.

The GLC set up a gay working party, and took active steps to oppose prejudice against gays and lesbians at County Hall. It also gave grants to gay liberation organisations, and became identified by association with a public campaign to normalise homosexuality. This last step went beyond the standard liberal position of opposing job discrimination, and entailed actively combatting homophobia.

Where the GLC charged in, some other left-wing authorities held back. Local Labour politicians could not fail to be aware of the extent of antipathy to gay men, especially at the time of the AIDS panic. In 1987, three out of four people in Britain said that homosexual relationships were 'always' or 'mostly' wrong.[31] Even old-style liberals, like Noel Annan (the first full-time Vice-Chancellor of London University), felt uneasy about the new phenomenon of gay liberation. 'Who were these hard-left creatures', he wondered, 'in dungarees, trumpeting Time Out values, sporting pink triangles and glowering instead of camping?'[32]

In this hostile climate, the Inner London Education Authority promoted supportive counselling of gay teenagers and acted against the victimisation of gay teachers, but stopped short of publicly campaigning against anti-gay prejudice in schools. Other councils moved discreetly, opposing discrimination against gays and lesbians in council jobs and housing, while being careful not to draw attention to their work through the setting up of gay and lesbian committees. The one major exception to this caution was Haringey Council, which initiated a 'positive images' campaign in schools that opposed homophobia by asserting the moral equivalence of gay and straight lifestyles. The campaign was eventually abandoned in response to press and public protest.[33]

The 1960s influenced radical municipal politics in another way. It was a time when irreverence and distrust of authority found expression in ground-breaking television political satire, a youth-led fashion for long hair and casual clothes and the 'power to the people' rhetoric of radical student politics. This tradition lived on in the town-hall politics of the 1980s. Young, left-wing councillors often came casually dressed to public meetings, in contrast to their older colleagues, and most contemporary Labour MPs and trade union officials. They shocked their elders by the 'individualistic' way they were ready to vote against the party line in council meetings. Radical councillors in the 1980s also developed a critique of bureaucratic power which echoed the arguments of 1960s radicalism. It had become the convention, they argued, for councils – whether under Labour or Conservative control – to be run by council leaders and their cronies in conjunction with the 'officer corps' of council officials. This concentration of power sidelined ordinary councillors, and excluded the public. It needed to be replaced by a more open and inclusive process of decision-making.

The sixties generation were strong believers in do-it-yourself politics. In the 1960s and early 1970s, there had been a great mushrooming of radical civil society groups – organisations like Amnesty International, Shelter, Crisis, Child Poverty Action Group, Help the Aged, the Disablement Action Group and the Playgroups Association. This belief in the virtues of organised action outside the bureaucratic structures of the state lived on, and gave rise to the new urban left's sponsorship of local participation in the 1980s. Left-wing councils introduced specialist committees, serviced by staff often recruited from the voluntary sector. These committees co-opted community activists and instituted processes of ongoing public consultation. Above all, left-wing councils gave grants to activist groups so that they could become more effective agencies representing the local community.

This approach was epitomised by the GLC's extensive patronage of the community sector. For example, County Hall funded local groups so that they could formulate plans for urban development, and challenge those advanced by commercial developers. In the case of the widely reported Coin Street project, the GLC blocked the developer's plans, bought the vacant land and involved the tenants' organisation in supervising what became a successful, much-lauded residential development in a prime London site.

Similarly, the GLC also funded some workers' groups to formulate plans for the restructuring of their companies, invested in their development and placed worker representatives on the board of directors.[34] Borough-wide groups were also given the resources to monitor the police as a way of influencing how the police operated in their local communities. In addition, the alternative arts movement was also funded by the GLC partly because the arts were viewed as an important way in which disadvantaged groups could cohere, express in imaginative ways their concerns and communicate these to a wider public.

Promoting community groups laid the municipal left open to the charge of crony politics, while the incorporation of community activists into the structure of local authority decision-making proved to be much more difficult, and also rancorous, than the new urban left had anticipated. However, these experiments came out of the idealistic, anti-statist, radical populism of the 1960s. Other threads of radical sixties culture are also discernible in the fabric of 1980s local socialism. The defining issue of radical politics in the 1960s – opposition to the Vietnam War – seemed far removed from the concerns of local government. However, this radical legacy prompted GLC councillors to assume the mantle of peace campaigners. They nominated 1983 as 'peace year', and publicised the devastation that would result from a nuclear attack on the capital. They also engaged in a public dialogue with Sinn Fein during a period when IRA bombs were being detonated in London. A political solution, they argued, had to replace a policy of attempting to suppress insurgents through force.

Another concern of sixties' radical culture was the environment. It found expression in a desire to lead a simple life, free of capitalist pressures and consumerist superficiality – a yearning that had a long history in British culture.[35] It also took a politicised form of growing anxiety about the negative effects of noise, pollution, traffic congestion, urban sprawl, the erosion of energy resources and the destruction of wildlife, giving rise to the founding of Friends of the Earth in 1970 and Greenpeace in 1971. This radical inheritance was central to the GLC's programme, which arrested the decline of public transport use in the capital by subsidising transport fares, and imposed greater restrictions on private motorists.

This legacy was resurrected when the Greater London Authority, under Ken Livingstone's leadership, introduced in 2003 controversial congestion charges on private motorists driving into central London.

Thus, the politics of the new urban left – its anti-racism, defence of gays, feminism, environmentalism, concern with peace and distrust of bureaucracy – reflected the formative influences of the 1960s. The urban left's rise also represented the emergence of a new political generation – the sixties generation – in the foothills of power. The alternative magazine, Frendz, had consoled itself in the dying days of 'sixties' culture (1972) with the thought that 'if flower power has gone to seed then germination must soon begin. And what King Weeds they'll be'.[36] These 'King Weeds' first made their appearance in mainstream politics during the early 1980s, between the grand colonnades of London's town halls.

Yet, the youngish men and women who took control of County Hall, and elsewhere, were all 'politicos'. This made them almost by definition aberrant products of the 1960s, partly disconnected from its hedonism. They were also conditioned by membership of the Labour party, which had a collectivist ethos embodied by the trade union movement (with special rights of representation and great prestige within the party). Leading members of the new urban left (including key figures like Ken Livingstone and Tony Banks) could deploy at times rather traditional, left rhetoric in grassroots publications like London Labour Briefing and Labour Herald. They also made common cause for a time with older, soberly dressed members of the far left like Ted Knight, leader of Lambeth Council. The London left was always a coalition made up of different elements.

That the GLC belonged, in some ways, to a traditional mould is demonstrated by its spending commitments. One of its top priorities became the growing number of Londoners who were made redundant as a consequence of de-industrialisation. It set up the Greater London Training Board (the word Manpower in the original title was hastily dropped) to enable workers to acquire new skills. In a major new departure, it also established the Greater London Enterprise Board (GLEB), and allocated to it £60 million over three years, in a bid to regenerate the local economy.[37] Originally, a major concern of GLEB was to promote innovative forms of ownership (in particular co-operatives); encourage worker representation in the companies that it backed; bring into being socially useful work, and foster through the provision of expertise and financial assistance the planned growth of specific sectors of the London economy. However, the urgent need to save desperately needed jobs in an economic downturn came to dominate the work of the organisation. GLEB became a lender of last resort to failing companies, sometimes in response to pressure from trade unions attempting to avert imminent redundancies. That GLEB sometimes 'fell captive to bad managements',[38] leading to a relatively high failure rate, brought into sharp relief the 'old Labour' presence that lurked inside the new urban left. Its commitment to job creation through direct investment in the local economy was of course a standard social democratic policy. This increasingly eclipsed GLEB's more innovative goals of promoting economic democracy and creating socially useful work.

In short, the urban left experiment came about as a consequence of the conjunction of new social movements and a new political generation conditioned by 1960s' values. This took place inside a political party, with a strong ideological tradition and union presence, operating within a parliamentary system. What resulted was significantly different from the fragmentary identity politics that took shape in the United States, during roughly the same period in response to similar cultural changes to those in Britain.[39]

The new urban left's strategic approach was also more traditional than it was sometimes represented to be. Critics argued that the new urban left was solely intent on creating a 'rainbow coalition' represented by ethnic minorities, gays, feminists and greens, and that this was doomed to failure because these minorities did not add up to a majority. But, in fact, the new urban left sought merely to extend Labour's core base of the organised, white working class, not to replace it. Radical councillors fought elections: their approach was often guided more by 'Reading pads' for knocking up supporters than critical social theory.

## Clash of ideologies

The municipal left were big spenders. This put them on a collision course with the Thatcher government, elected in 1979, one of whose principal objectives was to reverse the rise of public spending. The new government argued that public profligacy had fuelled inflation, 'crowded out' private investment and fostered a 'dependency culture' that undermined individual self-reliance. Labour's allegedly wasteful ways had also given rise to punitive rates of tax that discouraged enterprise and initiative. Soaring public spending and punitive taxation were, in the official view, a major cause of Britain's relative economic decline. It was something that the government was determined to rectify.

However, the Thatcher government quickly discovered that this was easier said than done. Rising levels of unemployment in the early 1980s led to an unavoidable increase in expenditure on social security. The central administration also found that it had very little control over the rising spending of local government, the main dispenser of public services. The worst 'culprits' were left-wing authorities in London. In 1983 the GLC and IlEA accounted for 40% of local government 'overspend'.[40] To reduce public expenditure, the government had to find a way of reining in these local authorities.

Fuelling this conflict over the appropriate level of public spending was disagreement about what local councils should do. The urban left believed that local government should regenerate the local economy, foster a progressive sense of community, combat prejudice, improve public services and transfer resources from the rich to the poor. It wanted, in other words, to expand what councils sought to achieve. By contrast, the government wanted to limit councils to managing the cost-efficient delivery of essential services. In particular, the radical right within the government favoured the outsourcing of services to private enterprise. The Conservative Environment Minister, Nicholas Ridley, hoped that eventually local councils would only meet once a year to allocate contracts to private providers.[41]

Underlying this clash was a conflict of political philosophies. The new urban left was broadly collectivist, whereas the government was increasingly wedded to free-market individualism. Although this divergence reflected profound political differences, it was also a response to differences of economic interest. Labour drew its support disproportionately from the working class, the Conservatives disproportionately from the middle class (despite making inroads into Labour's heartland support).[42] The implications of this became all too apparent in 1990 when the graduated council rate based on property values was replaced by a flat-rate, community charge (popularly known as the poll tax) on each adult resident. A key argument advanced by ministers for this reform was that it would bring more low-income groups within the local tax net, and encourage them to vote for prudent council administrations. The days of profligate, redistributive councils voted in by rate-exempt, 'dependent' citizens would be over. Critics objected that the poll tax made the millionaire pay the same amount as the shop assistant. What this angry debate made explicit, in other words, was class-based differences about who should pay and who should benefit that sometimes lurked behind differences over the role and organisation of local government.

The Thatcher administration sought to establish central government control over local government in a more direct way than had been attempted before. This meant repudiating the convention – then more often invoked by the right than the left – that the autonomy of local councils should be preserved as a check on central government (and 'elective dictatorship'). The new urban left responded by seeking to mobilise public support in defence of local democracy and the maintenance of local services. Both sides appealed to the public through the media in a historic battle over how the governmental relationship between the centre and the locality should be structured.

This was bound up with a broader debate about the reform of local government. The new urban left and new right were both critics of local government, as it was then constituted. The left's critique of local council 'paternalism' led it to explore new ways of involving and empowering the public. By contrast, the new right's diagnosis of local government ills was more damning, and its prescription more far-reaching. It argued that local councils were 'monopolistic' providers of services that put the interests of bureaucracy and staff unions before those of the public, and were consequently costly and inefficient. It also maintained that councils under left-wing control were not fully accountable in local communities dominated by Labour.[43] Therefore, their operation had to be restructured through privatisation, competitive tendering, local tax reform and central financial controls.

Both sides were trying in different ways to 'improve' local government. This led to a running battle over the level of public spending, the role and autonomy of local government and the organisation and management of local public services. How this conflict was reported, and how the public responded, was to influence the development of municipal politics and local government for a long time to come.

## Generational war

However, the battle between the urban left and new right was not simply an extension of the clash between collectivism and neoliberalism, and of the class-based constituencies these two traditions represented, to the area of local government. What gave this clash an added bitterness was that it was caught up in a war between generations. In 1985, the elders in the government, such as the Prime Minister (Margaret Thatcher), Deputy Prime Minister (William Whitelaw) and Education Minister (Sir Keith Joseph), were in their sixties. The coming men of the radical right, like Norman Tebbit and Cecil Parkinson, were in their fifties. So, too, were all five Environment Ministers between 1979 and 1989 (Heseltine, King, Jenkin, Baker and Ridley) with the partial exception of Heseltine in the early part of his watch. The overwhelming majority of the 1983 cabinet reached their majority in the 1940s and 1950s.[44]

The leading personalities of the mid-1980s government had grown up at a time when Britain ruled an empire; young men were taught discipline through national service in the armed forces; patriarchal values were entrenched; gay sex was criminalised; and much of the media were subject to strict moral regulation. The new generation that came of age in the 1960s partly turned its back on this legacy – its shared values, cherished memories, sense of hierarchy and stifling conformism. This had provoked a cultural clash between generations. Many in the older generation resented what they saw as the rejection of their values, and the withholding of respect. They had deferred to their parents, and not been accorded the same deal by their children's generation. Indeed, the youth culture of the 1960s very publicly and pointedly satirised the notion that age brought wisdom through accumulated experience.[45]

In the early 1980s, a section of the older generation struck back. It argued that the sixties cultural revolt had undermined authority and promoted indiscipline, selfishness and anti-social behaviour. This attack was led not by disgruntled letter-writers from Cheltenham, but by the democratically elected leadership of the country.[46] Their assault was both explicit and eloquent. Thus, Rhodes Boyson, a fifty-seven-year-old Conservative politician (and former head teacher) proclaimed in 1982: 'the permissive age, which blossomed in the late 1960s ... has created a pathless desert for many of our young people'. Sixties permissiveness, he continued, had fostered debased morals and false values, encouraged the break-up of stable families, and given rise to growing crime. 'Society', he warned, 'has reaped dragons' teeth' sown in the sick decade.[47] The same theme, and even the same imagery, was repeated by the Prime Minister, Margaret Thatcher, when she responded to a national debate about the causes of urban riots and the rise of 'black crime'. 'We are reaping what was sown in the 1960s', she warned, when 'the old virtues of discipline and self-restraint were denigrated'.[48] Her protégé, Norman Tebbit, then Trade and Industry Minister, reprised the same argument, with the same imagery, in a well-received public lecture. In the 1960s 'was sown the wind: and we are reaping the whirlwind'. The 'permissives' of the 1960s, he warned, had laid the foundation for 'today's violent society'.[49]

These jeremiads, delivered by middle-aged, right-wing politicians, were supported by the outpourings of middle-aged, right-wing journalists.[50] Thus, fifty-five-year-old George Gale proclaimed that Britain's riots in 1981 were caused by a 'revulsion of authority and discipline' that had taken place during the 'permissive revolution' of the 1960s.[51] Colin Welch, in the Spectator, also thought that the broadly defined 1960s generation had much to answer for. 'The decade of the 1960s (or perhaps more precisely '65–75)', warned Colin Welch, had 'injected poisons' into society that 'course still through its veins'. Indiscipline was rife because 'the revolting students of the 1960s' had become 'the revolting teachers of today'.[52] Christopher Booker, an ambivalent figure in the culture war,[53] reworked the same theme in a more apocalyptic mode for *Daily Mail* readers. 'The demons of drugs, pornography, violence and permissiveness in all its forms, are now raging out of control', unleashed, he argued, by the forces first set in motion during the 1960s.[54]

The 'sixties' became a code word in this generational backlash. It symbolised for some all the negative changes that had taken place in the recent past: the country's decline in the world, the rise of crime, the erosion of a sense of community, young people with more money than sense, the decline of courtesy and respect. Indeed, a growing legion of folk devils – black muggers, punk rockers, flying pickets, Irish terrorists, football hooligans, single parents, illiterate youngsters and 'race' rioters – came to be viewed as facets of a common problem: the loss of authority and erosion of tradition that had begun in the 1960s.[55] Some called for an all-encompassing solution – a return to the values of Victorian Britain, its social discipline and sense of order.

The indignation expressed by middle-aged ministers and journalists at the 'antics' of the new urban left in the early 1980s should be understood in the context of this generational conflict. Young politicians like 'Red Ken' were the unrepentant representatives of sixties culture. They promoted its values, advanced its political agendas, and even lavished taxpayers' money on organisations that perpetuated its transgressive legacy. These unreconstructed councillors were viewed as incorrigibles stuck in a time warp of the past, seemingly oblivious to the damage that they and their kind had wreaked and apparently determined to thwart the will of parliament. If the cancer of the 1960s was to be treated effectively, then chemotherapy had to be directed towards the infected cells of local government.

While this generational conflict drew upon manifold and sometimes unrelated discontents, it was in essence rooted in a genuine value conflict. This was especially the case in relation to the high-voltage issues of race/nation, homosexuality and gender.

In the late 1970s, ageing traditionalists recalled a time when there was a strong sense of national unity based on ethnic oneness, a shared culture and common heritage. They attributed the erosion of that world, in part, to mass immigration. John Biffen (a member of Thatcher's first cabinet) wrote bitterly in 1978 that 'the scale of immigration that has transformed the heartland of many English cities ... has not been willed by the British people'.[56] His concerns were spelt out by Margaret Thatcher in a pre-election interview:

> If we went on as we are, then by the end of the century there would be 4 million people of the New Commonwealth or Pakistan here. Now, that is an awful lot and I think it means people are really afraid that this country might be swamped by people with a different culture. And, you know, the British character has done so much for democracy, for law, and done so much throughout the world, that if there is a fear that it might be swamped, people are going to react and be rather hostile to those coming in.[57]

Margaret Thatcher spoke up for traditionalists fearful that their culture would be 'swamped' because she instinctively understood their fears, and was seeking their electoral support. With equal empathy, she understood the denting of pride which traditionalists of her generation experienced when Britain so hurriedly discarded its empire between 1947 and 1964. It was this elegiac feeling of loss and uncertainty that Thatcher addressed in her historic speech to a euphoric crowd of some 5,000 people celebrating the Falklands War victory:

> There were those who thought we could no longer do the great things which we once did. Those who believed that our decline was irreversible ... those [who feared] that Britain was no longer the nation that had built an Empire and ruled a quarter of the world. Well, they were wrong. The lesson of the Falklands is that Britain has not changed and that this nation still has those sterling qualities that shine through our history. This generation can match their fathers and grandfathers in ability, in courage and in resolution.[58]

The Falklands War confirmed to conservative commentators that Britain was still a force to be reckoned with, and that its bulldog spirit was undiminished. The victory had a powerful resonance because it entailed rescuing distant kith and kin from foreign despotism. 'If the Falkland islanders', wrote Peregrine Worsthorne in the *Sunday Telegraph*, 'were British citizens with black or brown skins, spoke with strange accents or worshipped different gods it is doubtful whether the Royal Navy and Marines would ... be fighting for their liberation'.[59]

The Thatcherite sense of community was that of a nation, bonded by its ethnic unity, proud heritage and resurgent confidence. It was an image of Britain as a recuperated country that had resumed its rightful place in the world. While this was only one part of a complex discourse,[60] it was informed by nostalgia and a backward-looking desire to restore what had been lost. It was thus at odds with the new urban left's attempt to come to terms with the past in a different way – by building a new sense of community. Thatcher's evocation of an organic nation, bounded by tradition, united by the Union Jack and secure in its

'British character', implicitly conflicted with the municipal left's desire to celebrate London's rich mixture of peoples and traditions, its cosmopolitanism and its identity as a global city.

The Thatcher government, and the forces it represented, also became locked into a confrontation with the new urban left over sexuality. The traditional right viewed homosexuality with visceral hostility. It entailed in their view unnatural acts, a view endorsed by conventional morality and Christian proscription. However, there was a liberal strand within traditional Conservatism that favoured 'live and let live' tolerance, and had supported the decriminalisation of sex between consenting adult males. These two strands of Conservatism came together in opposition to radical councils because both were affronted by the left's active support for gay liberation. This was harmful and dangerous, in their view, because it 'pretended' that homosexuality was a valid alternative, and was liable to confuse the young and impressionable. This merging of hardline and liberal strands of conservatism is perhaps best illustrated by the views of Max Hastings, a leading, one-nation, Conservative journalist (and, later, editor of the *Daily Telegraph*). In 1983, dining with his family at a Knightsbridge restaurant, he noticed that three men at a neighbouring table were wearing make-up. This galvanised him into putting his thoughts on paper in an impassioned article that had as its main target the new urban left. 'A powerful and influential section of opinion makers', he warned, has gone beyond 'seeking just sympathy for homosexuals in their misfortune, and now seeks to persuade us that homosexuality and heterosexuality are equally desirable states'. This is dangerous and misguided, he argued, because adolescents 'should be given every encouragement to choose heterosexuality' since 'it is obvious to any but the most absurd militant that the lives of homosexuals are frustrated and tormented, not because of outside persecution, but because of the very nature of their predicament'. Hastings concluded with a rhetorical flourish:

> When we lack the courage to declare this, when we allow ourselves to be intimidated by the threat of denunciation as 'reactionary', when we tolerate the granting of public money without protest to 'gay' groups in the sacred name of minority rights, then we shall have become not only a cowardly and hypocritical society, afraid to express the obvious, but also a truly decadent one.[61]

Battle lines over gender, by contrast, were not as clear cut as they were over sexuality. The urban left had chauvinist elements,[62] while the radical right in Britain was less centrally involved in the backlash against women's liberation than its counterpart in the United States.[63] This was partly because the leader of the new right in Britain, Margaret Thatcher, was a woman who had surmounted patriarchal attitudes in the Conservative Party to become the nation's first female prime minister. Yet, as Stuart Hall convincingly argues, the discourse of the British new right in the 1980s had as 'a continuous subterranean theme, the restoration of the family, the bulwark of respectable society and conventional sexualities with its fulcrum in the traditional roles for women'.[64] This was conveyed through attacks on single mothers, and through nostalgic references to Victorian values when women's place was recognised to be in the home. It was also mobilised through negative portrayals of feminism. Indeed, one of the ways in which the urban left was attacked was to portray it as the sponsor of 'loony' feminist follies such as 'judo mats for lesbians' in Islington.

However, the portrayal of the conflict between the new right and urban left as a generational war needs to be qualified. The radical right included anti-statist libertarians whose outlook was influenced by 1960s' values, while the urban left included authoritarian traditionalists. Both groupings were coalitions containing different elements. Moreover, while generations tended to differ in terms of their general orientation towards social issues, groups within each generation opposed the attitudes prevailing among their contemporaries. There were fogeyish young people, and ageing radical libertarians. This said, the clash between central and local government in the 1980s was in part a battle between middle-aged ministers whose world-view was formed by the immediate post-war period, and younger councillors who were products of the 1960s' cultural revolt. This cultural conflict was mainly over issues to do with race, gender, sexuality, tradition and authority. The bitterness it engendered stemmed from the fact that the two sides were set on a collision course. One side was seeking to turn the clock back and undo the harm that it felt had been wrought by a misguided generation; the other was intent on using town halls to promote progressive cultural change in their local communities.

## Retrospect

In brief, the battle between the new right government and the new urban left in the early 1980s was a confrontation between dynamic opposites. The new right was seeking to regenerate Britain through the fostering of an enterprise culture, while the new urban left was seeking to change local communities as a prelude to transforming society. The struggle that ensued between the Conservative government and radical town halls was one between opposed political philosophies and the different social constituencies these represented. It also became a contest about what local government should do, with both sides disagreeing fundamentally about its role and purpose. Above all, what imbued this struggle with added bitterness was that it was a clash over cultural values between two generations.

At this point, it is worth introducing the magisterial verdict of local government academics.[65] The new urban left, they argue, introduced some new policies that influenced subsequent local administrations. But the new urban left is also criticised for being prone 'in some instances to a degree of zealotry',[66] although this is an issue which, according to some,[67] is clouded by media mythology. More generally, new urban left councils are portrayed as attempting to do too much without adequate administrative experience or financial controls. They are also accused of failing to recognise conflicts of interest between council staff and trade unions ('producer groups') and users of council services. Above all, they are portrayed as failures. They were tamed by central government controls, and lost support within their own party. By 1990, the leaders of most left-wing councils were distinguished from their predecessors by 'the more modest nature of their political agenda'.[68]

The first limitation of this dismissive verdict – though it has some substance on its own terms – is that it is framed narrowly in terms of local public administration. Local government academics seem unaware that a culture war was being conducted between the new right and new urban left. This had its origins in the 1960s, and was to be played out over the next half-century with an unexpected outcome.

The second flaw in their verdict is that it was written shortly after the developments they describe. It was in effect a first draft of history with no knowledge of what was to come. Yet, the people who were so soundly defeated in the 1980s – and who were written off by local government specialists as architects of an interesting but failed experiment – supplied the future leadership of the Labour party. They turned out not to be career 'losers' after all.

## Notes

1 In a lecture delivered in 1978 (reprinted in M. Jacques and F. Mulherne (eds), *The Forward March of Labour Halted?* (London: Verso, 1981)), Eric Hobsbawm pointed to the long-term economic and social changes that seemed set to halt Labour's hundred-year rise. His warning was followed by Stuart Hall's celebrated essay, 'The great moving right show', (*Marxism Today*, January 1979), which highlighted both the failings of Labour's leadership and the populist appeal of the radical right. These two essays implicitly anticipated Labour's defeat in the 1979 general election, and strongly influenced the left's post-mortem. A good collection arising from this extended inquest is S. Hall and M. Jacques (eds.), *The Politics of Thatcherism* (London: Lawrence and Wishart, 1983).

2 D. Butler and G. Butler, *Twentieth-Century British Political Facts*, 8th edn. (Basingstoke: Macmillan, 2000), pp. 234–8.

3 D. Massey, L. Segal and H. Wainwright, 'And now for the good news' in J. Curran (ed.), *The Future of the Left* (Cambridge: Polity/New Socialist, 1984).

4 'Left alive: Labour and the people debate', *Marxism Today*, December 1984, p. 19: cf. B. Campbell and M. Jacques, 'Goodbye to the GLC', *Marxism Today*, April 1986.

5 'Interview with David Blunkett, Leader of Sheffield Council', in M. Boddy and C. Fudge (eds.), *Local Socialism?* (Basingstoke: Macmillan, 1984), pp. 254–5. Blunkett subsequently became a right-wing Labour politician (and Home Secretary).

6 H. Butcher, I. Law, R. Leach and M. Mullard, *Local Government and Thatcherism* (London: Routledge, 1990), pp. 123–4; cf. D. Hatton, *Inside Left* (London: Bloomsbury, 1988), p. 89.

7 R. Porter, *London: A Social History* (London: Hamish Hamilton, 1994), p. 346.

8 Porter, *London*, p. 347.

9 There was a shift to the left in the grassroots of the Labour Party in other parts of Britain during this period, partly for the reasons that applied in London. See P. Seyd, *The Rise and Fall of the Labour Left* (Basingstoke: Macmillan Education, 1987).

10 H. Wainwright, *Labour: A Tale of Two Parties* (London: Hogarth Press, 1987), pp. 20–1 illustrates this in relation to Newham.

11  S. Goss, *Local Labour and Local Government* (Edinburgh: Edinburgh University Press, 1989).
12  Butler and Butler, *British Political Facts*, pp. 238, 261.
13  S. Lansley, S. Goss and C. Wolmar, *Councils in Conflict* (Basingstoke: Macmillan, 1989), p. 144.
14  Porter, *London*, p. 354.
15  I. Benjamin, *The Black Press in Britain* (Stoke-on-Trent: Trentham Books, 1995); S. Quisrani, *Urdu Press in Britain* (Islamabad: Mashal, 1990); P. Martin, *Black Press, Britons and Immigrants* (Kingston, Jamaica: Vintage Communications, 1998).
16  P. Gilroy, *There Ain't No Black in the Union Jack* (London, Routledge, 2002); P. Fryer, *Staying Power* (London, Pluto, 1984); S. Humphries and J. Taylor, *The Making of Modern London, 1945–85* (London: Sidgwick and Jackson, 1986).
17  H. Butcher, I. Law, R. Leach and M. Mullard, *Local Government and Thatcherism* (London: Routledge,1990), p. 121.
18  J. Weeks, *Sex, Politics and Society* (Harlow: Longman, 2nd edn, 1989), p. 285.
19  Weeks, *Sex*, p. 286.
20  T. Sanderson, *Mediawatch* (London: Cassell, 1995).
21  Wainwright, *Labour*; M. Boddy and C. Fudge, 'Labour councils and new left alternatives', in M. Boddy and C. Fudge (eds), *Local Socialism?* (Basingstoke: Macmillan, 1984); J. Gyford, *The Politics of Local Socialism* (London: Unwin and Hyman, London, 1985).
22  S. Rowbotham, *Promise of a Dream* (London: Verso, 2001).
23  Lansley, Goss and Wolmar, *Councils*, p. 124.
24  F. Bianchini, 'Cultural Policy and Political Strategy: The British Labour Party's Approach to Cultural Policy with Particular Reference to the 1981–6 GLC Experiment', University of Manchester unpublished Ph.D. thesis, 1995.
25  C. Geraghty, 'Women and sixties British cinema: the development of the "Darling" girl', in R. Murphy (ed.), *The British Cinema Book* (London: British Film Institute, 1997); G. Murphy, 'Media influence on the socialization of teenage girls', in J. Curran, A. Smith and P. Wingate (eds), *Impacts and Influences* (London: Methuen, 1987); J. Winship, *Inside Women's Magazines* (London: Pandora, 1987), among others.
26  Goss, *Local Labour*; Lansley, Goss and Wolmar, *Councils*.
27  Lansley, Goss and Wolmar, *Councils*, pp. 144–5.
28  The principal organisation undertaking research for London borough councils during this period was MORI: copies of its reports are retained in its archives.
29  K. O. Morgan, *The People's Peace*, 2nd edn. (Oxford: Oxford University Press, 1999).
30  *London Evening Standard*, 18 August 1981; *Sun*, 19 August 1981; *Daily Express*, 19 August 1981.
31  L. Brook, 'The public's response to AIDS', in R. Jowell, S. Witherspoon and L. Brook (eds.) *British Social Attitudes: The 5th Report* (Aldershot: Gower, 1988), p. 73.
32  N. Annan, *Our Age* (London: Fontana, 1991), p. 205.
33  See Chapter 6.
34  M. Mackintosh and H. Wainwright, *A Taste of Power* (London: Verso, 1987).
35  R. Williams, *The Country and the City* (London: Chatto and Windus, 1973); J. Brewer, *The Pleasures of the Imagination* (London: HarperCollins, 1997); J. Richards, *Films and British National Identity* (Manchester: Manchester University Press, 1997).
36  Frendz (32, 1972) cited in E. Nelson, *The British Counter-Culture 1966–73* (New York: St. Martin's Press, 1989) p. 120.
37  Lansley, Goss and Wolmar, *Councils*, p. 84.
38  Mackintosh and Wainwright, *Taste of Power*, p. 430.
39  T. Gitlin, *The Twilight of Common Dreams* (New York: Henry Holt, 1995).
40  B. Pimlott and N. Rao, *Governing London* (Oxford: Oxford University Press, 2002), p. 38.
41  Lansley, Goss and Wolmar, *Councils*, p. 196.

42 A. Heath, R. Jowell, J. Curtice, G. Evans, J. Field and S. Witherspoon, *Understanding Political Change: The British Voter 1964–1987* (Oxford: Pergamon, 1991).

43 For a good critical exposition of Conservative arguments about local government, see J. Gyford, S. Leech and C. Game, *The Changing Politics of Local Government* (London: Unwin Hyman, 1989), especially Chapter 8.

44 Information about the composition of cabinets, and ages of ministers, has been derived from Butler and Butler (2000), pp. 38–47 and 84–133.

45 This was typified by 1960s films aimed at the youth market such as *A Hard Day's Night* (1964), *Help!* (1965), and *The Knack* (1965).

46 This draws upon D. Edgar, *The Second Time as Farce* (London: Lawrence and Wishart, 1988).

47 Cited in Edgar, *The Second Time as Farce* (1988), pp. 94–5.

48 The *Guardian*, 28 March 1982.

49 *Daily Mail*, 25 July 1985.

50 Journalists' ages are derived from D. Griffiths (ed.), *The Encyclopedia of the British Press* (London and Basingstoke: Macmillan, 1992).

51 *Daily Express*, 7 July 1981.

52 *Spectator*, 20 October 1983.

53 Booker had been involved in the development of political satire in the early 1960s, as a writer for the BBC television series *That Was the Week That Was* and the satirical magazine, *Private Eye*. But like many of these early 1960s pioneers, he became increasingly conservative. In 1983, he was aged forty-seven.

54 *Daily Mail*, 10 November 1983.

55 A. Gamble, *The Free Economy and the Strong State: The Politics of Thatcherism* (Basingstoke: Macmillan, 1988), pp. 197–8. Key contributions to this general argument are provided by S. Hall, C. Critcher, T. Jefferson, J. Clarke and B. Roberts, *Policing the Crisis* (London: Macmillan, 1978); P. Golding and S. Middleton, *Images of Welfare* (Oxford: Martin Robertson, 1982); G. Murdock, 'Reporting the riots: images and impacts', in J. Benyon (ed.), *Scarman and After* (Oxford: Pergamon); S. Hall, *The Hard Road to Renewal* (London: Verso, 1998); and C. Critcher, *Moral Panics and the Media* (Buckingham: Open University Press, 2003).

56 Cited in Edgar, *Second Time*, p. 112.

57 Cited in K. Teare, *Under Siege* (London: Penguin, 1988), p. 71.

58 Cited in R.Weight, *Patriots* (London: Macmillan, 2002), p. 624.

59 Cited in P. Gilroy, *There Ain't No Black in the Union Jack* (London: Routledge, 2002), p. 54.

60 It was linked to a modernising discourse centred around neo-liberal themes. For an insightful analysis of the way in which contradictory Thatcherite themes were combined in a compelling synthesis, see S. Hall, *The Hard Road to Renewal* (London: Verso, 1988).

61 *Daily Express*, 25 February 1983.

62 Goss, *Local Labour*.

63 L. Segal, 'The heat in the kitchen', in Hall and Jacques (eds.), *The Politics*.

64 Hall, *Hard Road*, p. 90.

65 G. Stoker, *The Politics of Local Government*, 1st edn. (Basingstoke: Macmillan, 1988); and 2nd edn. (Basingstoke: Macmillan, 1991); H. Butcher, I. Law, R. Leach and M. Mullard, *Local Government and Thatcherism* (London: Routledge, 1990); J. Kingdom, *Local Government and Politics in Britain* (Hemel Hempstead: Philip Allan, 1991); D. King, 'From the urban left to the new right: normative theory and local government', in J. Stewart and G. Stoker (eds), *Local Government in the 1990s* (Basingstoke: Macmillan, 1995); A. Cochrane, *Whatever Happened to Local Government?* (Buckingham: Open University Press, 1993); J. Gyford, S. Leech and C. Game, *The Changing Politics of Local Government* (London: Unwin Hyman, 1989); S. Duncan and M. Goodwin, *The Local State and Uneven Development* (Cambridge: Polity, 1988); J. Gyford, *The*

*Politics of Local Socialism* (London: Unwin and Hyman, London, 1985); M. Boddy and C. Fudge (eds), *Local Socialism?* (Basingstoke: Macmillan, 1984). Lansley, Goss and Wolmar's *Councils* is not part of this mainstream local government studies tradition.

66  G. Stoker, *The Politics of Local Government*, 1st edn. (Basingstoke: Macmillan, 1988), p. 210.

67  B. Pimlott and N. Rao, *Governing London* (Oxford: Oxford University Press, 2002); Butcher, Law, Leach and Mullard, *Local Government;* Lansley, Goss and Wolmar, *Councils*.

68  G. Stoker, *The Politics of Local Government*, 2nd edn. (Basingstoke: Macmillan, 1991), p. 48.

# 3

# GOODBYE TO THE CLOWNS

*James Curran*

The claim that those on the left of politics are mentally impaired is not new.[1] This abuse became particularly virulent in the 1970s, a time when political discourse coarsened, and was directed against radical MPs who questioned the prevailing political orthodoxies.[2] Tony Benn was called 'round-the-bend Benn' and 'Barmy Benn' when he moved to the left.[3] An early example of the phrase 'looney left' (then spelt with an e) appears in a *Sun* cartoon (4 October 1975) about three prominent left-wing MPs: Barbara Castle, Tony Benn and Ian Mikardo. The cartoon featured them floundering in the sea after their boat, with a tattered sail on which was written 'Ship-Wrecked Looney Left', had foundered on a rock, represented by the smiling face of the Prime Minister, Harold Wilson. A variant of the phrase 'loony left' – 'The Loons' – appeared in another cartoon (*Daily Express*, 10 April 1981). Again, it was applied to prominent left-wing MPs (Michael Foot, Eric Heffer and the ubiquitous Tony Benn). However, the phrase 'loony left' had not yet become firmly established as a standard part of the political vocabulary. Nor had it acquired its specific association with a new kind of left. All this was to change by the mid-1980s.

## Genesis of a political crusade

During the late 1970s, national tabloid newspapers seldom paid any attention to local government, save for fleeting references during local election campaigns. Councils were viewed in Fleet Street as being part of a dull, fustian world where local worthies dealt with parochial, uncontroversial issues. 'News' did not happen in local town halls.

However, some national papers reported in May 1981 that Ken Livingstone had been elected leader of the Greater London Council (GLC) by his council colleagues, shortly after the local election, ousting the right-wing Labour veteran, Andrew McIntosh. Livingstone's supporters justified the switch on the grounds that newly elected councillors were entitled to choose a new leader, and that Labour's GLC manifesto was the basis of their democratic mandate. This claim did not impress a number of national papers which questioned the legitimacy of Livingstone's 'coup'.

However, the event that put the tabloid press on full 'Red Ken' alert was a fresh outbreak of disorder in Brixton in July 1981. A major riot, accompanied by arson and looting, had occurred in Brixton in April. During the preceding three months, there had also been 'race' riots in Bristol and Liverpool, and significant disturbances elsewhere. To some alarmed commentators, the latest trouble in Brixton seemed to be part of a general pattern in which law and order was beginning to break down in inner city areas where there was a large concentration of disaffected black and Asian British youths.[4]

These disturbances coincided with major upheavals within the Labour Party. In January 1981, the left secured a change in the rules that, for the first time, gave union and party activists a major say in the election of the party leader. In March, an influential group of right-wing Labour MPs broke away to form the Social Democratic Party (SDP). In April, Tony Benn, the left's standard bearer, announced that he would contest the party's deputy leadership in a move that was widely seen as his opening bid to lead the party. The popular press's response to these developments was typified by the *Daily Express's* (22 May 1981) standfirst: 'Why Labour leaders tremble at the relentless advance of Benn's army. Torn apart by the politics of fear'. What made the rise of the left still more dramatic was that Labour stayed ahead in the polls, while the Conservative Party slipped to third place throughout most of the summer of 1981.[5] Fleet Street journalists began to contemplate the possibility that a left-dominated Labour Party could conceivably be elected to political office during a period of recession and mass unemployment.

Ken Livingstone became an emblematic figure symbolising for right-wing papers a dual nightmare: the breakdown of social order in the inner cities and the rise of the Labour left. He had already been marked down, in the words of one Fleet Street journalist, as 'a platoon leader of the advanced party of Bennite shock troops'[6] when he became leader of the GLC. What transformed him into a public enemy, following short bursts of bad publicity, were his outspoken public comments about the causes of the Brixton disturbances. These were the product, he claimed, of years of neglect, high unemployment, resentment against racial discrimination and insensitive, racist policing.[7]

Although his analysis was later echoed – in more restrained language – by the official enquiry headed by Lord Scarman,[8] it was judged at the time to be the height of irresponsibility for London's first citizen to be offering 'sympathy to rioters' (*Daily Express*, 16 July 1981) and acting as 'a cheer leader to trouble' (*News of the World*, 12 July 1981) Underlying this outrage was the belief that the riots were the work of hooligan and subversive elements, and that the best way to maintain order was to use whatever force was required. Livingstone stood accused of bestowing a mantle of respectability around urban thugs, and of engaging, in the words of the *Sunday Express* (19 July 1981), 'in a ruthless campaign ... to destroy good race relations between the police and the local community'. It was even suggested that he was trying to exploit lawlessness to bring down the government. Livingstone and his friends on the left, according to Max Hastings in the *Evening Standard* (20 July 1981), wanted to 'wreck the Tory government – and clearly the riots are useful stepping stones in this direction.' The article was accompanied by a photograph of a policeman, carrying away a rioter, with the caption: 'In charge – but for how long?'

Following the Brixton disturbances, Ken Livingstone and his GLC colleagues were subjected to a sustained press assault. This mobilised the standard rhetoric against the Labour left, derived from the polemics of the Cold War. It depicted the GLC administration as marxist, authoritarian and undemocratic, symbolically placing it outside the pale of legitimate politics.

In actual fact, the GLC administration elected to office in 1981 was a political coalition. While it included marxist councillors, these were only a minority within a minority. They were part of the left faction led by Ken Livingstone, which depended in turn on a centrist group of Labour councillors (people like Kinnock-supporting John Carr) to win the vote within the Labour group. Livingstone himself was an intelligent, radical populist – something that is clearly revealed in his political reminiscences,[9] revealing interviews with left inquisitors[10] and a good, pioneering biography.[11] His politics were the product both of his generation, and of an empirical, ethical tradition prominent in the British Labour Party.[12] It contrasted with the more theoretical tradition of far left organisations which instruct their members in marxist analysis in order to equip them for their role as vanguard leaders.

The politics of the GLC administration was also hybrid. Its radical arm, the Greater London Enterprise Board (GLEB) sought to promote co-operatives and economic democracy, and was influenced by the radical left. However, GLEB increasingly functioned in practice as a 'state capitalist' agency propping up ailing companies.[13] More importantly, the main thrust of the GLC's programme took it in a different direction, away from class politics and in the direction of personal politics: women's emancipation, gay liberation, and anti-racism. The GLC also championed environmentalist and 'anti-bureaucratic' initiatives, which were not part of the traditional repertoire of the old left. The GLC represented something new: a radical council that owed more to the 1960s counter-culture than to methodism or marxism.

However, the right-wing tabloid press initially foisted on Livingstone and his colleagues an identikit image of the left derived from the 1920s and 1930s. Livingstone was denounced as the 'Trotsky of County Hall' (*Daily Express*, 6 December 1982), 'the Commissar of County Hall' (*Daily Mail*, 30 July 1981) and in a bulging, portmanteau image as 'Ken Livingstone and his coterie of Marxists, Communists and Trotskyists' (*Sun*, 9 February 1983). The marxist tag was often accompanied by adjectives underscoring its negative symbolisation, as in the GLC's 'hardline Marxist ideologues' (*Daily Mail*, 5 June 1985) and 'Ken Livingstone and his grubby pack of marxists' (*Sun*, 9 February 1983). The implication was that they did not share the core values of democracy, something that was sometimes made explicit. Livingstone 'wanted the street demonstration to replace the ballot box', explained the *Sun* (10 June, 1984). In a similar vein, the *Daily Mail* (30 March 1984) warned that 'the real assault on the democracy of this country is by the Fascist left, which has gained a menacing hold on the power structures at union and local level within Mr. Livingstone's Labour Party'. The *Daily Express* (30 April 1984) was more direct: 'Citizen Ken Has No Time For Democracy'.

## Political subversion

This image of the GLC administration as marxist and undemocratic was reinforced by its depiction as being politically subversive. The Livingstone regime was repeatedly attacked in the tabloid press for undermining law and order, endorsing Irish terrorism and supporting Britain's enemies abroad.

The GLC's stance on the police anticipated what was later to become part of a political consensus. The GLC argued that the Metropolitan Police should not answer only to the Home Office but, like other police forces in Britain, should be accountable to representatives of the local community. Since the government refused to relinquish sole control of the Metropolitan Police, the GLC-funded police monitoring groups represented the only available way of exerting community pressure. The GLC maintained that local accountability fostered communication and co-operation essential for effective policing and the fight against crime. The stock complaints of monitoring groups – that violent assaults on women and ethnic minorities were not being taken seriously enough – were, in the GLC's view, legitimate concerns that the police should address. Indeed, a Conservative Home Secretary, Kenneth Clarke, argued subsequently that the Metropolitan Police should be made locally accountable. This paved the way for the Blair government's introduction, in 2000, of a Metropolitan Police Authority, with elected representatives. By then, a 'community policing' approach, involving ethnic minorities, had become a new orthodoxy.

However, what became mainstream politics in the 2000s was viewed by right-wing tabloids twenty years earlier as political extremism. The GLC was portrayed as wanting to 'handcuff' the police (*Evening Standard*, 20 July 1981) or, worse, 'destroy' the police (*Sun*, 31 March 1982). The tenor of this coverage (markedly different from that of the broadsheet press) is best conveyed by the way in which the *Sun* (15 July 1981) reported the GLC's funding of a police monitoring unit in Tower Hamlets. The decision was announced under the emotive headline 'Council Gives Cash to Fight Bobbies'. This was accompanied by a photograph of a policeman standing in front of a blazing building with the caption, 'Burning Britain'. The short report was given over largely to an impassioned attack on the GLC by the Police Federation Chairman, Jim Jardine, who was quoted as saying: 'I'm disgusted at public money going to fanatics who pursue allegations against the police. We are constantly bedevilled by political agitators fighting against us.' There was no attempt to clarify the composition of the monitoring group beyond the description given by Jardine, nor to provide a balancing comment from another source. By contrast, the broadsheet *Daily Telegraph*'s report (14 July 1981), though critical in tone, explained that the monitoring group included representatives from the churches, the Commission for Racial Equality and trades councils, and quoted a spokesman defending the unit's work.

Portrayed by right-wing tabloids as an enemy of the police, the GLC was also cast as a friend of the Irish Republican Army (IRA). The GLC administration argued that it was right to engage in talks with the IRA. Although the council condemned the IRA's bombing campaign (which had recently come to London), it also claimed that dialogue represented the way forward because the conflict in Northern Ireland could only be solved through a political rather than military solution.

This position seems less controversial now than it did then. We now know that the Thatcher government did in fact have secret, mediated talks with the IRA. A political, as distinct from a military, solution to the conflict in in Northern Ireland was what subsequently transpired. But in the early 1980s, the GLC's position was widely viewed as irresponsible and subversive. The British government defined the conflict in Northern Ireland as a struggle between the forces of law and order and criminals. This reflected the all-party consensus in parliament, and was the dominant framework for reporting IRA terrorism in television news and current affairs programmes (though this interpretation was contested in some television dramas).[14] The IRA bombing outside Chelsea barracks in October 1981 had also raised the political temperature, prompting the Prime Minister, Margaret Thatcher, to describe the IRA bombers as 'sub-human'.[15]

Livingstone and his colleagues were thus perceived to be stepping outside the framework of understanding – shared by government, the opposition leadership, and mainstream media – that the only way to respond to terrorists was to crush them with all means at the government's disposal. Livingstone's punishment was to be pilloried, and – whether wilfully or not – misrepresented in a way that made him look callous and foolish.

Some tabloid newspapers refused to accept that speaking officially to the IRA could mean anything other than covert approval. To engage in dialogue meant, in their view, 'backing' terrorism. Thus, when Livingstone met at County Hall the children of a woman murdered by the IRA, the *Daily Mail* (22 August 1981) reported the encounter as 'Victims Face IRA Backer'. Similarly, the GLC's invitation to two Sinn Fein members of the Northern Ireland Assembly for talks to discuss the end of bombing in London was hailed as 'Backing for Terror' (*Sun*, 6 December 1982).

The full ferocity of tabloid disapproval was unleashed in reports of a meeting of the Cambridge Tory Reform Club in October 1981, when Livingstone was asked a question about Northern Ireland. He replied that the IRA were no ordinary criminals but militant nationalists; and that the only way to deal with the crisis in Northern Ireland was to work towards a political settlement. It is not possible to determine for certain whether Livingstone's spontaneous answer used the phrase 'not just criminals' or 'not criminals' in relation to the IRA. Livingstone said that he used the conditional 'not just';[16] the *Daily Mail* reporter, Richard Holliday, who was present at the meeting, backed him up;[17] but an anonymous agency reporter, relied upon by most newspapers (without attribution) took a different view. Whether or not Livingstone made a slip of tongue, it is clear from all reports of the meeting that he explicitly condemned IRA violence. He also rushed into television and radio studios the next day to 'clarify' what he had said: 'I at no time said that people who set off a bomb aren't criminals ... Quite frankly, I wouldn't agree with what I was quoted as "saying"'.[18] He then repeated his usual line that there could only be a political rather than military solution to the Northern Ireland crisis.

The right-wing popular press used Livingstone's alleged gaffe at the Cambridge meeting to attempt to bury him as a politician. On its front page, the *Sun* (13 October 1981) began its report: 'This morning the *Sun* presents the most odious man in Britain'. It concluded with a demand that Livingstone be sacked '**right this minute**' (original emphasis). This theme was taken up by the *Daily Express* (13 October) which declared rhetorically 'London has endured fire, plaque and the blitz. It should not have to endure Mr. Livingstone at the head of affairs for one more minute'. The strongest condemnation came, however, from the *Daily Mail* (13 October) which proclaimed that Livingstone was 'a man who through Marxist dogma has become an alien in his own land'. It concluded by declaring that 'he is certainly not fit to rule Britain's capital city'. Furthermore, it was not only the right-wing press which set out to destroy Livingstone. The pro-Labour *Sunday Mirror* (18 October) also felt compelled to warn the public that 'this man is dangerous'.

The image of Livingstone as the ally of Fenian terror, apologist for black rioters and opponent of the police was rounded off by tabloid portrayals of him as unpatriotic or a Communist fellow traveller. His opposition to the dispatch of British troops to the Falklands was misrepresented as 'Red Ken Backs Junta' (*Sun*, 10 April 1982). The GLC's refusal to implement the government's civil defence plans as part of its anti-nuclear stance was interpreted by the *Sun* (9 September 1982) as revealing that Livingstone's loyalties lay elsewhere. 'Where will you be', asked the paper, 'should the Russian stormtroopers march through the streets of London ... in the streets welcoming them with open arms?' (original emphasis). The *Daily Express* (29 August 1983) suggested that Livingstone should emigrate to Communist Eastern Europe. The *Sun* (10 July 1985) extended the geographical range of this familiar taunt by accusing Livingstone of wanting to turn Britain into a 'Cuba of the North Sea' with 'the likes of the IRA and Vietcong' as a volunteer army.

## Moral subversion

In fact, the new urban left differed from a significant strand of the old left in being anti-Soviet. The identification of Ken Livingstone as a fellow-travelling Communist sympathiser merely revealed how little the right-wing press understood the phenomenon that it was reporting. However even when mechanically deploying Cold War rhetoric, some right-wing journalists sensed that the GLC represented something new, something that they did not quite understand.

Their first inkling that the GLC leadership was different occurred when Ken Livingstone addressed a meeting of the Gay Unity Group in Harrow in August 1981. In his speech, Livingstone attacked the bigotry of all the political parties, and promised to oppose discrimination against sexual minorities. This fuelled speculation about Livingstone's own sexual preferences. The *Sun* (19 August 1981) reported 'Red Ken Speaks Up For The Gays – I'll Get Them Jobs and Homes, He Says', and published a photograph of the GLC leader with the nudge-nudge caption: 'Red Ken ... would not talk about his private life last night'. However, subsequent journalistic enquiries revealed that Livingstone was heterosexual.

The popular press's reaction was to attribute Livingstone's support for gays and lesbians to his personal freakishness. Although initially viewed as a newt-loving eccentric, Livingstone came to be regarded as both morally and politically subversive. This view was summed up in the *Sunday Express's* denunciation of him as an 'IRA-loving, poof-loving Marxist' (27 October 1981).

However, it also dawned on journalists that it was not just Livingstone who was different: so were the people around him. Personal attacks on Livingstone broadened to a sustained assault on the GLC as a morally subversive institution. The GLC, declared the *Daily Express* (29 May 1984), is 'the Boy George of Local Authorities', a reference to the androgynous, lipstick-wearing pop star. According to the *Daily Telegraph* (23 January 1985), the GLC is 'out to confuse the many by perverting all normal feelings and turning all accepted ideas upside down'. It is against the natural order of things, warned columnist Lynda Lee-Potter, even wanting to close down beauty salons and make 'women strip down lorries instead' (*Daily Mail*, 2 November 1985). The GLC's championship of personal freedom was portrayed as a new form of oppression in which the young and vulnerable were being indoctrinated. 'Children as young as five', warned the *Daily Mail* (2 November 1984), 'are being taught by lesbians and militant feminist teachers to question the traditional value of the sexes'.

When the Inner London Education Authority (technically a branch of the GLC) endorsed the right of gay teachers to 'come out', its decision was angrily attacked on the grounds that it would corrupt and confuse the young, and weaken classroom control. 'Standards of education may fall relentlessly', warned the *Daily Express* (28 June 1983), to the point where 'codes of discipline and decent behaviour may hardly exist'. Where the *Express* anathematised, the *Sun* (28 June 1983) chuckled with the headline, 'Gay Sirs' Charter To Cuddle In Schools'. But its editorial that day called for the GLC to be closed down.

## Patrons of deviance

The theme of political subversion thus had as a counterpoint the theme of moral subversion. These two themes were brought together, and given a dramatic unity, through a tabloid focus on GLC grants to organisations that were deemed to be deviant.

The GLC administration developed a policy of financially supporting community groups as a way of enhancing their activities and assisting their participation in public life. This was in line with the new urban left's belief that local government should facilitate and enable, not just administer.

However, this policy became the target of right-wing newspapers in a sustained campaign in which newspapers repeatedly drew attention to GLC grants awarded to 'controversial' organisations. Articles often referred also to allegedly contentious organisations that the GLC had previously funded in order to cue reader indignation. The same names featured in a regular roll call: the English Collective of Prostitutes (a pressure group), London Lesbian and Gay Centre, Babies Against the Bomb (a child-minding group in north London), the Marx Memorial Library, Spare Rib (a feminist magazine) and the Rastafarian Advisory Centre. These favourites fell into four categories of undeserving 'other': ethnic, feminist, homosexual and radical organisations. Hostility was also engendered through the use of emotive rather than neutral language: with words such as 'handouts' rather than 'grants': 'snoopers' rather than 'monitoring group'; 'queers' lib' rather than 'gay rights'.[19] The undeserving 'others' were also rolled into a generic category as in 'loony lefties and fringe groups' (*Sun*, 23 February 1984) or distilled in an ironic caricature, as in 'black lesbians against the bomb' (*News of the World*, 15 April 1984).

Tabloid reporting exaggerated greatly the financial burden that GLC grants represented. In this way, two potential sources of resentment – towards outsider groups and towards paying rates – were brought together in a synergy designed to increase public anger. 'Terroristic rates … have produced a rash of bankruptcies and a flight of firms and offices', thundered the *Daily Mail* (19 May 1983) because 'the militant lesbians, babies for peace, Irish and black extremists, prostitutes' collectives, left-wing theatre groups and revolutionary 'creators' of all kinds have soaked up millions of ratepayers' money'. This dual message – the ratepayer burdened by undeserving outsiders – was succinctly conveyed through the description of the GLC as 'a hand-out machine for the feckless and freaky' (*Star*, 27 July 1984). It was also imparted in numerous headlines designed to cue a critical response: 'The Livingstone Follies' (*Daily Express*, 23 February 1983), 'The Crazy Things They Do With Your Rates' (*Daily Mail*, 16 February 1983), '£220,000 Hand-out For Prostitutes, Gays and Daft Plays' (*Sun*, 23 November 1982), 'Red Ken Livingstone Hands Out Cash With Gay Abandon' (*News of the World*, 21 February 1982). Angry reactions were solicited through the way in which news reports and features were written. 'GLC leader Ken Livingstone was once again yesterday doing what he does best – giving London's ratepayers' money away to bizarre minority groups' was a characteristic opening line of a *Daily Mail* feature article (16 February 1983).

The popular press published news reports and specially commissioned articles that conveyed the impression that there was a gathering storm of anger directed at the GLC. The right and the sensible left, it was implied, were united in a shared sense of outrage. Thus, the Conservative Party Chairman, John Selwyn Gummer, complained bitterly in the *Sunday Express* (11 August 1985) about the way in which GLC 'extremists have their hands in YOUR pockets'. His indignation was echoed by the retired, trade union leader, Frank Chapple, in the *Daily Mail* (27 March 1986). 'The GLC', he wrote, 'has made London the laughing stock of local government by opening its doors to every no-hoper, Marxist trouble-maker, political scrounger, foreign terrorist and sexual pervert who wanted a public handout'.

In fact, GLC grants accounted for only a small proportion of the council's total budget. And the grants that gained tabloid attention accounted in turn for only a small proportion of GLC grants. The Conservative Home Office Minister, David Waddington, estimated in 1984 that only 1.8% of the GLC's grants went to controversial organisations.[20]

## Crystallisation

The right-wing popular press thus began by projecting a standard identikit of the left, derived from the Cold War, onto the GLC. It then superimposed a new layer of signification centred on the GLC's alleged moral deviancy. This resulted in old and new structures of representation being merged together in an uncertain, fluctuating synthesis.[21]

However, this blurred vision gradually gave way to a pathological explanation of a new, unhinged left that was different from the 'traditional' left. An early attempt to pathologise the new urban left appeared in the *Daily Mail* (20 August 1981). It commissioned a clinical assessment of Livingstone's mental condition from 'three leading psychologists', who suggested that Livingstone was an emotionally damaged publicity-seeker. One unnamed 'senior woman psychologist' was quoted as saying that 'it is most likely' that his overworked parents were unable to give him enough attention. A named psychologist, Dr. Dougal MacKay, was also quoted as saying: 'Probably the only way in which he could get it was to be a naughty boy – which he still acts like'. The doctor continued by saying that 'the desperate need for attention is the hallmark of the hysteric. Mr. Livingstone is in the same category as a punk rocker who wears outlandish clothes'.

Dr. Mackay protested subsequently that words had been put into his mouth. 'When I was approached by the reporter concerned', he claimed, 'I made it clear that, although I was prepared to discuss a particular type of personality phenomenon with him, I was not willing to comment on any one individual'.[22] According to Dr. Mackay, he spoke only in hypothetical terms. He did not even know who Ken Livingstone was until he read the article quoting his comments.

However, mental instability was not at this early stage a central, organising theme in the depiction of Livingstone and the GLC. It was just one among a number of tabloid taunts, with echoes from the school playground. Thus, Livingstone was attacked as 'the pipsqueak leader of the GLC' (*Sun*, 23 July 1981), 'little twit' (*Sun*, 19 August 1981),'this weird creature' (*Daily Mail*, 20 August 1981), 'a puffed-up crackpot' (*Sun*, 27 July 1981), 'this fathead' (*News of the World*, 7 July 1983), 'a doctrinaire clown' (*Daily Mail*, 24 July 1983) and 'the Mickey Mouse of British politics' (*Daily Mirror*, 29 August 1983). The theme of mental instability was not in itself new. It had been used, as we have seen, in relation to other left-wing politicians in the past. It did not have traction in 1981, because the necessary foundation of identifying and characterising the new urban left had not yet been established.

But in the course of 1982–5, the GLC came to be identified repeatedly with 'crackpot', 'loopy', 'barmy', 'potty' and 'fringe' people, especially in the reporting of its grants policy. Jostling among these epithets were various workings of a single leitmotif: 'Red Ken and the loony left of the GLC' (*Daily Star*, 26 July 1983), 'a haven for political loons and crackpots' (*Daily Star*, 24 July 1984), 'rate loonies' (*Daily Express*, 7 September 1984), 'loony lefties and fringe groups' (*Sun*, 23 February 1984), 'Greater Loonification Council' (Keith Waterhouse in the *Daily Mirror*, 8 April 1985), 'Labour Loony Left' (Cummings cartoon, *Daily Express*, 26 June 1985); 'the loony left' (*Daily Express*, 25 April 1984). This was a time of trial and error when well-paid columnists, cartoonists, sub-editors, feature writers and leader writers experimented with different lexical forms. They only collectively settled for one form in late 1986, after the GLC had been closed down. However, the groundwork for designating – and de-legitimating – a new kind of left had been laid in the preceding five years. The succinct, alliterative phrase, 'loony left', merely crystallised an understanding of a new political phenomenon – the rise of a 'crackpot' left more concerned with minorities than with class – that had evolved during the course of the anti-GLC crusade.

## Political Retribution

Not all papers joined this crusade. The broadsheet press (apart from the *Daily Telegraph*) largely held back. The pro-Labour Mirror group of popular newspapers also tended to stay on the sidelines (although the *Sunday Mirror* was one of the first papers to call for the GLC's abolition, and subsequently ran an editorial urging its abolition to be speeded up).[23] It was primarily the right-wing popular newspapers which launched a jihad against the GLC. However, they accounted for 63% of national daily circulation in 1983.[24] Their firepower was sustained and relentless. Hardly a week went by between July 1981 and June 1983 when right-wing popular dailies failed to draw attention to a fresh GLC 'outrage'. Their efforts were reinforced by the capital's monopoly daily paper, the *Evening Standard*, which initially campaigned against the GLC, and joined the chorus for it to be closed down.

The opening barrage of press attacks generated in 1981 increased tensions within the GLC Labour administration, and gave rise to a leadership crisis. Some councillors complained that Livingstone's controversial pronouncements on issues unrelated to the GLC undermined support for the council and deflected attention from its achievements. Others (including some left-wing councillors) felt that the media focus on Livingstone detracted from the principle of collective leadership to which they were committed. In October, this rumble of complaint grew into open rebellion, with twenty councillors circulating a round-robin letter attacking Livingstone. The GLC leader declared subsequently that the absence of an obvious successor helped him to survive. Even so, it was a close-run thing. 'I might very well have been replaced as leader', he acknowledged, 'if the AGM, with its secret ballots, had been due in October 1981 rather than April 1982'.[25]

The popular press crusade also helped to turn Londoners against their council. An Audience Selection poll in August 1981 found that 51% disapproved of Livingstone as GLC leader compared with only 11% who approved. Still more devastatingly, the poll reported that 38% of those who had voted Labour in the May GLC election now regretted doing so.[26] The battering that the GLC received was so relentless, and the loss of public confidence so great, that Ken Livingstone privately concluded in the autumn of 1981 that he had 'blown it', and that the GLC administration was damaged beyond repair.[27]

A mid-term poll in April 1983 offered a glimmer of hope for the beleaguered administration. It indicated that the GLC had regained some lost support, but still remained deeply unpopular. Only 30% of Londoners said that they were satisfied with the GLC, compared with 49% who were dissatisfied. More than twice as many people disapproved of Livingstone as leader of the GLC as approved. Significantly, the poll revealed considerable opposition to those GLC policies which the press had targeted. Fifty-one per cent opposed the giving of 'financial aid to fringe and minority groups', with only 24% in favour; the GLC's police accountability proposals were rejected by 50% and supported only by 27%; and 69% also condemned the GLC's invitation to Sinn Fein representatives to come to London.[28]

Meanwhile, the political campaign against the GLC took off. In 1982, right-wing papers began demanding that the GLC be closed down. Their editorials were supplemented by feature articles and news reports, reinforcing the same message.[29] A growing number of organisations publicly declared that the GLC should be abolished, including the London Boroughs Association, the Institute of Directors and the Confederation of British Industry. In January 1983, the influential London Conservative Group of MPs joined this hue and cry, arguing that the GLC's abolition would be a vote-winner. Margaret Thatcher seems to have shared this opinion: she told MPs on 5 May 1983 that 'there are many people who would find abolition attractive'. After the Conservative General Election manifesto had already been drafted, a late addition was inserted that committed the party to closing down the GLC and the six Metropolitan County Councils.

In its hour of need, the GLC appeared to be without friends. Senior figures in the Labour Party had come to regard County Hall as a political liability. Michael Foot, the Labour Leader, blamed Labour's poor showing in the 1981 Croydon North-West by-election partly on the GLC.[30] Neil Kinnock, who was later to succeed Foot as Leader, complained about the damage caused to Labour by the GLC's high rates.[31] Labour MPs told lobby journalists in 1982 and 1983 that the GLC was alienating 'ordinary voters' by turning London 'into an adventure playground' for 'a variety of zany left-wing causes'.[32] London's Labour Mayor, Ken Livingstone, was told not to visit the Labour Party's national headquarters during the 1983 general election, as a mark of official displeasure.[33]

Indeed, the Labour Party commissioned a private survey during the general election campaign to see how much damage the GLC was doing to Labour's chances in the capital (only to find out that it was having no discernible effect). However, the survey also showed again that more people were dissatisfied with the GLC than were satisfied, and that over twice as many people disapproved of Livingstone as GLC leader than approved.[34]

In short, the GLC had become a pariah among local authorities. Crucified by the press, a source of embarrassment to the Labour Party, seemingly unpopular with its electors, it could be closed down – so it seemed in 1983 – with the minimum of difficulty.

## Notes

1 Research for this chapter was supported by a small grant from Goldsmiths, University of London. My thanks to Jane Fountain for her assistance.
2 This coarsening of public debate was partly a response to the breakdown of political consensus during the 1970s, and the rise of new right press controllers. See J. Curran and J. Seaton, *Power Without Responsibility*, 8th edition (London: Routledge, 2018).
3 For the tabloid pathologising of Tony Benn, see Mark Hollingsworth, *The Press and Political Dissent* (London: Pluto, 1986).
4 The anger and fear engendered by these disturbances are well anatomised in two studies of media coverage: G. Murdock, 'Reporting the riots: images and impact', in J. Benyon (ed.) *Scarman and After* (Oxford: Pergamon, 1984) and S. Cottle, *TV News, Urban Conflicts and the Inner City* (Leicester: Leicester University Press, 1993). The imagery deployed in reports of these disturbances drew upon the lexicon of outrage developed in response to a succession of moral panics in the preceding two decades.
5 The *Gallup* voting intention poll first put the Conservatives third in March 1981 (with the Liberals and Social Democrats added together). The Conservative Party stayed third for most of the ensuing twelve months. See D. Butler and G. Butler, *Twentieth–Century British Political Facts*, 8th edition, (Basingstoke: Macmillan, 2000), pp. 274–5.
6 J. Carvel, *Citizen Ken* (London: Chatto and Windus, 1984), p. 13.
7 *Daily Mail*, 11 July 1981; *Daily Express*, 11 July 1981; *The Times*, 11 July 1981.
8 *The Brixton Disorders* 10–12 April 1981 (HMSO, 8427: London, 1981) [Scarman Report].
9 K. Livingstone, *If Voting Changed Anything, They'd Abolish It* (London: Harper-Collins, 1987); K. Livingstone, *You Can't Say That* (London: Faber and Faber, 2001).
10 K. Livingstone and T. Ali, *Who's Afraid of Margaret Thatcher? Tariq Ali in Conversation with Ken Livingstone* (London: Verso, 1984); 'Local socialism: the way ahead. Interview with Ken Livingstone', in Martin Body and Colin Fudge, *Local Socialism?* (Basingstoke: Macmillan, 1984).

11  Carvel, Citizen Ken [2nd edition was published in 1986].
12  G. Foote, *The Labour Party's Political Thought*, 2nd edition. (London: Croom Helm, 1986).
13  Part of the intellectual parentage of GLEB was social democratic, reflecting an overtly state capitalist conception embodied in S. Holland (ed.) *The State as Entrepreneur* (London, Weidenfeld and Nicolson, 1972). For an account of the attempt to make it an agency of radical change, see M. Mackintosh and H. Wainwright (eds.) *A Taste of Power* (London: Verso, 1987); and for an assessment of its ultimate social democratic evolution, drawing on a major internal review, see S. Lansley, S. Goss and C. Wolmar, *Councils in Conflict* (Basingstoke: Macmillan, 1989).
14  P. Schlesinger, G. Murdock and P. Elliott, *Televising Terrorism* (London: Comedia, 1983).
15  *Daily Mail*, 13 October 1981.
16  Livingstone, *If Voting*, p. 167.
17  Richard Holliday's report, in the *Daily Mail* of 13 October 1981, records Livingstone as saying that the IRA bombers were 'not "just criminals, murderers and psychopaths"'.
18  BBC2 TV, Newsnight, 14 October 1981.
19  *Daily Mail*, 19 May 1983; *Daily Mail*, 22 April 1983; *Sun*, 20 September 1984, et passim.
20  Cited in J. Gyford, *The Politics of Local Socialism* (London: Allen and Unwin, 1985), p. 55.
21  Conflating different groups into one negative category is a standard rhetorical technique. New Labour supporters (and their press allies) subsequently represented diverse sections of the Labour movement not judged to be fully behind their project, as 'Old Labour'. See Chapter 8.
22  *The Press and the People: 29th/30th Annual Report of the Press Council* (London: Press Council), p. 178.
23  *Sunday Mirror*, 18 October 1981; *Sunday Mirror*, 15 January 1984.
24  Audit Bureau of Circulation, July–December 1983.
25  Livingstone, *If Voting*, p. 174.
26  Audience Selection Survey, August 1981.
27  Conversation with the author.
28  Market Opinion Research International [MORI], April 1983.
29  For example, *Evening Standard*, 23 September 1982; *Daily Telegraph*, 2 March 1983; *Daily Mail*, 10 May 1983; *Daily Express*, 27 December 1982; *Evening Standard*, 14 January 1983; *Daily Express*, 21 January 1983; *Times* 26 January 1983, *Evening Standard*, 27 January 1981; *Daily Express*, 6 May 1983; *Evening Standard*, 23 September 1982; *Daily Telegraph*, 3 January 1982.
30  *Daily Mail*, 9 November 1982.
31  *Evening Standard*, 23 October 1981.
32  Carvel, *Citizen Ken*, p. 165.
33  *New Socialist*, 37, 1986, p. 31.
34  B. Worcester and L. Gilbert, MORI, 'Voters in Greater London', Confidential Memorandum to the Labour Party (14), 26 May 1983.

# 4

# PRESS BOOMERANG

*James Curran*

The decision to abolish the GLC, announced in October 1983, was not greeted with the public enthusiasm that the government had expected. Indeed, shortly after the government's announcement, 54% of Londoners opposed the GLC's closure, while only 23% approved.[1] Opposition strengthened in early 1984, with many former 'don't knows' siding with the GLC. By April 1984 almost two-thirds of Londoners were against the GLC's termination, while less than a quarter were in favour. This one-sided distribution of opinion persisted, with occasional fluctuations, until County Hall closed in April 1986.[2]

How did all this happen? How did a politically isolated, reviled socialist council take on a popular right-wing government, re-elected in 1983 with a landslide majority, and win the propaganda battle? The answer advanced by numerous politicians, journalists and commentators at the time was that the GLC mounted a successful advertising campaign funded by a disgraceful misuse of taxpayers' money. This much-repeated argument encouraged the government to introduce new legislation that outlawed political advertising by local authorities.

However, the claim that Londoners were only won over by a slick advertising campaign is a myth. The majority of Londoners opposed the abolition of the GLC before its advertising campaign even began. The true explanation is more complicated and also more interesting.

## Hidden roots of resilience

The GLC was not as discredited in 1983 as it was widely thought to have been. Although it had been attacked by Fleet Street for two years, and its unpopularity had been recorded in successive opinion polls, it was damaged rather than fatally holed below the water line. This helps to explain why the GLC was able to rally public support behind it.

Opinion polls can be misleading because they can record instant, summary judgements without shedding light on the ambivalences that can sometimes inform opinions. This was true for example of the Labour Party's private poll in May 1983, mentioned earlier, which reported that 49% of Londoners were dissatisfied with the way the GLC was running London, compared with only 30% who were satisfied. The dissatisfied outnumbered the satisfied in every sub-group apart from those aged between eighteen and twenty-four. The poll also reported widespread disapproval of GLC leader Ken Livingstone. This poll thus recorded, like other polls that preceded it, a seemingly clear-cut public indictment of the GLC.[3]

However, another survey, which asked more questions during the same month, provided a more complex and insightful picture of Londoners' attitudes.[4] It found that much opinion was clouded by uncertainty: 78% of respondents said that they knew very little or not very much about the GLC, and what it did. This survey also revealed that some people were in two minds. On the one hand, the majority had negative perceptions of the GLC as being 'too political' (72%), too bureaucratic (55%) and out of touch (52%). On the other hand, more thought well of the council than the opposite on a number of counts. The GLC was thought to act in the best interests of Londoners by 44%, compared with a dissenting 37%; to have a clear idea of what it was doing by 42%, compared with a critical 37%; and to be go-ahead and progressive by 41%, with 31% taking the opposite view. These results thus indicated that some hostility towards the GLC was 'soft'. It was conflicted or uncertain, and therefore potentially susceptible to change.

## Broadcast shield against the press

Public confusion about the GLC arose partly from the contradictory accounts of the council supplied by rival media. In 1981–3, the tabloid press portrayed the GLC in overwhelmingly negative terms, whereas television and radio were much more inclined to report the GLC in terms of a neutral or implicitly positive news agenda. The national quality press was situated between these two polarities, while the *London Evening Standard* published an idiosyncratic combination of routine news reports that were often neutral or favourable to the GLC, and a smaller number of feature articles that were strongly critical.

Perhaps the simplest way of conveying the divergent nature of media coverage is to examine news coverage in a single week, 20–26 November 1982. Television and radio broadcast eighteen items about the GLC during this week, of which ten featured the GLC embarking on new initiatives to benefit the community. Thus, regional or national television featured the GLC as trying to save Riverside Studios, staging the Spirit of London Exhibition, planning the opening of the Thames Barrier and campaigning for the low paid, while radio featured the GLC as battling to save a breast cancer clinic, seeking to conserve for posterity the artist William Morris's home, improving the capital's sporting facilities, and protecting wildlife in the capital. Only one out of the eighteen broadcasting stories had an overtly anti-GLC theme. By contrast, all nine stories about the GLC published in the popular press during this week were negative.[5]

The contrast between regional television and the popular press was especially significant because both reached large audiences. Almost half of Londoners claimed in 1983 to watch regularly Thames News on ITV, while 29% claimed to regularly watch its BBC rival. 17–18% said that they regularly watched the two weekly TV current affairs programmes, *The London Programme* and *Reporting London* (with much larger proportions saying that they watched occasionally). The popular press accounted for about three-quarters of national daily paper readership in London. By contrast, the monopoly evening paper, the *Standard*, was read only by an estimated 7% of people in the GLC area in 1983.[6]

The media reported the GLC in divergent ways partly because they were subject to different regulatory regimes. The popular press was unregulated and partisan, whereas broadcasting was required by law to inform and display due impartiality. However, the more important, but related, cause of the divergence arose from differing news values. The popular press, selling nationwide, reported the GLC as an exemplification of a national story – the growing threat posed by the Labour left – and were interested primarily in stories about the council that fitted this agenda. By contrast, 'local' radio catered for all of London, while regional television served a region that had London at its centre. They were oriented towards local community stories that were of little interest to the national press.

The GLC deliberately exploited this difference. From July 1981 onwards, County Hall gave preferential access to television, radio and the broadsheets, in terms of interviews and briefings, as part of a conscious strategy of fighting back against hostile popular papers.[7] This engendered a relationship of growing reciprocity between County Hall and local broadcasting. Understaffed local radio and regional television news rooms were fed stories by a large GLC public relations department which made it a priority to identify items that would appeal to them. This policy paid off in the sense that the Livingstone administration received very much more broadcasting coverage than the previous Cutler administration had done.[8] Individual broadcasters who might easily have been hostile to the GLC were won over. For example, Roger Clarke, a Radio London reporter who described himself as a 'liberal Conservative', concluded that the GLC's leadership was 'high-powered', and insisted that the GLC was in reality 'not an extreme organisation'.[9] Similarly, Anne Jones, who was later to report Brent Council in a highly critical way for BBC television, viewed Ken Livingstone as someone who was 'head and shoulders above most people in local government'.[10] Thus, the GLC had developed a shrewd public relations strategy of cultivating metropolitan media as a shield against national media attacks.

## Partial rehabilitation

The Livingstone administration had, by mid-1983, also connected to other sources of support. Its 'new politics' of environmentalism, feminism and support

for ethnic minority and gay rights had won good will among a younger, affluent section of the local population (who were then predisposed, as a group, not
to be Labour supporters). At the same time, the Livingstone administration also
cultivated its traditional Labour, working class base through policies such as con-
cessionary fares for pensioners and job creation through the Greater London
Enterprise Board.

This coalition was inherently unstable because the GLC's working class base
and new supporters had, in important respects, different politics.[11] In a normal
context, the council administration could easily have fallen between two stools:
alienating some of its traditional, working-class supporters with policies they
disliked (such as funding gay and lesbian groups) without fully winning over the
new constituency. However, the government's determination to close down the
GLC changed the dynamics of this coalition. Its two wings came together and
united, providing an extended base of support for the GLC.

By 1983, the GLC had also gained a second wind after its initial, traumatic
mauling by the popular press. The key issue that helped to rehabilitate the GLC,
and win it grudging respect, was its battle over transport. In 1981, the GLC
introduced a 25% reduction in bus and tube fares funded out of the rates. The
council argued that something had to be done to persuade people to return to
public transport in order to ease traffic congestion in central London. Cheaper
fares would improve London's environment, and also assist those on low incomes
to travel more often and get more out of what the city had to offer.

This policy was successfully challenged in the courts by Conservative-
controlled Bromley council, one of the few boroughs not served by London's
underground transport network. The Appeal Court and the House of Lords
ruled that the fares reduction and GLC's supplementary rate were unlawful on
the grounds that London Transport should be run 'economically'. This produced a public outcry, including outspoken criticism from some papers usually
strongly hostile to the GLC. Why should unelected judges, it was asked, be
able to override a council administration elected by the people, especially when
its cheap fares policy had been a prominent part of its election manifesto. The
impolitic wording of some of the legal judgements that were handed down did
little to enhance the public reception of their Lordships. Lord Denning (then
aged eighty-two) argued that the GLC should set its election mandate to one
side and 'consider what it was best to do', while Lord Justice Watkins referred to
the council's 'abuse of power, which totally disregarded the interests of the ratepayers'.[12] Their judgements were subsequently criticised with great eloquence by
Robert Carnwath (now a Supreme Court judge), who voiced concerns about the
erosion of local democracy.[13]

But while the GLC's cheap fares policy was struck down in 1981, a more
modest version of it was allowed to go ahead in 1983. The GLC's policy did in
fact lead to an increased use of public transport, reversing a downward – and,
some had argued, unalterable – trend that had begun in the 1950s. The evident
success of this policy, and the obstacles that had been placed in its path, altered

public attitudes. In 1981, 77% of Londoners were opposed to public transport fare reductions funded from the rates.[14] Yet, by 1985, 78% of Londoners (including 77% of Liberal/SDP voters and 69% of Conservative voters in the GLC area) were in favour.[15] A once controversial initiative had become consensual.

The GLC was also a centre of power in its own right. Its political leadership possessed the democratic legitimacy of being directly elected by Londoners. Its officials had more information and expertise about governing the capital than Whitehall – something that was important in the battle for elite opinion. Immediately after the 1983 general election, the GLC was also placed on a war footing. Direct lines of control were established from the leader's office over all areas of the GLC in order to extract the greatest possible political and public relations benefit from everything it did.[16] The GLC also found itself with an overflowing war-chest. It had imposed a sharp increase in the rates to support its cheap fares policy. But this policy had been trimmed, due to a court ruling, creating surplus revenue to fund new initiatives and defend the GLC against the government. Tony Wilson, the council's public relations chief, estimated that the total cost of the 'Save the GLC' campaign, over two-and-a-half years, was approaching £30 million (of which its anti-abolition advertising campaign accounted for £12 million).[17]

In short, the GLC was not the broken-backed institution that it appeared to be in 1983. The council commanded considerable resources. Press attacks had been offset by more positive broadcasting coverage. The council administration could call upon support from its Labour base, and was earning a widening circle of goodwill among the young middle class and the minorities it championed. Attitudes towards the council were critical but often not entrenched.

What followed next is worth documenting in detail since it offers a classic case study of an effective political campaign.

## Benefits of victimhood

What really transformed the GLC's position in the community was the government's decision to close it down. The GLC became a symbol of London pride, and of resistance to an autocratic government.

The GLC appealed to local patriotism in the elevated register of defending local democracy. It argued that a city as big as London needed a council to oversee its affairs, and represent its interests. If the GLC was abolished, London would be the only major capital in Europe without a council. This was both a telling argument, and also an emotive call to local civic pride. Many people living in the capital thought of themselves as Londoners rather than as members of a local borough (as, for example, Mertonians, Islingtonians or Lewishamites), though this was less true of people living in some of the outer suburbs. A strong London identity underpinned the belief that London should have its own local government, and led to widespread rejection of the government's claim that the GLC was not needed. Thus, in April 1984, 68% of Londoners disagreed with the view that 'the GLC is an unnecessary level of local government', while only 20% agreed.[18] The influence of a metropolitan identity is also apparent in later survey evidence. In 1985, the second most often given reason for opposing the GLC's abolition in response to an open-ended question was that the council was 'specially for Londoners/knows our needs'.[19]

The GLC also took advantage of the mistrust of the Thatcher administration, and of central government more generally. It argued repeatedly that the plan to close down County Hall was intended to silence a political opponent, and not, as the government claimed, to improve the management of London services. This argument had a wider resonance because it chimed with growing criticism of the prime minister's 'dictatorial style' that extended beyond a Labour-voting minority. In 1984–5, substantial majorities disapproved of the government's rate-capping of local councils, its banning of trade unions at the intelligence communications centre GCHQ, and its attempt to suppress the BBC Real Lives television documentary about Northern Ireland.[20] Between 1983 and 1985, there was also a significant increase in the number of people who predicted that the government's term of office would result in less personal freedom.[21]

Above all, the GLC's claim that it was a victim of a political vendetta was also widely believed because it accorded with how the authority was represented in the right-wing press. Abolishing the GLC, the *Daily Express* (29 September 1983) bluntly explained, was a way of 'jettisoning the extremist rubbish'. 'The government does not need to produce arguments for killing off the GLC', declared the *Sun* (5 December 1984) since 'Red Ken's antics says it all'. 'The abolition of the Greater London Council' the *Daily Telegraph* (18 January 1984) concluded approvingly, 'is a sentence of execution for bad behaviour'.

This rhetoric from the government's press supporters undermined the credibility of the government's claim, set out in its White Paper, that it was closing down the GLC only in order to simplify local administration in the interests of better democracy and greater efficiency.[22] Instead, Conservative press outbursts strengthened the impression – fostered by County Hall – that the government's real agenda was to suppress political opposition. Londoners' responses confirmed that the Conservative press campaign against the GLC 'boomeranged', and hit the Conservative government rather than its intended target. In January 1984, 54% of Londoners agreed with the view that the GLC was being abolished 'to silence a political opponent', while only a quarter disagreed. By contrast, a mere 21% thought that 'the government was trying to abolish the GLC in the interests of Londoners', whereas 59% dissented from this view.[23]

## Classic advertising campaign

The government compounded its credibility problem by announcing that it intended to cancel the 1985 GLC elections. The government feared that a re-elected Livingstone administration would spend public money with reckless abandon in the last year of the GLC's life. It therefore proposed that joint boards, made up of nominees from the London borough councils, should be installed to manage the council's affairs in its last year. This meant cancelling elections that the Conservatives might well lose, and imposing a Tory regime of nominees at County Hall since the majority of London borough councils were then Conservative-controlled. This proposal thus reinforced the impression that the government's policy towards the GLC was both partisan and undemocratic. It aroused wide-spread criticism not only from the government's opponents but even from within the Conservative party itself. In the words of the former Tory Prime Minister, Edward Heath, the government's plan laid 'the Conservative Party open to the charge of the greatest gerrymandering of the last 150 years of British history'.[24]

The Livingstone administration exploited this apparent own goal through a skilful advertising campaign masterminded by the leading advertising agency, Boase, Massimi and Pollitt (BMP). Most Labour councillors had wanted the advertising campaign to focus on how the GLC's abolition would undermine the council's services to the capital.[25] However, the agency persuaded the GLC that there was another, more effective way of mobilising public support. BMP focus groups revealed that most people did not know about the government's plans to cancel the GLC elections and install a Tory regime at County Hall, but that those who did tended to strongly disapprove, regardless of which party they supported. This suggested, the agency argued, that the advertising campaign should draw attention to the government's cancellation plans with the slogan, 'Say No to No Say'. The slogan conveyed the subliminal message that the council's abolition would permanently remove the people's 'say'.[26]

This was a classic agenda-shifting strategy. To have focused on the loss of GLC services to the community – as GLC councillors proposed – would probably have renewed controversy about council policies, and elicited a polarised response. By redefining the terms of the debate, and shifting attention away from the tabloid agenda of left-wing excess to local democracy, it communicated a powerful message which people were already predisposed agree with: that their right to vote should not be curtailed. It also invited a bipartisan response, enabling Conservative- and Liberal Alliance-supporting Londoners to side with the GLC without modifying their views. And it reached out to people who did not know that the government was intent on cancelling the GLC elections, and sought to persuade them through imparting additional information.

The first phase of the advertising campaign focused on the cancelling of elections. It was typified by a large poster of Ken Livingstone, with the headline 'If You Want Me Out You Should Have the Right to Vote Me Out'. This proved to be highly effective. Between January and April 1984, there was a sharp increase of unprompted awareness of the government's plans for the GLC; a significant reduction in the number of people who were undecided on the issue; and a rise of twelve percentage points in the proportion of Londoners who opposed the GLC's abolition.[27] However, it is important to reiterate that the campaign, which began in March 1984, merely strengthened opposition to abolition: it did not create it (see Table 4.1).

**TABLE 4.1** Londoners' Attitudes Towards GLC Abolition, from 1983–5

|  | % Approve | % Disapprove | % Don't Know |
|---|---|---|---|
| bOct 1983 | 23 | 54 | 23 |
| bJanuary 1984 | 19 | 50 | 30 |
| cMarch 1984 | 23 | 54 | 23 |
| bApril 1984 | 18 | 62 | 20 |
| bMay 1984 | 17 | 64 | 18 |
| bJuly 1984 | 18 | 66 | 16 |
| bSeptember 1984 | 17 | 62 | 20 |
| aSeptember 1984 | 17 | 74 | 10 |
| aMarch 1985 | 22 | 62 | 16 |

Data is from market research companies: aHarris Research Centre; bMORI; cAudience.

The second phase of the GLC's advertising campaign depicted the alternative to the GLC as more central government control, with the implication that it would be more bureaucratic and expensive, and less responsive to the needs of Londoners. It featured images like a bowler-hatted snail, a bowler-topped brick-wall, and poster boards bound with red tape, with the slogan 'Imagine What London Would be Like Run by Whitehall'. Its centralisation message failed to convince the majority: in September 1984, only 40% thought that abolition would result in the GLC's functions coming under central government control.[28] At best, this second phase may possibly have deflated the government's counter-message that the abolition of the GLC would promote better, more localised democracy. But it had nothing like the impact of the first phase.

The third phase of the campaign focused on the extent of support for the GLC. It was summed up in the poster slogan '74 per cent say No'. This was a misleading reference to a rogue result that was out of kilter with other polls (which indicated that just under two-thirds rather than three-quarters of Londoners disapproved of the GLC's abolition, with a significant minority abstaining). The main purpose of this third phase was to strengthen opposition to abolition in Parliament.

## Community campaigning

When the Livingstone administration turned to an advertising agency, celebrated for its promotion of Smash Instant Mashed Potato (Cadbury Schweppes) and John Smith's Yorkshire Bitter (Courage), to mount a political advertising campaign against the government, it was breaking new ground. It also innovated by funding and choreographing public events in order to promote its new politics. It recruited professional impresarios – with experience in organising rock festivals and concerts, but in some cases drawing inspiration from royal jubilee celebrations and other royal pageants[29] – to stage major public events for Londoners. These were dismissed by critics as concealed bribes designed to win approval for the GLC at public expense. In fact, they operated at a more sophisticated level than these critics grasped: they were more than just free entertainments, the equivalent of Roman 'bread and circuses'.

The GLC used festivals as a way of promoting specific political campaigns (Fares Fair in 1982, Peace Year 1983, London Against Racism 1984, Jobs Year 1985 and Farewell celebrations 1986). The council also mounted other events such as the family-oriented Thames Day Festival and London Horseshow, conveying the message that the council was for everyone. A typical GLC festival took the form of an extended pop concert accompanied by political side-shows, street theatre and stalls of all kinds. They usually communicated a political message through visual means. For example, the Jobs Festival had a maze in which doors displaying government policies led nowhere, while those featuring GLC policies provided the way out. However, the unifying meaning of all these major public events – and their prime significance in terms of the anti-abolition campaign – was that they affirmed a communal London identity. They were occasions of festivity when normal conventions of separateness and reserve were set aside in favour of a liminal sense of togetherness (in which people talked freely to strangers). They also expressed a sense of community in ways that celebrated the cultural diversity of the capital – through the eclecticism of the music (from advanced rock to black gospel and jazz), through the different cuisines (from Chinese to Caribbean) on offer, and above all through the mass participation of people (several hundred thousand in some cases) drawn from different parts of London and from different ethnic groups. They were thus 'social rituals' that fostered a plural, multicultural understanding of what it was to be a Londoner.[30] Their implicit message was also that the GLC was the institutional embodiment of London, and needed to be defended against central government and its allies.

When the government attempted to champion local borough government against the GLC, County Hall moved swiftly to supplement these major events with smaller ones in local boroughs. GLC organisers fanned out from County Hall, offering financial backing and practical help to any local group willing to mount a public event that explicitly opposed the abolition of the GLC. Their reports back to County Hall read like those of nineteenth-century Christian missionaries: full of hope, frustration, and (one suspects) overstated success. However, the scale of their activity, when it was in full swing, can be gauged by what happened in March 1985: County Hall's 'link team' organised or intervened in thirty-four local meetings, events and festivals (as well as nine general, London-wide events) in one month.[31]

The GLC also broke new ground by becoming a major sponsor of the voluntary sector. Its funding of self-organised groups rose from around £6 million in 1980 to over £50 million in 1984.[32] By the time the GLC was closed down, it was funding over 2,000 organisations. These included not only feminist, ethnic minority, gay and left-wing organisations – that generated so much tabloid hostility – but a much larger number of 'mainstream' organisations such as myriad local community associations, crèches, playgroups, nurseries, law centres, training centres, groups for the handicapped and disabled, pensioners' groups, tenants' groups, sports and recreational associations and organisations linked to the churches.[33] Their unaligned character is further underlined by the correspondence that took place between GLC-funded organisations and County Hall in 1983–4. Numerous organisations refused to submit a formal objection to the GLC's closure, as part of the government's consultation exercise, on the grounds that they did not want to get involved in politics. Yet, some funded organisations were drawn into the GLC's orbit and supplied helpers to organise local borough and other events. Though this was not the original intention (since, initially, the GLC's grants policy was an expression of its sixties distrust of bureaucracy) the council developed what amounted to a quasi-clientelist system of patronage. It was effective precisely because it extended beyond the left to take in a large swathe of the voluntary sector, and won goodwill among public spirited, community volunteers who were often significant sources of personal influence.

The Livingstone administration also found other ways of expressing the political message not conveyed by its advertising campaign. The range of services provided by the GLC for the community was advertised by 'branding' all buildings and vehicles with the GLC logo. Voluntary groups were asked to display 'GLC-funded' declarations as prominently as possible. Above all, the GLC's press office sought to promote two key themes in its dealings with broadcasters: that the GLC offered important services to the community, and that these were threatened by the GLC's closure. This public relations strategy met with growing success. The more the GLC was in the news – vilified by the tabloids, and championed in parliament – the easier it became to secure local broadcasting coverage of routine GLC activities.

This is borne out by media coverage of the GLC in a single week, 1–7 June 1985, during the height of the GLC battle.[34] Although the GLC was still the target of tabloid attack (with six out of ten tabloid stories in this week featuring the GLC's alleged left-wing excesses), the council was still reported very differently by broadcasting. Eleven out of sixteen items on radio, and five out of seven on television, were about GLC services to the community, some with a subsidiary theme that these services were threatened by the GLC's closure. Some of these stories probably originated from County Hall's publicity machine: for example, a 'visual' story about the GLC re-introducing owls into London as part of its policy of restocking the capital's wildlife, or a report of the council's visionary plan (in a context when the council was due to close in nine months' time) to establish seaside homes for the elderly. Only one 'negative' story reported in the tabloids – about a plan said to be under consideration by the council for the twinning of London with the Nicaraguan capital Managua – was covered on broadcasting (BBC TV's *London Plus*).

The effectiveness of these different forms of communication – political advertising, music-based public events, sponsorship of the voluntary sector and skilful public relations – contrasted with the results of more traditional left-wing methods of campaigning. The GLC organised a 'Democracy Day' of demonstrations, stoppages and meetings, which mobilised only a radical minority and generated predictably unfavourable press coverage. It attempted to stage a mini-referendum by causing a number of by-elections to occur at the same time. However, these were boycotted by the Conservative Party, and were widely viewed as a meaningless stunt; they resulted in a 'GLC' victory on a low poll. The council also distributed a regular free publication, *The Londoner*, which was negatively perceived as too political.[35] In addition, the GLC organised a mass petition, which, according to one opinion poll, 36% of Londoners were asked to sign.[36] This last at least provided an opportunity for GLC activists to put the anti-abolition case to Londoners on a one-to-one basis, even if it had very little wider impact.

However, the net effect of the GLC's multiple forms of campaigning was only to stabilise its support during 1984–6 after its initial surge in the spring of 1984.

## Government's failure

Another way of viewing the battle over the GLC is to examine why the government failed to win more support. Six months after publication of its White Paper, which set out the reasons for closing down the GLC, the government had the backing of only about one in five Londoners. Nothing that the government did subsequently succeeded in reclaiming significant lost ground.

Yet, the government's case was far from negligible. In essence, it was that the GLC did not do very much, cost a great deal for what it did and its functions could be easily transferred in ways that made for better and cheaper local administration. London borough councils were already responsible for social services and housing, while the Inner London Education Authority (ILEA) managed education. The GLC was relieved of its main responsibility, control of London Transport, in 1984. Indeed, the GLC was responsible, according to the government, for only 16% of total expenditure on local services in London in 1983,[37] and 'less than 11 per cent of services' in the capital by 1985.[38] Its small range of responsibilities did not seem to justify its large staff and overheads. Local government in London could be simplified, in the official view, by being concentrated in borough councils and their representatives.

This was not just a way of rationalising political sectarianism. A very similar case had been advanced in 1979 by an able, young councillor who declared: 'I feel a great deal of regret that Marshall [1978 Inquiry] did not ... say "Abolish the GLC" because I think that it would be a major saving and would have released massive resources for productive use'.[39] He continued, 'I do not believe you need two tiers of local government'.[40] The young councillor's name was Ken Livingstone. He became celebrated for arguing exactly the opposite opinion.

However, all the key elements of the government's argument were rejected. Londoners were unconvinced, as we have seen, that the GLC was 'unnecessary'. They were not persuaded that its closure would make for better local administration. In April 1984, 62% said that services would get worse after abolition, while only 9% thought they would improve.[41] Similarly, 55% thought that abolition would make for less efficiency, compared with 14% who thought that it would result in more.[42] Indeed, the government did not even communicate effectively its most basic argument – that GLC services would be transferred rather than abolished. In 1985, the most cited reason given for opposing abolition in an open-ended question – given by 34% – was that London would lose GLC services.[43]

## Media logic

The government failed to get across its managerialist case for abolishing the GLC partly because it was seldom reported. Its case did not fit the populist agenda of right-wing popular newspapers. Thus, the *Daily Mail* rejected the anti-GLC article, which it had commissioned from the Environment Minister, Patrick Jenkin, on the grounds that it was too dull to publish. Right-wing journalists believed that their assault on the GLC was more persuasive than the government's technocratic rationale. In any case, they sensed that their readers – drawn from all over the country – had little interest in the details of local government reform in London. Their jihad was more attuned to what their readers would find interesting – and angry-making.

The government's case was also marginalised, with one notable exception,[44] in television current affairs programmes about the GLC's abolition.[45] These were framed in terms of the tabloid case that GLC was a threat to the public vs. the GLC's argument that its abolition was an assault on local democracy. For example, presenter Gavin Weightman introduced the London Weekend Television's *The GLC Abolition* (4 November 1983) by summarising the tabloid case for abolition: 'Ken Livingstone's GLC is perceived by Conservatives as a high-spending Marxist council, making free with ratepayers' money to support strange causes like the IRA and lesbians'. He concluded by summarising the GLC's anti-local democracy argument: 'The view that the long arm of Whitehall will be reaching into every recess of local government is gaining ground … It seems likely that many more people will raise the cry that the passing of the GLC has heralded the arrival of a Ministry for London'. Within the main body of the programme, the government's case was marginalised, and presented in such a condensed form that it would have been difficult to comprehend without background knowledge.

This TV marginalisation was partly a consequence of 'media logic'. The tabloid case against the GLC was more dramatic and attention-grabbing than the government's administrative rationale. Balancing the tabloid case against the GLC's case also made for symmetry. The opposing arguments – lunacy vs. democracy – dovetailed with each other, and were easy to communicate and understand. It made for 'good television'.

The second reason for the marginalisation of the government's case is that the GLC won the news source battle. How TV journalists reported and commented on the news was very strongly influenced by the elite actors they spoke to. TV programmes about the GLC paraded a succession of prestige sources supporting the GLC. They included critical Conservative MPs and peers (including a former Prime Minister, Foreign Minister and Environment Minister), senior opposition politicians, cross-bench peers, rebel Conservative GLC councillors, representatives of numerous London groups (of which the arts lobby was the most vocal) and accredited experts (notably local government academics and broadsheet journalists). By contrast, very few sources backed the government's case, and these tended to be low status: loyal backbench Conservative MPs, London Conservative borough councillors and the Thatcherite Institute of Directors (but not the Confederation of British Industry (CBI) which stopped campaigning against the GLC, nor the London Chamber of Commerce which backed the GLC). In the chess game of competing sources, the GLC had most of the pieces.

The government was thus very badly served by the media. As argued earlier, press partisanship backfired on the government. Its case for closing down the GLC was made to look spurious: pretending one thing while the Conservative press expressed the real, undemocratic reason for shutting up 'Red Ken'. In addition, the government's claim that the GLC was a lightweight, almost functionless authority was implicitly contradicted by the tabloids' representation of County Hall as a powerful, menacing Politburo-on-the-Thames. The prominence given to the GLC in the national press also rendered it more newsworthy, and made it easier for the council to secure extensive coverage from local radio and television.

## Losing the elite debate

The only part of the media which extensively reported the government's case was the quality press. Yet, the government failed to win over even most of these predominantly Conservative newspapers.

This was for four main reasons.[46] The government did not prepare the way for change through the time-honoured mechanism of a public enquiry or Royal Commission. There was thus no prior elite consent for what it proposed.

The government was intellectually outgunned because it knew less about local government in London than GLC officials. For example, a reluctant civil servant supplied to the Environment Minister, Tom King, a 'ballpark figure' for the savings that the GLC's abolition would achieve.[46] This figure was then paraded by government spokespersons, only to be publicly withdrawn when it was revealed to be totally implausible.

The government's third problem was that there were intellectual tensions at the heart of its case. Although the government made a technocratic case for cheaper, more streamlined local government, it was in actual practice trying to curb the 'profligacy' of the new urban left – a political objective. And while it argued for greater devolution of decision-making to the local borough level, it was also increasing central government control over local government. These contradictions were exposed in the heat of public debate.

The fourth problem was that there was an underlying intellectual case for having a central co-ordinating agency to manage a conurbation as large and complex as London. Academic experts repeatedly made this argument in the public domain.

In the event, five out of seven national quality papers either supported the GLC or asserted the need for a directly elected authority for the capital. This reflected a wider failure on the part of the government to win over informed opinion.

## Failed counter-attack

The government belatedly attempted to mount a counter-attack. In January 1984, the Prime Minister's Press Secretary, Sir Bernard Ingham, set up a committee to better co-ordinate the government's anti-GLC offensive. This was followed in April 1984 by the launch of Efficiency in London, an anti-GLC campaign group led by London local borough Conservative politicians. In September 1984 Kenneth Baker, a more feline and populist politician than Patrick Jenkin, was drafted in as Local Government Minister. He replaced Jenkin as Environment Secretary in the following year.

Yet, nothing the government did seemed able to turn the tide. This was partly because the GLC consciously set about softening its radical image. By 1984, people in County Hall weeded out grant applicants that might afford easy targets for press attacks (but sometimes recommended informally that the organisations concerned might consider changing their names in order to improve their chances of securing a GLC grant). In 1981, Livingstone had boy-cotted the marriage of Prince Charles and Lady Diana Spencer out of repub-lican principle: three years later, he invited the Queen to open the Thames Barrier, spoke warmly of her 'real sense of service to the people' and claimed that she was on the GLC's side. His press officer, Nita Clarke, arranged for Ken Livingstone's royalist mother to meet the Queen, and set up heart-warming media interviews afterwards. When Livingstone opposed resistance to rate cap-ping in 1985 (and fell out with his radical Deputy, John McDonnell),[47] the resourceful Nita Clarke used this to portray Livingstone to journalists as a member of the 'cuddly left'.[48]

Livingstone's pragmatic radicalism elicited a rueful compliment from the Deputy Prime Minister, William Whitelaw. 'There is no doubt', he commented, 'that Red Ken who, for years I thought was an invention of Conservative Central Office, has, in fact, really won practically every trick so far in the game'.[49]

Even the press assault against the GLC began to falter in the heat of bat-tle. The *Mirror* group of newspapers backed the GLC in 1984, with the *Sunday Mirror* reversing its support for abolition. The *London Standard* also backtracked by supporting the creation of a directly elected London council. Even, the *Mail on Sunday* and *Daily Express* broke ranks and opposed the cancelling of the GLC elections. Among the dailies, only the *Sun* and *Daily Mail* maintained with undiminished vigour their anti-GLC campaign until the very end.

## Victory in defeat

Worse still, the government faced a growing rebellion in parliament, fanned by the professional lobbying firm, with strong Conservative connections, employed by the GLC. The government's first reverse was over its 1984 'Paving Bill' to replace the GLC and the six metropolitan county councils with interim joint boards. A rebellion in the Commons, backed by senior Conservatives, and a still larger revolt in the Lords, forced the government to back down. Its next reverse was when it was forced to withdraw its proposal to close down the Inner London Education Authority.[50] The final showdown was over a rebel amendment to the 1985 Local Government Bill abolishing the GLC.

The amendment proposed that the GLC should be replaced by a directly elected London authority. It was immediately dubbed the 'son of Frankenstein' by government supporters. Yet, the amendment was defeated in the Commons by only twenty-three votes, with over a hundred Tory MPs voting against their government or abstaining. This was followed by a fraught debate in the Lords where a similar amendment was defeated by only four votes. The government, with large majorities in both Houses of Parliament, only just scraped through.

But if the government, backed by parliamentary whips, eventually won the parliamentary battle, it lost the political argument. The most enduring legacy of the GLC abolition campaign was that it consolidated a consensus among Londoners in favour of an elected London council (see Table 4.1). In 1991, a MORI poll reported that 64% approved of an elected authority for London[51] – a figure very close to the 62% who disapproved of the abolition of GLC in its last week in 1986.[52]

No less important, the GLC won elite political support for its resurrection. In 1983, the leaders of the Labour Party, Social Democratic Party (SDP) and Liberal Party had all been deeply hostile to the GLC regime, with the SDP being officially in favour of the council's abolition. The SDP subsequently reversed its position, and all three parties on the centre-left rallied behind the GLC, while major rifts opened up on the right. Consent was not secured within the political class for London to be without a London-wide local authority.

In 1991, the Labour Party announced its intention to establish a new London-wide council. In 1998, the Labour government (elected in 1997) held a London Referendum, in which it recommended the establishment of a directly elected London authority. The proposal was carried by 72% of the poll. In 2000, the GLC (albeit in a diminished incarnation) was reborn as the Greater London Authority, and the role of GLC leader was replaced by that of directly elected mayor. The person first elected, and then re-elected, as mayor was none other than Ken Livingstone.

The campaign on behalf of the GLC thus turned defeat into victory. It paved the way for its subsequent resurrection.

## Blocked legacies

For a time, it also looked as if the GLC battle would have two further legacies. GLC policies became increasingly popular in the council's last phase. Two surveys conducted by the Harris Research Centre in 1983 and 1985 reveal the remarkable shift that had taken place (although part of this shift might have been due to a change of wording in the 1985 questionnaire).[53] In 1985, the majority of Londoners backed all the GLC's major policies, with the exception of its anti-racism policies about which they had reservations and its pro-gay policies which they still opposed. The majority also said that they wanted the local council to generate jobs, protect the environment, hold the police to account and promote equal opportunities. What seems to have happened is that the GLC benefited from a 'halo effect'. First, Londoners rallied to its cause, then they reassessed more favourably what the council was doing.

It also appeared as if the political alignment of the capital had shifted. London had long been a barometer of the national political weather. In the June 1983 general election, for example, the Conservative lead over Labour in London was only two percentage points below that in the country as a whole. But between June 1984 and March 1986, Labour's lead over the Conservatives in the capital surged to between thirteen and twenty-two percentage points above the national average.[54] Some believed that London would become a flagship for a new kind of politics that was both progressive and popular,[55] (a belief that was eventually borne out in the 2017 general election when Labour under Jeremy Corbyn won 55% of the popular vote in London compared with the Conservatives' 33%, although much water was to flow under the bridge before this happened).[56]

Another seeming outcome of the GLC battle was that it brought into being a powerful political alliance determined to defend local democracy. This drew support from across the political spectrum: from councillors in all parties alarmed by the extension of central government control; from critics of 'new right' authoritarianism, among the liberal right as well as left; and above all from 'constitutionalists' who viewed the autonomy of local government to be a safeguard against democratic centralism. This last tradition was more strongly embedded within the Conservative Party than in the Labour Party (since the latter tended to defend centralisation as a way of securing uniformly high standards of public service provision across the country). Indeed, it was Conservative constitutionalists like Sir Geoffrey Rippon – a former Environment Minister who in 1984 called for the introduction of constitutional curbs against excessive state centralisation – who were, in some ways, the doughtiest defenders of local autonomy as a core principle during the GLC battle.[57]

In the event, these developments proved short-lived. The new urban left in London became discredited. The pro-Labour tide in the capital receded. Above all, the cross-party alliance opposing increased central government control fell apart. Indeed, senior politicians in all parties became reluctant to champion local government autonomy because it became such a tarnished cause. How all this happened is explored further in the chapters that follow.

## Notes

1 Market and Opinion Poll Research Centre (MORI), *Attitudes of Londoners to the Abolition of the GLC* (London: MORI, October 1983).
2 Ibid., table 3.1, p. 65.
3 B. Worcester and L. Gilbert, MORI, 'Voters in Greater London', Confidential Memorandum to the Labour Party (14), 26 May 1983.
4 Harris Research Centre, *Survey of Public Opinion in London* (Richmond: Harris Research Centre, June 1983).
5 This analysis is derived from articles archived each day by the GLC Public Relations Department, and 'Telex Monitors Radio and TV Log' undertaken for the GLC by Radio and Television News Service for Record and Research (RTNS), London. The latter data set provides only a brief note about each programme item, and, to judge from our own research, omitted some current affairs programmes. But despite these defects, its log still provides a valuable insight into the news agenda of TV and radio reporting of the GLC.
6 Harris, *Survey of Public Opinion* (1983).
7 Interview with the late Veronica Crichton, formerly press officer to the Majority Party, County Hall, by the author.
8 However, the available broadcasting logs relate only to the last phase of the Cutler administration.
9 Interview by the author.
10 Interview by the author.
11 The difference between economic and social radicals during this period is a central theme of R. Waller, *Moulding Political Opinion* (Beckenham: Croom Helm, 1988). It was a long-term problem of the left which the International Publishing Group grappled with unsuccessfully when it tried to launch the pre-Murdoch *Sun* in the 1960s. (See J. Curran and J. Seaton, *Power Without Responsibility*, 7th edition. (London: Routledge, 2010.)
12 Cited in J. Carvel, *Citizen Ken* (London: Chatto and Windus, 1984), pp. 132–3.
13 The Hon. Sir Robert Carnwath, 'The reasonable limits of local authority powers', *Public Law*, Summer 1996.
14 Audience Selection, August 1981. Opponents of rate-funded transport fare reductions decreased to 43% by 1983, but still outnumbered those in favour (25%), according to MORI, April 1983. The surge in support for cheap fares thus took place later but was preceded by a significant reappraisal in 1981–3.
15 Harris Research Centre, *London Attitude Survey* (Richmond: Harris Research Centre, 1985).
16 Interview with Bill Bush, formerly head of the Leader's Office, County Hall, by the author.
17 Interview by the author. Tony Wilson emphasised that this was an approximate estimate that took account of all forms of promotion, broadly defined.
18 MORI, *Attitudes of Londoners to the Abolition of the GLC* (London: MORI, April 1984).
19 Harris, *London Attitude Survey* (1985).

20  Ivor Crewe, 'Has the electorate become Thatcherite?', in R. Skidelsky (ed.), *Thatcherism* (London: Chatto and Windus, 1988).

21  Cited in Anthony King, 'Rumours of a revolt in a land that's not so free', The *Guardian*, 8 November 1985.

22  Department of the Environment, *Streamlining the Cities* (London: HMSO, Cmnd 9063, 1983).

23  Cited in MORI, *Attitudes of Londoners*, April 1984, p. 6.

24  Cited in A. Forrester, S. Lansley and R. Pauley, *Beyond Our Ken* (London: Fourth Estate, 1985), p. 67.

25  Interview with Tony Wilson, former Director of Publicity, GLC, by the author.

26  Interview with Chris Powell, Senior Partner of Boase, Massimi and Pollitt, by the author.

27  MORI, *Attitudes of Londoners*, April 1984.

28  MORI, *Attitudes of Londoners to the Abolition of the GLC*, September 1984.

29  Interview with Ken Hume, former GLC Festival organiser, by the author.

30  This draws on the interview with Ken Hume, and Franco Bianchini, 'Cultural Policy and Political Strategy', unpublished Ph.D. thesis, University of Manchester 1995.

31  GLC Events Diary (34), Campaign Link Team, 25 February 1985 (summarising the following month's events).

32  B. Pimlott and N. Rao, *Governing London* (Oxford: Oxford University Press, 2002) p. 35.

33  Computer printout of all organisations funded by the GLC on 28 February 1986, supplied to the author.

34  Same sources as cited in Note 5.

35  Harris, *Survey of Public Opinion* (1983).

36  MORI, *Attitudes of Londoners to the Abolition of the GLC*, June 1984).

37  Department of the Environment, *Streamlining the Cities* (London: HMSO, 1983), p. 4.

38  Kenneth Baker, *Reporting London*, Thames Television, 26 February 1985.

39  Cited in Forrester, Lansley and Pauley, *Beyond Our Ken*, p. 43.

40  Cited in Ibid., p. 103.

41  MORI, *Attitudes of Londoners*, April 1984.

42  Ibid.

43  Harris, *London Attitude Survey*, 1985.

44  *Reporting London*, 26 February 1985.

45  The *GLC Abolition* (The London Programme), London Weekend Television, 4 November 1983; *The House of Lords and the GLC* (The London Programme), London Weekend Television, 26 April 1985; *A Week in Politics*, Channel 4, 13 April 1984; *A Week in Politics*, Channel 4, 21 March 1986. The left-wing extremism versus local democracy framework was modified in the final stage of the GLC's life to left-wing extremism versus the council's struggle to preserve services after its closure.

46  Interview with former Environment Secretary, Lord Jenkin (Patrick Jenkin), by the author.

47  This is described in detail in K. Livingstone, *If Voting Changed Anything, They Would Abolish It* (London: Collins, 1987), pp. 308–35.

48  Interview with Nita Clarke, former press officer of the GLC Labour Group, by the author.

49  William Whitelaw, *Reporting London*, Thames Television, 25 October 1984.

50  ILEA was eventually closed down in 1990.

51  MORI London poll (June) reported in the *Sunday Times*, 27 July 1991.

52  Harris, *Final Day Poll*, March 1986.

53  The wording of the lead-in to a key set of questions in the 1985 Harris survey (*London Attitude Survey*) encouraged a positive response ('I am going to read out some specific propositions which some people think might improve things in London. Could you tell me how strongly you approve or disapprove of each bearing in mind that any

money necessary would have to come from rates and taxes.') There was no comparable lead-in in the 1983 Harris survey (*Survey of Public Opinion in London*).

54  Waller, *Moulding Public Opinion* (1988), table 12.4, p. 86.
55  'Goodbye GLC', *New Socialist*, 37, April 1986; Beatrice Campbell and Martin Jacques, 'Goodbye to the GLC', *Marxism Today*, April 1986; 'The big yin versus carry on up the Khyber', *Tribune*, 11 April 1986.
56  J. Colombeau, 'The 2017 General Election – the numbers behind the result', figure 3, London Datastore (Mayor of London) available in: https://data.london.gov.uk/apps_and_analysis/the-2017-general-election-the-numbers-behind-the-result/ (accessed December 30, 2017).
57  For example, Sir Geoffrey Rippon interviewed in *A Week in Politics*, Channel 4, 13 April 1984.

# 5

# 'NOT FUNNY BUT SICK'

## Urban myths

*Julian Petley*

## Latter-day folk devils

Attempts by right-wing British newspapers to demonise sections of the left are as old as the left itself. Long before Mrs Thatcher so egregiously labelled the striking miners of 1984–5 as the 'enemy within', the majority of Britain's press had perfected a way of representing the ideas and personalities associated with socialism as so deranged and psychotic that they represented a danger to society. Thus defined as modern incarnations of folk devils and placed outside the parameters of what many politicians and most papers would be prepared to recognise as 'proper' and 'acceptable' political debate, they have been rendered effectively illegitimate and other, and consequently fair game for what can be described only as sustained editorial hate campaigns (see Figure 5.1a and b.)

Within weeks of Labour winning control of the Greater London Council on 7 May 1981, its leader, Ken Livingstone, was regularly being described by newspapers as 'barmy' and 'loony' and GLC policies were being stigmatised as 'crazy'. This line of attack was gradually extended to include various Labour-controlled local councils in London; for example, Islington earned the sobriquet 'Bananas republic' in the *Sunday People* (13 March 1983) and was featured as 'The mad mad mad mad world of Islington' (*Mail on Sunday*, 13 February 1983). But this kind of rhetoric did not really gain momentum and crystallise around the alliterative phrase 'loony left' until *after* the Tories' vindictive abolition of the GLC in 1984. Significant moments in what was, in effect, a prolongation and intensification of the campaign against Ken Livingstone and the GLC were the London local council elections of May 1986, the Greenwich byelection of February 1987 (in which Rosie Barnes won Greenwich for the Alliance from Labour) and the runup to the general election later that year. After that the torrent of stories gradually slowed, although the phrase has

(a)

(b)

FIGURE 5.1 Conservative-supporting newspapers have habitually used grotesque caricatures as a means of demonising and de-legitimising the left. "I don't know what effect my troops will have on the enemy, but by God, they frighten me!" by Michael Cummings. (a) 1 October 1973, *Sunday Express*, courtesy of Express Syndication Ltd. (b) 8 February 1987, *Sunday Express*, courtesy of Express Syndication Ltd.

since become firmly embedded in press (and by no means simply tabloid) parlance and still surfaces quite regularly. For example, in the *Sun* (3 July 2017) in an article headed 'Corbyn mob rule will spark a Labour war', Trevor Kavanagh warned that 'the loony left are out of control, hysterically raising their fists against a democratically elected Tory government'. Its decline from the heady days of 1986–7 can at least partly be explained by changes in Labour policy and image after its 1987 defeat (changes not unconnected, of course, with the party's desire to lose the 'loony left' tag), although the stories may also simply have lost their novelty value and been replaced by equally ideologically loaded myths about the Human Rights Act 1998 being a 'villains' charter,[1] the European Union 'imposing' all sorts of crazy regulations on Britain[2] and Muslims allegedly demanding the banning of Christmas, Easter and piggy banks.[3]

'Loony left' stories in the press have two prominent themes: Labour councils are irrationally obsessed with minority and fringe issues, and in particular are paranoid about racial and sexual 'problems' which do not actually exist outside their own fevered imaginings. This characterisation enables their policies, and especially their antiracist and equal opportunities ones, to be dismissed as 'loony', it strips councillors of their legitimacy as elected representatives by reducing them to the status of unrepresentative freaks, and, by thus denying their democratic status, it facilitates their portrayal as authoritarian ideologues attempting to impose their crazed views on the public. Significantly, many of the 'loony left' stories are about children – that section of society least able to defend itself from indoctrination and most vulnerable to unscrupulous manipulation.

This demonisation of Labour councils contained a powerful, though initially implicit, call for retribution: the government should 'do something' – curb their spending, curtail their antics or transfer their powers to 'responsible' central government. Both implicitly and explicitly, singly and together, these various stories represented calls for the diminution of the powers of local government, and thus echoed Tory policy at the time. So, for example, and as described in the subsequent chapter, the controversy over positive images of gays and lesbians in Haringey was exploited as evidence that local education authorities had far too much power over what happened in individual schools, and was utilised to reinforce the argument that those powers should be largely redistributed amongst a combination of parents, school governors and, of course, central government.

In this chapter, however, we are concerned not with such a 'grand narrative' but with a number of smaller stories published in 1986–7. These are typical of a vast number of similar stories[4] published in the press during the period in question: we have simply chosen some of the more prominent. We investigated each of these stories in detail, examining the background to the reports, talking to the sources quoted in them, and, wherever possible, to the journalists concerned.[5]

It has to be admitted, however, that as far as this last task was concerned, we were largely unsuccessful when it came to the national press in particular. Often stories were not bylined – hardly surprising since so many were straight lifts from other papers. But even on the few occasions we managed to track down the authors of stories, most of them simply refused to answer our questions. Unfortunately, the motto of far too many journalists on national newspapers is 'never apologise, never explain', leading Will Hutton to remark in the *Observer* (17 August 2003) that 'Britain's least-accountable and self-critical institutions have become the media – and the way they operate is beginning to damage rather than protect the society of which they are part'. Thus, whilst in their 'loony left' stories (and elsewhere too) journalists have endlessly harped on about the importance of transparency and public accountability in every institution about which they write, they are habitually utterly unwilling or unable, when challenged, to subscribe to these values in their own profession. We did occasionally encounter responses along the lines of 'I'd like to talk to you but it's more than my job's worth', and this, of course, explains why so many critical books about the British press, such as the recent *Mail Men*,[6] are chock-full of anonymous quotes from journalists. However, the climate of fear which seems to prevail amongst the employees of most of Britain's national newspapers sits extremely oddly and uncomfortably with those papers' endlessly repeated claims to represent the Fourth Estate.

Haringey, and especially Bernie Grant, Britain's first black council leader, were favourite targets of the press, and they feature prominently in several of our selected stories.

## The 'racist' bin liner

The first of these concerns an allegedly 'racist' bin liner. Under the headline 'The racist bin liner is blacked', Chester Stern claimed in the *Mail on Sunday* (2 March 1986) that 'black bin liners have been banned at Bernie Grant's leftwing Haringey Council because they are "racially offensive"'. This was supported by a statement from an anonymous 'storeman at the North London council's central depot' and by a quote from a councillor who said that 'there was no written ban on the use of black sacks' – but added that the council had 'a strong antiracist policy'. Stern ended his piece thus: 'The council has now changed over to grey sacks – to avoid offending West Indian workers in the cleaning department'.

The report, notwithstanding the citing of a typically anonymous source, is quite without substance. In short, the council had not banned black bin liners at all. Indeed, days after the article appeared, and as a council minute confirms, the Civic Services Committee had accepted a tender from a local supplier of black liners, since these were the cheapest on offer. Of course, Stern could not have known about this decision, since it was taken after he wrote the report, and, atypically, he did in fact discuss the story with us, accepting that he was in error to claim that the banning of black bin liners was Haringey policy. However, he added that his story was 'not wholly false'. It was based, he said, on a oneoff incident when a storeman at the council's central depot in Hornsey High Street refused to accept an order for bin liners from two parks department staff because the order contained the word 'black'. The storeman claimed the black bin liner 'ban' was council policy. The park staff complained to their local (Labour) councillor, Brian Bullard, who recounted the incident at a subsequent council meeting. When we spoke to Bullard, he stated that the story had come to him from a park attendant, who had been informed by another staff member of the remark allegedly made by the storeman. Bullard's own retrospective opinion was that the story had originated in a joke which had been misunderstood, and that the whole affair was entirely without foundation.

The story about the storeman was originally relayed to Stern by a local freelance journalist, and he accepted this testimony as sufficient evidence for the existence of a ban. The council were not contacted for verification. The *Mail on Sunday* claimed that this was because the story was supplied to them on a Saturday when there are no council spokespeople available for comment. In turn, the council denied this and said that its spokespeople could be contacted on a Saturday via the council switchboard.

On 9 March 1986, the *Mail on Sunday* published a small and misleading update on the bin liners story. Under the headline 'Race peace in the bag', we learn that 'black dustbin liners at the centre of a council race storm are not to be banned after all'. Thus, in a typical journalistic move, what had previously been erroneously presented as fact was now re-presented as a proposal which had been subsequently withdrawn as a result of its being revealed by the paper. However, having its cake and eating it, it continued to publish indignant letters by readers who had apparently not read of this new twist to the story.

## 'Barmy' Bernie Grant

Grant himself crops up in another story concerning alleged antiracist measures, only here the subject is language. On 25 May 1986 the *Mail on Sunday*'s Liz Lightfoot ran a piece under the headline 'Bernie's banter is baffling', with the strap 'Parents' fury at Caribbean dialect lessons'. The article claimed that: 'Bernie Grant, controversial leader of Haringey council, has caused uproar over a scheme to teach West Indian dialect in the borough's schools. Black parents have told him they want their children taught English and maths instead of the dialect known as creole'. Condemnations by the West Indian Leadership Alliance and the local Conservative opposition leader were also reported, and Lightfoot's piece concluded with various examples of creole: 'An angry bus conductor might say "Gwan girl, yo too jerky pickmount. Me doing dis work for me eyes deh a me knees" or: "Stop being such a fussy old woman. I've been doing this job since I was kneehigh to a grasshopper"'.

The story was picked up by a number of other papers. For example, the *Sun* (27 May) ran a leader entitled 'Barmy party', which introduced

> the latest wheeze from Barmy Bernie Grant. The leader of London's Haringey Council wants children to be taught the West Indian dialect Creole and they will be understood in the backstreets of Kingston, Jamaica, and probably nowhere else in the world .... But don't imagine that Bernie's antics will afflict only one suffering part of London. Remember he is a parliamentary candidate for Labour at the next Election ... Labour is now the Official Barmy Party!

Illustrating the way in which these stories regularly travelled outside London, it also appeared in provincial newspapers, including the *Shropshire Star* (30 May) under the headline 'Now time he was agoing'. 'What I want to know,' the writer asked, 'is when Bernie Grant and his friends are going? The sooner and the farther the better. That may be Double Dutch. But do you get my drift?'

This story appears to have been based on reports in local newspapers about a conference held in Haringey on the subject of Caribbean languages in schools. Originally, the *Weekly Herald* had reported the conference under the headline 'Creole for kids?' (15 May). This reported, correctly, that the conference was organised by Haringey Community Relations Council (and not by the London Borough of Haringey, as Lightfoot asserts). Moreover, the conference had the support of a number of black parents' groups and was not universally opposed, as the *Mail on Sunday*'s report insisted. This aspect had come out quite clearly in the *Times Educational Supplement*'s 23 May report on the conference, headed 'Black parents in Creole campaign'. Haringey went to considerable lengths to counter the allegations, even calling Liz Lightfoot into the press office and going through the copy line by line with her. In her defence, Lightfoot claimed that her report had been cut, and so may not have been 'too clear' in its final form, which raises the suspicion that, at the sub-editing stage, the story may have been deliberately 'modified' in order to suit the paper's ideological position on matters such as this – not exactly an uncommon occurrence in sections of Fleet Street.

The *Sun* managed to couple Bernie Grant to one of English society's most routinely demonised groups, namely travellers.[7] In an article on 4 November 1986 entitled 'Bernie spends £½m on toilets for gypsies', Phil Dampier reported that 'Barmy council leader Bernie Grant is planning to spend nearly £½m of ratepayers' money on 24 superloos for gypsies. The loony leftie is splashing out on behalf of roving Irish tinkers, even though many of his longterm council tenants have no INSIDE toilet'. Local Conservative councillors were quoted as denouncing such moves as 'outrageous and extravagant'. Readers were also informed that, at one site, '12 families will each be treated to private bathrooms at a cost of £395,000'.

The story, which would have been highly likely to outrage those Haringey tenants with inadequate toilets, is highly inaccurate and misleading. Far from buying bathrooms at a cost of some £33,000 each, as suggested, the council had moved to spend a total of £395,000 over the next twelve months on all facilities for all travellers' sites. Of this sum, £333,000 was to be spent on the construction of twelve permanent pitches on Wood Green Common in accordance with the council's statutory obligations under the Caravan Sites Act 1968 (in line with increasing hostility to travellers on all fronts, these obligations were later abolished by Section 80 of the Criminal Justice and Public Order Act 1994). The remaining £60,000 was to be spent on improving the existing temporary sites. Phil Dampier declined to comment on his article.

A more extensively reported story attempted to link Grant with another favourite target of the Tory tabloids, namely the then newly elected government of Nicaragua. Under the headline 'Barmy Bernie is going coffee-potty', with the strap 'Staff must drink Marxist brew', the *Sun* (5 December 1986) reported that 'the leftwing council led by "Barmy" Bernie Grant has ordered its workers to show "solidarity" with Nicaragua… by drinking the Marxist country's grotty coffee'. 'Only beans from the red Central American state will be bought by the council', it claimed, and 'a spokesman for "Barmy" Bernie said, "We have decided to purchase this type of coffee as a gesture of solidarity"'. The *Sun* reporter assessed the merits of this decision by asking the opinion of a 'top Mayfair coffee-seller', and reported that the Nicaraguan blend, while costing the council 'an extra £820 a year', was of inferior quality. However, the article did contain an official denial from 'a spokesman for "Barmy" Bernie'.

In fact, *all* the central claims of the report are false. Neither the council nor Bernie Grant had issued an instruction for only Nicaraguan coffee to be drunk. However, the story received wide coverage in other tabloids. The *Mail* ran the story on the same day as the *Sun* under the banner 'Marxist beans Bernie's cup of coffee'. The Labour-supporting *Mirror* also ran a nearly identical story, under the by-line of John McShane, on the same day under the familiar-sounding headline 'Barmy Bernie goes coffee potty', with the strap 'Council's cuppa must be Marxist'. The same fictitious 'order' was cited and the same Mayfair coffee merchant apparently sought out, duly to deliver the identical words. 'The decision', McShane noted, 'is likely to leave ratepayers with a bitter taste because it will cost them an extra £820 a year'. However, he gave a more detailed contextualisation than had been forthcoming in the *Sun*. The view of the leader of the local Tory opposition was reported ('absurd'), and the piece concluded by making a link to other examples of the council's alleged folly:

> Haringey may soon have more staff to sample the true brew, however. The council is on the lookout for eight recruits to work in its gay services unit at a cost of £100,000 a year. Bernie Grant hit the headlines in October when he refused to condemn the rioters at Tottenham, where a policeman was stabbed to death. He said the police 'got a bloody good hiding'.

However, although the words allegedly uttered by Grant have been endlessly reiterated by the right-wing press and have come to occupy pride of place in a certain kind of demonology, they were taken entirely out of context and presented in such a way as to represent Grant in the worst possible light.[8]

This was another story that also spread to various provincial newspapers. The *Manchester Daily Star* (5 December) ran the story as 'Bernie backs red coffee'. The nonexistent 'order' was referred to yet again, and the piece concluded by pointing out that Haringey ratepayers 'will also have to find more than £100,000 a year for eight new staff in a unit being set up to help local gays and lesbians'. Wolverhampton's *Express and Star* followed suit with 'Bernie's coffee bar' (7 December). Here, the 'order' by the 'idiotic "Barmy" Bernie Grant' was said to have been enforced 'despite the fact that his loony council faces ratecapping for overspending, and is £28 million short in its budget'. As if this were not enough: 'Grant and his comrades have still committed £120,000 to a homosexual and lesbian unit. Life is certainly funny in Grant's Marxist Haringey, but the joke is on the ratepayers' (the story of the unit is analysed in detail in the subsequent chapter on Haringey).

The *Sunday People* ran a story on 8 December 1986 entitled 'Nuts to you and your coffee, Bernie', which, in the space of four short paragraphs, discussed the 'order' in terms of 'Barmy Bernie Grant … brewing up more trouble', 'coffee potty Bernie', 'Bernie old bean' and 'the loopy council leader'. The conclusion ran: 'Mind you, I'd have thought he would have felt much more at home with coffee from Brazil. That is, after all, where nuts come from'. The *Weekly Herald* (12 December) featured 'Coffee controversy stirs a bitter brew', concentrating upon the taste of the coffee and the local Tory reaction, but not reproducing the fictitious 'order'. Not so, however, the *Birmingham Post*'s 'Bitter taste' (19 December). This quoted Peter Bruinvels, Tory MP for Leicester East, to the effect that 'it is just as daft and offensive as poor old Leicester City Council now trying to pair with Nicaragua'. The 'order' by Grant, 'widely criticised recently for his comments on the riot at Tottenham's Broadwater Farm estate', was also presented for comment to Timothy Eggar, a junior minister at the Foreign Office. Eggar remarked that 'I understand the comment was made that the coffee has a distinctive taste, which may not please the majority unless they are used to it. I think the same can be said of Mr. Bernie Grant'. Further reproduction of these statements by two national Tory politicians featured the following day in Greenock's *Telegraph* ('Coffee move slammed'), the *East Anglian Daily Times* ('Coffee choice not to Tory's taste') and Newcastle-upon-Tyne's *Journal* ('Daft claim').

## 'A total tissue of lies'

Brent was a favourite subject of 'loony left' stories, and is the subject of a whole chapter in the previous edition of this book. Thus, for example, on 26 February 1987, the *Sun* claimed that the borough was providing cash to enable black youths

to visit Cuba free but that the cash was not available to white ones, a story absolutely calculated to stir up resentment amongst white people. Billed as 'Another
*Sun* exclusive', it was headlined 'Freebie trip for blacks but white kids must pay.
Barmy Brent does it again!' Written by David Jones, it alleged that the council
would spend at least £9,000 to make good any shortfall in the funds raised by
the group organising the trip. Those chosen to go had to be unemployed, on low
pay or rehabilitating after conviction for a crime. The article quoted the leader
of the Brent Conservative group as saying: 'For a hard-up, rate-capped borough
like ours to waste cash like this is ridiculous'. 'Youth worker Shirley Williams'
was quoted to the effect that 'blacks are getting the subsidised places because we
really only want to take them'.

The article begins by stating that: 'A Loony Left council is splashing out at
least £9000 to send a group of black teenagers on an all-expenses paid jaunt to
communist Cuba'. However, there is absolutely nothing in the article itself to
back up such an assertion. Indeed, as the article itself admits, the whole event
was being organised by a group called Caribbean Exchange, who were holding
a series of fund-raising events to pay for the trip. Our own researches showed
that the group's only connection with the council was that they were affiliated
to its Youth and Community Services, just like hundreds of other groups in the
borough, including the scouts and guides. Brent told us that they allowed the
group to use council premises for fund-raising activities but made it clear that
they had not applied for a grant to help pay for the proposed trip, although they
were eligible to do so. There was no evidence that Caribbean Exchange was
favouring black youths at the expense of white ones, nor was rehabilitation after
conviction a condition of going on the trip. Furthermore, we could not find any
youth worker named Shirley Williams in Brent, although David Jones insisted to
us that he did speak to such a person. We did manage to track down a youth and
community worker for Brent Council named Lynne Williams, who had indeed
been phoned by Jones, but she flatly denied making the statement attributed to
'Shirley Williams'. She also told us that she had informed the Brent press office
that the *Sun* was after a story, and that the press office wrote a very detailed statement about the trip, which they then checked with her before sending it to the
*Sun*. She described the story which actually appeared as 'racist', 'vicious' and 'a
total tissue of lies'. Caribbean Exchange told us that the story had made it much
more difficult to raise funds for the trip because it had sown racial divisions and
exerted a highly destructive effect on the project.

Caribbean Exchange actually complained to the Press Council about this
story. In an unusually tough adjudication, the Council stated that:

> The headline, which was provocative and potentially racially divisive, was
> unsupported in the story below it by anything more than an assertion by
> the newspaper. On the evidence presented to it, the Press Council finds
> that the headline was inaccurate and misleading. The article contained
> inaccuracies, some of them significant, and unsupported assumptions.

In the Press Council's view it was loosely written and had not been investigated as closely as such a story should have been before a newspaper
decided to publish it. The paper's overall presentation was misleading and
the complaint against the *Sun* is upheld.

## 'Now the Lefties bar manholes'

Another allegedly 'loony' council frequently in the news was Hackney. For
example, on 27 February 1987 a story attributed to 'a *Standard* reporter' and
headlined 'Taking "sexist" man out of manhole' appeared in London's *Evening
Standard*. Its substance, insofar as it had any at all, was that the council's equal
opportunities committee had proposed banning the term 'manhole' and that
this was now council policy. The article quoted four people: an anonymous
council spokesman, sewage worker Tom Jordan, Tory councillor Joe Lobenstein
and deputy council leader Jim Cannon. It claimed that the council's engineers
and sewerage workers would in future have to use the words 'access chambers'
instead of 'manhole covers'. Jordan was quoted as complaining that:

> It's absurd. We have a memo from the council telling us about the change.
> I can't imagine calling manholes anything else, least of all an access cham-
> ber. Where on earth do they dig that description up? But I suppose we
> shall have to comply with the regulations – even though we all think it's a
> joke. Most of us are sexist anyway – we love the topless models which the
> council hates. So they are asking us to be hypocrites.

The council spokesman states that: 'It is our policy to use non-sexist language.
The word manhole clearly defines it. It is an insult to women. Why not call them
womenholes?' Lobenstein denounces the whole idea as 'potty' and 'a total waste
of money'. The most extensive quotation, however, is from Jim Cannon, who
states that:

> I don't see anything wrong with calling a manhole an access chamber.
> Language reflects people's attitudes. At the moment it reflects a man's point
> of view. Talking about manholes and access chambers strikes me as a mar-
> ginal issue. But it should be looked at in the context that language should
> make women more confident of their own position and take away the
> restrictions that only men can do certain things.

The following day, the *Sun* ran a short piece under the headline 'Now manhole
is a dirty word' and the *Standard* headed its equally short article 'Loony'. The
*Star*, however, carried a full report by a '*Star* reporter' entitled 'Now the lefties
bar manholes'. The story is almost identical to that in the previous day's *Standard*,
except that Jim Cannon is also quoted as saying that: 'I am at the stage when the
use of the word man grates with me'. A *Sun* editorial (1 March), headed 'Not

again', opined that Hackney councillors were not fit to hold public office, adding that: 'As for the idiot who first thought of banning "manholes", we suggest he puts his head down the nearest access chamber and keeps it there'. The story also formed the subject of Keith Waterhouse's column in the Labour-supporting *Mirror* (3 March), under the headline 'The silly tendency', in which he lumps in the Hackney councillors with those from Lambeth who had changed street names and declares them all to be 'barking mad' and a 'gang of lunatics'. The story was also repeated in the *Cumberland Evening News* (3 March), *Peterborough Evening Telegraph* (4 March), *Nottingham Evening Post* (6 March), *East London Advertiser*, *Southend Evening News* and *Municipal Journal* (all 7 March). Letters about it featured in the *Standard*, *Birmingham Evening Mail*, *Sunday Telegraph* and *Ilford Recorder*.

However, as our own research showed, Hackney council had never in fact issued any instruction, memo or report about the use of the word 'manhole', nor had the word been the subject of any formal discussion within the council, although it did have a policy of avoiding words such as 'fireman' and 'foreman' which might give the impression that certain jobs were reserved specifically for men. Nor did the council employ anyone named Tom Jordan. So where did the story actually come from? Our researches eventually led us to the Fleet Street News Agency, which circulated the story on 27 February. Its then editor, Leif Kalfayan, who was shortly to move on to the *Mail*, admitted that his recollection of the story's origin was poor, but insisted that it had come from the *Hackney Gazette*. However, our own researches show that the paper had never run the story, and when we raised the matter with its local government correspondent, Tim Cooper, he vehemently rejected Kalfayan's claim and insisted that the story had originated from the agency.

Whatever the case, it's important to note that the source which was used by both the *Standard* and the *Star* to boost the credibility of the story was the deputy leader of Hackney Council, Jim Cannon. However, the quotation from Cannon by no means confirms the story, since nowhere does he state that the council has banned the use of the term 'manhole', simply remarking that: 'I don't see anything wrong in calling a manhole an access chamber'. Cannon told us that that he returned home one night at 1 a.m. to find a message asking him to ring a journalist 'urgently'. When he did so, he was surprised to be asked how he would react if the council were to ban the use of the word manhole. He recalled saying that he thought the use of language a serious issue, adding that the journalist surely had more important issues to investigate. Now, anybody who has ever been interviewed by a journalist absolutely determined to elicit a quote which will fit the story they've already written (as well, of course, as suit their newspaper's political line) will understand the difficult position in which Cannon found himself. However, it also needs to be borne in mind that he was relatively inexperienced in these matters, having only just been made deputy leader of Hackney, a borough in which there may well have been Labour supporters so ideologically pure that they did indeed believe that all language should be purged of any conceivable sexist or racist connotations. In these circumstances, Cannon may well have wondered if the word 'manhole' really had been banned, or perhaps he was unwilling to alienate any Labour purists by stating outright that if the council were to pass such a ban it would make itself a laughing stock. But, for whatever reason, he made the absolutely fatal error of answering a hypothetical question in such a guarded and equivocal manner that it enabled the journalist to stand up (after a fashion) the highly dubious story which they were clearly determined to publish.[9]

## 'Baa Baa Black Sheep': Hackney

The most well-known of all the 'loony left' myths is undoubtedly that of the alleged 'ban' on schoolchildren singing the nursery rhyme 'Baa Baa Black Sheep'. This story first appeared under the by-line of Bill Akass in the *Star* (15 February 1986) with 'Now its Baa Baa Blank Sheep'. According to Akass:

> Toddlers have been ordered to stop singing Baa Baa Black Sheep ... because it is racist. Staff at a nursery school in Hackney, London, claim the traditional nursery rhyme is offensive to blacks. At first they wanted the 30 children aged between one and three – only two of whom are black – to sing Baa Baa White Sheep instead. But now it has been banned altogether at Beavers Nursery in De Beauvoir Road. Leaders of Left-wing Hackney council welcomed the ban last night. A spokesman said: 'We consider playgroups and nurseries should be discouraged from singing the rhyme. It reinforces a derogatory and subservient use of the word "black" among our youngsters in their formative years. This is particularly important because the majority of children in our nurseries come from black and ethnic minority communities'.

This view was contrasted with that of 'one outraged mum' who stated that 'I think it's bloody stupid. What will they do next?'

The *Star* story was taken up by Tim Cooper in the *Hackney Gazette* (18 February). Under the headline 'Baa Baa banned', with the strap 'Councillors object to ancient rhyme being recited in nurseries', this stated that 'children in Hackney have been banned from reciting the nursery rhyme – because Labour councillors think it is racist'. It then goes on to quote the above council spokesman. However, what happens here is that the *reaction of* the council spokesman on being presented by Bill Akass with his original story has metamorphosed into the *reason for* the imposition of the alleged 'ban' in the first place. However, the story also contains a quote from one of the playleaders to the effect that 'we're run by parents and if they want us to stop singing it, we would. But there have been no complaints so far, though someone once suggested it could be racist'. In other words, no such ban had been imposed by the nursery school, as claimed by Akass, whatever impression may have been given by the Hackney spokesperson.

Entirely typically, the *Sun* simplified all of these ambiguities. Under the headline 'Lefties baa black sheep' (20 February) it asserted that 'Loony leftwing councillors have banned children from reciting the nursery rhyme ... because they claim it is racist. One nursery has even reacted by writing new words which begin Baa Baa White Sheep'. This version of the story duly appeared in the Irish paper the *Sunday World* (23 February), which also suggested some galumphingly unfunny new nursery rhyme possibilities, such as Senior Citizen MacDonald Had a Rural Collective, Old Socially Disadvantaged Single Parent Hubbard Went to the Cupboard and other such would-be witticisms.

The story received further attention in the letters columns. In the *Hackney Gazette* (28 February) a correspondent suggested a new version of the rhyme: 'Baa Baa Black Sheep, censored by a fool. Yes sir – yes sir, another sheepish rule'. On 4 March the *Gazette* ran a contribution from another reader:

> Some Labour, Militants and SWP are trying to create a racist problem where it does not exist ... Stop this phoney antiracist campaign. Banning Baa Baa Black Sheep, black coffee, white coffee, etc. ... is to reduce a noble battle for justice and equality for all races to a trivial pursuit in semantics.

The *Gazette* published yet another letter three days later, offering 'Baa Baa Grey Sheep, have you any wool? Yes person, yes person, three containers full (bags is an offensive term for women)'. The *Ilford Recorder*, 6 March, featured a letter under the headline 'Baa! Protest that has no rhyme or reason', whose author exclaimed:

> What about this latest nonsense in Hackney about children learning 'Baa Baa Black Sheep'? It's as pathetic a complaint as wanting to remove from the marmalade pot the friendly golly kids love ... What of the many white people whose surname is Black? ... And some black people whose surname is White? ... Will we be expected to feel odd when buying a ticket to – dare I say it – Blackfriars, or even Whitechapel?

Later, the story was even to appear as the subject of a spoof in *Knitting International* (4 April), drawing explicitly on the *Sun*'s report. This reported the activities of a 'Campaign Regarding Equal Tonality in Natural Sheep', under the headline 'The white sheep of the family'.

The story thus enjoyed considerable and widespread, indeed global, coverage. But despite constant repetition, evidence was nowhere adduced to make the story stand up. Nor were those, journalists and letter writers alike, who repeated the story able to point to any solid, factual evidence which backed up their assertions. Only the black paper, *The Voice*, emphatically rejected the story and offered an explanation of its genesis and purpose. Under the headline 'Hackney humbugged', it argued that 'the row over Hackney Council's alleged banning of the nursery rhyme ... is not so much a storm in a teacup as a deliberate attempt to discredit the work that the council does in increasing racial awareness'.

The actual facts of the story are as follows. When Bill Akass discovered what he alleged to be a ban at Beavers Nursery on 'Baa Baa Black Sheep', he rang Hackney press office in order to find out the council's view on the matter, even though the nursery was run by the parents, and not by the council (as Akass' story could be read as implying). Furthermore, as can actually be judged from the *Hackney Gazette* article, there was never any ban on 'Baa Baa Black Sheep' at the nursery; instead, and for reasons quite unconnected with racism, 'Baa Baa White Sheep' had occasionally been sung simply as an alternative version of the rhyme, and with numerous other lines changed for humorous effect. Martin Bostock, at that time press officer for the council, takes up the story:

> It was possible for the council to say: 'We don't know what this nursery is doing, but whatever they're doing it's up to them'. This was the advice we took to the then leader of the council [Tony Millwood]. I had a long discussion with him. He, however, wanted to take a bullish attitude and show support for the alleged ban at Beavers. And, between us we arrived eventually at a statement saying that we supported what they'd done, although making it quite clear that it was not a council nursery and not a council ban.

From here, of course, it was but a short step for Tim Cooper of the *Hackney Gazette* to visit Beavers and ask parents for their reaction to Hackney council's apparent support for the alleged ban; indeed, as Cooper himself said to us:

> I think [the council] really shot themselves in the foot. I think they issued the statement because they, or the council leader at the time, believed the ban was in force and tried to justify it. I think they were wrong. There was no ban in the first place. By issuing the statement they virtually created the story, which obviously snowballed from there.

And, in many respects, Martin Bostock agrees:

> The council allowed itself to be led by the nose into the story in the first place ... We allowed ourselves to be drawn in and comment on it. We didn't have to, but we did. However, I think that the newspapers concerned were guilty of turning our support for the alleged ban into a council ban. We were accused of instituting a ban, but, however naïve we may have been as a council, and I think we were over this one, we did not ever say that we had banned or wanted to ban the rhyme.

Thus, the genesis of this story has a great deal in common with that about manholes analysed above, and can be explained not only in terms of certain newspapers' news values and ideological/political positions, but also of a certain ideological rigour and rectitude on the part of certain council representatives themselves. To quote Bostock again:

> There was a tendency to compound what were in my opinion undoubtedly conspiracies by some journalists to create these stories. We, the Labour councils, I'm afraid to some extent compounded that by being more than happy to jump in and comment and add our voices to things that had not been properly checked out. And that we had no need to comment on at all. A story can be quite easily fabricated in that way. Someone denying something immediately becomes a story instead of just having nothing to do with it.

On the other hand, one really does have to consider why on earth such minor parochial matters in certain London boroughs should be considered newsworthy by national newspapers in the first place

## 'Baa Baa Black Sheep': Haringey

However, this episode in Hackney was only the beginning. According to Anthony Doran, writing in the *Mail* (9 October 1986), under the headline 'Baa Baa, Green (yes green) Sheep!', Haringey Council had ordered playgroup leaders to attend a racism awareness course, on pain of grant withdrawal if they refused, at which they were instructed that the council had banned the rhyme as racist. In future, children would have to sing 'green' sheep instead. An anonymous playgroup leader is credited with the story. Parents, teachers and Kenneth Baker at the Tory conference in Bournemouth, were quoted as condemning the alleged ban.

The story appeared the same day in the *Birmingham Evening Mail*, where it featured twice, under the headlines 'Silly bleat' and 'Green sheep? They've got to be joking'. In the latter, a local race relations leader is called upon and denounces the alleged ban as 'ridiculous' and as raising 'a great danger of turning the whole subject into a joke'. The story also appeared in the *Liverpool Echo* ('Black sheep in the dog house') and the *Yorkshire Evening Press* ('So sheepish'), which advised its readers to 'enjoy laughing at this potty behaviour. But let's not be too carried away with hilarity. It's funny, yes. But is it not also sinister?' The *Birmingham Post* (10 October) followed suit with 'Racist sheep are a joke', an article in which local parents were quoted as deriding the 'ban'.

The *Sunday People* (12 October) likewise reported on the 'ban' and the 'compulsory course', commenting that: 'With loonies like this running the schools, the future for education in Haringey looks extremely black. Sorry. Extremely green'. The same day's *News of the World* announced a 'Green sheep take over' in an article which began with the words: 'Labour has promised to step up the numbers of coloured immigrants. That's a mistake'. Following this introduction, the 'green sheep' story is reported, along with the aside: 'But what if it turns out

Martians are green?' A Tory MP in Birmingham lamented in the *Sunday Mercury* that 'it makes you weep that loonies get elected to councils'. Carlisle's *Evening News and Star* (13 October) ran the story beneath 'Bernie bleat barmy', claiming that the alleged ban 'will probably cause a storm of protest on Mars'. The Yorkshire *Evening Courier* (14 October) also carried the story, warning: 'But it is no joke that parents must watch the thinking that has abnormal sexual quirks as acceptable and should be taught so in schools, that political indoctrination is part of their social studies'. The *Liverpool Echo* (15 October) returned to the story with 'Just barmy', whose author opined that 'I'm surprised they haven't also condemned it on grounds that to subject a sheep to intrusive personal questioning over whether it has any wool is an offence against animal rights'. The same day Ipswich's *Evening Star* ran 'A load of wollies!'

The facts of the story, which were never reproduced outside the black press, were that the racism awareness course had been requested by playgroup leaders in Haringey, that attendance was not compulsory and that the council had issued no such ban. There is no evidence that the rhyme was ever mentioned on the course. Haringey went to great lengths to counter the 'green sheep' allegations, initiating legal action against the *Mail* (which, as so often happens in such cases, it was forced to drop for financial reasons), and taking statements from fifteen people alleged to have been involved in the 'ban'. What appears to have happened is that a number of playgroup workers who attended the course did not appreciate what they took to be some of its arguments about the racist connotations of everyday language. They then complained to the *Mail*, infamous for its vigilance for the merest hint of a 'loony left' story, that next they would probably be forced to stop children singing 'Baa Baa Black Sheep'. In its sustained attempts to stand up the story, the *Mail*, as is its wont, phoned or door-stepped about twenty playgroup workers, one reporter claiming to be a Haringey parent looking to place a child in a playgroup which did not practice racism, and others posing as Marks and Spencer or Tesco managers wanting to put on racism awareness training courses. Most disobligingly, none confirmed the alleged ban on 'Baa Baa Black Sheep'.

The council's considerable efforts to defend itself were ignored by the press for some time. In the *Haringey Advertiser*'s 'Black sheep still in evidence' (16 October), the council's rebuttal made its first appearance in print. A council spokesperson was quoted as saying that 'the frequency with which stories like this appear in the *Mail* seems to suggest that it is trying to discredit the council'. But the fiction had by now been uncritically reproduced across the entire country. That same day, it even appeared in a satirical piece in *Men's Wear*, which pointed out the need to don 'green ties' for formal occasions. Three days later *The Sunday Times* (19 October), featured a letter beneath the headline 'The blacking of Comrade Black Sheep'. Haringey was subjected to a mock critique for failing to realise that the rhyme 'encapsulates the socialist principles at the heart of our caring, loving society ... Green sheep don't exist. If they did they would probably live in a world far removed from our galaxy, probably called Haringey, whose cultural heritage would be rather different from ours'. Auberon Waugh, writing the same day in the *Sunday Telegraph*, used the 'ban' to demonstrate how, compared to the US, Britain is 'pretty well a nation of loonie lefties'. Two days later a *Times* leader, 'Exploiting race', warned that 'it is a common fallacy to suppose that what is funny must be harmless'.

The story cropped up yet again on 23 October in the *Hendon Times* under the headline 'Stop stirring up trouble'. *The Sunday Times* (26 October) featured a letter headed 'Colour bar' which claimed: 'It is clearly no longer permissible to black a job ... To describe a certain skin affliction as blackheads is completely unacceptable'. That same day the *Mail on Sunday* featured a similar letter, which argued that an example had been set for 'fellow lefties' in the north, with Manchester now to be noted for its 'Green Pudding'. On 30 October, the *Mail* returned to the 'story' with a leader drawing parallels between Haringey Council, the Spanish Inquisition and Nazi Germany. The Haringey playgroup leaders themselves issued a statement deriding this editorial in particular and pointing out the hypocrisy of the fact that the *Mail* itself had ardently supported Hitler right up until the outbreak of the Second World War. This statement attempted to set the record straight on 'Baa Baa Black Sheep', but was reproduced only in the black press (*Asian Herald*, 3 November; *West Indian News*, 5 November). Nothing daunted, however, the *Economist* (1 November) was perfectly happy to feature the story among the list of 'loony sins' that Tory Central Office could use to pin on the 'ever-so-moderate Mr. Kinnock'.

## 'Baa Baa Black Sheep': Islington

On 20 February 1987, the story resurfaced in the staunchly anti-council *Islington Gazette* under the headline 'Bye bye black sheep', with the strap 'Mum's fury over ban on "racist" nursery rhyme'. Attention, this time, was focused on an angry mother's removal of her handicapped son from an Islington council nursery because his teachers objected to his singing 'Baa Baa Black Sheep'. The article quoted from the child's report which stated that 'we do not encourage the rhyme Baa Baa Black sheep because it has been identified as racially derogatory and is actively discouraged by Islington Council'. It then went on to give a good deal of space to the mother's negative reaction to her son's report, and the piece concluded with a council spokesperson stating that 'it is not council policy to ban Baa Baa Black Sheep, but if individual nursery workers find it offensive the council is not in the business of forcing them to teach that rhyme rather than others'. It also added that 'the council appointed an anti-racist adviser for the under-fives in 1985'.

What appears to have happened in this case is that the staff of Beacon Day Nursery really *did* believe that it was Islington council policy to discourage the rhyme, but because the nursery staff refused to talk to us, we do not know why this was the case. However, given the veritable flood of stories about Baa Baa Black Sheep and other alleged anti-racist initiatives appearing in both national and local papers at the time, a perfectly plausible explanation is that these stories had fuelled and confirmed just such a belief. On the other hand, the council spokesman's equivocal statement quoted above, and their refusal to issue a forth-right denial of any such ban, left the door open, just as in the Hackney examples analysed earlier, for the absolutely inevitable deluge of press stories which fol-lowed the *Gazette* piece.

The *Daily Express* (20 February) ran the story on its front page under the head-line 'School bars boy's Baa-baa Black Sheep "racist" rhyme'. This report was very similar to that of the *Islington Gazette*, save that the writer, Michael O'Flaherty, failed to report the council's reaction. That the council had appointed an antira-cist adviser for the under-fives is all that we hear about the local authority, thus letting the nursery workers' entirely mistaken impression of council policy set the framework of the piece. The *Telegraph* (20 February) did however conclude its article headed 'Boy's first rhyme upsets nursery staff' with the council state-ment. The same day's *Mirror* ran a short piece, 'Baa Baa blacked', in which the statement is abbreviated to: 'If they find it offensive we're not going to make them teach it'. In the *Mail*, Ruth Gledhill wrote a piece entitled 'The little boy who made the mistake of humming Baa Baa Black Sheep', which at least includes a quote from local Labour councillor Chris King to the effect that:

> There is clearly a problem somewhere, down the line, and we are going to look into it. We have over 6,000 staff and on this occasion someone clearly got hold of the wrong end of the stick. It was an overzealous interpretation of our equal opportunities policy. We have a strong equal opportunities policy, but no member of this council has ever resolved that Baa Baa Black Sheep is to be actively discouraged. We have a lot of staff and we cannot – and nor should we – control everything they do.

However, the way in which the story is written, and, in particular, laid out, gives the strong impression that the ban was indeed council policy. For example, it includes a photograph of what it calls the offending 'coldly official comment' written by a member of the nursery staff, with the entirely erroneous caption: 'What the council said'. Islington complained to the Press Council about this article, but it rejected the complaint, supporting the contention of the *Mail*'s associate managing editor that 'the story was not about Islington Council's policy but about how one member of its staff interpreted the policy and the actions she took', and apparently regarding the quotation from Councillor King as an ade-quate representation of the council's position, even though it occupied a relatively small space in a long article which was otherwise almost wholly critical of it.

The *Sun*'s first report, 'Baa Baa nursery ban on sad little Dan' (20 February) began with the words: 'Handicapped tot Daniel Griffin delighted his mum by reciting Baa Baa Black Sheep but loony leftie teachers banned it – for being rac-ist!'. This prepared the ground for the *Sun*'s leader the next day, 'The vile hard left', which stated that 'Loony left councils have given us a good laugh over the years. But Islington's ban on a retarded five year old ... is not funny but sick ...

Islington's callous treatment of little Daniel and his parents earns them the title of vilest council in this country'.

Like the remarkably tenacious, press-created myth that the film *Child's Play 3* was responsible for the death of James Bulger,[10] the myth that Islington council banned children in its schools from singing Baa Baa Black Sheep has proved quite extraordinarily resilient, and sections of the press have been determined that it remain so. Thus, for example, *The Sunday Times* (8 February 1998), in an article entitled 'Champagne socialist toasts family windfall', claimed that the former leader of Islington council, Margaret Hodge, 'banned the singing of Baa Baa Black Sheep in nurseries'. On 4 October 1999, the *Daily Mail* enlivened an article about Hodge's nursery education policies (she was then Education Minister) by reporting that: 'Under her ten-year leadership, the north London council became a byword for "loony left" local government, notoriously backing nursery school staff in 1987 who told off a mentally handicapped five-year-old for humming Baa Baa Black Sheep as it was considered "racially derogatory"'. Shortly after Labour had lost control of Islington to the Liberal Democrats, the *Standard* (6 July 2000) ran an article on the new council's policies, reminding readers that Islington 'was once one of the country's most celebrated loony Labour councils. A place that symbolised the worst excesses of the left, where … Baa Baa Black Sheep was banned for being politically incorrect'. And when Hodge became Children's Minister, the *Sun* (14 June 2003) told its readers that her 'Loony Left council once banned kids from singing Baa Baa Black Sheep'. Later that year, as part of its 'MPs Rich Report', the *Mail* (28 September) spiced up its entry on Hodge by stating that 'as a councillor [she] helped ban the nursery rhyme Baa Baa Black Sheep in primary education in Islington'.

## 'Fake news'

Looking back on these stories from the perspective of 2017 inevitably raises the question of whether or not they constitute what has come to be called 'fake news'. Of course, the term itself is an oxymoron and has been greatly overused in recent times. As David Mikkelson, the founder of the myth-busting website Snopes, put it: 'Fake news was a term specifically about people who purposely fabricated stories for clicks and revenue. Now it includes bad reporting, slanted journalism and outright propaganda. And I think we're doing a disservice to lump all those things together' (quoted in *The New York Times*, 25 December 2016). But, however unwieldy and unsatisfactory the term, it's possible to distinguish four different kinds of journalistic activity which have variously been labelled as 'fake', namely:

- 'News' which has been quite deliberately made up for purely commercial purposes (clickbait of the kind emanating from Macedonia, for example).
- 'News' which has been quite deliberately made up for political or ideological purposes.

- 'News' which is not entirely made up but is seriously inaccurate, either through lack of journalistic rigour, or because of deliberate bias, or both
- 'News' which is quite deliberately made up for the purposes of media critique.

'Loony left' stories of the kind analysed in this chapter and that on Haringey fit largely into the third category, although a few belong firmly in the second. Such kinds of stories are, unfortunately, a major stock in trade of sections of the English national press. As Jim Waterson pointed out on *Buzzfeed* (24 January 2017) in an article aptly entitled 'Britain has no fake news industry because our partisan newspapers already do that job': 'Fake news sites [of the "Macedonian" variety] have struggled to take hold in the UK political sphere, seemingly because traditional British news outlets are already incredibly adept at filling the market with highly partisan news stories that stretch the truth to its limits'.[11] This is not an achievement of which newspapers should be anything but thoroughly ashamed, and 'loony left' stories demonstrate just how very damaging such journalism is to the democratic process, since what are at very best half- and quarter-truths about local and, by extension, national politics serve only to poison the wells of political debate and to misinform citizens about the policies and activities of those they have elected or are about to elect. In this case, the motive for publishing such stories is not exactly hard to ascertain: as pointed out in the chapter on Haringey, 'loony left' stories were meat and drink to the Conservatives and the client press in the run-ups to the London local elections of May 1986 and the general election of June 1987, and local papers in particular were relentlessly scoured by the nationals for the merest hint of 'lunacy' that could be exploited on a UK-wide scale.[12] In the case of certain papers, such as the vociferously anti-Labour *Hornsey Journal* and *Islington Gazette*, the reason for publishing such stories may indeed have been straightforwardly political and ideological, but one should also never underestimate the role of an infantile conception of news values which is ingrained in sections of the British press and which regards these (and similar) stories as simply entertaining and amusing copy without the slightest concern for or awareness of their political consequences.

What these various stories all too clearly demonstrate is exactly what happens when local and national politicians, aided and abetted by politically supportive newspapers, make a concerted effort to demonise those with different political viewpoints and aspirations from their own. Stories are manufactured out of thin air, or stood up on the flimsiest, most dubious of grounds. Thus, drawing on an already well-stocked reservoir of anti-socialist demonology, certain councils are effectively allotted pariah status: once cast beyond the democratic pale and isolated as politically 'other' and alien, they can be relentlessly subjected to sustained campaigns of distortion and vilification. Given the considerable wealth of the newspapers, the financially straitened circumstances of the councils, the financial risks of undertaking legal action, the intimate relations between the Tory government and its press allies, the vicissitudes of defamation law and the utter ineffectiveness of press 'self-regulation', there was very little which councils could do when faced with such an onslaught. As John Walker, press officer for Haringey during this period, put it:

> If you create a climate where an authority is seen to be 'loony', anything becomes plausible, and therefore journalists feel they have *carte blanche* to write whatever they want. There's a whole range of issues where we've been at the end of that kind of treatment, simply because if it sounds daft enough therefore we will have done it.

As we have been at pains to point out, certain local councils stigmatised as 'loony' by the press did not, either through ineptitude, inexperience, ideological purity or a combination of all three, help their own cause by the way in which they sometimes dealt with the newspapers attacking them. However, this should not be allowed to obscure the plain fact that, in pursuit of frankly political/ideological goals, a significant number of newspapers had clearly decided to throw their considerable weight behind the Tory campaign to de-legitimise London's Labour councils, which, like the abolition of the GLC, was part of a wider strategy to wipe socialism off the British political map.[13] In such a situation, it is frankly difficult to see how even the most sophisticated of press and PR operations could have prevented or discouraged newspapers from printing stories which they were clearly quite determined to publish, whether true, partly true or wholly false.

## Notes

1 J. Petley, 'Podsnappery: or why British newspapers support fagging', *Ethical Space*, 3 (2), 2006, pp. 42–50; D. Mead, '"You couldn't make it up": some narratives of the media's coverage of human rights', in K. S. Ziegler, E. Wicks and L. Hodson (eds), *The UK and European Human Rights: A Strained Relationship?* (Oxford: Hart Publishing, 2015), pp. 453–72.

2 P. Anderson and T. Weymouth, *Insulting the Public? The British Press and the European Union* (London: Routledge, 1999); D. MacShane, *Brexit: How Britain Left Europe* (London: I.B. Tauris, 2016); H. Dixon, 'Facts as newspapers saw them: Ipso's role – and a weak BBC', in J. Mair, T. Clark, N. Fowler, R. Snoddy, and R. Tait (eds), *Brexit, Trump and the Media* (Bury St Edmunds: Abramis, 2017), pp. 107–22. For detailed analyses of all the Euromyths peddled by the English national press since 1992 see http://blogs.ec.europa.eu/ECintheUK/euromyths-a-z-index/. This is an extremely useful resource, but it is absolutely shaming that the European Commission in the UK should have been forced to waste valuable resources constantly correcting falsehoods and distortions circulated by newspapers in their long-running, and ultimately successful, campaign to remove the UK from the EU.

3 P. Oborne and J. Jones, *Muslims under Siege: Alienating Vulnerable Communities* (Colchester: Democratic Audit, University of Essex, in association with Channel 4, 2008); H. Muir, J. Petley and L. Smith, 'Political correctness gone mad', in J. Petley and R. Richardson (eds), *Pointing the Finger: Islam and Muslims in the British Media* (Oxford: Oneworld, 2011), pp. 66–99.

4 In his memoir *Exclusive: The Last Days of Fleet Street: My Part in its Downfall* (London: Biteback 2017), p. 200, Maurice Chittenden notes that when he was at *The Sunday Times* in the 1980s, the Murdoch-appointed editor, Andrew Neil,

set out to expose the left-wing posturing of Labour councils who were spending their ratepayers' money on political propaganda rather than much-needed services. It was decided to form the London Boroughs' Unit (LBU) to look into authorities in the metropolitan area. It was not long before an office wag converted its initials into 'Leftie Bashing Unit' and it was a name that stuck with us.

Chittenden's chapter on the LBU is a fascinating insight into how an ideologically committed journalist, one who openly admits to loathing the left (p. 212), routinely attempted to make the news, rather than simply resting content with reporting events that took place of their own accord. For example, Chittenden tells this story of his time at the *Sun*: 'I had rented a grotty flat in Dalston and tapped Kelvin MacKenzie for regular payments on expenses to pay the rent while trying to get a grant from Islington Council for my bogus police monitoring group' (p. 201). The fact that this ploy failed makes it no less reprehensible.

5 This chapter draws upon research carried out by Chris Bertram, Luke Martell and Brennon Wood, as well as the present author, all of whom were members of the Goldsmiths Media Research Group, which published the report *Media Coverage of Local Government in London* in June 1987. This was commissioned by the Association of London Authorities.

6 A. Addison, *Mail Men: The Unauthorized Story of the Daily Mail* (London: Atlantic Books, 2017).

7 R. Morris, 'Gypsies, travellers and the media: press regulation and racism in the UK', *Communications Law*, 5 (6), 2000, pp. 213–19; J. Richardson, *The Gypsy Debate: Can Discourse Control?* (Exeter: Imprint Academic, 2006); K. Bhopal and M. Myers (eds) *Insiders, Outsiders and Others: Gypsies and Identity* (Hatfield: University of Hertfordshire Press, 2010); J. Richardson and R. O'Neill, '"Stamp on the camps": the social construction of Gypsies and Travellers in media and political debate', in J. Richardson and A. Ryder (eds), *Gypsies and Travellers: Empowerment and Inclusion in British Society* (Bristol: The Policy Press, 2012), pp. 169–86.

8 Grant was questioned about this remark at the independent inquiry into the Broadwater Farm disturbances which was chaired by Lord Gifford QC in 1986. As the report, *The Broadwater Farm Inquiry* (1986), makes clear, Grant 'explained that he had been putting forward the view not only of young people, but of a substantial section of the community' (p. 127). The report concluded that:

> Instead of avoiding the problem by distancing himself from Black youths, he tried honestly to articulate their position. In doing so he walked a tightrope, for as an elected leader he represented others also. The words quoted above were not well chosen and should not have been said. He knew as a political leader that the press would seize on an ill-considered phrase; and in this case they did, leading to the impression that Councillor Grant revelled in the defeat of the police. However, we are impressed with the honesty and courage which Councillor Grant showed in trying to articulate the grievances which had led to the disturbances, and in particular the death of Mrs Jarrett, rather than evading the issue with bland statements.
>
> *(p. 128)*

9 A disturbing, but accurate, picture of press practice is provided by Martin Bostock, a former press officer for Hackney:

> There were some particular journalists who would use all manner of tricks to make sure their story 'stood up', as they say. In other words, don't give anyone a chance to prove that it's not true. The kind of technique that people used were to call very late in the afternoon just before the paper's going to bed, when they know that the chances of you being able to research the story and get an authoritative answer and perhaps knock it on the head are remote. You will then get a

call five minutes after the first one, often with a very irate journalist, often giving people a very, very bad time. I've seen people reduced to tears by browbeating journalists who want a response immediately to a story they've probably been working on for a couple of days, or in some cases much more, but they expect the press officer to have chapter and verse immediately at half past six in the evening.

10  J. Petley, 'In defence of "video nasties"', *British Journalism Review*, 5 (3), 1994, pp. 52–7.
11  www.buzzfeed.com/jimwaterson/fake-news-sites-cant-compete-with-britains-partisan-newspape?utm_term=.ptLbQGDBqp#.vqRJkagOoy
12  Local papers generally gave Labour councils in their catchment area a fairer hearing than did the national press (although some, such as the *Hornsey Journal* and *Islington Gazette*, were as vehemently anti-Labour as the *Sun* and *Mail*). Local papers have to bear in mind that their readers, unlike the far-flung ones of national press, are liable know what is happening in their boroughs and are thus better able to distinguish fact from fiction. Nonetheless, certain journalists on local papers did sell 'loony left' stories to the national press, and more than one Fleet Street career was established on such foundations.
13  As Mrs Thatcher put it in her speech to the Scottish Tories on 13 May 1983:

> The choice facing the nation is between two totally different ways of life. And what a prize we have to fight for: no less than the chance to banish from our land the dark, divisive clouds of Marxist socialism and bring together men and women from all walks of life who share a belief in freedom.
>
> *(www.margaretthatcher.org/document/105314)*

And again, in an article in *Newsweek*, 27 April 1992:

> I set out to destroy socialism because I felt it was at odds with the character of the people. We were the first country in the world to roll back the frontiers of socialism, then roll forward the frontiers of freedom. We reclaimed our heritage; we are renewing it and carrying it forward.
>
> *(www.margaretthatcher.org/document/111359)*

# 6

# 'A WAVE OF HYSTERIA AND BIGOTRY'

## Sexual politics and the 'loony left'

*Julian Petley*

## Introduction

In this chapter, I want to examine how a specific set of 'loony left' stories, namely stories about how certain London councils and local education authorities were allegedly trying to 'promote' homosexuality in the schools for which they were responsible, were mobilised by Conservative politicians and newspapers in order to try to damage Labour's chances in the London local government and Inner London Education Authority (ILEA) elections of 8 May 1986 and the general election of 11 June 1987. How successful this initiative was in its own terms is debatable, but three points may be made with absolute confidence. First, these stories formed part of a more general assault by moral campaigners, many of whom were active Tories, against the forces of what they termed 'permissiveness'. Second, such stories played a major role in the Labour leadership's decision to distance itself considerably from the London-based municipal left in order to try to limit what it perceived as the fall-out from what came to be known as the 'London effect'. And third, these stories led directly to the creation of the measure which would become the highly controversial Section 28 of the Local Government Act 1988, which outlawed the 'promotion' of homosexuality by local authorities and in state schools. Thus, the story told in this chapter is not simply one of a campaign against Labour at both the local and national levels by the Conservative party and press, but it is also an analysis of the role that the press can play in the creation and successful passage of legislation. This is not, of course, to argue that 'it's all got up by the press', but, rather, to point to the ways in which newspapers and politicians interact on occasion in pursuit of common policy aims. Defenders of the idea of the Fourth Estate might argue that this is just as it should be, as long as both sides are acting in the public interest, but the overwhelming bias to the right of Britain's national press means that only certain *kinds* of policies can benefit from this alliance, which in turn suggests that it is not the public interest which is being served in such instances, but rather the interests of certain *sections* of the public and of specific *shades* of the political spectrum.

## Setting the scene

The London local elections of May 1986 were a watershed for Labour's initiatives on lesbian and gay rights, with various councils making manifesto commitments on the subject, some involving sex education in schools. Contemporaneously, the government had decided to take a tougher line on what many of its members and supporters – not least in the press – regarded as far too 'permissive' an approach to sex education, against which they had been campaigning, increasingly vociferously, ever since the Tories came to power.

At this time, the heat was on education at the national level. First, teachers were involved in a long-running pay dispute. Then, on 21 May, Kenneth Baker took over from Sir Keith Joseph as Secretary of State for Education and was soon to become a newspaper hero, promising radically to reduce local government responsibility for education (which he did first in the Education Act (No. 2) 1986 and then in the Education Reform Act 1988). The educational inspectorate had recently released their annual report on education, and this had highlighted a deterioration in teachers' ability to understand and cater for students' needs, as well as the negative effects of budget cuts. However, many newspapers had very different explanations for the poor state of education, and they rapidly enrolled sex education in their battle against the local education authorities. Thus, in its 7 May editorial, the *Mail* complained that:

> Education in Britain is a disaster area .... As education has slipped into the hands of the teachers' unions and the local authorities we have seen it visibly deteriorate. Examination performance is down while political indoctrination is up. In place of discipline and skill in basics we now have peace studies and anti-racism. Text books, we are told, are in short supply; but not the glossy books which teach boys to behave like girls, or show children in bed with gay 'parents'.

On local election day itself, *The Times* editorialised on behalf of parents 'who do not want equal-value indoctrination of homosexuality' and against the very notion of heterosexism, whilst a whole page of comment in *Today* urged voters to 'root out' of local government the 'extremists' who have infiltrated the ranks of 'decent' Labour people and are 'squandering' rate-payers' money on 'an unpleasant assortment of unworthy causes' such as 'a £9,800 grant by Hackney Council towards an open day for gays and lesbians' and 'a £120,000 Lesbian and Gay unit set up by Haringey'. On 1 May, under the headline 'Love books Bernie

wants to be banned', the *Standard* told its readers that 'normal sexual relationships between men and women are under attack in the borough of Haringey run
by Labour leader Bernie Grant. The Labour Party's women's manifesto for the
borough elections which take place next week wants heterosexual books banned
from libraries'. No such proposal was in fact ever advanced, and, as in the case
of most articles on this subject, there is an elementary confusion between anti-
heterosexism and hostility towards heterosexuality itself.

The May 1986 local elections in London thus presented a perfect opportunity
for the Tory press and party at both national and local level to mount a concerted
scaremongering campaign against local Labour initiatives on gay and lesbian
rights, and to represent 'loony left' boroughs as microcosms of Britain under a
Labour government. This campaign was able to build effectively on the demon-
ologies which had already been created around similar policies pursued earlier
by the GLC, and during the 1982 Bermondsey by-election which Peter Tatchell
fought (and lost) for Labour, described by *Gay News* (March 1982) as 'the most
homophobic by-election of our times'.[1]

Journalists and politicians were also able to draw on another already-existing
construction: that of AIDS as a 'gay plague'. It was thus argued that councils
pursuing rights for gays and lesbians were effectively encouraging people, and
especially young people, into sexual 'deviance' and thereby exposing themselves
to the danger of contracting AIDS. Inevitably, British national newspapers had
been at the forefront of this construction in the first place.[2]

During the local elections, one book achieved totemic significance in the
Tory campaign: *Jenny Lives with Eric and Martin*, an English translation of a
Danish book about a little girl who lives with her father and his male partner. This continued to play a key role in Tory demonology long after the elections, being made to stand for everything that was anathema to the opponents of
London Labour councils' alleged policies on sex education. Starting with a story
on 2 May in the *Islington Gazette*, a paper which decisively negated the tendency
for the local press to take a more balanced approach than the nationals to council
matters, the myth was created that this book was homosexual propaganda and
was widely available in London schools. The Tory peer Baroness Cox[3] raised
the matter in the Lords on 7 May 1986, and this was but the first of its many
parliamentary appearances. But for all the lurid stories splashed across the newspapers, the truth was that ILEA did not consider the book suitable for general
use in primary schools and thus decreed that it should not be available to pupils.
Indeed, the Authority had only one copy, which was held at a teachers' centre
and could be used only with older pupils, and even then only in exceptional
circumstances after their parents had been consulted.[4] However, this did not stop
Baker, according to the *Mail* (16 September) 'demanding its immediate withdrawal', or the *Telegraph* (19 September) stating that *Jenny* was 'widely stocked
in schools and libraries', or the *Mail* (22 September) reporting that it 'was being
circulated by the Inner London Education Authority'.[5]

## 'Putting the gay in Haringey'

Labour's local election manifesto in Haringey, a London borough outside the ILEA area and thus with sole responsibility for education, committed the council to upholding the right of educational workers to be 'openly lesbian or gay at work' as well as to supporting students 'realising their own gayness'; it also committed the council to beginning 'the process of ensuring lesbianism and gayness are treated positively on the curriculum'. In all, there were five mentions of 'positive images' in the manifesto. For this, the council would be subjected to what Les Levidow has described as 'Britain's best organised, most intense manifestation of homophobia'[6]. In what follows, I have inevitably been able to present only a fraction of the negative press coverage which the borough received between 1986 and 1988.

Haringey is divided into two constituencies: Hornsey/Wood Green and Tottenham, each with its own Conservative Party Association. The former was represented in Parliament by the relatively moderate Conservative Sir Hugh Rossi. Tottenham, however, had been a Labour stronghold since the war, and in 1987 it elected as its MP Bernie Grant, who, as leader of Haringey council from 1985, had come in for vitriolic abuse from the Tory party and press, and had been nicknamed 'Barmy Bernie'. At the time of the events described in this chapter, the Tottenham Conservative Association was dominated by hardline Thatcherites, and its chairman, Peter Murphy, a local councillor, ardent Roman Catholic and overt homophobe, was a major player in the events detailed here. Largely white and working-class, Tottenham was precisely the kind of area which Thatcher considered crucial to her electoral success, and this is one reason why the anti-Labour battle was so bitterly fought there by the Tory party and its press allies.

In response to Labour's manifesto, the Tottenham Conservatives focused heavily on the lesbian and gay issue – in particular on AIDS and positive images. Slogans abounded such as 'We do not believe in prejudicing young minds. AIDS is a killer', 'You do not want your child educated to be a homosexual or lesbian', and 'A child of 3 being taught that homosexualism [sic] is normal is turning the world upside down'. One of their leaflets claimed that: 'This is the order from the Homosexual Unit [sic] – "children must be educated from nursery to secondary in a manner designed to 'promote' Lesbians and Homosexuals"', and another presented as 'quotes' from the Labour manifesto: 'Heterosexual is pernicious' and 'We will campaign against normal sex'.[7] The campaign also utilised press articles, for example reprinting one from the *Express* (14 April 1986) headed 'Storm over "Barmy" Bernie's new gay teach-ins'. Not to be outdone, the *Hornsey Journal* (9 May), at that time an extremely anti-council paper which, like the *Islington Gazette*, clearly negated the tendency for local papers to take a more balanced approach than the nationals to council matters, ran a screaming front page headline: 'Lesbians to adopt kids. Schools to get lessons about homosexuals. HarinGAY!' Murphy was quoted as saying that: 'No person who believes in God can vote Labour now. It is an attack on ordinary family life as a prelude to revolution', whilst the paper's editorial shrilled: 'We are on the edge of an abyss. We call on all decent, ordinary people to have an "uprising" of their own – at the ballot box'. Indeed, so keen was the paper to influence the election result that it actually brought forward its publication date by a day, and it played a key role in the events described in this chapter, giving full rein to the council's critics, providing the national press with ample 'loony left' fodder in its columns, and frequently misrepresenting or simply failing to report Council policy.

However, in spite of the campaign waged by the *Journal* and much of the national press, at the local election the Tories in Haringey lost seven of their twenty-two seats, with Labour gaining six of them. Significantly, though, Labour lost four seats in Tottenham. But it now had forty-two seats, and the Conservatives only sixteen on the local authority.

## Positive images

Just before the election, the council had formed a Lesbian and Gay Unit within the Community Affairs Department, which had a staff of seven and a budget of £100,000. One of its first acts was to write to all local head-teachers advising them of Labour's manifesto commitment that 'we will encourage [equal opportunities practice] by establishing a fund for curriculum projects from nursery through to further education which are specifically designed to be anti-racist, anti-sexist and to promote positive images of lesbians and gays, and of people with disabilities'.[8] Local objectors to the council's gender policies then formed themselves into the Campaign for Normal Family Life (CNFL), which operated out of the Tottenham Conservative Association's offices. One of their leaflets stated: 'Protesting against plans to introduce homosexual education throughout Haringey. Our demands are: Completely abolish the present policy. A return to normal family values. An end to ridiculous words such as sexist and racist and a return to normality'.[9] In September, supporters of the council's gay and lesbian initiatives founded the counter-movement Positive Images.

As already noted, the topic of sex education was already firmly in the Tories' sights and high on the press agenda. In June 1986, following the lead given by Viscount Buckmaster in the Lords in May (see below), Baker introduced a new clause into the Education (No. 2) Bill requiring local authorities to ensure that sex education would encourage pupils 'to have due regard to moral considerations and the value of family life'. This was, in fact, very much in line with the government's 1985 White Paper, *Better Schools*, and the 1986 schools inspectorate document, *Health Education from 5 to 16*. However, the latter also noted that: 'Teachers need to remember that many children come from backgrounds that do not correspond to this ideal [of family life], and great sensitivity is needed to avoid causing personal hurt and giving unwitting offence'. It concluded:

> Given the openness with which homosexuality is treated in society now it is almost bound to arise as an issue in one area or another of a school's curriculum. Information about and discussion of homosexuality, whether it involves a whole class or an individual, needs to acknowledge that experiencing strong feelings of attraction to members of the same sex is a phase passed through by many young people, but that for a significant number of people these feelings persist into adult life. Therefore it needs to be dealt with objectively and seriously, bearing in mind that, while there has been a marked shift away from the general condemnation of homosexuality, many individuals and groups within society hold sincerely to the view that it is morally objectionable. This is difficult territory for teachers to traverse and for some schools to accept that homosexuality may be a normal feature of relationships would be a breach of the religious faith upon which they are founded. Consequently, LEAs, voluntary bodies, governors, heads and senior staff in schools have important responsibilities in devising guidance and supporting teachers dealing with this sensitive issue.[10]

However, the measured tones of the inspectorate conspicuously failed to find an echo in the pages of the *Hornsey Journal* and much of the national press in their reporting of Haringey, in which the battle between the opponents and proponents of positive images was becoming decidedly more heated. The *Sunday Telegraph* (6 July 1986) ran an article headed 'Putting the gay in Haringey' which announced that:

> Courses on homosexuality are to be introduced into the 78 schools of one London borough by the end of the year despite fierce protests from parents. Head teachers in Haringey have been instructed by the Left-wing council to develop courses designed to 'promote positive images of lesbians and gays'. Nursery and primary schools are not exempt from this order. Conservative councillors condemned the plan last week as an attempt to 'turn the world upside down by making the abnormal appear normal and the normal seem abnormal'. They accused the ruling Labour group of 'dangerous social engineering'.

This highly inaccurate account of the council's positive images policies was faithfully repeated in the next day's *Telegraph* under the headline 'Outrage over homosexual classes plan'. The article began: 'Courses on Homosexuality and Lesbianism for all pupils from nursery schools to further education have been proposed by the London Borough of Haringey, led by Mr. Bernie Grant, which has decreed that "heterosexism is pernicious". The plan has outraged parents'.

The article also included a quote from Peter Murphy stating that 'I am raising the issue, as a Catholic, with Cardinal Hume. It represents an open attack on family life'. A *Sun* article, 7 July, headed 'Bernie kids get lessons in gay love', stated that:

> Courses to teach children about homosexuality and lesbianism are to be started in schools run by Barmy Bernie Grant's Left-wing council. And Haringey council may even extend the scheme to nursery and primary schools. Head teachers have been ordered to start the courses to counter the 'pernicious effects' of straight sexual relations. The scheme, decided by the North London council's women group, is official policy. They call for the promotion of positive images and practices of lesbianism and gays.

The *Mail* followed suit on 9 July, calling the plan 'Upside down idiocy' and commenting that:

> The courses on homosexuality and lesbianism for all pupils from nursery schools to further education no doubt will be followed by lessons propounding the theories that thuggery can be fun, stealing is the right of the unemployed, if you're black you can't be bad and heterosexism is pernicious.

On the same day, George Gale in the *Mirror*, in a column entitled 'Lessons that threaten life', called the plans a 'left-wing conspiracy to brainwash children into the subversive belief that homosexuality is just as good, natural and desirable as heterosexual activity.' He concluded that Haringey council wanted not only to 'subvert the entire political structure in which we live,' but, through a 'perversion of the natural order', to 'subvert the human race as well.' On 18 July, the *Hornsey Journal* quoted the Tottenham Conservatives as stating that the council's policies on sex education were 'a bigger threat to normal family life than the guns and bombers of Adolf Hitler'.

What is common to all these articles, and to the many succeeding ones, is the lack of any hard facts about the council's actual policy. But what is central to them is the implicit or explicit suggestion that children of all ages are to be encouraged to become gay or lesbian. However, no statements or documents from the council remotely bear out any such interpretation, and no directives of the kind suggested by the *Telegraph* et al. were ever issued. What the council did make clear, however, was that its educational aims and objectives included the following: encouraging teachers to prevent name-calling such as 'lezzie' and 'poof'; supporting lesbian and gay staff who are open about their sexuality; training staff to understand and cope with this issue in the classroom; not avoiding mention of lesbians and gay men in teenage sex education; making students aware of the positive contribution lesbians and gay men have made to society in music, sports, politics and entertainment, where relevant; and presenting a 'positive image' of lesbian and gay relationships as one of the many lifestyles that students will come across. As Labour councillor and education committee chair Bob Harris pointed out in the *Times Educational Supplement* (24 October):

> We are not trying to force children or young people to be lesbian or gay. We are not saying children in primary or secondary schools are to have homosexuality thrust upon them. The concept of 'gay lessons' is a nonsense. What we are saying is that lesbians and gay men have a right to be treated as equals in a society which does not discriminate against them.

Unexceptionable, even worthy, sentiments, one would have thought – but not to the massed ranks of a significant section of Fleet Street, as was becoming clearer by the day.

## 'Freedom fighters of the angry suburbs'

The *Mail* (17 September) carried an article entitled 'Hit squad of parents to burn gay schoolbook' which focussed on threats by the Parents Rights Group (PRG, which had been formed in August as the successor body to the CNFL) to burn any copies of *Jenny Lives with Eric and Martin* which they found in Haringey libraries. Two days later, the *Hornsey Journal* ran a front-page story headlined 'Toddlers' library shock – PARENTS TO BURN GAY BOOK'. Significantly, in the *Mail* article, PRG leader Pat Headd justified their actions by stating that 'the Minister's message in your paper was a signal for us to act, and to use our own initiative'. This was a reference to an interview with Baker in the *Mail* (16 September) headed 'Baker acts over gay school book', in which he stated that:

> Parents – and I'm a typical one – find this material [*Jenny*] grossly offensive. The cartoons are blatantly homosexual propaganda and totally unsuitable for use in classroom teaching or school libraries. Unfortunately, I cannot order an education authority to stop circulating such a book. But I can make the strength of my views known to them and ensure that the public are also aware of my thinking.

The *Mail* (18 September), under the headline 'Boycott threat over gay books', quoted Headd as stating that 'we will take our children out of the schools if it is taught that homosexuality is acceptable'.

These were two of the earliest appearances in print of the PRG, a group dominated primarily by working class women, many from an Irish Catholic background, whose attacks on the council's policies, book burning and school boycotts and pickets would, over the following months, garner very considerable publicity and support in sections of the press. Indeed, in Conservative papers which are stridently opposed to all forms of direct action by those with different political views from their own, they would achieve the status of martyrs and folk heroes, and, in a highly resonant phrase coined by Geoffrey Levy in the *Mail* (3

February 1987), 'freedom fighters of the angry suburbs'.[11] Considerably less attention would be paid by these papers to a number of inconvenient issues, such as: the alleged role of certain members of the group in assaults on and intimidation of supporters of the council, the sources of their funding, their extensive network of contacts in both the Lords and Commons, the increasingly acrimonious splits within the group (for example, the formation of the Haringey Parents Association by those alienated by the PRG's stridency and hard-line approach), and to the support of extremist groups such as the National Front, British National Party, Committee for a Free Britain[12] and the Moonie-related New Patriotic Movement (given a whole column in which to air their views in the *Mail* (23 January 1987)). In other words, little or no attention was given to anything that failed to fit the heroic image of bullied and embattled 'ordinary' parents struggling against a local authority apparently attempting to corrupt their children.[13]

On 30 September, Haringey's Education Committee, having heard deputations from both sides of the spiralling dispute, formally agreed to initiate a policy of positive images. The recommendations were, however, minimal: setting up a working party to develop educational resource materials, and establishing a forum for consultation with parents and the gay and lesbian community which would examine how best to implement the policy. The *Mail* (1 October), however, entirely ignored these recommendations and concentrated solely on events at and before the meeting: 'As parents burned a copy [of *Jenny*] they were jeered by homosexuals and lesbians entering the building. Inside, parents were bombarded with missiles and spat on from the public gallery as they spoke against the Labour council's "anti-heterosexist" policy'. The story was also covered by the *Mail's* then stable-mate the *Standard* on the same day under the headlines 'Gays scuffle with book row parents' and 'We were pushed, shoved and sworn at, claims protest leader'. The story is presented entirely from the point of view of the liberally quoted PRG, and also peddles the falsehood that 'Haringey Labour chiefs have agreed to put the book … in the children's section of borough libraries'.

These scenes were repeated on a far larger scale at a full council meeting on 20 October, at which the council had agreed to meet deputations from the PRG, who wanted to present a petition against what they took to be Haringey's sex education policies, and Positive Images. Supporters of the former numbered about fifty, and of the latter over 1,000. Given the already boiling tensions in the borough, the scene was set for conflict. As Sue Reinhold describes the scene:

> During the meeting, supporters of the policy in the gallery pelted the Parents Rights Group and Conservative councillors with eggs. Two Conservative councillors were ejected after making inflammatory comments, and one extremely right wing Conservative councillor [Peter Murphy] was ejected after throwing a pillow cushion which, in an extraordinary moment of creation of symbolic capital, hit a Black lesbian Council worker on the head. Outside, an opponent of 'positive images' threatened the crowd of supporters with a machete. At the end of the meeting, as a

Labour councillor drove away from Town Hall, the back window of his car
was smashed in by an opponent of the policy wielding a crowbar.[14]

However, if both sides were to blame for this clash, the report of the incident
by the *Standard*, 21 October, did its best to represent it simply as a spectacle of
uncontrolled lunacy – as, of course, befitting a 'loony left' borough. The list of
events which opens the article – 'bayonet wielding, egg hurling, cushion throw-
ing, shoe banging, flag waving, a bomb scare, much abuse, and one arrest' –
makes no attempt to explain which side was responsible for each of these actions,
and, although this does become clear in the course of the article, it is also equally
clear that the paper's sympathies lie entirely with the PRG, whose members, the
article relates, were 'heckled and abused from the gallery when they tried to put
their point of view. They were called bigots and fascists'. What the paper failed to
report was that PRG supporters described gays and lesbians as 'sick animals' who
didn't deserve to live, and as 'warped, abnormal individuals', that PRG solicitor
Gerrard Tumany described Labour's actions as 'akin to Nazi Germany', and that
after the meeting a Labour councillor's car was attacked with a crowbar.[15]

As luck would have it, the very next day an amendment to the Education Bill,
relating to sex education, was being debated in the Commons, and Haringey
was mentioned nearly twenty times during the three-hour debate. Particularly
significant was a remark by Sir Hugh Rossi, which serves only to emphasise both
the one-sidedness and the political impact of the *Standard* report of the council meeting:

> Virtually all hon. Members will have seen in their evening papers a report
> of the disgraceful and scandalous scenes which occurred in the council
> chamber of the London borough of Haringey last night, when a group
> of parents calling themselves the Parents Rights Group—they are of all
> political parties and of none—went to the council to ask whether they
> could be heard in regard to the education of their children. They were
> shouted down, spat upon and urinated upon. Every conceivable obscenity
> was hurled upon them, and threats of physical violence were made.[16]

Equating the positive images initiative with 'definite and aggressive proselytisa-
tion by gays and lesbians to bring as many people as they can into their camp',
and condemning the 'entryism ... that has resulted in the Haringey Labour party
becoming what it is',[17] Rossi argued that 'unless parents have ... the right to
withdraw their children from classes in schools where that sort of thing is taught,
we shall have a very unfortunate generation of children'.[18] However, Rossi, who
handed the PRG's petition directly to the Secretary of State for Education, presented extracts from the Lesbian and Gay Unit's above-mentioned letter to head-
teachers as if they were quotes from Labour's local election manifesto.

The highly selective and partisan account of the meeting presented by the
*Standard* and repeated by Rossi was to be endlessly regurgitated during the next

two years nearly every time sex education was debated at Westminster, and, in particular, as the measure which would eventually become Section 28 of the Local Government Act 1988 began to take shape, as will be explained below.

## Labour on the defensive[19]

Given the sheer scale and ferocity of the attack on Haringey's positive images policy, and its consequences for the Local Government Act 1988, the question of whether the council could and should have handled matters differently clearly needs to be raised. According to Stewart Lansley et al., a campaign which went beyond arguing simply for gay and lesbian rights and, by positing the equivalence of different lifestyles, challenged the 'normality' of heterosexuality, could not be undertaken through a process of peremptory policy changes and gestures. It required a longer time-scale, and a far more sophisticated approach to the process of changing ideas'. In support of this view, they quote Chris Smith – the first openly gay Labour MP – to the effect that sections of the left had overloaded their commitment to sexual equality 'with a lot of language about heterosexist attitudes and a series of gestures that don't really benefit the lesbian and gay community. The overloading has instead served to alienate people – it's done a basic disservice to the basic cause'.[20]

It is certainly the case, as one of the architects of the positive images initiative, the Labour councillor Davina Cooper herself admits, that the Lesbian and Gay Unit's initial letter to the borough's heads was sent without consulting the education department and

> took Haringey council and the borough Labour Party by surprise. The council leadership and education service were furious that the unit had ignored the 'proper' procedures. They argued the policy should have been developed slowly and gradually with education taking the primary responsibility. That way, it was claimed, opposition would have been minimised. The unit, and lesbian and gay activists, disagreed. Had they not taken immediate action on the basis of manifesto commitments (subsequently council policy), nothing would have happened.[21]

The delay in establishing the curriculum working party, which, as noted above, had been agreed on at the council meeting on 30 September, may indeed lend weight to the final sentence. Whatever the case, it's hard to disagree with her judgment that:

> The inability of Haringey education service to come forward with an authoritative version of what 'positive images' would mean, practically, in classrooms and schools was a major strategic blunder which left the opposing forces free to provide their own interpretations of events and to set the terms of the debate.[22]

In this respect, she concludes that:

> Haringey council leadership and senior officers lacked confidence in how
> the policies, even if 'accurately' conveyed, would be received by the general
> public. They also feared how such information might be used by the right.
> As a result, their response tended to be defensive; emphasis was placed on
> protecting the council from attack rather than on effectively conveying the
> reasons why a policy such as 'positive images' was necessary.[23]

Reinhold quotes a Labour councillor who supported the positive images policy as
stating that the Council was not 'putting out information. They were actually going
in on themselves', and an officer of the Lesbian and Gay Unit to the effect that:

> The Council refused to answer questions, they refused to answer the press.
> They wouldn't actually put council statements out when inaccuracies were
> printed in the local and national newspapers, they stuck their heads in the
> sand and hoped it would go away. Which of course it wouldn't.[24]

Cooper alleges that when journalists approached the council looking for interviewees to talk about the issue, press officers tended to be reluctant to refer them
to groups such as Positive Images, which they, along with the council itself, saw
as having an ancillary function; they may also have feared what such groups
might say. On the other hand, as Cooper not altogether unsurprisingly reveals,
journalists from the mainstream media were simply not interested in interview-
ing supporters of gay and lesbian rights in the first place; as she says of members
of Positive Images and Haringey Black Action: 'Their very identity as gay, Black
and radical was perceived by the media as affording them no legitimacy or credibility as spokespeople'.[25]

However, given the evidence amassed elsewhere in this book, and particularly
in Chapter 5 on urban myths, it's extraordinarily unlikely that the press pack
would have behaved any differently even had the council adopted the strategies suggested by Cooper. As even the more critical Lansley et al. note, Labour
councils which pursued far less radical approaches than Haringey to gay and
lesbian rights found their policies 'grossly distorted by opponents'.[26] Not only
was most of the national press highly supportive of the Thatcher government's
onslaught against 'permissiveness', not only were its ideological antennae finely
attuned to the merest hint of 'loony leftism', but here was a story which can only
be described as a Tory editor's wet dream. It could so obligingly be presented in
such a way as to combine a heady brew of political 'extremism', the corruption of
childhood, the threatened nuclear family and the subversion of the heterosexual
norm, with the 'ordinary mums' of the PRG as the much put-upon populist
paragons, always prepared to lay on a newsworthy event such as a book-burning,
picket or school boycott, and with Education Secretary Kenneth Baker ever-
ready with an appropriate response to what the press told him was Haringey's

latest outrage. In such a situation, *any* pronouncements, even the mildest, on gay and lesbian sexuality emanating from the council were all too liable to be distorted out of all recognition and added to the ever-growing demonology of the 'loony-left'. Thus, for example, Davina Cooper recalls how she was contacted by a children's counselling service and asked whether it was true that copies of *Jenny* would be delivered to every household in the borough, and notes that:

> I was amazed that anybody could think a London borough like Haringey had the resources (even if it had the political will, which it didn't) to buy and distribute approximately 80,000 copies of the book. The concept of the Town Hall waist-deep in such literature made me realise that, thanks to right-wing attacks, many people had no idea what to believe; their sense of judgement about what was plausible or likely had evaporated; thus they were suggestive to the most ludicrous and ridiculous possibilities. Even among people sympathetic to lesbian and gay equality, many, accepting that there must be some truth in what they heard, felt councils like Haringey were going too far.[27]

## 'Kicked into line'

Pat Salim, one of the Conservative councillors who was thrown out of the Council meeting on 20 October for fighting with the Labour deputy leader and hurling sugar lumps at the mayor, had shouted:

> No civilisation in the world is trying to do what this Labour Council is trying to do ... I have never come across such evil incarnate as this Council ... My firm opinion of this movement that you are supporting is not for your own good, not for the good of the people – it is for the purpose of social revolution. If these people, in the power of the land, take any notice, you will be the first to be kicked into line.[28]

This was to prove remarkably prophetic, in terms of the Education Reform Act 1988 and the Local Government Act 1988.

As already noted, Baker was always quick to capitalise on stories in the press about sex education, however distorted and inaccurate. On the other hand, there were many in his own party for whom his proposed measures were far too weak. Amongst them was Rhodes Boyson, the MP for Brent North and Minister for Local Government, who believed that homosexuality 'is wrong biblically ... It is unnatural. AIDS is part of the fruits of the permissive society. The regular one-man, one-woman marriage would not put us at risk in this way. If we could wipe out homosexual practices, then AIDS would die out'.[29] Boyson and like-minded MPs such as Peter Bruinvels argued vociferously that parents should be allowed to take their children out of sex education classes, and that the government should compile a list of sex education books to be banned from schools. Such views were vociferously supported in large sections of the press.

The *Guardian* (21 August) reported that Baker had written to Ealing and Haringey councils asking for details of their policies on teaching children about homosexuality. In particular, a reference in the letter to Section 23 of the 1944 Education Act appeared to suggest that the councils' policies in this area might run contrary to their duty to provide a balanced curriculum. The *Express* (22 August) reported Baker's actions as 'Clampdown on "gay" lessons', whilst the previous day's *Telegraph* wrote of 'a deliberate attempt to molest the sexual education of children without their parents' consent' and called for government action.

In October, at the Conservative Party conference at Bournemouth, Baker was given a standing ovation for a speech in which he condemned the 'bigotry and intolerance' of Labour education authorities and stated that that the Education Bill would include an amendment removing, according to the *Hornsey Journal* (10 October),

> control over sex education … from teachers and local authorities and given to the new-style governing bodies which have more parents on them and be answerable to an annual parents' meeting. The Governing body will decide what, if any, sort of sex education they should offer, and whether the school should allow particular parents to withdraw their children from particular sex education lessons.

Referring to the ubiquitous press stories about Brent and Haringey, he was quoted in the *Telegraph* (8 October) as stating: 'This is nothing to do with education but is bigotry masquerading as equality and intolerance masquerading as freedom'. Entirely typically, he also attempted to tar Labour at the national level with the local 'loony' brush by arguing that 'this is not a tiny minority of fanatics and cranks. It is Mr. Kinnock's supporters applying Labour education policy'. The same day's *Express* gave considerable prominence to the Bournemouth debate under the headline 'Maggie blitz on schools' and the sub-heads 'Left wing cranks will be curbed' and 'More parent control on sex education'. According to a leader in the same day's *Sun*: 'At last, Education Secretary Kenneth Baker is curbing the poisonous flow of homosexual propaganda into the schools … Sensible parent power will take over from the left-wing crackpots'.

Other ministerial speeches also developed this theme. Deputy Leader and Chancellor of the Duchy of Lancaster Norman Tebbit condemned the immorality of 'ILEA distributing explicit books no decent parents would wish their children to see.' Nicholas Ridley, Secretary of State for the Environment and therefore responsible for local government, ridiculed the local 'loony left' for creating 'independent Socialist republics', adding that certain local authorities 'challenge the very basis of society, actually teaching homosexuality and lesbianism in nursery schools'.[30]

On 14 October the *Mail* devoted highly sympathetic coverage to those Tory MP's, now numbering over 100, for whom Baker's plans were inadequate and who were urging him to compile a mandatory blacklist of 'corrupting' sex books, sack any teacher who used such books, and give parents the right to withdraw children from sex education lessons. But the symbiotic relationship between such politicians and the client press was nowhere more clearly demonstrated than by events later that month. Thus, on 21 October, Peter Bruinvels cited in Parliament an article on sex education books which had been published in the *Mail*, 23 September. Books mentioned in the article which were name-checked by Bruinvels were *Jenny*, *Make It Happy*, *The Rights of Children*, *The Playbook for Kids about Sex*, *Biology for Life*, *Growing Up: A Guide for Children and Parents* and *Talking Sex*. Bruinvels' descriptions of these books were nearly identical to those in the *Mail's* annotated list, except that minor but significant tweaks made them sound even more dubious. Thus, for example, while the *Mail* reports that *Make It Happy* 'discusses masturbation, group sex and bestiality', Bruinvels states that it 'encourages' these activities, and in the *Mail's* description of *Sex for Beginners* the book 'professes to set out "sensible" rules for experimenting with bondage', whereas according to Bruinvels it 'calls for experiments in bondage'. But the echo chamber was in operation yet again the day after Bruinvels' speech when the *Mail's* sister paper, the *Standard*, devoted the entirety of its front page to a story headed 'Beware this dirty dozen', with the strap 'MP condemns "too sexy" school books'. The article, such as it was, consisted of virtually nothing but an edited version of the annotated list of the books first published in the *Mail* and then partly regurgitated by Bruinvels, who, the article explains, 'is calling on parents to write to him or Education Secretary Kenneth Baker with the names of books which they believe should not be used by teachers'.

The *Express* (7 November), in an article entitled 'Rape of the innocent minds', which comprised part of its 'Wrecking of our schools' series, also turned to the subject of sex education, arguing that 'the full extent of the pollution of children's minds can be gauged by the wide selection of sex guides and advice now available in some classrooms ... Books reveal a new chapter in moral corruption'. Entirely unsurprisingly, *Jenny*, *The Playbook for Kids about Sex*, *Make It Happy* and *Growing Up* are all featured. The series had started on 25 October with an article which listed 'the seven deadly sins' of which Labour authorities were guilty: the first two were anti-racism and anti-sexism. Summing up the series on 21 November, the paper concluded:

> We have shown how extremist Labour councils are exploiting pupils for their own warped political ends. How gay rights watchdogs and race commissars are appointed in their schools ... And above all how a wide range of sex guides are recommended for schools, seemingly to undermine family life by glorifying homosexuality while not warning of its dangers.

But here Baker was able to seize the initiative from his Tory critics, concluding, in the course of a lengthy and supportive interview that illustrates all too clearly the symbiotic relationship between the Tory party and sections of the national press:

> What I can do is subject these schools and local education authorities to the critical glare of publicity. But at the end of the day, it is parents who must

use their power to turn out the race and sex commissars who are imposing their dictates in some of our schools. The fact that all the awful examples spotlighted by the *Express* are taking place in Labour authorities is the clearest illustration of what will follow nationally if a Labour Government, containing many of the same extremists, is elected and given power to control the entire education system.

## From Haringey to the Lords

However, it was in the Lords that reaction to press stories about sex education in Haringey began the process that would eventually lead to the enactment of Section 28.

On 15 April 1986, Viscount Buckmaster, an independent peer but member of the Conservative Family Campaign, introduced an amendment to the Education Bill, which stated that:

> It shall be the duty of each local education authority, and of the head teacher and governing body of every school, to ensure that any teaching, books, materials or other teaching aids concerned with sex and human reproduction, whether given in specific sex education lessons or elsewhere in the curriculum, shall not advocate any illegal act or act of obscenity, and any such teaching shall comply with the religious and moral beliefs of the parents of children at the school and shall be given in the context of enduring family life.
>
> It shall be the right of every parent to be informed in advance of the content of any sex education to be given at the school, and notwithstanding the provisions of subsection (1) above it shall be the right of any parent to withdraw his child from any sex education to which that parent objects.[31]

He claimed that 'a great deal of the sex education today, particularly in our maintained schools, is amoral, if not downright immoral, dealing, as it does, with human reproduction in the most provocative and explicit way, with no element of moral guidance'.[32] He also raised the issue of 'the appalling sexual crimes that are apparent nowadays, the increase in rapes, the attacks on children. Is there not perhaps some connection between these and this appalling sex education?'[33] In his view:

> This Bill surely comes at a fortunate time. It comes at a time (does it not?) when discipline and self-discipline are under increasing criticism, when any restraint on acts or word is considered totally unnecessary. It comes (does it not?) at a time when moral standards are flying away like straw in the wind and the sins of Sodom and Gomorrah are rampant in the land.[34]

For the Government, Baroness Hooper called the amendment 'impractical', but also assured the House of the Government's 'sympathy' for the amendment's intention, and claimed that 'the Government do not believe that the door is closed on this topic'.[35] Thus reassured, Buckmaster withdrew the amendment.

However, he returned to the Lords on 20 May with an amendment which stated that 'such sex education as is given in schools shall have due regard to moral considerations and the promotion of stable family life'.[36] Resuming his attack on sex education, he expressed concern that:

> There are certain themes which appear to be running through much of this education, and particularly in London. These are that homosexual relations are just as acceptable as heterosexual relations; that there is nothing basically wrong with under-age sex provided one takes the appropriate precaution; and that incest can on occasions be regarded as a loving relationship.

*Jenny* was invoked as evidence of this form of sex education, and the Viscount confidently asserted that the book was 'issued by an authority in north London' and 'was designed for use by six- to eight-year olds'.[37] For the Government, Baroness Hooper stated that:

> I believe that many who have supported the amendment are in favour of the intention behind it, as indeed are the Government. What we have been trying to show is that the whole point of the present Bill before your Lordships is to seek to ensure that the curricular policies of individual schools will be more flexible and more responsive. The new governing bodies with substantial parent representation and accountable to the full parent body should play a major role in ensuring that schools adopt a sensitive and commonsense approach to controversial issues such as sex education. Nevertheless, in view of the feeling expressed in the House this evening I shall undertake to take back this particular issue and reconsider it before the next stage of the Bill.[38]

Again reassured by this indication of government policy, the Viscount withdrew his amendment.

Two days after Buckmaster's question, Sir Hugh Rossi wrote to his constituents asking them to join him 'in condemning Haringey Council's proposals to promote images of homosexuals in local schools'. He stated that he had received over forty letters from parents on the subject, and, according to the *Hornsey Journal* (1 August), 'vowed to raise the issue in the House of Commons' during the final readings of the Education Bill in the autumn. Thus the matter had arrived in Parliament within a mere three months of the campaign mounted by the Tottenham Conservative Association, and within two weeks of the earliest public protest over the issue.

On 28 July 1986 the crossbencher Lord Monson asked whether the government approved of 'Haringey Borough Council's plans for compulsory lessons intended to promote "positive images" of homosexuality in nursery, primary and secondary schools in the borough'. For the government, the Earl of Swinton admitted that the Secretary of State for Education 'was disturbed to see press reports of Haringey council's plans'; he also revealed that Baker was 'making enquiries of the authority to establish the facts' and to discover how it proposed to pursue its policies with schools. Although admitting that 'there have been a number of rather exaggerated press reports', he also added that he thought Haringey's policies 'pretty horrific'.[39] The *Telegraph* (29 July) duly reported the debate under the headline 'Homosexual teaching in schools deplored'.

## 'Promoting homosexuality': Haringey and the genesis of section 28

A few months later, on 18 December, another crossbencher, the Earl of Halsbury, who had played a key role in in the 1977 campaign to defeat Lord Arran's bill to reduce the age of consent for homosexual acts from twenty-one to eighteen, proposed the Local Government Act 1986 (Amendment) Bill, entitled 'An Act to restrain local authorities from promoting homosexuality'. This was intended to apply to local authority activities in general, and to schools in particular, and, as finally amended, sought to prohibit 'the teaching ... of the acceptability of homosexuality as a pretended family relationship'. In his opening remarks he complained that:

> We emancipated races and got inverted racism. We emancipate homosexuals and they condemn heterosexism as chauvinist sexism, male oppression and so on. They will push us off the pavement if we give them a chance. I am, in their jargon, a homophone [sic], a heterosexist exploitationist. The whole vocabulary of the loony Left is let loose in a wild confusion of Marxism, Trotskyism, anarchism and homosexual terminology.[40]

This set the tone for a debate which Stephen Jeffery-Poulter rightly describes as sinking to 'new levels of intolerance' and which 'in terms of reactionary hysteria equalled the homosexual law reform debates in the 1950s'.[41] During its course, Haringey was mentioned seventeen times, which was hardly surprising given the press furore and the extent of lobbying by the PRG of both Houses.[42] The Tory peer Lord Campbell of Alloway, who had actually drafted the Bill, attacked 'the provision of explicit books of certain types' to children. He also translated the presentation of positive images of gays and lesbians into 'the promotion of homosexuality as this so-called family relationship' and condemned it as a 'direct attack on the heterosexual family life'.[43] Another Tory peer, Lord Bellwin, quoted from the *Standard* (10 December) about 'a cri de coeur from a priest who has vowed "to fast from New Year's Day unless Haringey Council reverses its policy of positive classroom images of homosexuals"'.[44] Recalling a theme mentioned at the start of this chapter, Lord Fitt, the former Social Democratic and Labour Party MP who now sat as an independent socialist, announced that 'I have absolutely no doubt that a significant number of present AIDS carriers within our society were given positive education in homosexuality when they were at school'.[45] Baroness Cox complained of 'the active promotion of positive images of homosexuality and outright attacks on the concept of the normality of heterosexuality'[46]. Both she and the crossbencher, Lady Saltoun, cited a leader published, most conveniently, in that day's *Times*. Headed 'A grass roots rebellion', this is yet another excoriation of Haringey council and paean to the allegedly much-persecuted PRG, which is represented as standing bravely against 'malignant causes' and 'the extremists in charge of the local council' who want to subject children 'to what amounts to sexual propaganda'. As proof of such propaganda, the leader cites *The Playbook for Kids about Sex*, apparently available from the Lesbian and Gay Unit, which

> includes an introduction of small children to homosexual relationships and could even be construed as conditioning children so that they will not object to sexual abuse. From the children's shelves of a public library, a 15-year-old schoolgirl obtained a book which is simply homosexual pornography. And the campaign, as described by its own advocates, is designed to subject the school curriculum to homosexual proselytising.

The leader also notes that 'most of the protesting parents are Labour voters. But they have come to believe that their own party has become a cover for the anti-democratic left which abuses the education of their children to undermine the family and democracy'. Hammering home the party political point, it recounts:

> The Haringey mothers wrote to Mr Neil Kinnock but got a five-line letter from his office saying he could not intervene. They have taken the point. Today the House of Lords is debating a private member's bill, introduced by Lord Halsbury, which would seek to forbid local authorities from giving financial aid for the promotion of homosexuality. It is of riveting interest to the mothers of Haringey.

The leader was also quoted by Lord Denning, who revealed, in a telling insight into the attitudes of the unelected to the elected:

> I looked up the Book of Genesis again. 'But the men of Sodom were wicked and sinners before the Lord exceedingly'. And the Lord destroyed Sodom and Gomorrah. When I read the article in *The Times* this morning, I thought of altering those words and saying: 'But the councillors of the Borough of Haringey were gay, and corrupted the children of the borough exceedingly'. And, I should like to add, after this Bill, 'The Lords destroyed those councillors'.[47]

The only Labour peer to oppose the Bill was Lord Graham of Edmonton, head of the Association of London Authorities, which represented Labour-controlled authorities in the capital. Predicting, quite correctly, that 'perhaps mine will be the only voice in the debate that is not in favour of giving this Bill a Second Reading', he went on to state that:

> I do not stand here with any brief either for homosexuality or for lesbian-
> ism. I fully share all the criticisms that have been made about the behaviour
> of some councils and councillors in pursuing what they believe to be their
> duty to their ratepayers and citizens.[48]

However, he also warned that 'there is a great danger, if this amending Bill is passed, that it will seek to repress the honest and open discussion of these matters at a time when, in my view, they ought as never before to be discussed seriously and sensibly in our schools'.[49] On the other hand, he concluded his speech in the same vein with which he had commenced it:

> If anyone here with responsibility on this side of the House believes that the
> image of the Labour Party or of Labour in local government is aided and
> assisted by the performance or behaviour of some individuals or collectively
> in certain parts of the country, then they are not correct .... I very much
> hope that when we hear what the Minister has to say he will sympathise
> with the situation in which a great many people find themselves, but share
> my view that a Bill of this kind is not the way to proceed.[50]

And indeed, the Minister agreed. For the Government, Lord Skelmersdale stated that 'it is extremely disturbing to see some of the material which is published or made available by local authorities and I should like to endorse the aims underlying the proposals in the Bill and the tenor of today's debate'. He also noted that:

> The Government believe unequivocally that to promote homosexuality
> as a normal way of life – to anyone, let alone children – is to go too far
> and to create the serious risk of undermining those normal family rela-
> tionships which are the very fabric of our society. There is no doubt, in
> my mind at least, that this is the effect of some councils' spending of their
> ratepayers' money. Some would say that it is the reason for it, and as it
> increases it makes even my simple mind wonder whether this is not in fact
> the truth.[51]

However, he also made it clear that, in the Government's view, Halsbury's measure was unnecessary, because what it sought to ban had already been outlawed by new legislation. Thus, under the Education (No. 2) Act 1986 (itself largely the result of Lords, backbench and newspaper pressure):

> All those responsible for the provision of sex education in county, volun-
> tary and maintained schools will be required by law to ensure that any

teaching offered is set within a clear moral context and is supportive of family life. Full control over the content and organisation of sex education will be placed in the hands of the new-style school governing bodies, which the Act establishes. These have increased parental representation and are answerable to an annual meeting of parents.[52]

He also noted that:

The Government's policy is that schools should be prepared to address the issue of homosexuality, provided they approach it in a balanced and factual manner, appropriate to the maturity of the pupils concerned. The issue cannot be ignored by schools when it is widely discussed in society and when pupils may well ask questions about it.

In his view, the distinction between 'proper teaching about homosexuality' and teaching which set out to 'advocate or encourage it as a normal form of relationship … cannot be drawn sufficiently clearly in legislation to avoid harmful misinterpretation', a risk that the Government was unprepared to take.[53] For these reasons, he did not offer Government support for the Bill. However, it passed without a formal vote and started its progress through the parliamentary system.

The Bill made its first appearance in the Commons on 8 May 1987, where it was introduced by the veteran right-wing and anti-'permissive' campaigner, Dame Jill Knight, the chair of the Lords and Commons Family and Child Protection Group and active member of the Monday Club. Her case for the Bill reads like a compendium of every 'loony left' story about sexuality ever published in the press. Thus, she told the Chamber that 'there is evidence in shocking abundance that children in our schools, some as young as five years, are frequently being encouraged into homosexuality and lesbianism', not least by books such as *The Playbook for Kids about Sex* and *The Milkman's on His Way*. Inevitably, *Jenny* is cited as being 'made available by education officials in and for junior schools'.[54] According to Knight, 'there is a pile of filth, and it is shocking when one considers that it is all paid for by the rates', particularly when 'some of that which is being taught to children in our schools would undoubtedly lead to a great spread of AIDS. Even the knowledge of the danger of AIDS has not stopped the promoting of homosexuality among little children'.[55] Knight confidently asserts that '95 per cent of those who start AIDS come from the homosexual section',[56] but her sources are not only wildly inaccurate stories from local and national papers, but also an article from the *Catholic Herald*, 23 January 1987, by Rachel Tingle, a prominent member of the right-wing group the National Association for Freedom[57] and author of the publication *Gay Lessons: How Public Funds Are Used to Promote Homosexuality amongst Children and Young People* (1987).[58] Knight doesn't acknowledge this source, but as Reinhold[59] points out, parts of her speech are a verbatim lift from it, and, like her source, she mistakenly refers to the PRG as the Parents Action Group.

Knight also cited a more recently minted myth:

> Recently, the lesbian and gay development unit of Haringey council made a video called *How to Become a Lesbian in 35 Minutes*. Under the aegis of the council, it was shown to mentally handicapped girls, of whom one was aged eighteen, one was aged sixteen, and the others were much younger.[60]

The only accurate parts of this story, which was repeated by the *Mail* and the *Evening News*, are the title of the video, which was, of course, an ironic joke (admittedly a most unwise one, given the circumstances), and the fact that it had been made by the unit. However, this is actually part of another story, first told by *The Times* (17 March) and repeated by Lady Saltoun in the Lords on, entirely fittingly, 1 April. According to the paper, 'a pregnant woman was taken to hospital after she claimed she was punched in the stomach at a gay and lesbian unit meeting'. From a report in the *Hornsey Journal* (28 March), it is clear that this meeting was the video screening mentioned by Knight. The woman was Mrs. Rosemarie Thomas-Johnson, a black member of the PRG who had already been involved in various public altercations with Bernie Grant. The story then escalated when, following a miscarriage she blamed on the alleged assault, she failed in her private summons against the man she claimed had attacked her at the screening. This led to an inevitable storm in the press, with headlines such as 'I lost my baby in lesbian protest!' (*Sun*); 'The perverts who control London' (*Evening News*); 'Mum "lost baby in gay attack"' (*Star*); and 'Pregnant woman "was punched at gay meeting"' (*Independent*) (all 22 April). However, the police did not charge anyone with assault in the first instance or manslaughter in the second, and her prosecution failed because she could not recognise the man she had named as her attacker when he appeared before the court. The council denied the entire story, and according to eyewitnesses interviewed by Reinhold,[61] when Thomas-Johnson had tried to attend the meeting she was politely told that it was only for people under twenty-one. She refused to leave, stating that she wanted to know what videos they were showing and how they were corrupting young people. In the end, she was taken firmly by the arm and escorted out by a black male. None of this, of course, made its way into the national press, which did, however, name the man who was summoned to court, with inevitable consequences for him.

The Minister for Local Government, Rhodes Boyson, argued that although the proposed measure 'goes over ground that Parliament has recently traversed',[62] in his view 'the clause should stand as part of the Bill'.[63] However, it failed because, as less than forty members had taken part in the division, the Chamber was not quorate, but at Prime Minister's Question Time on 14 May 1987, Mrs. Thatcher stated it was a 'great pity' it had not passed, assured Knight of her government's support for its objectives and expressed the hope that she would bring it back into parliament following the election.[64] The headline in the *Standard* that evening was 'Government plans blitz on gays'. The election was called the following week.

As the chapter 'Slaying the Dragon' makes abundantly clear, the Labour leadership was thoroughly rattled by what it was now calling the 'London effect', and especially by the flood of stories about sex education, gays and lesbians. This chapter has focussed on a just a few of them, but the total number was enormous, which may lead some to conclude that the leadership's concerns were more than justified. It also needs to be borne in mind that the Tory party and press played the 'loony left' card for all it was worth in the Greenwich by-election of 26 February 1987, when Labour lost the seat to the SDP. The Labour general election manifesto made no attempt to set the record straight about the actual policies of London Labour councils towards gays and lesbians, although it did promise that a Labour government would 'take steps to ensure that homosexuals are not discriminated against'.[65] As Sue Sanders and Gill Spraggs put it, Labour's response to Tory attacks on lesbian and gay rights policies was to 'keep its head well below the parapet and hope the issue would go away'.[66] Which, of course, it didn't.

The election took place on 11 June 1987, after a campaign in which, as Anna Marie Smith puts it: 'The construction of the equivalence, Labour = "excessive" local government = high rates = "loony left" = permissiveness = radical blackness, queerness, feminism = erosion of the entire social order, was central'.[67] A particularly unpleasant feature of the election campaign was a Tory poster which presented an image of the books *Police: Out of School, Young, Gay and Proud*, and *The Playbook for Kids about Sex*, posing the question: 'Is this Labour's idea of a comprehensive education?' In Haringey, only one constituency swung away from Labour, and that, significantly, was Tottenham, where Peter Murphy halved the Labour majority to 4,000 with a 6.8% swing from Labour to Conservative. But the other, Hornsey and Wood Green, saw Sir Hugh Rossi's majority halved to 2,000, with a swing from Conservative to Labour of 5.4%.

At the Tory party conference in October 1987, the newly re-elected Mrs. Thatcher, in an attack on 'hard-left education authorities and extremist teachers', declared that: 'Children who need to be taught to respect traditional values are being taught that they have an inalienable right to be gay'.[68] And in November 1987, the Department of Education and Science published a circular on the two 1986 Education Acts. This was sent to all Local Education Authorities and included guidance on the interpretation of the sex education clauses in the legislation. In particular, it stated that 'there is no place in any school in any circumstances for teaching which advocates homosexual behaviour, which presents it as the "norm", or which encourages homosexual experimentation by pupils'.[69] The difference in tone and import from the 1986 DES document quoted earlier is extremely clear, and it would seem highly likely that the change was brought about by the events described in this chapter.

## 'A sordid role'

Up until this point, the Government had, as noted above, actually opposed the Halsbury Bill, because it believed – quite correctly – that the 'promotion' of homosexuality was outlawed by various already-existing statutes and that the legislation was not, and probably could not be, drafted so as to avoid harmful misinterpretation. However, in the light of Mrs. Thatcher's above remarks, it is altogether unsurprising that, on 8 December, the Bill re-appeared in the Commons, in a very slightly modified form, as an amendment to the Local Government Bill at its Committee Stage. It was proposed by David Wilshire and Jill Knight, apparently with the Prime Minister's personal blessing. At first numbered Clause 14, then 27, it eventually became the much-reviled Clause 28. Entitled 'Prohibition on promoting homosexuality by teaching or publishing material', it originally stated that: 'A local authority shall not − (a) promote homosexuality or publish material for the promotion of homosexuality; (b) promote the teaching in any maintained school of the acceptability of homosexuality as a pretended family relationship by the production of such material or otherwise'.[70] This time, the government supported the measure,[71] local government minister Michael Howard stating:

> The promotion of homosexuality, particularly in schools, by local authorities is an unacceptable development. In view of the worry that has been expressed about that development in the House, in another place, and in many representations made to us by the general public, the Government wish to support the progress of the proposal. Legislation should make clear that the promotion of homosexuality, particularly in schools, by local authorities is not permissible.[72]

During the debate, Haringey was mentioned sixteen times, the borough being singled out specifically for criticism by both Wilshire and Howard. Various Labour MPs raised fears that the amendment might outlaw far more than was apparently intended and also encourage negative attitudes to homosexuals, and Bernie Grant, now MP for Tottenham, forcefully defended the council's policy, quoting at length from a council document which Howard had cited only highly selectively, detonating various myths about books which were allegedly available to children in Haringey library, and criticising the amendment as 'a disgraceful attack on a minority group'.[73] Howard in turn twice condemned Grant's speech as 'disgraceful' and attempted to pin the 'loony left' tail on the Labour donkey by stating that 'it is not possible for the Labour party to dissociate itself from [Grant] and his observations' and that 'his continued membership of the Labour party is a badge of shame for the Opposition to wear'.[74] But although Jack Cunningham, the Shadow Secretary of State for the Environment, defended Grant as a 'welcome member of the Labour party',[75] expressed reservations about the measure and indicated that Labour would be seeking to amend it at its next stage, particularly regarding the matter of 'acceptability', he also made it abundantly clear, twice, that 'it is not, and never has been, our policy to encourage local authorities or education authorities to promote homosexuality in schools or in any other place' and stated that he would vote for the amendment.[76] These remarks were to be gleefully regurgitated on numerous occasions by the measure's supporters in subsequent debates in both Houses whenever Labour members opposed it.

The Clause reached its Report Stage on 15 December, at which point amendments were moved by Simon Hughes (who had opposed the clause the previous week) and Archy Kirkwood for the Liberals, and by various Labour MPs, all of whom were concerned that the measure would censor artistic creativity, endanger education and counselling in relation to sexual health, and infringe the rights and liberties of gays and lesbians. This reflected the worries voiced by a very large number of organisations and individuals, including twenty local authorities and the National Council for Civil Liberties, following the Committee Stage. The proposers of the amendments were also angry that the Government had simply abandoned its earlier position, Hughes accusing it of playing a 'sordid role'[77] and engaging in 'an effort to capitalise on a populist view and to gain the maximum political advantage from the scares and fears about AIDS'.[78] Similarly Cunningham stated: 'We must know what has made the Government change their mind. What events, influences and legal advice have brought the Government to find not only acceptable, but necessary, something that was totally unacceptable only twelve months ago?'[79]

A highly plausible answer would surely include the ongoing flood of 'loony left' stories in the press, which would undoubtedly have led to a swelling of MPs postbags, and assiduous lobbying by the PRG. Evidence for the latter is provided by Dame Jill Knight, who pleaded on behalf of 'parents such as those who contacted me when they wished to complain about the way in which their children were being dealt with in schools promoting homosexuality. Those parents were hit, spat upon, urinated on and one, who was pregnant, was punched very hard in the stomach'.[80] Just as at the Committee stage, Wilshire cited the alleged availability of *Jenny*[81] and Howard claimed that:

> The London borough of Haringey has published a leaflet containing an approved reading list. One book on the list calls for a ban on the wearing of wedding rings by teachers and on teachers talking to their pupils about their husbands and wives. Another book entitled *Young, Gay and Proud* is recommended as suitable reading for children aged 13 and older. The leaflet describes it as 'very helpful to everyone'. It describes homosexual acts in considerable detail.[82]

However, these and similar assertions by no means went unchallenged by Labour members. Thus, Clive Soley pointed out that the stories quoted by the Clause's supporters 'were known to be and had been found to be lies by newspapers. Those lies have now been picked up by certain people who have used them to create hatred and fear'.[83] Similarly, Chris Smith argued that:

> It might help our debates on these sensitive and important matters if we based our arguments on facts rather than on general statements and assumptions

which have appeared in the popular press and are immediately taken by some Conservative Members to be the truth, which they are not.[84]

Ken Livingstone, who had weathered numerous similar attacks as leader of the GLC, noted that:

> Conservative Members are responding to a wave of hysteria and bigotry that has been whipped up by the popular press. It has been absolutely disgraceful. Some people have the misfortune to believe what they read in the *Daily Express*, the *Daily Mail* and the *Sun*. They have come to accept that in some areas children are being taught how to be lesbians. It is easy for those outside who live with the day-to-day prejudice against lesbians and gay men to laugh it off, but that pernicious lie has bitten deep into the popular conscience.

Citing specifically press stories about *Jenny*, he asked: 'Should such nonsense be the basis of legislation?',[85] and Jeremy Corbyn followed a similar line, asking Tory MPs

> to think for a moment before they vote. They know about the way in which the media have manipulated this issue, about the self-fulfilling prophecies and lies peddled by the Murdoch press and others, and about the fears about the alleged promotion of homosexuality in schools, of which there is not one shred of evidence.[86]

During the debate there were a number of interruptions by gays and lesbians in the public gallery, which gave the *Sun* the next day the opportunity to run the headline 'Screaming gays bring Commons to a halt!'

## A perfectly circular process

However, the dissenters' warnings all fell on deaf ears, and the amendments were defeated. The role played by events in Haringey (and, more particularly, by the way in which these were represented by sections of the press) simply cannot be overestimated. As Peter Murphy wrote in a letter to the *Hornsey Journal* (8 January 1988) the clause

> came about through the work and dedication of a few Tottenham parents who have fought magnificently to bring this to the attention to the Government and the nation as a whole … This shows that a small group of dedicated people can change the course of such an evil policy as proposed by Haringey Councillors.

As the Clause made its way steadily onto the statute books, all the myths exposed in this chapter, and many more besides, were paraded with quite mind-numbing regularity by its supporters. A great deal of well-informed debunking by Labour and Liberal MPs and peers, and a massive campaign of protest by a very wide range of individuals and organisations, including the Arts Council, proved to be of no avail whatsoever. Neil Kinnock publicly condemned the clause on 29 December 1988, but it was all too little too late.

Nor, indeed, had the opponents of positive images finished their work.

Members of Positive Images sometimes met at Reading Matters bookshop in Haringey, which also served as the contact address for the group. It was an independent bookshop but at that time received council grants to enable it to participate in activities such as providing stalls at school book fairs. Because it stocked gay literature, among other kinds of reading material, it had long been a target for the Tottenham Tories, and also for the PRG. Indeed, during the 1987 election campaign, the aggressive behaviour of members of the latter was such as to cause them to be banned from the shop. Nothing more happened until February 1988, when the Haringey Tories tabled a motion demanding that the Council 'immediately cease all Grant Aids to Reading Matters Bookshop and any other homosexual group'.[87] A few days later, the shop began to receive visits from journalists, one from the *Sunday Express* saying that he had received a package of books containing *Young, Gay and Proud*, *School's Out* and *Gay Communism* from a group calling themselves 'Concerned Residents of Haringey'.[88] Then, on 28 February, the *Sunday Telegraph* ran a front page story on the bookshop headed '"Tintin" sells riot and anarchy on the rates'. The article began:

> Children as young as five are being encouraged to read anarchist cartoon books and homosexual propaganda by a children's bookshop funded by a left-wing Labour council. Reading Matters bookshop, in Tottenham, stocks a cartoon book that celebrates the murder of PC Keith Blakelock, who was hacked to death a few hundred yards from the shop during the Broadwater Farm riots.

The article asserted that the shop also stocked *Jenny* and *The Playbook for Kids about Sex,* claimed that it was 'dependent on funds from Haringey council', was 'run particularly for children', and regarded by Tory Councillors as the 'centre of a 'sinister left-wing network' in the Borough. It also mentioned that the shop was the contact address for Positive Images, which 'promotes the introduction of lessons on homosexuality', and was set up 'not only by Left wingers from the Labour Party but also by activists from the Communist Party, the Trotskyite Socialist Workers Party and from the Revolutionary Communist Party'. The paper had presented its story to Michael Howard, who was quoted as duly responding:

> This is appalling. Parents of children who are exposed to this kind of activity need to be able to point to a law which makes it illegal. They soon will be able to do just that. Clause 28 of the Local Government Bill will prevent this kind of abuse.

As in the case of so many articles examined in this chapter, most of the contents of this story are inaccurate, innuendo-laden and calculated to provoke and inflame.[89] Reading Matters was not a children's bookshop – it was a general-interest community bookshop, which, like most bookshops, had a children's section, although this one was multi-cultural and catered for the variety of different languages spoken within the borough. The cartoon book, *The Scum*, was not a children's book, but a paper produced by print workers angry at their treatment by the police during the Wapping dispute. Whilst the shop was indeed a contact address for Positive Images, it also performed the same function for many other local groups. As noted above, it did receive grants from the Council for certain educational activities, but it was by no means fully funded by it.

The following week, the story was picked up by the *Mail*, *Sun* and *Star*, although, like the *Sunday Telegraph*, none bothered to contact the shop in order to check the facts of the case. Indeed, the *Mail* compounded the errors in the original by calling *The Scum* 'a junior guide to subversion … on display with books like *Postman Pat*' in an article headed 'Tintin in "sick" book on riot PC's killing'. On 29 February, in a debate on the Local Government Bill, Baroness Blatch, responding to Lord McIntosh of Haringey's point that the Education Act already prevented local authorities from 'promoting' any subject in a classroom, stated that 'a way round that has been found by funding with ratepayers' money organisations such as the Reading Matters bookshop, which does all the promotion that the positive images policy would have done within the local authority'.[90] By this time, the hate mail and bomb threats had started, and people, including two Tory councillors, had been coming into the shop and hurling insults at the staff. However, the minds of the supporters of Section 28 were on other things. Thus, on 1 March, in response to a question about whether an amendment could be introduced to the Local Government Bill to prevent Haringey Council giving a grant to Reading Matters, Mrs. Thatcher stated that:

> Many people would be utterly revolted that any such thing [*The Scum*] should be on sale, let alone on sale from a bookshop which received a grant from a local authority … What is certain is that measures in the Local Government Bill will strengthen the ban on party political propaganda at public expense and will require local authorities to take proper account of the publicity code of practice that will shortly be placed before Parliament for approval.[91]

This gave the *Mail* (2 March) the opportunity to run a story headed 'Maggie in attack on Tintin hate book', which repeated the line that *The Scum* was a 'junior guide to subversion'.

On 8 March, Dame Jill Knight asked the Prime Minister about 'the reports last week that Haringey council was funding a bookshop selling anarchist literature to five-year-olds', receiving the response that the requisite department was looking into the matter 'with a view to taking action'.[92]

On 9 March, Clause 28 finished its progress through Parliament. A few days later, Reading Matters' windows were smashed.

## The magic of reiteration

This is not the place to trace the further history of Clause 28, nor its consequences.[93] But the subsequent debates[94] were characterised by exactly the same process that is so apparent in the debates cited above, namely one whereby myths about the alleged 'promotion' of homosexuality by 'loony left' boroughs, and Haringey in particular, were propagated locally, amplified by sections of the local and national press, made their way into Parliament, thereby giving rise to yet more press coverage and thence forming the basis for legislation. In such a situation, myths and falsehoods are created which, although ludicrous or demonstrably untrue, or both, are almost impossible to contest and dispel – not least because they are recycled, rehashed and embellished by the press on a daily basis. The myths thus become entirely self-perpetuating. As Anna Marie Smith points out apropos the parliamentary debates:

> Later speakers cite the same 'evidence' as if its legitimacy and significance were already well-known. In the final debates, the simple act of speaking the names of five local authorities, Camden, Haringey, Lambeth, Brent and Ealing, is deemed sufficient to evoke the figure of the 'promoter' of homosexuality.[95]

The press articles and parliamentary debates discussed in this chapter constitute classic examples of what Stuart Hall et al. have called a *signification spiral*, defined as 'a way of signifying events which also intrinsically escalates their threat … The activity or event with which the signification deals is *escalated* – made to seem more threatening – within the course of the signification itself'. One of the processes involved in the spiral they define as *convergence*, which occurs when

> two or more activities are linked in the process of signification so as to implicitly or explicitly draw parallels between them … Another, connected, form of convergence is listing a whole series of social problems and speaking of them as 'part of a deeper, underlying problem' – the 'tip of an iceberg', especially when such a link is forged on the basis of implied common denominators. In both cases, the net effect is *amplification*, not in the real events being described, but in their 'threat potential' for society.[96]

Thus, sex education which is based on a liberal, non-judgmental attitude to homosexuality and lesbianism is represented as encouraging young people to experiment sexually or even to 'become' homosexual or lesbian. In the case of men, it is alleged that this can lead to the spread of AIDS, and anything which discourages sex as being regarded as anything other than a means of procreation is represented as endangering the very continuation of life itself (as in Margaret Attwood's novel *The Handmaid's Tale*). Thus, in a series of discursive steps, we move from sex education in a North London borough to the end of the world.

The process analysed here also provides an excellent example of what has been called the 'magic of reiteration'.[97] In the case of 'loony left' stories about sex education, the 'magic' is made all the more powerful by the fact that the myths speak to deep-seated anxieties about sexuality, the family, childhood, the breakdown of the social order, and 'the end of life as we know it' and that they do so in terms which are at once both apocalyptic and 'commonsensical'. With regard to the latter, the opponents of Positive Images in the press and Parliament had the overwhelming ideological advantage of working entirely within what Hall calls 'the dominant circle of ideas' and 'ruling conceptions of the world'. These are 'the horizon-of the taken for granted' and set

> the limit to what will appear as rational, reasonable, credible, indeed sayable or thinkable, within the given vocabularies of motive and action available to us. Their dominance lies precisely in the power they have to contain within their limits, to frame within their circumference of thought, the reasoning and calculation of other social groups.[98]

They thus come to exercise 'symbolic dominance' over competing accounts of the world. It goes without saying that the mainstream media play an absolutely crucial role in this process – particularly when they are as ideologically homogenous and combative as is the bulk of the national press in the UK. Any individuals or groups attempting to assert alternative ideological strategies are thus at a very considerable disadvantage from the start because they are engaged in a massively unequal struggle. In such circumstances, any ideological challenge, if it is to have the remotest chance of success, has to have an extremely clear idea of exactly what it wants to achieve and needs to employ a highly sophisticated political strategy in order to try to do so. As noted earlier, it can be argued that Positive Images failed on both counts.

Such a political strategy will involve, among other things, making allies with more mainstream political and ideological forces and enlisting the aid of those media which are not totally opposed from the outset to the cause in question. Positive Images certainly found willing and energetic allies in the left and gay press, but, inevitably, these publications spoke only to the already-persuaded. However, the liberal and/or Labour-supporting press was quite another matter, as it fully reflected the concerns felt by the Labour leadership over the 'London effect', and especially the gay issue, as noted above and explored in more detail in the 'Slaying the Dragon' chapter. Thus, for example, an editorial in the *New Statesman* (13 March 1987) argued that, although many 'loony left' stories are baseless or tenuous, they nevertheless 'fit a stereotype' and 'are immeasurably aided by ultra-leftists who have taken civil rights for minorities to a position where their impossibly extreme application becomes a test of socialist principles and personal integrity'. In the same edition, John Lloyd and John Rentoul argued that the gay issue 'has become a badge of leftism' and that 'the hard left and the Trotskyist groups have taken it up with an uncompromising moralism which brands as homophobic those who do not agree that it should be at the front of all campaigning'. And in the *Guardian* (January 14 1988), Polly Toynbee averred that 'gay rights as a cause was dead once it had been purloined by the left from the liberal establishment', arguing that 'moderate non-political people need to get back into these organisations, seize them from the extremists, remove them from the grip of the left-wing authorities and start to campaign effectively'. Such sentiments were routine in publications such as these.

On the other hand, as I have tried to illustrate in this chapter, there were those on the Labour side in Parliament, who, along with Liberals such as Simon Hughes, were fully prepared to call out the positive images press stories as either wholly untrue or highly inaccurate, and it is particularly significant that one of these was Jeremy Corbyn, who, as Labour leader, has demonstrated that his public criticism of the Tory press is not the electoral liability that many of his predecessors feared. Indeed, in his speech to the Labour conference in 2017, reported in the *Guardian* (27 September) he openly goaded *Mail* editor Paul Dacre by saying:

> The day before the election, one paper devoted fourteen pages to attack- ing the Labour party. And our vote went up nearly 10%. Never have so many trees died in vain. The British people saw right through it. So this is a message to the *Daily Mail*'s editor: next time, please could you make it 28 pages?

Furthermore, it can be argued convincingly that in December 1987 Labour made a crucial tactical error by allowing itself, as explained above, to be pushed by the Tory government and press into supporting the embryonic Clause 28, thus ally- ing itself with the most reactionary forces in Parliament whilst profoundly alien- ating many members of precisely that liberal establishment so lauded by Toynbee.

At the time, while the policy pursued by the Labour leadership and its allies in the liberal media may have seemed advisable, indeed necessary, given the daily press onslaught and the Tories' absolute determination to tar the party as a whole with the 'loony' brush, there are two major objections to such a stance. The first is pragmatic, and argues that the 'London effect' was in fact nothing like as widespread or pronounced as the leadership feared. This argument could also pray in aid Prime Minister Stanley Baldwin in 1931 and Jeremy Corbyn in 2017 in order to point out that political leaders who are the targets of vicious press campaigns do not necessarily suffer crushing defeats at the ballot box. But the second objection is a principled one, and involves the extent to which politicians in a representative democracy should allow themselves to be swayed by partisan newspapers. This applies equally to those who supported Section 28 on both the Labour and Tory sides, whatever their various motives. As this chapter has attempted to demonstrate, the stories which led to the creation of Section 28 were either wholly untrue or wildly inaccurate and massively one-sided. Whether these were invented by the newspapers themselves, or whether those newspapers were amplifying stories which they had been told by their sources, is irrelevant, since, in the latter case, normal professional journalistic practice should have required that such stories were checked for their veracity before being published. However, the adage 'never let the facts get in the way of a good story' is nowhere more assiduously observed than in Britain's highly partisan national press, and particularly when the pack is in full cry in pursuit of a left-wing fox. Whether journalists should behave in this fashion is, of course, a matter for debate, but equally important is the question of the extent to which politicians should allow themselves to be swayed in policy matters by such newspapers – let alone to exploit partisan newspaper stories for their own political ends.

The complaint is frequently heard today in Britain that newspapers exert too much power over the political agenda, but, if indeed they do, then that is largely because politicians allow them to do so – either because of ideological and political affinities, or for fear of what newspapers might do to them if they endorse policies with which those papers disagree. Either way, the result threatens to be what Bruce Page has called 'a dance of death for democracy'.[99] In her Reith Lectures, Onora O'Neill argued that 'the press has acquired unaccountable power that others cannot match',[100] and writing about his book *Who Runs This Place?* (in which the chapter on the press is entitled 'Unelected Legislators') in the *Independent* (13 April 2004), Anthony Sampson stated that 'Parliament without a press is now unimaginable, but a press without an effective Parliament is an invitation to demagogy and rule by unaccountable new elites'. More recently, Lord Justice Leveson concluded that relationships between the press and politicians had become 'too close to give sufficient grounds for confidence that fear and favour have not been operative factors', and argued that this had given rise to 'legitimate perceptions and concerns that politicians and the press have traded power and influence in ways which are contrary to the public interest and out of public sight'.[101] I would argue that the events analysed in this chapter fully bear out all these words of warning.

## Notes

1 For accounts of the press role in this campaign see M. Hollingsworth, *The Press and Political Dissent: a Question of Censorship* (London: Pluto Press, 1986), pp. 140–69; P. Tatchell, *The Battle for Bermondsey* (London: Heretic Press, 1983).

2 K. Wellings, 'Perceptions of risk – media treatment of AIDS', in P. Aggleton and H. Homans (eds), *Social Aspects of AIDS*, (London: The Falmer Press, 1988), pp. 83–105; V. Berridge, *AIDS in the UK: the Making of Policy 1981–1994* (Oxford: Oxford University Press, 1996).

3 Cox was and continues to be a ubiquitous campaigner against numerous progressive and liberal causes, particularly in education. In 1976, she and her fellow authors Keith Jacka and John Marks published a vitriolic attack on left-wing lecturers and students at the institution in which they worked, *Rape of Reason: the Corruption of the Polytechnic of North London* (London: Churchill Press, 1975) and she was a member of the Hillgate Group and the Conservative Philosophy Group, both of which included Roger Scruton. She also contributed to attacks on current educational practice in works published by the CIA-backed Institute for the Study of Conflict, and was director of the Centre for Policy Studies and chair of its Education Study Group. Such indefatigable ideological labour brought her to the attention of Mrs. Thatcher, who recommender her for a peerage in 1982, and her ongoing campaigning on the education front caused *The Times*, 5 May 1988 to note: 'All the most formidable and mysteriously named little groupings are to be found on the right [and] Lady Cox seems to be on the steering committee of almost every one of them' (quoted in D. Callaghan, *Conservative Party Education Policies 1976–1997: The Influence of Politics and Personality* (Brighton: Sussex Academic Press. 2006), p. 32). However, her strong anti-EU sentiments caused her to rebel over the Maastricht Treaty, and, in May 2004, she and three other Conservative peers signed a letter published by the UK Independence Party urging voters to support it in the elections to the European Parliament. The then Conservative leader, Michael Howard, immediately withdrew the party whip, and she subsequently sat as a crossbencher, increasingly devoting herself to campaigning against sharia law. In February 2009, she and UKIP peer Lord Pearson invited Dutch Freedom Party leader Geert Wilders to show the anti-radical-Islam film *Fitna* to the House of Lords. However, Wilders was prevented from entering the UK on the instructions of Labour Home Secretary Jacqui Smith. For a general overview of Cox's career see http://powerbase.info/index. php/Caroline_Cox#cite_note-20, and for a hagiography, which entirely ignores her role in the creation of Section 28, see A. Boyd, *Baroness Cox: a Voice for the Voiceless* (Oxford: Lion Publishing, 1998).

4 As the Press Council confirmed, in upholding a complaint against an article in the *Sun*, as reported in *UK Press Gazette*, 16 February 1987.

5 For further details of press coverage of *Jenny*, and of the political response to it, see pp. 162–5 of the first edition of this book.

6 L. Levidow, 'Witches and seducers: moral panics for our time', in *Crises of the Self: Further Essays on Psychoanalysis and Politics*, B. Richards (ed.) (London: Free Association Books, 1989), pp. 181–215.

7 S. Reinhold, Local Conflict and Ideological Struggle: 'Positive Images' and Section 28, unpublished DPhil thesis in Social Anthropology, University of Sussex, 1994, pp. 55–6. I am extremely grateful to Sue Reinhold for allowing me to draw on her thesis, which, amongst much other highly useful material, contains interviews with many of the main Haringey players discussed in this chapter. A short account of her work on Haringey can be found in S. Wright and S. Reinhold, (2011), '"Studying through": a strategy for studying political transformation. Or sex, lies and British politics', in C. Shore, S. Wright and D. Però (eds), *Policy Worlds: Anthropology and the Analysis of Contemporary Power* (Oxford: Berghahn Books, 2011), pp. 86–104.

8 Quoted in ibid., p. 53

9 Quoted in ibid., p. 57.

10 The report is available at www.educationengland.org.uk/documents/hmi-curric-matters/health.html.

11 This is the title of a lengthy paean to Patrick Harte, who had just formed the Belmont Parents Rights Group, whose aim was to prevent Haringey Council 'introducing

the teaching of homosexuality as an acceptable alternative to heterosexuality and the teaching of positive images of gays and lesbians throughout the curriculum in Belmont Junior and Infant Schools'. It actually reads like a *Private Eye* parody of *Mail* journalism, with Harte being described as 'a folk hero for innocence' with 'a cup of tea at his elbow' and married to 'wee Scots lassie' Alison. In fact, this is Wolfie Smith and the Tooting Popular Front as re-imagined by the *Mail* – except totally devoid of the humour of John Sullivan's TV series *Citizen Smith*.

12  This was a right-wing libertarian organisation chaired by the shadowy, Lord Lucan-lookalike David Hart, who had taken a highly active role in defeating the striking miners in 1984–5, advising Thatcher and the National Coal Board and funding the Union of Democratic Mineworkers (UDM). The Campaign produced a newsletter, *British Briefing*, which was edited by former MI5 officer Charles Ewell and partly funded by Rupert Murdoch. During the run-up to the 1987 election, the Campaign published a number of virulently anti-Labour advertisements in the national press (S. Milne, 'Rightwing campaigners come out of the bunker', *Guardian*, 23 June 1987, p. 6). One of these, which ran twice in the week before the election, featured the vice-chair of the PRG. Beneath her picture, the advertisement read: 'My name is Betty Sheridan. I live in Haringey. I have two children. And I'm scared. If you vote LABOUR they'll go on teaching my kids about GAYS & LESBIANS instead of giving them proper lessons'. The advertisements were placed by the solicitors White and McDevitt, whose address was shared with the right-wing pressure group Aims of Industry, which has also paid for anti-Labour advertisements in the national press. Earlier, in January 1987, the PRG had announced that it was going to mount a legal challenge to Haringey's policy on sex education, and hired as their solicitor David Negus, whose legal manoeuvrings on behalf of working miners during the strike had paved the way for the creation of the UDM. An article in the *Standard* (24 January) quoted UDM general secretary John Liptrott as telling a PRG meeting: 'Your fight is the same as ours was. It's a battle over who controls the country. Arthur Scargill wanted us to be Stormtroopers for the revolution. We said no. So must you'. The next day's *Mail* took up the story under the headline 'Pit rebels fight left over "gay lessons"', which quoted Liptrott as stating: 'There's a saying: corrupt the morals and you defeat the people'. However, the legal challenge never materialised. Hart played a key role in establishing contacts between the PRG and Westminster politicians, and the Campaign's members included, inevitably, the ubiquitous Baroness Cox (see endnote 3).

13  For example, on 15 October 1986, Peter Simple wrote in the *Telegraph*: 'I have a great dislike of demonstrations, picketing and other such activities. But a columnar award goes to the parents of children at Devonshire Hill primary school in Wood Green who demonstrated against Haringey borough council's policy of "positive images" for homosexuals'. But a few days later, on 23 October, the *Guardian* published a letter from Arthur Phillips, the chairman of the governors of that school, in which he complained that the protestors were not parents of pupils but a 'politically motivated flying picket, bent on disrupting primary schools in the area and making scurrilous remarks, as I myself have witnessed, about the teachers at the school'. In the *Haringey Advertiser*, 27 November, he was quoted as saying that 'I personally heard parents being told that the teachers in the school were lying to them. This took place in front of the children who were with their parents'. And the chair of Haringey's education committee, John Moore, stated that he had seen PRG pickets 'clapping when a child has run away from the gates crying' (*City Limits*, 30 October). No such sentiments ever appeared in those national papers cheerleading for the PRG. For more details of the PRG see M. Durham, *Moral Crusades: Family and Morality in the Thatcher Years* (New York: New York University Press, 1991), pp. 111–18; Reinhold, Local Conflict, pp. 70–8, 149–54.

14  Reinhold, Local Conflict, p. 4.

15  J. Hughes, 'Putting the boot in for God', *City Limits*, 30 October 1986.

16 House of Commons, 22 October 1986, col. 1083. This litany would be endlessly recycled and repeated in Parliament during the following months – for example, by Jill Knight in the debate on Clause 28 on 15 December 1987 (House of Commons, col. 1000), by Baroness Cox in a debate on the Local Government Bill as a whole on 11 January 1988 (House of Lords, col. 1013), and by Knight again in a debate on the Bill on 9 March 1988 (House of Commons, col. 386).

17 House of Commons, 22 October 1986, col. 1084.

18 Ibid., cols. 1084–5.

19 For an analysis of Labour reaction at the national level to these local events, see Chapter 8 'Slaying the Dragon' in this book.

20 Quoted in S. Lansley, S. Goss and C. Wolmar, *Councils in Conflict: The Rise and Fall of the Municipal Left* (Basingstoke: Macmillan, 1989), p. 173.

21 D. Cooper, *Sexing the City: Lesbian and Gay Politics within the Activist State* (London: Rivers Oram Press, 1994), p. 105.

22 Ibid., p. 110.

23 Ibid., p. 136

24 Reinhold, Local Conflict, p. 84.

25 Cooper, *Sexing*, p. 139.

26 Lansley et al., *Councils*, p.172.

27 Cooper, *Sexing*, pp. 122–3.

28 Quoted in Reinhold, Local Conflict, p.8

29 Quoted in J. Weeks, *Against Nature: Essays on History, Sexuality and Identity* (London: Rivers Oram Press, 1991), p. 126.

30 All quoted in Reinhold, Local Conflict, pp. 97–8.

31 House of Lords, 15 April 1986, col. 646.

32 Ibid., col. 647.

33 Ibid., col. 649

34 Ibid., cols. 649–59.

35 Ibid., cols. 650–2.

36 House of Lords, 20 May 1986, col. 225.

37 Ibid., cols. 225–6.

38 Ibid., col. 230.

39 House of Lords, 28 July 1986, cols. 552–4.

40 House of Lords, 18 December 1986, col. 310. Given Halsbury's persistent, some would say obsessive, pursuit of matters such as these, it was surely odd that his obituary in the liberal *Guardian* (1 February 2000) contained no mention at all of this aspect of his life, noting instead, at the climax of a glowing encomium, that 'Halsbury's influence on our nation was considerable … He was greatly respected and greatly loved'. But not by everybody.

41 S. Jeffery-Poulter, Stephen, *Peers, Queers and Commons: The Struggle for Gay Law Reform from 1950 to the Present* (London: Routledge, 1991), p. 210.

42 Reinhold, Local Conflict, pp. 133–5.

43 House of Lords, 18 December 1986, cols. 312–13.

44 Ibid., col. 318.

45 Ibid., col. 330.

46 Ibid., col. 320.

47 Ibid., col. 25.

48 Ibid., col. 326–7.

49 Ibid., col. 328.

50 Ibid., cols. 328–9.

51 Ibid., cols. 332–3.

52 Ibid., col. 335.

53 Ibid., col. 336.

54 House of Commons, 8 May 1987, col. 997.

55 Ibid., col. 998.
56 Ibid., col. 999.
57 This was re-named the Freedom Association in 1978. It first came to prominence through its strike-breaking activities during the bitter and premonitory 1976–8 Grunwick dispute in Brent, and later campaigned in support of the right of England cricketers to tour in apartheid-era South Africa, and against the BBC licence fee, the UK's membership of the EU, and the Royal Mail's erstwhile monopoly. Inevitably, Caroline Cox is a member of its Council. For a critical account of the Campaign's early years see J. Jennings, *Enemy Within: The Freedom Association, the Conservative Party and the Far-Right* (London: Campaign for Press and Broadcasting Freedom, 1980), and for a general overview http://powerbase.info/index.php/Freedom_Association.
58 The publication of this book was the occasion for yet another press furore. On 5 October 1986, the *News of the World* ran a story headed 'Storm over gay video in schools', which related to the video *Framed Youth: Revenge of the Teenage Perverts.* This, according to Tingle, 'encourages children to become gays', was being shown in schools, 'promoted' by the ILEA, and furnished proof that 'schools are now the prime target for gay propagandists'. Not reported was the fact that in 1984 it had won the prestigious Grierson Award. Interestingly, one of those featured in this allegedly corrupting film was Richard Coles, now an ordained priest in the Church of England and something of a 'national treasure'. Tingle's book was also featured in *The Times*, 6 October, ('Schools "targets for gay lib propaganda"'), the *Mail*, 6 October, ('Gays "use sex lessons to promote their own lifestyle"') and the *Telegraph*, 7 October, ('"Gay is natural" fight in schools'). Tingle's entry on the Forum of Christian Leaders boasts that 'her booklet, *Gay Lessons: How Public Funds are Used to Promote Homosexuality Among Children and Young People* led directly to the Section 28 legislation in Britain' (http://foclonline.org/user/253/webinars).
59 Reinhold, Local Conflict, p. 175.
60 House of Commons, 8 May 1987, col. 997.
61 Reinhold, Local Conflict, p. 167.
62 House of Commons, 8 May 1987, col. 1004
63 Ibid., col. 1005.
64 House of Commons, 14 May 1987, col. 413.
65 www.politicsresources.net/area/uk/man/lab87.htm
66 S. Sanders and G. Spraggs, 'Section 28 and education', in *Learning Our Lines: Sexuality and Social Control in Education*, C. Jones and P. Mahony (eds) (London: The Women's Press, 1989), p. 94.
67 A. M. Smith, *New Right Discourse on Race and Sexuality* (Cambridge: Cambridge University Press 1994), p. 184; S. Hall, *The Hard Road to Renewal: Thatcherism and the Crisis of the Left* (London: Verso), pp. 259–67.
68 The full speech is available at www.margaretthatcher.org/document/106941.
69 Reinhold, Local Conflict, p. 199.
70 The final version stated: 'A local authority shall not (a) intentionally promote homosexuality or publish material with the intention of promoting homosexuality; (b) promote the teaching in any maintained school of the acceptability of homosexuality as a pretended family relationship'.
71 There is a particularly striking parallel here with the genesis of the Video Recordings Act 1984, and its amendment in 1994 in the wake of the murder of James Bulger, blame for which significant sections of the press attempted to pin on 'video nasties'. In both of these cases, the Conservative government actually tried hard to withstand increasingly shrill calls for legislation emanating from backbenchers and sections of the press, and in both cases they were eventually forced to cave in. (See J. Petley, *Film and Video Censorship in Modern Britain*, (Edinburgh: Edinburgh University Press, 2011), pp. 26–30, 90–3). Entirely unsurprisingly, many of the MPs and newspapers

that had played an active role in putting the Video Recordings Act on the statute book and later agitating for its tightening up were the same as those that helped to give birth to Section 28.

72 House of Commons, 8 December 1987, col. 208.
73 Ibid., col. 1226.
74 Ibid., col. 1230
75 Ibid.
76 Ibid., col. 1213.
77 House of Commons, 15 December 1987, col. 990.
78 Ibid., col. 993.
79 Ibid., col 998.
80 Ibid., col. 1000.
81 Ibid., col. 1008.
82 Ibid., col. 1017.
83 Ibid., col. 1008.
84 Ibid.
85 Ibid., col. 1010.
86 Ibid., col. 1025.
87 Quoted in Reinhold, Local Conflict, p. 217.
88 Ibid.
89 Indeed, the story about *The Scum* was fed to the press by Malcolm Glynn, a Haringey parent-governor and active right-wing campaigner who had tried repeatedly to get the shop closed down, including writing to the Charity Commissioners and demanding that its charitable status be revoked. See J. Dibblin, '"Burn it down"', *New Statesman* (11 March 1988); and 'Haringey bookshop faces vicious onslaught from press-inspired bigots', *The Pink Paper* (10 March 1988).
90 House of Commons, 29 February 1988, col. 74.
91 House of Commons, 1 March 1988, col. 817.
92 House of Commons, 8 March 1988, col. 186.
93 Those interested in doing so should refer to Sanders and Spraggs, 'Section 28'; M. Colvin and J. Hawksley, *Section 28: a Practical Guide to the Law and its Implications*, London: National Council for Civil Liberties, 1989); Jeffery-Poulter, *Peers, Queers and Commons*; Reinhold, Local Conflict; and Smith, *New Right Discourse*.
94 These were in the Lords on 11 January; 1, 2 and 29 February; and in the Commons on 9 March.
95 Smith, *New Right Discourse*, pp. 192–3.
96 S. Hall, C. Critcher, T. Jefferson, J. Clarke and B. Roberts, *Policing the Crisis: Mugging, the State and Law and Order* (London: Macmillan, 1978), p. 223.
97 The most infamous believer in this particular form of 'magic' was Adolf Hitler who in *Mein Kampf* (London: Hutchinson, 1969), stated that:

> The most brilliant propagandist technique will yield no success unless one fundamental principle is borne in mind constantly and with unflagging attention. It must therefore confine itself to a few points and repeat them over and over. Here, as so often in this world, persistence is the first and most important requirement for success.
>
> *(p. 168)*

98 S. Hall, 'The toad in the garden: Thatcherism among the theorists', in C. Nelson and L. Grossberg (eds), *Marxism and the Interpretation of Culture* (Urbana, IL: University of Illinois Press, 1988), pp. 44–5.
99 B. Page, *The Murdoch Archipelago* (London: Simon & Schuster, 2003), p. 479.
100 O. O'Neill, *A Question of Trust* (Cambridge: Cambridge University Press, 2002), p. 93.
101 L. J. Leveson, *An Inquiry into the Culture, Practice and Ethics of the Press: Report: Volume III*, (London: TSO, 2012), p. 1439.

# 7

# TOXIFYING THE NEW URBAN LEFT

*James Curran*

## Introduction

Extensive survey and experimental research over a seventy-year period provides the main source of evidence about media influence.[1] Its central argument is that people are not empty vessels filled only with media messages. On the contrary, people have values, opinions and understandings, formed by early socialisation, social networks and personal experience. This inclines people to understand, evaluate and retain media information in highly selective ways that accord with what they think already. Even when people are exposed to media information on a topic they know nothing about, they still have core beliefs and general orientations – 'interpretive schema' – that predispose them to 'process' selectively this information. People, in this view, are not easily manipulated, still less controlled by the media. This cautious assessment has been revised to acknowledge that the media can significantly affect what people think about ('agenda-setting') and influence frameworks of public understanding ('framing').[2] Even so, the central conclusion of this work is, still, that the media do not 'determine' public attitudes and behaviour.

Effects research is complemented by reception studies, a research tradition indebted to literary studies and the methodology of commercial focus group research. It argues that meaning is not fixed and inscribed in 'media texts' but is created through the interaction of audience and media. This active process of meaning-making is strongly influenced by the 'discourses' which audiences bring to their media consumption. Even more than effects research, this tradition emphasises the wayward and selective nature of audience responses.[3]

This cumulative academic work has done little to diminish the exaggerated public belief in the ubiquitous power of the media.[4] Yet, the conclusions of both effects and reception studies are – in broad terms – correct. They are supported once again in this overview of the consequences of media reporting of municipal radicalism in London. As we shall discover, the popular press did not determine the thinking of its readers. When it appeared to be dictating public policy, this was also sometimes an illusion.

Yet, academic exasperation with public perceptions of media omnipotence should not give rise to an over-reactive understatement of media influence. This chapter points to times when the media affected public attitudes. This, then, raises the question of why significant media influence was exerted on some occasions but not others. The answer, we will suggest, has usually to do with the pre-existing attitudes of audiences and the wider context in which the media operated.

A distinction also needs to be made between the influence of media on elites and the general public. We have already seen how the press influenced the passing of Section 28 of the Local Government Act 1988 designed to prevent local authorities from 'promoting' homosexuality.[5] This chapter also provides evidence that the press had a significant impact on politicians.

## Mirage of press power

At first glance, the sequence of events suggests that the press was mainly responsible for the closure of the GLC. Between 1981 and 1983, numerous papers campaigned against the GLC, and mobilised public and political pressure for the council to be closed down. It was seemingly rewarded with a last-minute addition to the Conservative party 1983 general election manifesto, committing the party to abolishing the GLC. This proved to be the council's death warrant when the Conservatives won the general election.

However, this imputation of press influence is based merely on inference and chronology. This is typical of the way in which media influence is mythologised. Yet, a detailed examination of the evidence in relation to the GLC's closure puts into perspective the role of the press. It was not as important as it seemed to be.

The assault on the GLC did not originate in the 1980s press but in local, right-wing animosity towards metropolitan government in London that had existed for over a century.[6] For a long time, this hostility was neutered politically by the lack of influence of Conservative activists within their own party. However, grass-roots opinion found an eloquent champion in the right-wing politician Enoch Powell, who published in 1955 a detailed plan for closing down County Hall. By the 1970s, party activists were becoming a significant force within a changing Conservative Party. Conservative London borough leaders lobbied inside their party in 1973 to such effect that the GLC might well have been abolished if the Conservatives, rather than Labour, had won the 1974 general elections.[7]

The abolition campaign temporarily lost momentum in the later 1970s when the Conservatives won the 1977 GLC elections, and reversed policies that right-wing activists had found especially objectionable. But opposition to the GLC among numerous London Conservative activists, councillors and MPs remained.

It resurfaced with increased intensity when the radical Livingstone administration took charge in 1981.[8]

By then, the GLC was already a widely criticised, weakened institution.[9] Central government had undermined the council's planning role by reversing key decisions. Local borough councils had obstructed the GLC's housing programme (which effectively came to an end in 1980 when most of the GLC's housing stock was transferred). The GLC's transport policy had fluctuated in the 1960s and 1970s from plans for a massive road-building programme to subsidised public transport, both of which had been abandoned, while traffic congestion in London grew steadily worse.

These failures prompted some people from the political left and centre to join right-wing critics in attacking the GLC. The council was inherently ineffectual, it was argued, because it was squeezed between an interventionist central government and resentful local boroughs, and immobilised by the competing demands of the inner city and the suburbs. Above all, it was claimed, the root cause of the GLC's deficiency lay in a failed political compromise. The London County Council had been redesigned as the GLC – with a broader electorate, and less power – in order to placate the right. But the right had not been won over, leaving Londoners with a weak institution that lacked legitimacy.

The GLC was further undermined by the deepening political conflict that developed in the Thatcher era.[10] Livingstone's regime redefined the role of the GLC. However, this put the council on a collision course with the government, which was moving towards a different – and fundamentally opposed – understanding of the role of local government. Public choice arguments in favour of a depoliticised, devolved system of local government that was cheap, efficient and more financially accountable had already gained ground in official circles in the early 1980s. Yet, the GLC wastefully propped up, in the government's view, loss-making companies; it subsidised an anti-business counter-culture; it was a superfluous talking shop with subversive views on defence, peace and Northern Ireland; and its ultimate justification was strategic planning, an 'illusion' inherited from the mocked Heath–Wilson era.

The key issue that brought this conflict to a head was public finance. Although the government had been elected in 1979 on a good housekeeping mandate, it had greatly increased public spending. Left-wing metropolitan authorities had contributed to this 'overspending' by sidestepping the government's new grant penalty scheme. Between 1978–9 and 1983–4, the GLC increased its expenditure in real terms (allowing for inflation) by 65% and the Metropolitan County Councils by 22%, compared with a 4% increase among other local authorities in England during the same period.[11] The government found itself in a further quandary. Although it had promised in 1979 to abolish the rates, it could not agree (at that time) on what should replace them. Yet, the Prime Minister Margaret Thatcher felt that the control of local government spending was an area where the government had fallen down, and that something had to be done about this. Abolishing profligate local authorities seemed the way forward.

As Patrick Jenkin, the minister charged with abolishing the GLC, recalls:

> In the end, the cabinet said, well, if we are going to have a credible local
> government policy – we can't abolish the rates – we have got to have rate
> capping, and we have got to get rid of the GLC and the six Met counties.
> It was the Prime Minister who led from the front on this one.[12]

The popular press gave impetus to this decision by making the GLC 'notorious', and mobilising support for its abolition. Above all – and this was perhaps its
most significant input – the press conveyed the impression that the abolition of
the GLC would be easy. According to Patrick Jenkin, the cabinet assumed that
the GLC was 'wildly unpopular', and that its abolition would present no political difficulty.[13]

However, the press's role was secondary. Demands for abolition were initiated not by the press but by right-wing activists, councillors and MPs. Indeed,
considerable political momentum had already built up in favour of abolishing
the GLC long before right-wing newspapers became belated converts to the
cause. This momentum became irresistible when the government, galvanised by
a sense of failure, decided to take effective steps to control local spending. Even
without the press's intervention, it is doubtful whether the GLC would have sur-
vived. After all, the six metropolitan county authorities – largely ignored by the
London-based national press – were also closed down in 1986 because they were
judged to be profligate and unnecessary.

The popular press cannot even be credited with winning public support for
the GLC's closure. Despite campaigning against the GLC for almost five years,
right-wing popular newspapers persuaded only one in four Londoners that the
GLC should be abolished. In fact, they may well have convinced some people of
the opposite. Their campaign undermined the government's administrative case
for closure by giving the impression that the council was really being closed down
out of political animosity. It also rendered the council more newsworthy, making it
easier for the GLC to secure broadcasting coverage. Indeed, there can be fewer better illustrations of the limits of the popular press's power than its failure both to bury
Livingstone as a politician, and to gain public approval for the GLC's execution.[14]

Yet, the popular press was not always so powerless. It was much more effective
in its campaign against the 'loony left' London borough councils. This highlights the contingent nature of press influence – the way in which press influence
depends upon the presence of other factors. It also highlights one further thing:
the press had an impact on political institutions, not just on the public.

## Press disrupts a divided party

The campaign against 'loony' boroughs began with Islington in 1983, intensified in
1985 in response to the Broadwater Farm disturbance and took off in the autumn
of 1986 with a press campaign over 'race commissars', centred on Brent Council's

suspension of a primary school head teacher, Maureen McGoldrick, for making an allegedly racist remark,[15] and over Haringey council's alleged 'promotion' of homosexuality in its schools.[16] The press assault on radical London boroughs thus overlapped with its crusade against the GLC but lasted longer.

A number of things made this campaign against the 'loony left' boroughs different from the assault on the GLC. Radical borough councils like Lambeth, Haringey, Camden and Brent lacked the resources of the GLC, and were less able to fight back. London regional TV journalists initially ignored most stories about them (privately doubting their veracity) with the paradoxical result that these councils lacked an effective platform to answer back. This benign neglect then turned into attack, when broadcasters framed the McGoldrick story in a way that was similar to the press.[17] Television and radio thus did not provide a shield against popular press attacks in the way that they had for County Hall.

What also made the later phase of the 'loony left' campaign different were the actions of the Conservative government. In 1983, the government had been taken by surprise by the GLC counter-attack. It was forced onto the back foot, and made to defend its decision to close down the council in the face of public hostility. But the 'loony' boroughs were a different matter: the Conservative government sensed that here was an opportunity to take the political initiative. In October 1986, Conservative Central Office sent out the first of its three 'research briefings' on the municipal left.[18] These reproduced popular newspaper stories about the alleged outrageous actions of radical London councils, and quoted denunciations from leading Conservative politicians. These denunciations were then reported in the popular press in an escalating spiral of opprobrium. Thus, 17 November saw a double-barrelled attack on radical councils by two senior Conservative politicians. Nicholas Ridley, Environment Minister, compared them to the totalitarian regimes of Poland and East Germany ('the knock on the door in the middle of the night'), while Norman Tebbitt, Conservative Party Chairman, linked them to the possibility of a 'Berlin wall ... erected around our country to keep us in'.[19]

The virulence of these attacks forced a reluctant response from the Labour Leader, Neil Kinnock. The first reaction of his publicity team had been to ignore these attacks. When this became untenable, the Labour leadership distanced itself from 'loony' borough councils in contrast to the way it had belatedly rallied behind the GLC. Kinnock's team was politically hostile to the radical London borough councils; at this time, they did not have lines of communication with them, so did not get their side of the story; they were furious with these councils for undermining their strategy of presenting Labour as a moderate party; and sought to limit, as they saw it, the damage that London's municipal left was inflicting on the party.[20]

Kinnock's attempt to distance himself from the 'loony left' produced a series of headlines in which he seemed to tacitly endorse the government's attack: 'Kinnock slams town hall wreckers' (*Daily Express*, 20 November 1986), 'Kinnock blast at "zealots" for helping the enemy' (*The Times*, 20 November 1986) and the more explicit 'Loony left told to button up' (*Independent*, 23 November 1986).

It was a foretaste of things to come. The right-wing press turned the Greenwich by-election into a public trial of the municipal left. It framed the run-up to the by-election campaign in terms of whether Labour would choose a 'loony' candidate or not, followed by news that it had done so (principally on the grounds that Labour's candidate, Deirdre Wood, had been a member of the Inner London Education Authority, attacked by the press as 'loony'). This was capped by reports of Kinnock's dismay over the decision. 'What a disaster it is for poor Mr. Kinnock', mocked the *Sunday Express* (15 February 1987), while the *News of the World* reported him as saying 'Oh God, not Deirdre'.[21] 'The lesson

The response of Labour managers was to keep Deirdre Wood on a tight rein, and attempt to shift the political agenda to unemployment and welfare. Their efforts were unavailing partly because the 'loony left' was constantly featured in the popular press. The Liberal/Social Democrat Alliance and, initially, the Conservative Party also made the 'loony left' a central theme of their by-election campaigns. When the Alliance candidate, Rosie Barnes, duly won the Greenwich by-election, not only the right-wing press but also most of the rest of the media hailed her victory as a public repudiation of the new urban left. 'The sins of the GLC', declared the BBC's political editor, John Cole, 'have been visited upon the Labour Party'.[21] 'The lesson of Greenwich', according to the pro-Labour *Daily Mirror* (27 February) was that 'the voters don't share the excitement of the zealots'.

In reality, Deirdre Wood's politics and union involvement made her more typical of the 'traditional' left than the new urban left. And although Labour had held Greenwich for forty years, its loss was not quite the bolt out of the blue that it was widely represented to be. Greenwich had become increasingly gentrified, and its politics had consequently changed. Labour had only won the constituency with 38% of the vote in the 1983 general election, making Greenwich one of Labour's twenty most marginal seats. Labour's by-election defeat was in fact less due to a decline of its vote (down four percentage points compared with 1983) than to a collapse of the Tory vote (down twenty-four percentage points). Rosie Barnes was an early beneficiary of tactical voting.

However, these complexities were lost in the febrile atmosphere of the contemporary Labour party. On the night the by-election result was announced, right-wing Labour MPs called for 'desperate remedies to prevent a national disease for the Labour party'.[22] Their appeal was taken up the next day by London trade unionists demanding 'a clean-up' of the London Labour Party in order, in the words of Brian Nicholson, National Chairman of the Transport and General Workers, 'to reassure our traditional supporters that Labour is not a party of lunatics'.[23] Similar views were expressed by Labour's former chief Whip, Michael Cocks, in the *Sunday Times* (21 March 1987), while BBC's *London Plus* (22 March 1987) reported 'an eleventh hour fight back against the hard left' by party 'moderates'.

The Labour leader, Neil Kinnock, lent his authority to this growing hue and cry. Speaking on BBC radio, he said that embarrassment was too 'mild' a word to describe his reaction to some left-wing activists in his party. In a formal statement of dissociation to the press, Kinnock declared that 'people at the fringe of our movement will have no influence, and get no influence on the leadership, our policies or the direction of the party'.[24]

These denunciations were levelled at unidentified left-wing activists. Those whom Kinnock had in mind were pinpointed in a confidential letter written by Patricia Hewitt, Kinnock's press officer, to Frank Dobson, Chairman of the London Group of Labour MPs, which was leaked to the *Sun* (6 March 1987). The letter seemed to vindicate the campaign against the 'loony left' by implicitly acknowledging that popular newspapers were voicing the concerns of ordinary voters. As Patricia Hewitt put it:

> It's obvious from our own polling, as well as from the doorstep, that the 'London effect' is now very noticeable. The 'loony Labour left' is taking its toll; the gays and lesbians issue is costing us dear amongst the pension-ers; and fear of extremism and higher taxes/rates is particularly prominent in the GLC area. Private and public polling is now showing very clearly that, whereas London at the height of the GLC campaign was pulling Labour's national average support up – London today is pulling Labour down. I think there are many in the London party who still fondly believe they are doing well – they need to be disabused.[25]

Following a briefing from Kinnock's office, Labour's leadership was depicted as being determined to wage war on its lunatic fringe. 'Kinnock war on left-ies' (*Star*, 6 March 1987); 'Kinnock tackles the loony left' (*Daily Mirror*, 6 March 1987); 'Gay left scares Kinnock (*Daily Mail*, 6 March 1987). 'A statement from the opposition leader's office', reported BBC TV's Six O'Clock News (6 March 1987), 'insisted that Mr Kinnock would make it crystal clear to a London Labour meeting that the few whose antics attracted sensational attention – in other words the loony left – had no influence'. Speaking later in the programme, a flustered Neil Kinnock said 'I won't tolerate the nonsense that goes wrong – er, on – in and around the edges of the Labour Party'. However, the *Sun* (6 March 1987) warned that the left would not roll over. 'Miss Hewitt's remarks about gays and lesbians will enrage', it reported, 'the lunatic fringe of the Labour party, which has adopted homosexuality as a political cause'.

The leaked letter led to an orgy of public recrimination within the Labour Party. The Labour MP, Frank Field, appeared on television that day to say that the party had come close to becoming unelectable and unworthy of being elected. He declared on BBC2's *Newsnight* (6 March 1987):

> Either we face the appalling prospect of the press picking them [the left] off between now and the election so that the electorate does not vote for them, and that means we do not have a Labour government. Or they get in under the cover of moderation, and totally transform the PLP [Parliamentary Labour Party] in the next parliament. Both prospects are pretty appalling.

This interview was followed by a studio debate between Jo Ashton, Labour MP and *Daily Star* columnist, and Russell Profitt, a left-wing parliamentary Labour candidate and race adviser to Brent council. Ashton angrily said that 'we are seething up in the north' because the London 'loony left' is paving the way for another Conservative victory. 'It is no good blaming the media', exclaimed Ashton. 'It is not the media who says you have got to ban Baa Baa Black Sheep ... and all the other nonsense'. Profitt replied that he was misinformed, and the exchange between them became increasingly acrimonious with each person raising his voice and interrupting the other. 'What chance have you of winning the election', asked Adam Raphael, the bemused programme presenter, 'if you carry on in this kind of vein?'

In the aftermath of the leaked letter, the Conservative press continued to stoke the embers of internal party conflict with a steady flow of 'loony left' stories, such as the alleged banning of 'wife jokes' by Camden Council, subsidised holidays for black pensioners in Lewisham, Bernie's 'barmy jobs for crooks' and a proposal for condom machines in council children's homes.[26] These 'revelations' were sometimes presented as being part of a bigger story in which the leader of the Labour Party was vainly trying to control the party's lunatic elements. This added a new dimension to the right-wing press representation of the 'loony left'. It came to symbolise not only left-wing excess, but also the party's internal turmoil, its weak leadership, its continuing extremism and total unsuitability for public office. While television did not endorse this narrative, it gave it an airing and portrayed the 'loony left' as an electoral albatross around the Labour Party's neck.

Despite behind-the-scenes attempts at peace-making, conflicts continued to simmer within the Labour Party, and were widely reported. Just the day before the announcement of the general election, Labour's left and right were still publicly blaming each other for the party's disappointing May local election results. Attacks on the 'loony left' from within the Labour movement even rumbled on during the general election campaign itself. Paul Gallagher, president of a leading right-wing trade union (EETPU), publicly blamed Labour's poor showing in the polls to:

> the perception that far too many people had of the Labour Party [as] a party dominated by fanatics, committed to extreme policies, catering exclusively to the most bizarre 'representative' minority causes, the advocacy of homosexuality, of inverted racism, of discriminatory feminism, of liaisons with terrorist organisations.[27]

The final phase of the 'loony left' press campaign, during the May–June 2017 general election campaign, had an almost ritual quality. It was claimed that the 'loony left', and its allies, were poised to take over the national leadership of the Labour Party, just as they had done at County Hall. Attention was focused in particular on two 'loony' parliamentary candidates, Bernie Grant (Tottenham) and Ken Livingstone (Brent East): they were among the five most photographed Labour politicians featured in the national daily press during the election campaign.[28] The 'loony left' also graced the Conservatives' opening poster campaign, a party political broadcast and numerous candidates' election addresses.[29] But by then, this hardly mattered. The Conservatives had won the 2017 general election before the official campaign had even begun.[30]

In short, the press 'loony left' campaign was, unlike the GLC battle, an unmitigated disaster for the Labour party. It contributed to prolonged bloodletting, and the party's total disorganisation.

## Pre-election influence

The standard way of measuring press's impact is to examine its influence in a four-week general election campaign. This has led to inconclusive results, suggesting at best only a modest effect.[31] However, this approach fails to consider the potential for much greater influence during the long lead-up to general elections.

The press campaign against the loony left's boroughs took off in the autumn of 1986, and reached its zenith in the aftermath of the Greenwich by-election (26 February 1987). This coincided with the downturn, and then collapse, of the Labour vote (see Table 7.1). Labour's support started to crumble in November 1986, and haemorrhaged in March and April 1987. In just seven months, those intending to vote Labour declined by a quarter. There was no recovery from this collapse. Labour's poor showing in the June 1987 general election – coming second with 31% of the poll – was a direct consequence of this pre-election decline.

That there was a connection between the 'loony left' campaign and Labour's pre-election decline is supported by the way in which perceptions of the Labour Party changed during this period. Some facets of the party's public image remained relatively stable. But perceptions that connected to the 'loony left' campaign shifted significantly. Thus, between October 1986 and April 1987, the proportion thinking that Labour was 'too extreme' increased by fifteen percentage points, while those who said the party was 'too divided' rose by twelve percentage points (see Table 7.2). Those concluding that Labour was poorly led rose by twenty-four percentage points, while those thinking that Labour was the 'only party that can turn out the government' dropped by 31%. The period of most pronounced deterioration in Labour's image was in the immediate aftermath of the Greenwich by-election when the party was convulsed by mutual recrimination.

However, to understand why the 'loony left' campaign had such a strong impact, it is necessary to take account of pre-existing attitudes towards the Labour Party. Labour's result in the 1983 general election – following its extended civil war in 1979–81, the 1982 Falklands War, and recollections of industrial strife and economic crisis during the Callaghan Labour government (1976–9) – had been abysmal. Labour won a smaller share of the vote per opposed candidate in 1983

**TABLE 7.1** Decline of Labour Party support, 1986–7

| Month: | 1986 | | | | | 1987 | | | | | |
| --- | --- | --- | --- | --- | --- | --- | --- | --- | --- | --- | --- |
| | Aug | Sept | Oct | Nov | Dec | Jan | Feb | Mar | April | May (1–14) | May (ave.) | G.E. |
| % Lab: | 37 | 39.5 | 40 | 38 | 36 | 38 | 36 | 32 | 30 | 30 | 32.5 | 31[1] |

*Source*: Monthly averages of MORI, Harris, NOP, Marplan and Gallup polls.

[1] D. Butler and G. Butler, British Political Facts 1900–2000, 8th edition. (Basingstoke, Macmullan, 2000), p. 239. The general election was held on 11 June 1987.

**TABLE 7.2** Perceptions of the Labour Party, 1985–7

|  | Jan '85 % | Jan '86 % | Sept '86 % | Oct '86 % | Jan '87 % | April '87 % |
|---|---|---|---|---|---|---|
| Too extreme | 65 | 60 | 49 | 52 | 53 | 67 |
| Too divided | 75 | 63 | 67 | 61 | 56 | 73 |
| Poor leadership | 65 | 51 | 53 | 45 | 53 | 69 |
| Economy worse under Labour | 46 | 44 | 46 | 48 | 41 | 55 |
| Lab. defence policy Dangerous | 70 | 57 | 62 | 62 | 60 | 66 |
| Looks after working class | 41 | 47 | 38 | 44 | 45 | 39 |
| Not clear what Labour stands for | 72 | 63 | 57 | 57 | 59 | 67 |
| Only party that can turn out government | 53 | 39 | 49 | 59 | 53 | 28 |

*Source*: Gallup.

than at any time since 1906, and came third or lower in 292 constituencies.[32] The party's own private research during the 1983 general election highlighted its crisis: it was widely judged to be economically incompetent, and was criticised on numerous other counts (including being both unprincipled and extreme). It seemed to be surviving perilously as a political force only because it was viewed as the party of the working class and the welfare state.[33]

Following Neil Kinnock's election as Labour leader in 1983, the party sought to reassure the electorate that Labour had become a more moderate party. This electoral strategy was pursued through symbolic changes, and supported by some shifts of policy. For a time, it seemed as if this strategy was working. There was a gradual, if chequered, recovery of Labour's position in the polls after 1983 until the winter of 1984–5,[34] when television showed recurrent – and influential – images of picket-line violence during the bitter miners' strike.[35] However, when the strike ended, Labour's recuperation gradually resumed and seemed to gather momentum in 1986. This recovery only faltered and went into reverse when the 'loony left' campaign took off in November 1986.

This campaign was effective because it activated latent misgivings about whether Labour had really changed. Negative images of Labour had receded during 1983–4, revived during the 1984–5 miners' strike, were allayed again in 1985–6, and then were greatly strengthened by the 'loony left' assault. This campaign thus brought to the surface and crystallised doubts that already existed.

Thus, the high proportions of people who viewed the Labour Party as extreme, divided and badly led in April 1987 – shortly before the general election – were in fact very similar to those saying the same thing in January 1985, during the height of the miners' strike (see Table 7.2). Mistrust of Labour revived.

There were multiple reasons why the Conservatives won the 1987 general election (of which their reputation for greater economic competence was probably the most important).[36] But negative perceptions of Labour as extremist played a part. No less than 42% of Labour defectors in the 1987 election gave the party's extremism as a factor that had influenced their decision to withdraw support from the party.[37] Another post-election survey found that dislike of the 'loony left' was the aspect of the Labour Party that repelled the highest proportion of non-Labour and ex-Labour voters alike. Among the crucial latter crucial group, 42% agreed with the statement that the '"loony left" would gain too much influence'.[38]

These last results should be viewed with caution since retrospective assessments do not always provide a reliable guide to motivation. Indeed, they probably inflate the importance of the 'loony left' campaign by providing an 'acceptable' reason for switching from Labour. But even if allowance is made for this, they still powerfully support the conclusion – backed by other evidence – that a toxified municipal left contributed to Labour's defeat.

## Delegitmating the new urban left

The press assault on the 'loony left' was a personally traumatic experience for the relatively young team – Neil Kinnock, Charles Clarke, Patricia Hewitt and Peter Mandelson – who were in the front line attempting to defuse its consequences. They found themselves powerless to prevent Labour's pre-election collapse in 1986–7, culminating in the party's third successive election defeat. This collapse reinforced, in their view, the need for a fundamental transformation of the party.[39] Labour moved much further to the right after the 1987 general election, and this helped to reconcile the Labour right to Kinnock's continued leadership. A successful press assault thus played a part in encouraging an accelerated transitional shift, under Kinnock's later leadership (1987–92), towards New Labour.

The new urban left also became a scapegoat for failure within the Labour party. It was not just leading members of the Labour right who blamed the 'loony left' for Labour's defeat. This view was echoed by the party's leadership, and was duly amplified by political correspondents. As the BBC's political editor, John Cole, put it: 'I have no doubt that he [Kinnock] would believe that it's the London Labour Party and people like it have got Mrs Thatcher's majority'.[40] Moreover, some members of the Labour left also joined in this chorus of condemnation. For example Tom Sawyer, Deputy General Secretary of the left-wing National Union of Public Employees (and a member of the inner group who had organised Tony Benn's deputy leadership bid in 1981) publicly rounded on the London left, warning that 'the politics of gender and politics of race are dynamite, and they have got to be handled carefully. Unless we learn that lesson Labour [may]never be elected to government again'.[41] Traditionalists on the far left also rounded on the new urban left. According to

Derek Hutton, former Deputy Leader of Liverpool Council (and a leading figure in the Trotskyist Militant Tendency), 'the London Left are more concerned
about black mayors and gay rights than about building homes' and 'more concerned that we called ... a manhole cover a personhole cover, than they ever
were about real issues'.[42] 'People as a whole – especially older Labour voters',
echoed a Scottish trade unionist in a militant rank-and-file paper, 'become
anti-Labour when they see councils in London ... subsidising all kinds of
odd activities'.[43]

During this period of extended recrimination, some members of the new urban
left begged forgiveness for their sins. Graham Smith, a radical Ealing Councillor,
wrote in *Tribune*: 'I plead guilty. I put my hand up ... We have to admit we were
wrong'.[44] Margaret Hodge, leader of left-wing Islington council (from whose Town
Hall a red flag had once fluttered), declared that the new urban left needed to
leave behind the politics of gesture.[45] Camden Council, explained its press officer
Jonathan O'Neil in 1991, had learnt the error of its ways. 'This tag as a loony left
authority', he explained, 'is one we're trying very hard to shake. It refers to nearly
ten years ago with a very different [Labour council] administration'.[46] 'We don't do
gesture politics now', echoed Camden's new leader, Julia Fitzgerald, 'which wasn't
always the case three or four years ago'.[47] The London Labour Party, declared its
senior organiser, Terry Ashton, had turned its back on the errors of the past.[48]

Labour's critics were not convinced. The right-wing press detected further manifestations of the 'loony left' virus in the late 1980s and early 1990s,
and issued fresh health warnings.[49] In this extended period of almost universal denigration of the 'loony left', opinions were revised. The GLC had
been widely praised, none more so than by Martin Jacques (editor of *Marxism
Today*) who wrote in 1986 that it was 'the *greatest* achievement of the labour
movement since 1979' (original emphasis) and had advanced 'a new set of
priorities – gender, race and sexuality – which will surely be a central part of
the agenda of the 90s'.[50] Writing in 1991, Martin Jacques (now a columnist
for the *Sunday Times*) expressed misgivings about 'gesture politics' and 'high-
profile stances on racism and sexism', although he praised the GLC's cheap
fares policy.[51]

Others were more acerbic. Ros Coward, a prominent feminist, scoffed at
those who remembered 'Red Ken's rule [at the GLC) as the heyday of the democratic left'. On the contrary, she declared in 1997, 'I remember it as the time the
lunatics took over the asylum'.[52] In the same year, the progressive journalist Polly
Toynbee implicitly acknowledged the new consensus by referring to the former
flagship of the London left as 'the old reviled GLC'.[53]

A movement that had been hailed by many on the left during the mid-1980s
as marking a way of reinventing radicalism in new times, and of connecting to
new social forces, was thus almost universally denigrated as a failed experiment
in the post-1987 period. This condemnation contributed to the weakening, sub-
division and increasing demoralisation of the left within the Labour Party that
facilitated the New Labour ascendancy (1994–2010).[54]

## Mythologising the 'London effect'

In Labour's post-election inquest, much was made of the fact that the Conservative Party's share of the vote rose in London, whereas it fell in most regions. This was taken to be conclusive proof that the London left had been decisively repudiated by the electorate. It was said to signify the new urban left's total unelectability, and to underscore the need for the Labour party to 're-connect' to the concerns of the public.

Central to this discourse of blame was unquestioned acceptance that there was indeed a 'London effect'. Paving the way for this conclusion was Patricia Hewitt's leaked letter reporting that it was 'obvious' from the party's own research that fear of extremism was 'particularly prominent in the GLC area'.[55] In fact, this was very far from obvious. The relevant survey, commissioned by the Labour Party,[56] reported that 3% more Londoners than the national sample said that a future Labour government would be 'too left-wing/communist'. This difference was within the statistical margin of sampling error. Furthermore, there was no consistent difference between the responses of Londoners and the national sample on a range of issues (such as rates) where a 'London effect' would be expected to operate. What in fact the party's polling evidence suggested, in an inconclusive way, was the possibility of a weak effect – not at all what Patricia Hewitt claimed.

The actual 1987 election results do not in fact demonstrate the existence of a powerful 'London effect' if other variables are taken into account. There was a 2% increase of the Conservative share of the vote in the capital. However, the Conservatives also increased their share of the vote in the south-east by the same amount. Both results could be attributed to the disproportionate growth of prosperity that took place in London and the south-east during the 1986–7 economic boom.

What most analysts also failed to notice was that Labour's share of the vote also increased by two percentage points in London in the 1987 general election. It was the Alliance, not Labour, which fell back in the capital. The erosion of the centrist rather than left vote was not what most commentators had in mind when they talked about the 'London effect'.

There was also no systematic voting trend against 'loony left' candidates and those standing in 'loony left' boroughs. Some left-wing candidates, like the former GLC councillor Tony Banks, did exceptionally well, as did some candidates in 'loony' boroughs, like Islington's left-wing Jeremy Corbyn. Conversely, some right-wing Labour candidates standing in right-wing Labour boroughs, like Newham's Nigel Spearing, did badly.

But while this was no systematic pattern of 'loony left' rejection, seven left-wing parliamentary Labour candidates underperformed in London. However, this was due to a number of factors. Four of these candidates were black in a general election where non-white candidates fared worse than average. Certain results could be attributed to sub-regional differences of swing within the metropolitan area (where Labour did better in south than in north London).

Furthermore, the adverse swings experienced by some radical candidates were not enough in most cases for Labour to lose a seat. The best available inference, derived from a very careful sifting of the evidence, is that – at most – the 'London factor' helped the Alliance to retain one seat (Greenwich), and the Conservatives to win another (Walthamstow).[57] In short, what the 'London effect' amounted to was the possibility that it affected the outcome of just two seats.

Of course, the damage that the 'loony left' campaign inflicted on the Labour Party extended across the country, including London. But this damage was made worse by the way in which the Kinnock team mishandled the press assault. They implicitly endorsed the attack, reinforcing its damaging impact. Only in the final phase, shortly before the general election, did the Labour leadership opt for the strategy that it should perhaps have adopted in the first place. It attacked some 'loony left' stories as lies, and sought to play down the whole issue as over-blown.[58] By then, it was too late.

## Absence of sustained retribution

If voters did not especially punish the London left in the 1987 general election in the way that was mytholgised, perhaps they exacted retribution in local council elections. After all, it was radical local councils in the capital that were at the centre of controversy.

Borough council elections in London were held in May 1986, when the popular press campaign against radical London councils had been running for several years. Those singled out for special press attack before May 1986 were Camden, Hackney, Haringey, Lambeth, and Islington councils. Yet, Labour's share of the vote in five out of these six 'loony' boroughs actually increased – in two cases by a margin of ten percentage points or more.[59]

The 1990 local election in London provided another opportunity for local electorates to send their 'loony' councillors packing. By then, the right-wing popular papers had branded some ten London councils as 'loony'. Yet, there were positive swings to Labour in seven of these boroughs, (whereas there was a 0.5% swing to the Conservatives in the capital as a whole). In only three of these local boroughs did Labour do worse than the London average.[60] This was perhaps due to the popular press's assault, although other factors were also involved.[61]

The absence of sustained local retribution in 1990 was probably down to three things. Some councils had radical constituencies; some made a pitch that they had moderated their radicalism; and there was widespread public distrust of the national popular press.

Thus, Islington was a radical borough of long standing. In 1987, the majority under the age of forty-five in Islington supported higher rates/taxes in order to try to reduce poverty in the borough. Two local polls – conducted in 1984 and 1987 – indicate that satisfaction with Islington council actually increased even though it continued to be the butt of right-wing press attacks.[62] In the event, there was a strong swing to Labour in the 1990 Islington Council election.

The credibility of the national press was low. In 1988, only 12% thought that tabloids like the *Sun* were truthful, and only 25% said the same of middle-market papers like the *Daily Mail*.[63] Furthermore, there were alternative sources of information. In local surveys, the most often cited source of information about local councils were the local councils themselves, the local weekly press, and friends and neighbours.[64]

But if the electorate in radical areas were often unmoved by the 'loony left' assault, this was less true of local political activists. The press's assault contributed to intense faction fights in some radical London councils in the later 1980s. It was personally traumatising for some, like Linda Bellos, leader of Lambeth council, who was deeply upset by the way in which she had been stigmatised in the press as a 'black lesbian'.[65] She dropped out of municipal politics.

A further reason why the new urban left project faltered in the 1980s was that rate-capping and the exhaustion of creative accounting (with no Labour government bailout in sight) heavily limited what left-wing councils could do. Councils became so neutered that immersion in municipal politics was judged by some radical activists to be a waste of time and energy.

## Decline of local democracy

During the 1980s, ten major statutes reduced the functions, resources or discretion of local councils and had the cumulative effect of extending central government control.[66] The financial autonomy of local councils was greatly curtailed; local council responsibility for housing and education was diminished; and local power to regulate and subsidise public transport was also limited. Competitive tendering for key local government services, first introduced in 1988, was greatly extended under John Major's administration (1990–7).[67]

This emasculation was justified partly by the need to curb the 'loony left', and address the underlying malaise that had allowed left-wing councils to flourish. Councils were elected, it was argued, on low turnouts. Low-income voters were exempted from paying local rates, and were free therefore to vote 'irresponsibly'. Council services were inefficient due to the absence of competitive market forces, and undue union influence. Above all, some council administrations went beyond their core role of delivering essential services. As Margaret Thatcher complained, a 'whole batch' of Labour councils are engaged 'not in crime prevention, but in police prevention', and seek to impose gay propaganda 'on innocent children'.[68]

Yet, a sustained attack on seemingly unpopular councils failed to win consent for the restructuring of local government. Although the poll tax was initially welcomed by a slim margin of 4% in June 1987, it soon became unpopular. Two-thirds of the public opposed it by late 1987, and almost three-quarters by early 1990.[69]

The government's plans for compulsory tendering of local government services encountered growing opposition. Although welcomed in principle by many in 1987, it was a different matter when it came to outsourcing in their

area. In 1988, the large majority opposed the sub-contracting of *their* local council services. Indeed, the majority of Conservative supporters believed that their
council would do a better job than private enterprise or central government in
administering all but one service.[70] MORI studies during this period show that
people opposed privatisation of local council services for three main reasons:
they feared that prices would rise, quality would decline and local community
control would be reduced.[71]

More generally, people showed little enthusiasm for escaping from the incompetent and oppressive town hall commissars of tabloid legend. In nine local studies between 1987 and 1989, the proportion of councils' tenants wanting to retain
council management ranged between 69 and 94%.[72] Although parents supported,
in principle, the right for schools to opt out of local authority control, successive
polls in 1987–8 showed that those wanting schools in their area to opt out were a
small minority.[73]

Two reforms – council house sales and the introduction of the national curriculum – won enduring public support. But what is striking is how little public
acceptance there was for most of the measures that eroded local democracy in the
1980s. Given the outpouring of official justifications for these measures, and the
scale of negative coverage of left-wing councils that legitimated local government reform, this lack of public support requires an explanation.

One reason was that many people were not as disenchanted with local government during the 1980s as critics on the right (and also on the left) imagined.
The Audit Commission survey of local government in England and Wales in
1986 found that 53% were satisfied with their local council, compared with 26%
who were dissatisfied.[74] Dissatisfaction with central government (52%) was in
fact double that for local government.[75] The level of satisfaction with local councils was also higher in 1986 than it was in 1981.[76] In short, there was no consensus
that local government needed to be 'fixed'.

The second reason was that the nature of the 'fix' – greater market provision and increased central control – did not accord with contemporary public
attitudes. In the 1980s, the majority disapproved of the privatisation of British
Gas, British Telecom, electricity and water supply.[77] This absence of a neo-liberal
consensus helps to explain why so many people were opposed to privatisation of
local government services.

The third reason is that people also did not favour a greater role for central
government in local affairs. In 1986, the large majority believed that increased
government control over local council spending would result in worse services
and reduced local accountability.[78] In 1987, only 15% said that councils should
be controlled more by central government.[79] And only 5% thought that national
government had too little power, compared with 48% who said that it had
too much.[80] This was at a time when there was growing criticism of government heavy-handedness.[81]

The fourth reason why many local government reforms lacked support was
that they were presented, especially in the later 1980s, as a way of curbing

'problem' councils. Reform did not seem relevant therefore to many people as a way of improving the unproblematic council in their area.

But if the public did not approve of the revolution in government that was inaugurated in the 1980s, this did not seem to register in official circles and much of the national press. Thus, Kenneth Baker, then Education Minister, talked confidently about the 'tremendous consensus we have got to be moving down this road [of local government reform]'.[82] Asked why Labour had made major gains in 'notorious' Haringey in the 1990 local elections, Baker expressed bafflement. 'Possibly in Haringey', he suggested, 'they are more insulated to the extravagances of Labour authorities than elsewhere'.[83] It was not just Conservative newspapers but also some prominent liberal voices who cheered the curbing of local government. For example, Alan Watkins, a much-admired *Observer* columnist, wrote of Margaret Thatcher: 'She has removed two fears, even hatreds, from the lives of working people: of trade unions and of Labour local authorities'.[84]

Sustaining this illusion of public approval for local government reform was a cumulative crisis of opposition. As noted earlier, the defence of the GLC had brought into a being a formidable political alliance, drawing support from across the political spectrum. This coalition fell apart in the later 1980s. It became politically difficult for Conservatives to rally to the cause of local democracy when it was embodied by the 'loony left' in London and Trotskyist Militants in Liverpool. It also became politically inexpedient for the Labour leadership to make too much fuss about creeping centralisation when this invited the media to identify it with 'indefensible' zealots in local government. The campaign against the poll tax in the late 1980s and early 1990s perhaps provided an opportunity to recreate a political coalition in defence of local democracy. However, a tactical decision was taken by Neil Kinnock to concentrate almost exclusively on the regressive nature of the poll tax.[85]

Local councils were forced to fall back on their own resources in defending local democracy. However, local authorities split along party lines, and did not present a united front. The municipal left itself split over how to respond to rate-capping. In some areas, polls indicated support for militant action. For example, 36% of Islington residents wanted in 1985 their council to refuse to set a lower rate 'even if this means breaking the law' and a further 37% wanted the council to resign in protest and call a special local election, while only 21% wanted the council to set a lower rate demanded by the government.[86] In neighbouring Southwark, 56% wanted their council to break the law over rate-capping.[87] However, left-wing councils in the 1980s did not have a mass movement to call upon, unlike the militants of Popularism in the 1920s.[88] They also lacked significant support in parliament and the media. There was really not much they could do to arrest the increasing centralisation of government.

In short, the right-wing press did not win public support for the emasculation of local government. But it deterred cross-party opposition to the erosion of local democracy, and strengthened the government's determination to outsource local government services and impose greater central control. Once again, the influence of the press was seemingly greater at Westminster than in the country as a whole.

## Notes

1 J. Curran, *Media and Power* (London: Routledge, 2002).
2 For overviews, see S. Iyengar, *Media Politics*, 3rd edition (New York: Norton, 2015), especially chapter 8; R. Nabi and M. Oliver (eds.) *Handbook of Media Processes and Effects* (Thousand Oaks, CA.: Sage, 2009); R. Preiss, B. Gayle, N. Burrell, M. Allen and J. Bryant (eds.) *Mass Media Effects Research* (New York: Routledge, 2007).
3 For an overview of this tradition, see J. Tulloch, *Watching Television Audiences* (London: Arnold, 2000).
4 Belief in the brainwashing power of the media is based partly on irrational fears and discontents. See M. Barker and J. Petley (eds.) *Ill Effects*, 2nd edition. (London: Routledge, 2001) and L. Blackman and V. Walkerdine, *Mass Hysteria* (Basingstoke: Palgrave, 2001).
5 See Chapter 6.
6 K. Young and P. Garside, *Metropolitan London* (London: Edward Arnold, 1982).
7 K. Young, 'The conservative strategy for London, 1880–1975', *London Journal*, 1, (1975); K. Young and J. Kramer, *Strategy and Conflict in Metropolitan Housing* (London: Heinemann, 1978).
8 A. Forester, S. Lansley and R. Pauley, *Beyond Our Ken* (London: Fourth Estate, 1985); K. Young, 'Metropolis, R.I.P.?' *Political Quarterly*, January–March, 1986; B. Pimlott and N. Rao, *Governing London* (Oxford: Oxford University Press, 2002).
9 Young and Garside, *Metropolitan London*.
10 B. O'Leary, 'Why was the GLC abolished?', *International Journal of Urban and Regional Research*, 1987; B. O'Leary, 'British farce, French drama and tales of two cities: reorganizations of Paris and London governments 1957–86', *Public Administration* 65, (1987).
11 Department of the Environment, *Streamlining the Cities* (London: HMSO, 1983), p. 4.
12 Interview with Lord Jenkin (Patrick Jenkin) by the author.
13 Ibid.
14 See Chapter 4.
15 This is documented in detail in chapter 5 of the first edition of this book (J. Curran, I. Gaber and J. Petley, *Culture Wars* (Edinburgh: Edinburgh University Press, 2005) and outlined in Chapter 10 of this edition.
16 See Chapter 6.
17 See Note 15.
18 Conservative Research Department, 'Red-print for Ruin: The Labour Left in Local Government' (London: Conservative Party, 1986); 'Labour in Power: Profiles of Municipal Militancy' (London: Conservative Party, 1986); 'Labour in Power: More Profiles of Municipal Militancy' (London: Conservative Party, 1986).
19 *The Times*, 18 November 1986.
20 Interviews with Peter Mandleson (Director of Labour Party Communication (appointed in 1985)), Patricia Hewitt (Press Secretary to Leader of the Opposition) and Charles Clarke (Chief of Staff, Kinnock's Office) by the author. All three subsequently became cabinet ministers.
21 BBC TV, Six O'Clock News, 27 February 1987.
22 *Daily Mirror*, 27 February 1987.
23 *Guardian*, 28 February 1987.
24 *The Times*, 8 March 1987
25 *Sun*, 6 March 1987.
26 *Sun*, 13 May 1987 *et passim*.
27 *Guardian*, 2 June 1987.
28 M. Harrop, 'Press', in D. Butler and D. Kavanagh, *The British General Election of 1987* (Basingstoke: Macmillan, 1988), table 8.3, p. 169.
29 Butler and Kavanagh, *British General Election of 1987*, pp. 212, 222–3 and 241.

30 W. Miller, H. Clarke, M. Harrop, L. Leduc and P. Whiteley, *How Voters Change* (Oxford: Clarendon Press, 1990).
31 For example, W. Miller, *Media and Voters* (Oxford: Clarendon Press, 1991); K. Newton and M. Brynin, 'The national press and party voting in the UK', *Political Studies*, 49 (2), (2001); A. Reeves, M. McKee and D. Stuckler, '"It's the Sun wot won it": Evidence of media influence on political attitudes and voting from a UK quasi-natural experiment', *Social Science Research*, 56, (2016), among others.
32 D. Butler and D. Kavanagh, *The British General Election of 1983* (London: Macmillan, 1984).
33 MORI private polling on behalf of the Labour Party, May–June 1983. Its devastating findings were succinctly summarised in internal memoranda by Adam Sharples.
34 D. Butler and G. Butler, *Twentieth-Century British Political Facts 1900–2000* (Basingstoke: Macmillan, 2000), p. 275.
35 G. Philo, *Seeing and Believing* (London: Routledge, 1990).
36 A more detailed analysis of the causes of the Conservative victory in 1987 is provided in chapter 9 of Curran, Gaber and Petley, *Culture Wars*, first edition.
37 BBC Gallup Survey, 10–11 June 1987.
38 IFF Post Election Survey, 1987, presented to Labour's National Executive Committee.
39 Kinnock, Hewitt and Clarke originated from the centre left, and for them this was an intellectual journey. Mandelson was by the early 1980s on the militant right of the Labour party.
40 Election '87, BBC1, 12 June 1987.
41 Quoted in J. Lloyd and J. Rentoul, 'Londoner's Diary', *New Statesman*, 10 July 1987.
42 D. Hatton, 'Kinnock kicks me out', *The Sunday Times*, 14 February 1988.
43 J. Connell, 'Open letter to Tony Benn', *Voice of the Unions*, October 1987.
44 G. Smith, 'Why Labour lost in Ealing', *Tribune*, 18 May 1990.
45 'Capital service', New Socialist, August/September 1990.
46 *Guardian*, 5 August 1991.
47 Ibid.
48 *Tribune*, 11 May 1990.
49 *Sunday Times*, 26 January 1992.
50 B. Campbell and M. Jacques, 'Goodbye to the GLC', *Marxism Today*, April 1986, pp. 8–10.
51 M. Jacques, 'From gesture to realism', *The Times*, 2 May 1990.
52 R. Coward, 'Now we are all children of the revolution', *Guardian*, 31 March 1997.
53 P. Toynbee, 'Interview' (with Chris Smith), *Independent*, 3 June 1997.
54 This was explored more fully in chapters 7 and 9 of the first edition published by Edinburgh University Press, and is developed here in Chapter 8.
55 *Sun*, 6 May 1987. This claim seems to have been based on some focus groups – based on tiny samples – which suggested that the GLC's championship of 'minorities' was having a negative impact on the Labour vote. See in particular 'Research De-Brief', March 1986, Kinnock Papers (KNNK-2-1-72), Churchill College, Cambridge. My thanks go to Colm Murphy for drawing this to my attention.
56 'Public Opinion and Choices', MORI, 23–27 January/6–10 February 1987, conducted on behalf of the Labour Party.
57 This draws on J. Curtice and M. Steed, 'Appendix 2' in D. Butler and D. Kavanagh, *British General Election of 1987* (Basingstoke, Macmillan, 1988).
58 For example, Neil Kinnock interviewed on *The London Programme*, Thames Television, 18 May 1987; Denis Healey debating with Shirley Williams in *World in Politics*, Channel 4, 15 May 1987; and Jo Ashton, 'Nailed – myth that cost votes', *Star*, 1 June 1987.
59 London Borough Council Elections 6 May 1982 (London: Greater London Council, 1982), table 3; London Borough Council Elections 8 May 1986 (London: London Residuary Body, 1986), table 3. The only press-targeted radical London council to

experience a swing against Labour was Islington where a large number of Labour councillors had defected to the SDP, establishing for a time a strong SDP presence in the borough splitting the progressive vote.

60 C. Rawlings and M. Thrasher, 'London council voters see beyond poll tax', *The Guardian*, 29 May 1990.

61 The three boroughs were Brent, Ealing and Waltham Forest. A number of factors were involved such as a large rate rise in Waltham Forest, producing an adverse reaction (see Waltham Forest Community Consultation, MORI, 1987), and press attacks on Ealing Council for its alleged 'loony' policy on sex education.

62 Public Opinion in Islington, MORI, 1984; Service Provision and Living Standards in Islington, MORI, 1987.

63 Gallup Political Index, April 1988.

64 For example, Public Opinion in Camden, MORI, 1985.

65 Interview with the author.

66 These were 1980 Housing Act; 1982 Local Government Finance Act; 1984 Rates Act; 1984 Housing and Building Control Act; 1985 Transport Act; 1985 Local Government Act; 1988 Local Government Finance Act; 1988 Housing Act; 1988 Education Reform Act; and 1989 Local Government Act.

67 K. Young and N. Rao, *Local Government Since 1945* (Oxford: Blackwell, 1997); G. Stoker, *Transforming Local Governance* (Basingstoke: Macmillan, 2004).

68 *Sunday Times*, 22 March 1987.

69 D. Deacon and P. Golding, *Taxation and Representation* (London: John Libbey, 1994), table 7.1, p. 190.

70 Gallup Survey, April 1988.

71 For example MORI surveys undertaken for Bristol Council (1987) and Nottinghamshire (1988).

72 B. Gosschalk and J. Curran, 'A hostile awakening', *Local Government Chronicle*, 8 September 1989, p. 18.

73 Gallup Survey, October 1987; Marplan Survey, February 1988; MORI, November 1988.

74 Attitudes to Local Authorities, Audit Commission/MORI, 1986.

75 Ibid.

76 Attitudes to Local Government, Association of Metropolitan Authorities/MORI, 1981.

77 I. Crewe, 'Has the electorate become Thatcherite?' in R. Skidelsky (ed.) *Thatcherism* (London: Chatto and Windus, 1988), table 4, pp. 41–3.

78 Attitudes to Local Authorities and Their Services, Audit Commission/MORI, May 1986.

79 J. Curtice, 'One nation?' in R. Jowell, L. Brook and S. Witherspoon (eds.) *British Social Attitudes: The 5th Report* (Aldershot: Gower, 1988), table 8.2, p. 147.

80 Curtice, 'One nation?'

81 Crewe, 'Electorate', table 4, p. 43.

82 Cited in B. Gosschalk and C. Game, 'Mrs. Thatcher's local revolution', unpublished ESOMAR Conference paper, February 1989.

83 The *Guardian*, 7 May 1990.

84 A. Watkins, 'Mr. Kinnock has still to find his big idea', *Observer*, 31 December 1989.

85 Interview with Patricia Hewitt (Kinnock's Press Secretary) by the author.

86 Public Opinion in Islington, MORI, 1985.

87 Public Opinion in Southwark, MORI, 1984.

88 N. Branson, *Poplarism 1919–1925* (London: Lawrence and Wishart, 1979).

# 8

# SLAYING THE DRAGON

*Ivor Gaber*

He [Ken Livingstone] praises Mr. Blair for running 'the government of my dreams' on issues such as race, female equality and sexual orientation. 'If you come out [as gay]' he says 'it almost guarantees you a junior ministerial post. It's wonderful',

*Jackie Ashley, the* Guardian *8 April 2004*

Today as an experiment, I have been asked to run a few job advertisements. These are not ordinary jobs. These are some of the nation's top jobs, none of which has ever been advertised before. So only extremely serious applicants, please ... Bogeyman of the Left. This symbolic post fulfils the very important function of giving the British electorate (or at least the British media) someone to fear. The British find it very hard to work out the ideas or aims of the far left (also known as the "far left", "loony left", "mad left", etc.), so they prefer to concentrate on one person, as this fits better into their idea of politics as soap opera. Previous holders of the post have been Tony Benn, Ken Livingstone, Arthur Scargill and (briefly) Derek Hatton, but the post is currently vacant. Candidates should have a strong but well-hidden sense of humour, a gift for oratory, a short name for headlines, and a minimum of one odd hobby, even if it is only newt-keeping or tea-drinking. The post is not paid, but there are considerable fees for broadcasts, interviews, articles, etc., and the incumbent will soon be able to move out of politics and become a well-loved character on telly.

*Miles Kington, the* Independent *28 March 1990*

This chapter uses a wide-angled lens to examine the part played by the media in the evolution of the Labour Party under the leaderships of Michael Foot and Neil Kinnock. But it takes as its starting point the sharp increase in the vituperative nature of the press attacks on Labour that coincided with the so-called winter of discontent in 1978–9 (when public sector workers rebelled against the pay limits being set by the then Labour Government). We also analyse two other aspects of press reporting of the Labour left. First, the ongoing narrative that characterised left-wing politicians as 'mad' with Tony Benn, in particular, being singled out for such treatment. And second, how the reporting of the winter of discontent, and the leadership of Michael Foot, can be seen as early exemplars of a particular UK variant of fake news. Whilst, as outlined in Chapter 4 and 5, some of the press reports of the left were based on straightforward untruths, some of it was based on the tiniest kernel of truth, which was then vigorously and distortingly spun, either by political campaigners, or the media, into a form which we label 'extreme spin' and ended up with the reader gaining a totally false impression of what had actually occurred.

The treatment of Foot by the press persuaded his successor, Neil Kinnock, to attempt to prevent this demolition from happening again. With the help of Peter Mandelson and Phillip Gould, Kinnock sought to modernise Labour, a process in which shedding the 'loony left' label was also seen as a key objective. Kinnock was only half successful – media attacks continued – but he did upgrade the Party's media and marketing campaigning. This paved the way for the arrival of New Labour in which Tony Blair, Gordon Brown, Peter Mandelson and Alastair Campbell played key roles. To ensure that the New Labour brand triumphed, it was important for its advocates to create, and then slay, the dragon that Old Labour (and its offspring, the urban left) was perceived to be. It has been argued that 'old Labour' never actually existed, except in the minds of those who sought to slay it, but its apparent 'slaying', combined with Blair's courtship of Rupert Murdoch, led to a period (1994–2003) during which Labour's relations with the media were the least problematic at any time in the past half century.

As a backdrop to this analysis, this chapter looks at what happened to the 'loony left', or more importantly to perceptions of the 'loony left', in the period between the demise of the GLC in 1985 until the 1992 General Election and the resignation of Neil Kinnock as party leader. It will describe how Labour's election defeat in 1987 was interpreted, both by the media and the Labour leadership, as a defeat for the notion of Labour as a left-wing party. This in turn gave impetus to those who were arguing that, although Labour had changed it had not changed enough and needed to travel further toward the political centre to regain power. It will then examine how the Labour leadership set about changing the party and its policies, initially through a process of political realignment known as the Policy Review Process, and then through organisational change, to create a party that would not only 'look different' from the previous model but would actually be different. The chapter will also analyse how this was achieved by the recruitment of a new cadre of political actors who were themselves, if not communication professionals then, at the very least, highly focussed on the importance of communications as central to the political project. And it will investigate how these professionals, charged with the task of making Labour more 'marketable', themselves became a new, powerful tier of leadership which assumed and dispensed, more real power than all but a few of the elected leaders they were supposed to serve.

However, it is important to indicate at the outset that it is no part of the argument being advanced here that the rise to power and influence by the left of the Labour Party was a media invention, nor would we deny that there were groups, particularly the Militant Tendency, whose ultimate aim was to take over the Party and transform it into a revolutionary organisation. No political party committed to democratic parliamentary politics can afford to ignore such developments. Nonetheless, such groups and their supporters played only a very minor role in the broad sweep of left politics that were characterised by the media as 'loony'.

It is commonly assumed that those who led the 'project' – the name given to the operation by Labour's self-styled 'modernisers' to capture the party and transform it into an election-winning machine – virtually created a new party, or at least a new brand i.e. New Labour. But in fact, consciously or otherwise, they created not one new party but two – New Labour (about which much has been written) and 'Old Labour' an artifice, taking in everyone from left urban activists, through Militant and other ultra-left groupings, to both right and left-wing backbench MPs and the entire trade union movement (in other words, from the ranks of the cynical right to the activist left). Old Labour had to be created because if one is wanting to be seen to be slaying a dragon then it is important to ensure that the dragon appear as terrifying and potentially dangerous as possible in order to make the act of dramatic regime change appear not just necessary but welcome. As Tim Bale notes: 'just as any improved version of a product must have an old, unimproved one from which it can be distinguished, New Labour needed old Labour'.[1]

The importance of this is that when the modernisers – led by Tony Blair, Gordon Brown and Peter Mandelson – were in the process of creating New Labour it was important for them to not just to be seen to be taking on the existing party and challenging its basic precepts and ways of working, but also for the party – or at least those sections characterised as Old Labour – to be seen to be resisting these changes. In his magisterial account of the Labour Party under Blair, Lewis Minkin attributes this tactic to Peter Mandelson which, he claims, was dubbed 'blood on the floor'. Minkin writes that this:

> was an attention seeking tactic said to be the brainchild of Mandelson, in which advance publicity heightened the sense of confrontation with unions, the left or the activists in order to lodge in the mind of the recipient the subservience of the targets and the dominance of the leader.[2]

It was based on the belief that, without controversy and dissent, the public would not accept that the transformation was either real or complete. Hence, opposition was an essential part of the process, and those doing the opposing had to be perceived as commanding significant support in the Party, or at least having done so in the past. Exaggerating the importance and success of the 'loony left' in its earlier supposed capture of the Labour Party was an important sub-text for the modernisers. Thus, supporters of the 'loony left', the modernisers and the right-wing press all, bizarrely, had a vested interest in making it appear to have been a far more significant player than was in fact the case, so that its defeat would appear to have a significance way beyond that which it probably deserved.

Paradoxically, much of the political agenda of the 'loony left' came to be accepted, even supported by New Labour, as the quotation from Ken Livingstone at the head of this chapter makes irreverently clear. This agenda included support for the raft of policies associated with the equality agenda – ethnicity, gender and disabilities – it also included other policy areas such as negotiating with Sinn Fein and, strangely enough, the Public Finance Initiative which had its origins in attempts by left Labour local administrations to raise extra cash by selling off unrequired buildings to cover the shortfalls in expenditure caused by the Conservative Government's policy of rate-capping.

Contemporary political history is always problematic to document, for the historian is dealing not just with what actually happened but also the percep-tions of those involved at the time – perceptions which are frequently clouded by current political arguments and positions. It is also complicated because political actors tend to believe that their own political stances have been constant, and it is the world around them that has changed. As Alan Finlayson has observed: 'investigation must also focus on how those with power come to forge their own understandings and on what shaped their illusions ... They interpret the world for us and then ask us to believe in their interpretation'.[3]

It is now commonplace to observe that Tony Blair and Margaret Thatcher shared certain personal and political characteristics; in particular, both Blair and Thatcher (and, for them as individuals, read they and the people close to them) embarked on ideological projects to re-make their parties. Both saw the need to push their parties rightwards – Thatcher further to the right of British politics and Blair to the centre and, in the process, pushing the whole centre of gravity of British politics further to the right. In order to achieve these tasks, both leaders had to stake out why their trajectory was the only possible one to follow – the 'no alternative' scenario. Finlayson provides a helpful explanation for the dynamics of this process:

> In order to provide a political project with a solid ground to stand on, it is always necessary to clear a space first. Parties, movements and ideologies do this by establishing a crisis to which they have the necessary answers, so that they are the only reasonable response. Thatcherism was part of a New Right reformulation, which posited the crisis of Keynesianism wel-fare state, blamed failure on socialism and hence advocated that socialism be 'smashed' and the state rolled back from the economy. Blair's established itself firstly within the Labour party, as a response to manifest electoral cri-sis. It blamed that failure on bad party management, inefficient, in-fighting and unworkable, un-sellable, policies.[4]

But Finlayson's analysis does not confine itself to the political; he goes on to make a persuasive argument as to how the modernisers, steeped as they were in the marketing paradigm, perceived the 'project' as something more than just political transformation:

> [the modernisers] also pointed to the inadequate and outdated branding of the party. The emotional connotations of the party were all wrong. The customer base, the electorate, had changed, and the party's image, structure and product would have to change if there was to be any hope of securing a market position. New Labour saw a shift in the market; it identified a new consumer need and a market opportunity. Through research, it developed a product and a strategy for placing it, found a chief salesman who could embody the company's values, and oriented itself so as to claim the future.[5]

The notion of Blair as Labour's 'chief salesman' is a compelling one, particularly if one thinks of the very determined attempts made by New Labour to market itself in a holistic way, even before Blair. It was under Kinnock that the party changed its trademark colour from the slightly strident traditional red and yellow (resurrected by the Conservatives in 2004 to remind voters of Old Labour) to pastel pink; of how the annual party conference was transformed from a political decision-making body into a sales convention (for Labour's policies and personalities) and the virtual handing over of the power to direct election campaigns from elected politicians to appointed officials.[6]

But the rise of New Labour was not just associated with the rise of the political marketing paradigm – a trend in itself that owed much to the privatisation of public life – a paradigm which saw voters as consumers, policies as products and parties as sales organisations. It was also associated with the near total dominance of electioneering via the media; so, as parties shifted from being organisations of volunteer leafleteers and door-knockers to professionalised organisations dedicated to persuading and mobilising the public, the defining of what was 'politically acceptable' to the electorate became something that became more and more dominated by the media rather, than as it had been in the past, a process that was the preserve of the political parties and their decision-making processes. In other words, the process of mediatization in which a media logic takes precedence over the formerly dominant political logic.[7]

The gradual process in which the Conservative party and their supporters in the press shifted their characterisation of Labour from representing it as their 'opponents' to representing it as their 'enemy' began in 1974 when Rupert Murdoch switched the *Sun* – the UK's largest selling newspaper at the time – from supporting Labour to the Conservatives and gained full momentum during the Winter of Discontent in 1978–9. The 'Winter' began with a nationwide lorry drivers' strike which soon led to stories in the press of the hardship being caused by the lorry drivers' action, including farm animals dying for lack of feedstuff. An ITN journalist, having been sent out to substantiate this story, reported back that that having visited five farms supposedly affected, she had found just one dead chicken that had died of fright when her camera crew switched on their lights.[8] This story did not make it on air but others, following similar unsubstantiated dominant narratives did, particularly in the Conservative-supporting press. For all the talk of people dying as a result of the public sector strikes, the only reported death associated with the action was that of a trade unionist who fell under the wheels of a lorry whilst on picket duty. Derek Jameson, then editor of the *Daily Express* (and a self-declared Labour supporter), said: 'We pulled every dirty trick in the book; we made it look like it was general, universal and eternal when it was in reality scattered, here and there, and no great problem'.[9]

The reporting of the subsequent 1979 election was vitriolic and provided textbook examples of what we are calling 'extreme spin'. Perhaps the most memorable was a *Daily Mail* front page featuring 'Labour's Dirty Dozen: 12 big lies they hope will save them'[10] which was a direct lift from a Conservative Party press release. One such 'lie' was that the Tories would double VAT from 8% to 16%; this claim was strenuously denied by the Conservatives at the time, but they went on to increase VAT to 15%, subsequently arguing that since Labour had said the rate would go up to 16%, then to call it a 'lie' was correct.

Following the 1979 election, Jim Callaghan resigned as Labour leader to be succeeded by veteran left-winger Michael Foot. He provided the press with a seemingly irresistible target; the daily humiliation of Foot was described as 'monstering', within what used to be known as Fleet Street. Through his three years in office, Foot was a constantly portrayed as an extreme left-winger, and a slightly 'bonkers' old man. Foot's background in newspapers – he was a former editor of the *Evening Standard* – did not protect him from the almost daily mocking for his allegedly left-wing views (which most left activists regarded as very much a thing of the past), for his slightly old-fashioned way of speaking but above all, simply for his appearance. He took over the leadership at the relatively old age of sixty-seven, but looked older. He walked with a stick, wore pebble-lens spectacles and dressed as befitted a man of letters (as he was) from a nonconformist background. Foot's dress-sense, or lack of, came sharply into focus when, attending the service of remembrance for the war-dead at the Cenotaph in London in 1981, he wore a coat (dubbed, incorrectly a donkey jacket) that appeared to be out of keeping with the solemnity of the occasion. Even the normally sympathetic *Guardian* described him as 'looking as if he had just completed his Sunday constitutional on Hampstead Heath'.[11]

Despite the hostility that he had received from the press throughout his political career, Foot never developed the sort of rugged defences against the media that Mrs Thatcher had installed around herself and as Tony Blair did too. Indeed, Foot's biographer, Kenneth Morgan described his press officer – Tom McCaffrey – as 'no Alastair Campbell spin-merchant, but a professional civil servant who broadly, gave the unvarnished facts and was fully trusted by journalists and the media'.[12] Morgan went on to outline Foot's pitifully small private office – 'nowhere near enough to help the leader impose his authority'.[13] But handling the media came low down Michael Foot's list of priorities during his time in office. Not that he (or more pertinently his team) didn't think it important, but it was because internal party matters – including a split to the right by the nascent Social Democratic Party and battles to the left with the Militant Tendency – made it difficult for Foot or his office to focus on these presentational issues.

Foot's lifestyle gave added grist to the mill of a hostile press. His daily habit of walking his dog Dizzy (named after one of Foot's heroes, the Prime Minister Benjamin Disraeli) made him a target for tabloid picture editors. Photographers could be guaranteed to get a picture of Foot as a lookalike of the fictional scarecrow 'Worsel Gummidge', simply by shouting his name from afar. Foot would return the 'greeting' by waving his walking stick in the air, which made for a great 'loony' photo. Indeed, according to Chippindale and Horrie, two former journalists who wrote a 'biography' of the *Sun*, photographers covering Foot were instructed 'no pictures of Foot unless falling over, shot or talking to militants'[14]

It would be fallacious to argue that the press representation of Foot as either shambling and unkempt, or a dangerous left-winger (because, for example, of his continued support for unilateral nuclear disarmament) was the cause of Labour's disastrous performance in the 1983 election. The Labour Party was in a state of internal war, which encouraged the press to emphasise the significance of the 'loony left' narrative. In 1981, Labour left-winger Tony Benn challenged Dennis Healey for the deputy leadership of the party. Benn had become a popular figure on the left – indeed Bennite was how the Labour left wing was almost universally described. Although not directly associated with the Militant Tendency, the group supported Benn and he, in turn, opposed their expulsion from the party. The media characterised Benn's deputy leadership campaign (which he narrowly lost) as representing the near takeover of the party by the far, or hard, left.

The notion of 'loony left' control was further cemented in the public mind when, in 1983, there was a parliamentary by-election in the South London constituency of Bermondsey. The local party selected a left-wing gay activist – Peter Tatchell – as their candidate, despite this being a traditional right-wing seat, dominated by London dock workers. The press, and the opposition parties, mounted a homophobic campaign against Tatchell; Labour's cause was not helped when Foot declared that Tatchell would never be the official Labour candidate. But Foot was overruled by an increasingly left-wing national executive and Tatchell stood. He was subsequently defeated, losing the seat to the Liberal candidate Simon Hughes, who himself subsequently came out and who, in 2006, apologised to Tatchell for the gay smears he had used in that by-election campaign.

None of this was the best possible preparation for the 1983 election in which Foot was no match for a Margaret Thatcher riding high on her victory in the war in the Falklands. James Thomas, in his study of post-war Labour and the tabloid press, described the 1983 General Election as 'the most hostile Press labour had experienced for 50 years'.[15] The attacks on Foot were merciless: 'Do You Seriously Want This Old Man to Run Britain' asked one *Sun* headline[16] Apart from the sheer personal abuse Foot sustained, the Labour Party was the victim of a number of 'fake news' stories. The *Daily Express* ran a story in which it claimed that marchers protesting against mass unemployment had 'refused' offers of work en route. The story was untrue – it was based on *Express* reporters checking out the vacancies on the job centres along the marchers' route. The *Daily Mail* carried a story claiming that the Japanese car-maker, Nissan, was threatening to pull out of the UK if Labour won, a claim strenuously denied by the company. The *Mail's* reporting was so slanted that journalists on the paper voted by six to one to condemn their own newspaper's election reporting. During the campaign, the *Sun* described Tony Benn as 'dedicated ruthless [and] bent on the destruction of Britain as we know it'.[17]

Following that defeat, Michael Foot stepped down and, waiting in the wings to take over, was another politician representing a South Wales constituency, someone whom Foot regarded as almost like a son, Neil Kinnock. The contrast between the two men, in terms of their attitude to the media could not have been more different, though both ended up being attacked, humiliated and pilloried by the Conservative-supporting press.

Kinnock was a familiar figure. Late at night in the conference watering holes of Blackpool and Brighton, in the years of Callaghan and Foot's leadership of Labour. A regular sight was the young Neil Kinnock drinking and carousing with party members and journalists alike. Kinnock was liked and admired by much of the press and was a good TV performer, not that any of this helped him when he took over the reins of leadership from Foot in 1983. Indeed, at the very Labour conference of that year, when Kinnock beat Roy Hattersley for the Labour leadership, the most memorable image of the conference was not a triumphant Kinnock waving to the adoring mases from the conference platform but instead, Kinnock being 'saved from the waves' by his wife Glenys became the headline story, as the 'ideal seaside photo opportunity' went horribly amiss when, as Neil and Glenys strolled along the water's edge, a sudden wave swept Kinnock of his feet. Conservative historian and *Daily Mail* contributor Dominic Sandbrook claimed that the picture became 'the abiding image of the conference, even of Kinnock's leadership – a man utterly out of his depth, shamelessly courting the media and making a complete fool of himself in the process'.[18]

Unlike Foot, Kinnock came into the leadership surrounded by a far more robust team of advisers. They had learnt harsh lessons about the media during Foot's leadership and went about applying these lessons ruthlessly, both during and even before Kinnock's ascent to the leadership. Many commentators see Tony Blair's successful bid for the Labour leadership in 1994 as the first New Labour campaign, but that was not the case. Kinnock was, if not propelled into power, at least substantially helped, by a cadre of former Labour student politicians, who had learnt their politics fighting the far left in the very hard school of politics that was (and is) the National Union of Students. They became Kinnock's praetorian guard, both in getting him elected and defending him both against the right (in the form of Ray Hattersley and his supporters) and also against the Militant Tendency and the Bennite left. This cadre of young supporters was mobilised and organised by politicians, later to become cabinet ministers, including Patricia Hewitt, Charles Clarke and, most crucially Peter Mandelson, who in 1985 was appointed the party's Director of Communications.

Kinnock's appointment of Peter Mandelson as the party's new Director of Campaigns and Communications in 1985 was a pivotal moment in the birth of New Labour. Almost as important was the role of Phillip Gould, a long-time Labour supporter with a marketing background. Gould is an important figure in understanding this period, not just because of his intrinsic importance in setting-up and running the Shadow Communications Agency – an organisation of volunteer PR, advertising and marketing experts, led by Gould and reporting to Mandelson – but because in his autobiography he sets out, with unabashed honesty, how he saw the making of New Labour:

> I saw the final betrayal of the people I had grown up with the people the Labour Party had been formed to serve but whom it had abandoned. Labour had not merely stopped, listening or lost touch: it had declared political war on the values, instincts and ethics of the great majority of decent, hard-working voters. Where were the policies for my old school-friends – now with families and homes of their own – in a manifesto advocating increased taxes, immediate withdrawal from the EEC, unilateral disarmament, a massive extension public ownership and import controls.[19]

Just months after Mandelson's appointment, Gould sent the new Director of Communications an analysis in which he set out how he perceived Labour in terms of its public standing and how, in marketing terms, it had to re-invent its 'brand' as an essential prerequisite to winning power. Gould's sixty-four-page analysis became a crucial text in the battle to transform Labour. In it Gould wrote:

> Positive perceptions of the Labour Party tend to be outweighed by negative concerns, particularly of unacceptable 'beyond the pale' policies and figures; the party sometimes acts in a way that confirms these concerns by scoring 'own goals'; there is some feeling that the Labour Party does not, as it once did, represent the majority, instead it is often associated with minorities; the party has something of an old-fashioned cloth cap image.[20]

Out of this report grew the Shadow Communications Agency (SCA), described by journalists Colin Hughes and Patrick Wintour as: 'Labour's secretive but influential image-makers. It was there, among aides and volunteers in the marketing and advertising world, that the idea of building a party fit for the millennium germinated'.[21] But it is unhelpful to view the SCA as having an autonomous existence separate from the Labour leadership. Admittedly, its terms of reference, as drafted by Gould, were wide-ranging, including drafting strategy, conducting and interpreting research, producing advertising and campaign themes and providing other communications support as necessary. But it was always Peter Mandelson's, and thus Neil Kinnock's, tool rather than their master. Gould and the SCA were providing the Labour leadership with what it wanted – the wherewithal to transform the Party from where and what it was to what they wanted it to be. And once the decision had to be taken to shift campaigning from traditional forms of political activity – meetings, leafleting and so on – to media-based campaigning, then it was inevitable that media and marketing professionals, in other words the SCA, would come to dominate Labour's policy-making processes, as well as its communications structures.

But if the Labour leadership thought that the SCA's new communications strategy had lanced the 'loony left' boil, they were to be sadly disappointed when, in the last months of 1986 as Labour was preparing for the coming General Election, the Conservatives (and the newspapers that supported them) stepped-up their onslaught against the Party, the spectre returned. This report from *The Times* was typical:

> Two Cabinet ministers last night launched one of the Conservatives' strongest attacks yet on Labour's 'loony left' council leaders. Mr Nicholas Ridley, Secretary of State for the Environment, told the Commons that some were behaving like Eastern bloc commissars ruling people by fear. And Mr Norman Tebbit, the Party Chairman, claimed that the 'loony left' was poised to take over the Parliamentary Labour Party. Mr Ridley said: 'I am told that people dare not speak out for fear of what might happen to them and their families. Perhaps they cannot really believe it is happening in England in the 1980s. It is more like Poland or East Germany: the knock on the door in the middle of the night. It is totalitarian, it is intolerant, it is anti-democratic, and it employs fear to control people. Every day's newspapers contained new horrors about the attack on local government by Labour-controlled councils. Town halls founded on civic dignity had become an arena for aggressive political posing, disruption, wild accusations, threats and fear. It is vicious, it is frightening, and it is deliberate.[22]

The Conservatives, whether consciously or otherwise, were aided by the Labour leadership itself. Two days after the Ridley/Tebbit onslaught, the *Financial Times* reported Labour as responding thus:

> Mr Neil Kinnock, the Labour leader, yesterday attacked extremist left-wing councils which he claimed attracted lurid headlines and obscured the real achievements of the majority of Labour-controlled local authorities. His comments, which acknowledge the potential electoral damage the activities of extremist councils could inflict on Labour, come immediately

after repeated government broadsides aimed at what ministers have dubbed the 'loony left.' The Government believes that in exploiting the well-publicised excesses of a number of local authorities they have found an important weapon with which to attack Labour in the run-up to the next general election. Mr Kinnock told a meeting of the Parliamentary Labour Party attended by nearly 90 MPs that the sensationalism attached to the actions of a few councils obscured the efforts of most of the Labour movement at local level. He said many Labour councils were working under near impossible conditions to turn their policies into practical help and the credit due to them was obscured by extremism. He added: 'It simply proves yet again that the greatest enemy of radicalism is zealotry. When idealism is made to look like extremism it is the ideals that are discredited.[23]

Labour's own research suggested that the Conservative's attack on the 'loony left' was well-chosen; it was telling them that the crucial swing voters saw Labour as 'a party in disarray', its leader as a 'very nice bloke' but pushed about and bullied by extremists, the unions, immigrants and homosexuals'.[24] It was this research, and the pressures emanating from the Conservatives 'loony left' campaign, which led to Labour's most traumatic moment in the run-up to the 1987 election – the Greenwich by-election.

By-elections were, in the 1980s, important media events – emblematic of the parties' public standing. The late Vincent Hanna, a BBC political reporter, had developed a mode of by-election reporting that transformed these seemingly routine political events into something akin to television entertainment. He baited weak candidates, challenged electors with their own apathy and dreamed up stunts, all with an eye to making by-elections into 'good television'. As a result, far greater public attention was trained on by-elections than had been the case in the past or was to be in the future.[25]

Thus, when a by-election was called in the South London constituency of Greenwich, there were great fears that the Labour candidate, almost irrespective of whom he or she might be, would be subjected to the sort of vitriolic attack that had been unleashed on Labour's candidate in the Bermondsey by-election the previous year (referred to above). The local party selected one of its own activists – Deidre Wood – to fight the by election. Up until that point, she had not been known as a particularly prominent member of the local 'loony left', but that was not the impression that would have been gleaned from contemporary newspaper accounts, as these examples from the *Guardian*, the *Financial Times* and *The Times* reveal:

Ms Deidre Wood is, her opponents say, the hard face of the London Labour left: full-time politician, husband of allegedly even wilder opinions, four sons of unknown opinions, lives in the East.[26]

Despite her refusal to have a political label attached to her, [Deidre Wood] is considered to be on the hard-left of the party … it is known that the party leadership, which is anxious not to alienate traditional supporters or to hand 'loony left' ammunition to its opponents, would have been happier to see a more moderate candidate emerge from the selection process.[27]

The selection of Miss Deidre Wood, a supposedly hard left member of the Inner London Education Authority, to fight the forthcoming Greenwich by-election had her political opponents rubbing their hands with glee last night'.[28]

It is worth noting, from these quotations (all from serious broadsheet newspapers), how Ms Wood's 'hard leftism' is, or is not, attributed. The *Guardian* attributes the description of her politics as 'the hard face of London Labour' to 'her opponents'; the *Financial Times* tells us that she is 'considered to be on the hard left of the party' (by whom, it is not specified) and *The Times* uses the word 'supposedly' to justify its description of Ms Wood as 'hard left'. However, among these non-attributions lies one important clue as to where it is all coming from. The *Financial Times* tells us that 'it is known that the party leadership ... would have been happier to see a more moderate candidate emerge.[29] And, if further proof were needed, it came from the BBC's Vincent Hanna who told the *Guardian* that the smearing of Deidre Wood had been started by elements in Labour's headquarters in Walworth Road who were keen to prevent her from being selected.[30]

Unsurprisingly perhaps, Labour lost the Greenwich by-election to the up and coming Social Democratic Party (that had split from Labour in 1981) and this led to the, now infamous' 'Hewitt letter'. This was the letter from Patricia Hewitt, then Neil Kinnock's Head of Policy, that was leaked to the *Sun* (at the start of its career as the receptacle of choice for New Labour secrets). The letter and its aftermath, discussed in the previous chapter, was a dramatic demonstration of just how concerned the Labour leadership was about what they termed 'the London effect'.[31]

Hughes and Wintour suggest that the leak – which was headlined in the *Sun* 'Gays put Kinnock in a panic: secret letter lashes loonies' – had come from Kinnock's office 'to put a bomb under the London left'.[32] And Heffernan and Marqusee are even more specific in their analysis of the Hewitt letter. They wrote: 'At a stroke, the entire Tory and media campaign against local Labour councils' equal opportunities initiatives were vindicated – by the Labour leadership itself'.[33] Right wingers in the Labour Party seized upon the defeat at Greenwich to push home their advantage. They used the media to reinforce Patricia Hewitt's warnings about a 'London effect'. The *Sunday Times* reported, in March 1987:

Senior Labour party moderates gave a warning yesterday that time was running out for Labour to avoid disaster at the next general election. They told the *Sunday Times* that unless Neil Kinnock acted immediately to curb London's 'loony left', Labour would be humiliated at the polls and Mrs Thatcher would be guaranteed a third term in office. ... Stuart Bell, Labour MP for Middlesbrough and secretary of the Solidarity group of

Labour moderates, said he will be warning all prospective parliamentary candidates against manipulation by the left, particularly in London. ... Moderates are alarmed at the prospects of the parliamentary party being dominated by the far left after the general election. Ken Livingstone, the former GLC leader and candidate for Brent East, is believed to be planning to run for the party chairmanship after the retirement of Jack Dormand, a veteran moderate from north eastern England.[34]

The Greenwich defeat was undoubtedly traumatic for the Labour leadership. One of Kinnock's close aides told the noted general election chroniclers David Butler and Dennis Kavanagh:

> What changed everything of course, was Greenwich and subsequent rows – all of which were peculiarly disastrous because they re-awoke fears which many potential voters still had about Labour extremism, divisions, unfitness for government and Kinnock's own leadership ability'.[35]

Hence, Labour went into the 1987 election as a bitterly divided party. On the ground, members, trade unionists and community activists still believed the Party to be a vehicle for achieving sweeping social change across a wide swathe of issues. Its economic policies were essentially redistributive, it favoured unilateral nuclear disarmament, the restoration of trade union rights and it was committed to an equality agenda covering gender, ethnicity, disability and sexuality. However, the party leadership viewed things somewhat differently. They fought a campaign based on convincing the electorate that the agenda of the grassroots was not shared by the leadership, that the Party in power would seek to represent the aspirations of middle Britain (a phrase not used at the time) and that it (rather than the SDP/Liberal Alliance) was the only viable alternative to the Conservatives.

Hughes and Wintour (seen at the time as journalists close to Blair) in the almost 'authorised version' of the birth of New Labour wrote:

> Mandelson and Phillip Gould succeeded not because they exploited slick advertising and media management more effectively than the Conservatives, but because they forged between themselves an approach to political strategy which has never before been seen – certainly in the Labour party, and arguably, ever in British politics. They welded policy, politics and image-creation into one weapon.[36]

In his perceptive analysis of the evolution of Labour's campaigns and communications strategy, Eric Shaw concluded that this meant that the Party concentrated its communications effort on:

> maximising the saliency of those matters where it was most in line with popular sentiment, such as health and education, and strive as far as possible

to neutralise or exclude from the agenda issues such as industrial relations and defence, where it had few hopes of evoking a supportive response.[37]

During any election campaign the party leader's itinerary is a crucial part of the planning process. This involves finding salient stories and strong pictures to illustrate the 'campaign theme of the day' – done effectively it means that the chosen theme will dominate the main television news bulletins and hopefully spill over into the following morning's headlines. Those planning the leader's tour were invoked to look for 'suitable' locations and interviewees. 'Suitable' meant finding upbeat televisual locations and 'reliable' (i.e. not associated with the 'loony left') local authorities and interviewees, in other word, avoiding, at all costs, anyone who might remind the electorate of what the Labour leadership saw as its negatives.[38] In the words of Patricia Hewitt, in charge of the planning:

> we want places that are modern, that show the best of Britain and, in particular, the best of what Labour councils are doing, places that encapsulate Kinnock's Britain. ... We do not want any closed factories, derelict housing sites, run-down hospitals, industrial wastelands or other wrecks of Thatcher's Britain ... people – bright attractive people presenting an image of the broader base Labour has too capture – not people who present an image of old-fashioned Labour die-hards.[39]

Recommendations for appropriate campaign visits by the leader reflected this desire to reflect the 'new' the 'modern' and avoid images and people associated with Labour's past. For example, in the North East region, one of the recommendations was for a visit to Newcastle's South Gosford transport interchange, which represented a good example of the advantages of an integrated transport system over a deregulated one. The report went on to note: 'A visit to the control centre would afford an opportunity of seeing how the system works, talking with the employees and being seen in a modern computer-controlled environment, built by a Labour local authority'.[40]

As the 1987 election approached, Phillip Gould undertook a series of presentations to leading Labour politicians (and then subsequently to MPs and candidates) outlining his analysis of why Labour was failing to capture public support.[41] Those attending were, understandably, desperate to win and were looking to Gould for reassurance. Gould spoke fluently, and in a language that many of the participants found baffling but impressive; he was passionate and convincing about his research. He showed slides that diagrammatically showed the image of the party, its leader and its policies. The research looked authoritative and it was difficult not to accept the validity of his findings. Out of these findings a reality was portrayed which might, or might not have been, the reality that existed out in the country, but it became accepted by Labour's leaders and thus became the new catechism.

The very first slide Gould presented, 'Key Findings from Research – Value Change', read: 'Shift from collective to individual values' It reflected the success, Gould argued, that Margaret Thatcher had had in shifting the centre of political gravity away from collectivist values to more to individual ones. Yet, the annual British Social Attitudes survey (which began in 1983) has consistently shown that throughout this period the values of the British electorate remained resolutely 'social democratic' – committed to those very values that the Labour leadership were being told no longer resonated with voters.[42]

The second slide presented by Gould was entitled 'Mood of the People' and reported findings that people felt personally better off but had long term doubts about the state of the economy and were worried about the quality of life. The third slide was 'What the People Think About the Parties' and indicated that the main finding about the Conservatives was 'Fears About the Future'; for the Liberal/SDP Alliance it was 'Untried but Inexperienced' and for Labour it was 'Fears About the Loony Left'. Thus, Labour's senior politicians were being told that the single most important issue they had to confront was people's fears about the 'loony left'. But if Gould's research had been faulty in identifying a shift from collective to individual attitudes, then perhaps it was also inaccurate in its portrayal that fears about the 'loony left' were the single most important facet of the public's perceptions of Labour?

The 1987 election can be seen as something of a watershed in terms of the supposed 'loony left' effect. By then, Neil Kinnock's control over the party machine was well-established with the left apparently defeated in all Labour's decision-making fora. Nonetheless, the 'loony left' remained a potent factor for the media, for the Conservatives and, perhaps surprisingly, for Labour as well. In the case of the latter, the 'misdeeds' of the 'loony left' were to be used to demonstrate just how far Labour had travelled since the days of Tony Benn's leadership campaign. It proved a useful as a stick to beat a recalcitrant party back into line whenever it appeared to be straying off-message – back the leadership or face the prospect of the return of the 'loony left' and life in the political wilderness, was the implicit message of many of the battles that both Kinnock and Blair embarked upon (and usually won). As Lewis Minkin notes:

> There was an uninhibited enhancement of the routine management practice, began under Kinnock, of focusing publicly on what was going to happen to sources of opposition – groups to be weakened, institutions to be curbed etc. An exaggeration of the political blood spilt on the floor in any significant victory (said to be the Mandelson doctrine) was used to heighten the impression of supremacy.[43]

Despite the popular conception of the 1980s as a period of left dominance of Labour, in fact the decade represented a period of retreat for Labour's left. Two leading left activists of that period – Richard Heffernan and Mike Marqusee – claim that the high point of the left (in terms of winning votes at party conference

and gaining seats on the National Executive Committee) was the party conference of 1980.[44] The following year, Tony Benn lost his challenge for the deputy
leadership of the party and, for Labour's left, it was downhill from there on, as
Lewis Baston has observed:

> The leadership had, by 1987, an exaggerated fear, even hatred, for the
> activities of the local left. This was a replay of the debates between Herbert
> Morrison and the supporters of Poplarism; Neil Kinnock feared that their
> antics would detract from Labour's statesmanlike image, and alienate tra-
> ditional working-class voters.[45]

Labour's defeat in 1987 was, for many in the Party, harder to take than the 1983
debacle. This time there were fewer excuses. To all intents and purposes, the left
had been defeated, the party had gone into the election with Neil Kinnock very
much in control of his party and on a manifesto which appeared to be acceptable to the traditional right in the parliamentary party. But Labour was defeated,
and badly. Despite there being a brief moment when the party was ahead in the
opinion polls – just a couple of months before polling day – it ended up still on
the opposition benches, having only reduced the Conservatives' majority from
144 seats to a still healthy 102.

Labour's defeat in 1987, unwelcome as it was, did enable the Kinnock leadership to 'take on' what they saw as the extremism of some (mainly London) local
councils. Labour had done particularly badly in London in the general election
(despite faring reasonably well in local elections in the previous year); although
no seats in areas covered by the so-called 'loony left' councils were lost. The
poor performance in the capital further strengthened the hand of the leadership in their battles to bring these councils into line. The leadership was also
strengthened in this endeavour by what, for some, was the surprise distancing
from the left of the Labour Co-ordinating Committee (LCC), seen as one of the
key pressure groups on the party's left flank. In an LCC pamphlet, called 'Labour
Councils in the Cold', published in 1978, the LCC criticised some of their erstwhile colleagues, claiming: 'They had come to see themselves as servants of
local authority trade unions and professional groups, rather than the servants of
their electors.'[46]

After the election, the Shadow Communications Agency commissioned a
research report – based on qualitative and quantative polling – entitled 'Labour
and Britain in the 1990s'. The qualitative focus group research found that the
majority of the electorate were yet to accept 'Thatcherite' values, nonetheless,
'Labour was too associated with the unions, the poor, the "disadvantaged".
Its greatest handicaps were its perceived "extremism" and "disunity"'.[47] The
quantative research claimed to have found that among non-Labour voters the
most important reasons for not voting Labour were perceptions of Labour as a
party of 'extremism' and 'division'; the perceived dominance of the Party by the

'loony left' was found to be the primary reason why the Party was thought of as 'extremist'.[48] Phillip Gould recalls:

> The polling was clear Labour lost because it was still the party of the winter of discontent; union influence; strikes and inflation; disarmament; Benn and Scargill. It lost because people thought they 'had left the party and the party had left them'. Labour and the voters were facing in different directions. The electorate looked onwards and upwards; they work hard; they 'want to do better for themselves and their families'. Labour looked downwards: 'Clawing back; turning the clock back; for Militant; anti-home ownership; strife; strikes inflation – not for me'.[49]

There was also evidence, not made available at the time to Kinnock, that his own persona was one of the main causes of Labour's lack of popularity and there was also more than a hint of anti-Welsh racism in some of the coverage of Kinnock. A *Sun* headline during the campaign read 'Get lost. Go spout to the valleys boyo'.[50]

Speaking at a post-election Fabian Society conference Peter Mandelson, then the party's campaign director, argued that ordinary voters felt alienated from Labour. *Guardian* columnist Terry Coleman reported Mandelson as talking about:

> people's fear of Labour. Fear is his word. He says it. People said Labour's not for them but for blacks, or for gays, or for losers. Labour too easily disqualified itself, and gave too many hostages.[51]

The 1987 result reaffirmed for Kinnock, and the leadership, that they had to, not just to change the party's image, but its 'product' as well. Thus began the attempt to refashion Labour's policies known as the Policy Review. It was intended to bring the party closer into line with what Gould, and others, identified as the aspirations of 'ordinary people'. There were to be no 'sacred cows', everything was to be examined. As Steven Fielding has observed:

> The basic object of the Review was to make the party more electable as the leadership believed Labour had to develop policies that appealed to those individualist values apparently embraced by many voters and distance itself from remedies that were overly reliant on the state. It is interesting to note that the Review was supposed to represent a clearing out of old and irrelevant policies to be replaced by polices that would make the party more acceptable to the electorate. But the Review was as much about changing the style, as the content, of Labour's policies. This is demonstrable by the fact that the basket of policies that came to be encapsulated in the phrase 'loony left' – in particular the equality agenda – played virtually no role in the Policy Review's deliberations or final publication. The only exception

being the policy of unilateral nuclear disarmament, supported by an over-whelming majority of party members, and this was largely left untouched by the Review.[52]

A series of policy review groups were charged with assessing 'relevance and cred-ibility of party policy' not on the basis of any ideological blueprint but on the basis of 'needs and concerns of voters' as defined by the Shadow Communications Agency. Ordinary party members were under no illusions as to the purpose of the operation. Hughes and Wintour describe the mood of the 1987 conference that accepted the proposal to initiate the Review as 'sullen ... There was no enthusiasm from constituency activists who made it plain that they believed the whole enterprise was a cloak for selling out'.[53]

After a year-long series of consultations with party members and (a few) members of the public, the new policy proposals were put in place. The consen-sus inside party headquarters was that, given the radical nature of many of the changes, they should be launched in piecemeal fashion, so as to lessen the antici-pated hostile reaction from left-wing party activists. However, Phillip Gould recalls, he argued for a different course of action. He wanted to introduce the new package of policies (which were being launched prior to the 1989 European Elections) in a blaze of publicity:

> I argued for a continuous five-month campaign ... At its heart was a central strategic recommendation: do not trickle out the policy review; instead make one, big-bang presentation... This was in complete defiance of the previous consensus about the presentation of the review, which had been to do it late, and do it gradually, in order to minimise the possibility of backlash and dissent. My view was the opposite: people would shift to Labour only if they were sure that it had changed, and only bold, demonstrable change would convince them of that. *Dissent in these circumstances did not reduce our electoral appeal, but heightened it. It was evidence of change* (emphasis added).[54]

This is a crucial quotation, central to the argument of this chapter, and rein-forced in Minkin's study of the Blair transformation of the Labour Party. Here was someone, a crucial 'insider', arguing that the Labour leadership needed the 'loony left' to be seen and heard in high profile and then seen and heard to be defeated. Thus, early in the process, confrontation with the left was sought, not avoided. This makes sense of how Labour handled the 'loony left' issue from the Greenwich by-election onwards, it also explains why Tony Blair subsequently appeared to go out of his way to 'take the party on' – whether over the very public abolition of Clause Four or the downgrading of the party's internal democracy.

Phillip Gould's role in the process is significant not just for its content but for what it tells us about the shifting balance of power in the party. For, parallel with the assault on the party's left, went the growing ascendancy of the appointed over the elected, with power clearly moving away from elected politicians – as symbolised by Labour's NEC – and moving towards the professional advisers.[55] These advisers were located either inside the Leader's office – Patricia Hewitt or Charles Clarke, for example – or appointed by Peter Mandelson (himself, at the time, an appointed official) to the Shadow Communications Agency.

Apart from their expanding role, in terms of campaigning and communications, appointed advisors were also making a far greater input into the selection of by-election candidates. This followed what, for Labour, had been the twin disasters of the Bermondsey and Greenwich by-elections – in which safe Labour seats had adopted left candidates who then lost to Liberal or SDP candidates respectively. As a result, the party leadership created a new process for selecting by-election candidates, a process designed to ensure that only those candidates that could be seen as 'media-friendly' (in other words, demonstrably not of the left) were selected. And selection, although nominally in the hands of a small group of members of Labour's national executive, was heavily influenced by the professional advisers who drew up the short-list of candidates for consideration and who also attended the selection interviews and provided advice. This new process led to a series of rows with local constituency parties (for example, in two areas seen as strongholds of the 'loony left' – Lambeth and Brent) in which local constituency activists found that they had candidates imposed on them who did not reflect their own political views. In a situation where Labour was seen by the leadership and the media as having a problem with 'extremists', attempts to rein in constituency parties and impose more 'sensible' candidates could helpfully be seen as part of a strategy of publicly defeating the 'loony left'.

Another change begun under the Kinnock leadership (and brought to fruition under Kinnock's successor John Smith in 1993) was intended to wrest control of the machinery from the (mainly left) constituency activists. This was to be achieved by the introduction of One Member One Vote (OMOV), an initiative to expand decision-making, in terms of policy and elections to Labour's National Executive, beyond the activists who attended meetings to the wider membership. One aspect of the change was that it gave considerably greater opportunity for the media to influence the result of these elections. In the past, decisions about which candidates to back had largely been in the hands of local party general management committees (GMCs) and, as often as not, the GMC would opt for one of the 'slates' – lists of candidates which had the support of one or other of Labour's factional groups. In the 1980s activists tended to support the candidates on the left-wing slates. However, the introduction of OMOV made these elections much more public affairs and bore fruit (for the leadership at least) as the membership of the National Executive Committee shifted from being dominated by left wingers, largely unsympathetic to the Kinnock leadership, to its dominance by MPs who could be relied upon to support the party leader.

In the run-up to the 1992 general election, the decision by the Conservatives to campaign around the 'loony left' issue was redolent of the fact that much of their campaigning in this period was based on exploiting perceived fears of the voters, a strategy that had served them well in the past. Their campaigns, in both

1987 and 1992, tended to focus on generating general fears about Labour which they combined with provoking specific fears about tax rises, trade union power and the 'hard left'. But there was also an unspoken fear that ran through much of the Conservative's campaigning and through Labour's response, which was fear of the 'other' – the outsider, the alien, the 'loony left'.

It is commonplace to observe that a great deal of political attitude formation and electoral behaviour is driven by fear of the 'other' – whether the 'other' be immigrants, homosexuals, young people or whatever. Fear of the 'other', and the use made of it by the Conservatives, can be seen at its clearest when considering the way that the party used race and racism in its election campaigning. In 1968, a senior Conservative, Enoch Powell, was sacked from the front bench by the then party leader, Edward Heath, for a speech opposing further immigration dubbed the 'rivers of blood' speech.[56] Ten years later in 1978, Margaret Thatcher then leader of the Opposition said that 'people are afraid that this country might be rather swamped by people of a different culture'.[57] And in 1995, the Conservative Party's then Head of Research (later to become a cabinet minister), Andrew Lansley, wrote: 'Immigration, an issue which we raised successfully in 1992 and again in the 1994 Euro-elections campaign, played particularly well in the tabloids and has more potential to hurt'.[58] In subsequent campaigns, including the referendum on Britain's membership of the EU, immigration and asylum have always been a presence – this has been the case from Michael Howard's 'Are you thinking what we're thinking?' campaign in the 2005 election to the latest findings from the British Election Study that it was one of the most important issue for electors in both the 2016 Euro referendum and the 2017 general election.[59]

In some real, and some imagined, ways the spectre of the 'loony left' was a useful code for race. Bernie Grant, who originated from Guyana and was at onetime Leader of Haringey Council, and subsequently MP for Tottenham, was a frequent target for attack by the national press (and some sections of the local press too).[60] Anti-racism was undoubtedly a key issue uniting the left (indeed it was an issue that united the whole Labour Party), and if voters perceived Labour and Labour's left as being 'in favour' of anti-racism and supporting ethnic minorities, then this was an accurate perception. But there was also a more subconscious fear captured in the pages of the *Daily Mail*, the *Sun* and other newspapers – a fear that something essentially 'British', or for perhaps something essentially 'English', was being destroyed. In the 1950s, the American Secretary of State, Dean Acheson, talked of Britain having lost an Empire but not having found a role; Acheson was talking about British foreign policy, but it also resonated at a more parochial level. This sense of a golden age rapidly being obscured from view by a haze of multiculturalism was captured by Conservative Prime Minister John Major in his selective quotation from Orwell, evoking maidens on bikes, warm beer and cricket matches on the green.[61]

Much was changing in post-war Britain, and one of the most visible signs of change was in the ethnic make-up of the population, particularly in London.

The municipal left saw race and race equality as important political, moral and electoral issues. The voting records of black and Asian electors had shown consistently high levels of support for Labour and, to some extent, their electoral support compensated for the decline in the white working class vote that had, in part, propelled Mrs Thatcher to power and, arguably, secured the referendum vote in favour of UK withdrawal from the EU some thirty years later.

So, Labour activists saw black and minority ethnic voters as electoral friends but also, as representing an important area of political activity. The inspiration might not have been drawn directly from the 'rainbow coalition' of the American civil rights movement but there was no shortage of both political theorists and electoral strategists who were opining that, as class and political de-alignment speeded-up, the left should be seeking to build a new coalition covering leftists, feminists, blacks, gays, people with disabilities and so on. Hence, the left was seen as heavily identified with black and ethnic minorities, and this provided grist to the mill of Conservative politicians and newspapers who wished to suggest, indirectly, that support for Labour equalled support for its far left which equalled support for black people and the consequent ending of their idealised notion of a golden-age Britain.

In 1986, one of Bill Clinton's political advisers, Joe Napolitano, was brought over to the UK by the Shadow Communications Agency to 'warn' Kinnock that Labour was 'seen as associated with extreme leftism racial worries and Labour's affinity for perceived "undesirables"'.[62] Almost ten years later (in 1995) another American pollster – Stan Greenberg, another of Clinton's polling advisers – told the Labour leadership much the same thing. He declared: 'One of the pre-occupations of Old Labour was a pre-occupation with what the public often saw as 'bizarre' issues: homosexuals, immigrants, feminists, lesbians, boroughs putting their money into peculiar things'.[63]

It is not an uncommon political phenomenon that groups, particularly those who feel they are under some sort of pressure, identify themselves not so much by who they are, as by who they are not. In this case, we see a notion of 'Englishness' being formed in opposition to those groups that Labour's left was seen to be representing – blacks, gays, trade union militants 'scroungers', travellers and so on – the 'folk devils' identified by Stanley Cohen more than thirty years ago.[64] The combination of Labour weakness, the astuteness of Conservative campaigning and the enthusiastic endorsement of the Conservative-supporting press, created a climate in which Labour was seen to symbolise something unedifying, un-English, almost alien. As Eric Shaw observes:

> The real significance of the Tory and tabloid 'loony left' assault was its invitation to voters to define themselves as white and respectable rather than as working-class, to identify with the Conservatives as the party of whites and upwardly mobile – and to reject Labour as the party of minorities and the failures. This strategy was pivoted on driving a wedge though Labour's working-class constituency, which effectively involved exploiting,

politicising and sharpening existing cleavage patterns and rival social identities, dividing the more affluent, socially mobile and owner-occupiers
from the poor, welfare recipients, one-parent families and so forth.[65]

In his account of the rise of New Labour, Phillip Gould relates how, quite uncon-
sciously, his focus group respondents associated Labour with 'black'. He writes:

> For the next fourteen years [after 1983] indeed until the very last days of
> the 1997 election, Labour became a party to be feared. One woman said
> to me just weeks before the 1997 election 'When I was a child there was
> a wardrobe in my bedroom. I was always scared that one night, out of the
> blackness, a monster would emerge. That is how I think of the Labour
> Party.'... Labour had become the party of the shadows; of deep, irrational
> anxiety. Only modernisation would save it.[66]

The Labour leadership, consciously or otherwise, played to these fears. In the
Party's crucial positioning document 'New Labour New Life for Britain', pub-
lished in 1996, there are more than two hundred of pictures of 'ordinary people'.
Of those who are clearly identifiable, 215 are white and just seven are black or
Asian – all of whom are 'unthreatening' babies, children or students. Clearly
Labour, in seeking to position itself for the forthcoming election, was deliber-
ately distancing itself from black and ethnic minority adults.

There is no suggestion that Labour was, at any time, deliberately 'playing the
race card'. What is being suggested is that the party, throughout this period, was
acutely aware of what it took to be its vulnerability on this issue and sought to
draw the sting out of the implicitly racist attacks that would almost certainly be
made on the party by the right-wing press. The Labour leadership believed that
the most effective way of countering these fears, (or at least so they were advised)
was to establish Labour's general 'trustworthiness' and then to hope this would
act as a neutralising agent over issues such as race and gender politics.

Hence, from 1987 onwards Labour's campaigning teams focussed on the goal
of convincing the British people that they were not 'extremists' and could be
trusted to run Britain in the way that it had always been. Gould recalls:

> As soon as I returned to London from the 1992 Democratic victory I wrote
> a long document ... Labour was perceived to be looking downwards not
> upwards and backwards not forwards; it was for 'minorities and not the
> mainstream' and it was 'not trusted to run the economy properly'.[67]

Patricia Hewitt, who was then Neil Kinnock's Head of Policy, wrote at the time:

> The essence of making Labour electable, is trust. Trust in Labour's leadership,
> in the team, in Labour's ability to manage the economy competently. Trust
> that Labour knows where it is going – and trust in the policies to take it there.[68]

Labour went into the 1992 general election campaign far more confident than it had been in 1987. It had continued the process of change begun in 1985; the party's decision-making structures, its policies and – it hoped – its image, had all undergone wholesale change. The spectre of the 'loony left' appeared to have been banished. But as election day approached, the Conservative-supporting press returned to the fray. Phrases such 'the loony left's bully boys',[69] 'It's the loony left again' and 'antics of the "loony left"',[70] began to appear in the right-wing press. In the months prior to the poll the *Sun*, for example, then the UK's largest circulation paper, on the day before the election, devoted its first ten pages to a slew of personal attacks on the Labour leader. Beginning with a front-page headline 'Nightmare on Kinnock Street' and ending with a full-page advert for the Conservative Party, the coverage included a psychic asking famous dead people how they would vote – Tory leader John Major received the 'votes' of Winston Churchill, Elvis Presley and Queen Victoria whilst Kinnock had to content himself with the 'support' of Mao, Marx and Stalin. The following day, the *Sun*'s front page consisted of a picture of Kinnock's head in a light bulb with the headline 'If Kinnock wins today will the last person to leave Britain please turn out the lights'. According to the *Daily Mail*'s post-election analysis:

'Far from making advances in the South, Labour were repulsed in nearly all the seats they thought they could capture. Clearly the 'London effect' of the so-called Loony Left still haunts voters who have had to put up with some of their crazy ideas'.[71]

David Hill, who was Labour's Director of Communications in 1992, agreed with this analysis. He told a post-election seminar:

Immediately after the election I said that the main reason why, when it came to the crunch, people felt that they could not vote Labour, was because they were concerned about Labour's history ... The problem for Labour has was that people had very long memories. Our canvassers discovered ... that people on the doorstep were remembering 1979. They were also remembering the arguments that took place in the Labour Party in the 1980's. These memories were fostered by the newspapers in particular. And people recalled, or thought they recalled, that Labour had a history of internal conflict and a history of chaotic government. As people saw it, they could not be confident that they could trust Labour ... they felt that Labour was a party which was no longer in tune with them that the Labour Party's approach to life was not consistent with third own perception of their aspirations, their outlook and their wish for success, for themselves and their families.[72]

However, the Butler and Kavanagh series of general election studies tells a somewhat different story. In their study of the 1987 general election, the term 'loony left' received seven index entries; the volume looking at the 1992 contained none. And the psephological analysis of the 1992 result appeared to question the Labour's leadership's belief that the main cause of their defeat was their failure to shake off the 'loony left' label. In a pre-election analysis in *The Times* Ivor Crewe investigated whether there was a 'loony left' effect at work – as the Conservatives had been claiming. Crewe reported that there was none, with London showing an above-average swing to Labour of 8%.[73] His view was supported by Colin Rallings and Michael Thrasher whose post-election analysis in the *Sunday Times* demonstrated that: 'Only four regions saw significant changes in the party profile of seats, with London accounting for more than a quarter of all Labour's net gains. The "loony left" image, which so damaged the party in 1987, has almost disappeared'.[74]

## Notes

1  T. Bale 'Managing the Party and the Trade Unions' in B. Brivati and R. Heffernan *The Labour Party: A Centenary History* (Basingstoke: Macmillan 2000).
2  L. Minkin *The Blair Supremacy: A Study in the Politics of Labour's Party Management* (Manchester: Manchester University Press 2014), pp. 58–9.
3  A. Finlayson *Making Sense of New Labour* (London: Lawrence and Wishart 2003), p. 19.
4  Ibid.
5  Ibid.
6  See Minkin op cit for the most comprehensive account of this process.
7  One of the earliest descriptions of this process can be found in G. Mazzoleni, & W. Schulz 'Mediatization' of Politics: A Challenge for Democracy? *Political Communication*, 16(3), 247–61, 1999.
8  Based on Gaber's personal experience whilst working as a journalist at ITN.
9  James Thomas *Popular Newspapers, the Labour Party and British Politics* (London: Routledge 2005), pp. 90–1.
10  *Daily Mail* 25 April 1979
11  Quoted in Owen P. (2010) Michael Foot: a life in pictures (obituary) *Guardian* 3 March 2010.
12  K. Morgan *Michael Foot: A Life* (London: Harper Perennial 2012), pp. 384–5.
13  Ibid.
14  C. Horrie and P. Chippendale *Stick It Up Your Punter: the rise and fall of the Sun* London, Heinemann p. 140
15  James Thomas, pp. 80–1.
16  Horrie and Chippendale op cit, p. 140.
17  Quoted in Thomas op cit, p. 90.
18  Sambrook, D (2009) What if … Neil Kinnock hadn't tripped? *New Statesman* 24 September 2009.
19  P. Gould *The Unfinished Revolution; how the modernisers saved the Labour Party* (London: Abacus 1989), p. 19.
20  Quoted in C. Hughes and P. Wintour *Labour Rebuilt: the new model party* (London: 4th Estate 1990), p. 50.
21  Op cit, p. 48.
22  *The Times* 18 November 1986.
23  *Financial Times* 20 November 1986. Interestingly this particular report appeared on the same day that a Gallup poll showed that Labour had regained its poll lead. It put Labour on 40%, the Tories on 36% and the (SDP/Liberal) Alliance on 22% compared

with the previous month when Gallup had Labour and Conservatives both on 38% with the Alliance on 22.

24 Quoted in E. Shaw *The Labour Party Since 1979 Crisis and Transformation* (London: Routledge 2002) p. 75.

25 Vincent Hanna passed away in 1996. It is, perhaps therefore no more than a minor footnote of political history, that it was Hanna's production company that was originally awarded the contract to undertake the research for Neil Kinnock's 1987 election tour (work which was subsequently sub-contracted to this author). The original negotiations took place between Hanna and Patricia Hewitt.

26 *Guardian* 5 February 1987.

27 *Financial Times* 4 February 1987.

28 *The Times* 2 February 1987.

29 *Financial Times* op cit.

30 *Guardian* 3 March 1987 quoted in Heffernan and Marqusee, p. 73.

31 *The Times* 6 March 1987.

32 Hughes and Wintour op cit, p. 19.

33 Heffernan and Marqusee op cit, p.74.

34 *Sunday Times?* 8 March 1987.

35 Butler and Kavanagh, p. 72.

36 Hughes C and Wintour, p. 183.

37 Eric Shaw, p. 61.

38 Based on Gaber's experience in 1986–7 as a media consultant working for Labour.

39 Quoted in Hughes and Wintour, p. 23, and the author's private correspondence.

40 Confidential report by I. Gaber 'General Election Location Searching' submitted to the office of the Leader of the Opposition 1986.

41 All quotes from copy of Gould presentation slides, in author's private collection.

42 National Centre for Social Research 'British Social Attitudes' http://natcen.ac.uk/our-research/research/british-social-attitudes/.

43 Minkin, p. 168.

44 See Heffernan and Marqusee *Defeat from the Jaws of Victory.*

45 L. Baston 'Labour Local Government 1900–99' in Brivati and Heffernan, p. 78.

46 Quoted in Hughes and Wintour, p. 156.

47 'Labour and Britain in the 1990s' NEC paper November 1990 quoted in Heffernan and Marqusee. p. 98.

48 This research was undertaken by LFF a market research firm then owned by Lord McIntosh, the Labour leader of the Greater London Council who was deposed by Ken Livingstone in 1980.

49 Gould 1998, p. 158.

50 *Sun* 14 March 1986 quoted in Thomas, p. 104.

51 Terry Coleman writing in the *Guardian* 7 December 1987.

52 S. Fielding *The Labour Party Continuity and Change in the Making of 'New' Labour* (Basingstoke: Palgrave 2003), p. 73.

53 Hughes and Wintour, p. 46.

54 S. Fielding, p. 73.

55 A process well-documented by Minkin.

56 S. Heffer *Like the Roman: The Life of Enoch Powell* (London: Orion 1999), p. 459.

57 Quoted in H. Young *One of Us: A Biography of Margaret Thatcher* (London: Pan1989), p. 111.

58 *Observer* 3 September 1995.

59 C. Prosser (2017) *What Was It all About? The 2017 Election Campaign in Voters' own Words* British Election Study www.britishelectionstudy.com/bes-findings/what-was-it-all-about-the-2017-election-campaign-in-voters-own-words/#.WYLsW4jyvIU.

60 Explored in more depth in Chapter 4.

61  J. Major *Speech to Conservative Group for Europe* 22 April 1993 www.johnmajor.co.uk/
    page1086.html. The full quote: 'Fifty years on from now, Britain will still be the
    country of long shadows on county [cricket] grounds, warm beer, invincible green
    suburbs, dog lovers and old maids bicycling to Holy Communion through the morn-
    ing mist'.
62  Gould, p. 69.
63  'Strategic Observations on the British Elections' [sic], report by Stanley Greenberg,
    8 June 1995, quoted in Gould, p. 258.
64  S. Cohen *Folk Devils and Moral Panics: Creation of Mods and Rockers* (London: Routledge
    2002).
65  Shaw, p. 193
66  Gould op cit, p. 20.
67  Gould, p. 175.
68  P. Hewit *New Statesman and Society* 14 August 1988.
69  *Daily Mail* 30 April 1992.
70  *The Times* 12 March 1992.
71  *Daily Mail* 10 April 1992.
72  D. Hill 'The Labour Party's Strategy' in *Political Communications: the General Election
    Campaign of 1992* I. Crew and B.Grosschalk (Cambridge: Cambridge University
    Press 1995), pp. 38–40.
73  *The Times* 24 March 1992.
74  *Sunday Times* 12 April 1992.

# 9

# THE BLAIR ASCENDANCY

*Ivor Gaber*

Following his defeat in 1992, Neil Kinnock stepped down as Labour leader. On the day after the election, the *Sun* front page famously declared: 'It Was the Sun Wot Won It'[1] which elicited Kinnock to respond:

> I express no bitterness when I say that the Conservative-supporting press has enabled the Tory Party to win yet again when the Conservative Party could not have secured victory for itself on the basis of its record, its programme or its character.[2]

The man who succeeded Neil Kinnock as Labour leader – John Smith – could not have been less like him, apart from sharing a Celtic heritage, although in the case of Smith this was Scots rather than Welsh. Smith was described by the then BBC's Political Editor, Andrew Marr, as 'Placid, secure, self-certain … a Gaitskell-supporting moderate'.[3] He had been Kinnock's Shadow Chancellor of the Exchequer and, apart from a falling out during the 1992 campaign, these two very different men had worked well together. Smith was the favourite from the start of the leadership campaign and eventually defeated Bryan Gould, seen as the 'soft left' candidate, by an overwhelmingly 90% to 10%, taking over the leadership in July 1992.

However, Smith did not subscribe to the Mandelson/Gould school of thought that the party needed to change still more radically if it was ever to be electable. Indeed, Smith was thought to share the sentiments of those in the party leadership who, following the 1992 defeat, felt that there had been 'too much glitz and not enough substance' and who believed that, following the Party's progress at the polls from 1983 to 1987 and then 1992, 'one more heave' was all that was required in order to get Labour into power.[4]

Smith adopted a less confrontational attitude to the party than had Kinnock. He did not believe that the party, or its polices, were in need of further radical surgery. He sought to avoid unnecessary confrontations, which resulted in him trying to introduce changes in policy 'surreptitiously'[5] for fear of antagonising either the party or the public. Referring to Peter Mandelson, Marr describes Smith as taking 'an instant dislike of the Mephistopheles of the modernisers' although Marr adds 'which may have been tinged with Scottish Presbyterian's homophobia'.[6]

In one sense, Smith was very lucky. Within weeks of winning the leadership, the Conservative Government had stumbled into a major financial crisis which forced the UK to withdraw from the precursor to the Euro, the Exchange Rate Mechanism, in September 1992, giving Smith the opportunity, in his maiden parliamentary speech as Labour leader, to describe Prime Minister John Major as 'the devalued Prime Minister of a devalued government'.[7] From that point onwards, the Conservative Government's fate appeared sealed although it took six months for Labour to move into a lead in the opinion polls; but once there the party remained in front. At the time of Smith's sudden death in March 1994, its lead over the Conservatives stood at 23%.

Despite his brief tenure in office, Smith was responsible for two major changes in terms of organisation and policy. Organisationally, after much prodding from party colleagues, he persuaded the 1993 Labour Party conference to abolish the trade unions' block vote and introduce a one-man-one-vote system for determining party policy; in policy terms he committed a future Labour government to establishing a Scottish (and subsequently Welsh) Parliament.

Whilst Blair and Brown remained in their front bench posts, Smith very deliberately excluded Mandelson and Phillip Gould from his inner circle. The Shadow Communications Agency was put into cold storage, as were the strategy and techniques of media management that the Party had developed under Kinnock. The advent of the Smith regime led to a deep sense of frustration and unease among the modernisers. Labour adviser Phillip Gould was, at the time, very concerned that if Smith continued to ignore the lessons that he believed the Party had learnt under Kinnock, then it was by no means guaranteed success at the next election.[8] Peter Hyman, who was to become one of Tony Blair's key aides wrote:

> I could sense too, and share, the exasperation that some had for the 'one more heave' strategy that John Smith employed, the assumption that if Labour held tight it would win next time round.[9]

In their post-election analysis of what went wrong for Labour in 1992, Patricia Hewitt and Phillip Gould's explanation of why Labour remained 'not trusted' was simple:

> The party had not changed enough … there were too many who went along with the Kinnock project of change not because they believed in the

need for change or in the kind of change he was offering, but because they thought it might win.[10]

They argued that voters were not fools and that they recognised that the party's grassroots had not gone through the same conversion process as its top leadership clearly had undergone – if the Party was not convinced, then why should the voters be, they asked? Much of the supporting evidence for this assertion came from a series of focus groups Phillip Gould conducted in the wake of the 1992 defeat.

Smith, who died suddenly in 1994, was succeeded by Tony Blair who resumed the modernising project begun under Kinnock. Blair, armed with Gould's focus group findings, clearly saw it as central to his mission to persuade voters that the Party had radically changed from the one that had previously been identified with the 'loony left'. Blair and his colleagues felt that Smith's leadership had been an interregnum in the long-term process of transforming the Labour Party from old to new Labour. Even as late as 1994 it was clear, or at least clear to them, that the party had still not succeeded in convincing significant sections of the electorate that the Labour's change was real and fundamental.

That this image might, or might not be, a false one engendered by a hostile media was of little consequence to Blair and his inner circle – their job was to get Labour elected. Thus, rather than challenge this image, he sought to exaggerate it so that the differences between 'old' and 'new' Labour appeared greater than they actually were. In Fielding's words: 'He [Blair] deliberately made the party's break with its past appear more apparent than it actually was'.[11] Blair believed that, whilst Kinnock had taken heroic steps in changing the Party, he had been less successful in persuading the British public that the changes were for real. Thus, Blair believed that by using the phrase 'New Labour' at every possible opportunity he was reinforcing the message that this was a different Labour Party from the one in voters' minds that was preventing them from supporting the Party at the polls.

Nonetheless, New Labour did argue in favour of gender equality – one area of 'loony left' politics that the leadership felt less uncomfortable with. This was both because they were instinctively, and generationally, committed to equality between the sexes but also because their polling was telling them that this was an effective way of closing the gender gap. Labour was seen as a male-dominated party that used macho language and adopted macho posturing, and anything that could be done to correct such a perception would be electorally beneficial. New Labour sought to bridge this gap by changing its policies and its organisation. An element of positive discrimination in favour of women was introduced into elections for the Shadow Cabinet in 1989 and four years later this was extended to the selection of parliamentary candidates. Thus, all-women shortlists, argued for vociferously by the Labour left, were put into effect under New Labour.

However, Lewis Baston is among doubters as to New Labour's real commitment to gender equality. He suggests that Labour adopted women-only
shortlists as a result of the momentum that had been built-up on the issue by
the left:

> The party leadership reluctantly came around to the view that all women
> shortlists were necessary in 1992–93, a step which would have been
> impossible had the local left not raised the profile of sex equality … The
> politics of social inclusion with which Labour successfully ends the cen-
> tury owes much to the initiatives that came through local government in
> the 1980s.[12]

Ironically, it was with the support of some of the more right-wing unions, keen
supporters of Neil Kinnock's leadership, that were persuaded that if Labour
was to ever win again then a real commitment – both in policy and internal
structures – had to be made to gender equality. Thus, on one raft of issues –
lone parents and increasing support for working mothers – New Labour pushed
the policy agenda into the terrain of the left. Indeed, according to Hughes
and Wintour:

> Labour reformers … insisted that the party would not be fully recon-
> structed until it had been imbued with feminism. Research prepared by
> the [Shadow Communications] agency for 'Labour and Britain in the
> Nineties' showed that for some time women had been less likely to vote
> Labour than men.[13]

Following its 1997 general election victory, the Blair government demonstrated
an overwhelming desire to retain the trust of the electorate with assurances
that it would not be embarking on any radical measures, which sometimes
overcame its genuine commitment to gender equality. Within the first few
months of the Labour Government coming to power, Harriet Harman, a politician formerly identified with London's 'loony left' and New Labour's first
Secretary of State for Social Services, was tasked with persuading her fellow
women MPs to support a cut in benefit for single parents – plans inherited
from the outgoing Conservative Government. Fiscally, the measure was an
irrelevancy, the amount of money being saved was minimal, but Blair and his
advisers saw this as an emblematic issue with which to demonstrate the extent
to which Labour had changed; how better to do this than to have the change
championed by someone formerly identified with the 'loony left'? A report in
the *Guardian* began:

> Tony Blair's honeymoon with his own party ended dramatically last night
> when 47 Labour MPs defied a three-line whip to stage an unexpectedly

emphatic vote against the lone parent benefit cut ... He had staked considerable authority on facing down the rebellion in the name of New Labour solidarity behind his election manifesto.[14]

However, given New Labour's publicly declared position on gender issues, and the fact that there were now over 100 women Labour MPs in the House, this token gesture engendered a great deal of hostility and bitterness and created a sense of distrust between the leadership and the Party at large. This was despite the fact that in the subsequent budget the Chancellor of the Exchequer more than made up for the symbolic cut that Harman had been forced to put through the House (she herself was shortly after sacked from the Cabinet – scant reward, it was suggested, for her apparent willingness to put herself in the front-line of New Labour's confrontation with lone parents).

In some ways, it could be argued that New Labour was a tribute to the perceived power of the focus group – a research tool that Phillip Gould was particularly attracted to. President Clinton was once quoted as saying: 'There is no one more powerful today than the member of a focus group. If you really want to change things and you want to get listened to, that's the place to be'.[15] Gould had been using focus groups as the basis of his understanding of what Labour needed to do to become electable ever since the establishment of the Shadow Communications Agency seven years earlier. Focus groups can be a very useful research tool, but they can also be illusory, particularly if the person leading the group is not the dispassionate researcher that the text books advocate. And Gould certainly was not. He describes his first encounter with a focus group:

> No one trained me, I just did it. And I loved it. I loved the direct contact with the electorate, the way that I could put arguments, hear arguments, confront arguments, develop ideas, feel the intensity of a point of view and hear the opinions, attitudes and emotions of ordinary members of the public .... I do not just sit there and listen. I challenge, I argue back, I force them to confront issues.[16]

Exciting stuff it might be, but objective research it certainly was not. If, and it's not a big 'if', Gould was convinced that one of Labour's major weaknesses was the perception that it was not trusted, and that the principle cause of this was that the Party was perceived to be dominated by the 'hard left', it is hardly surprising that he came back with the news that that was exactly what people believed – especially in the light of his own particular 'research method'. As one reads Gould's account of his encounters with focus groups, it is difficult to dispel from one's mind the image of a hapless group of focus group subjects sitting in a North London front room, being forced to 'admit' (a la 1984) that it was the 'loony left' that had kept them from voting Labour.

Gould recounts how he achieved these 'results'. He used a technique of 'show cards' and prodded respondents to talk about 'acceptable and 'unacceptable' fields of politics – an extremely problematic notion (who is defining 'acceptable and 'unacceptable'?). He reported responses such as: 'It's outrageous – they're spending a million pound on parks for gays and lesbians in Camden ... There are too many loonies'.[17]

Such responses cannot be divorced from the methodologies used to obtain them in the first place. It has been well-documented that one of the problems facing quantitative researchers is what Elizabeth Noelle-Neumann first characterised as the 'spiral of silence'[18] – certain attitudes and views become deemed as 'socially acceptable' and others 'unacceptable'. Thus respondents, when faced with researchers (particularly face-to-face), seek to give the 'correct' i.e. socially acceptable answer (in the 2015 election it worked against the Conservatives and in 2017 against Corbyn's Labour Party – which is perhaps a partial explanation as to why, in both elections, the pollsters underestimated the parties' respective votes). Thus, if the 'spiral of silence' effect operated during a phone or internet-based encounter, then how much more must it come into effect when focus group respondents find themselves in a room having to 'argue' with an enthusiast for the New Labour project? In essence (as a result of his enthusiasm for the 'project' rather than anything more malevolent), Gould was presenting the Labour leadership with the output of his 'research' as objective information when in fact it was more akin to the data garnered from old-fashioned political canvassing. The significance of this is that Gould's views about what voters were thinking carried significant weight in Labour's inner circles. In his own words: 'I was seen as the voice of the electorate'.[19] Gould's belief was not universally shared; indeed, Tony Blair notes in his memoirs: 'how extraordinary the confluence was between his (Gould's) own thoughts and what the groups seemed to say'.[20]

Whether Gould's interpretation of the 'voice of the electorate' was, or was not, accurate is a moot point but it what is not in doubt is the fact that Blair, despite his above-quoted cynicism, put a great deal of store by Gould's notion that the Party had to do more than simply create 'New Labour'. It also needed its mirror image – 'Old Labour'. This was because, even as late as 1994, it was clear, or at least clear to the modernisers, that the Party had still not succeeded in convincing significant sections of the electorate that the Party's change was real and fundamental. Thus, rather than challenge this image Blair worked with it and, to some extent, sought to exaggerate it so that the differences between 'old' and 'new' Labour appeared greater than they actually were. In Fielding's words: 'he deliberately made the party's break with its past appear more apparent than it actually was'.[21]

This process can be observed at work in the way that, shortly after his election to the leadership, Tony Blair launched his revision of Clause Four of the Party's constitution, the clause that, on paper at least, committed the party to public ownership of most major industries. In writing about his plan to confront the party with the abolition of Clause Four, Blair said that he was embarking on this course because: 'It's time we gave the party some electric shock treatment'.[22] Blair told Gould that the only way they could build trust with the British people was by showing them that the Party had changed and therefore could be trusted with government; this could be achieved only by dramatic measures, or at least dramatic gestures. Revision of Clause Four would demonstrate how much Labour had changed – it would not initiate change, but would signal that change was already underway. As Stephen Fielding observes: 'For Blair the point of revision was to cause a fuss ... It was precisely due to its symbolic significance that Blair wanted the clause revised'.[23] Tim Bale concurs with this analysis. He writes:

> A new rather audacious strategy was tried: rather than playing down its past difficulties, the Party would own up to them – and in spades. The encouragement of amnesia was replaced by the penitent's promise to have changed for the better, and for good ... demonstrating that New Labour had learnt its lessons and wiped the slate clean would boost both the electoral chances of the Party and what they hoped was their ever-tightening grip upon it.[24]

In conversation, in 1996, David Miliband, then Tony Blair's Head of Policy and later Foreign Secretary, was open and insistent that New Labour's plans for its first term in office would be based on an underlying strategy of reassuring the British people that Labour could be 'trusted' in office.[25]

In order to achieve this trust, New Labour had to continue to be seen to be confronting the Party's left but also had to neutralise the persistent hostility that emanated from the largely right-wing national press. This obliged them to hone still further the 'art' of political spin that Margaret Thatcher's Press Secretary, Bernard Ingham, had developed. To do this, Blair recruited his own version of Ingham – the formidable Alastair Campbell – who can largely be credited with shaping New Labour's communications' agenda. Whatever the complexities of the relationship between people's political allegiance and the media, it is undoubtedly true that since Margaret Thatcher, political communication had come to be seen as being at the very heart of government, and this trend accelerated under New Labour. Barely a year into office, Alastair Campbell told a House of Commons Select Committee: 'In opposition we made clear that communications was not something that you tagged on the end, it is part of what you do. That is something that we have tried to bring into government'.[26]

This mindset was, in its intensity, unique in the history of British governance. It had its roots in the mauling that the Labour Party – under Michael Foot, and then Neil Kinnock – had received over a long period at the hands of large sections of the Conservative-supporting press as recounted in earlier chapters. In particular, the mauling tended to focus on Labour's real, or imagined, far left policies, hence this was the virus that New Labour sought to neutralise. In the 1987 campaign, for example, the *Daily Mail* had reported that:

> Labour's hard left have revealed their hand on the programme they want Neil Kinnock to adopt if they win the election. A manifesto sent out yesterday details a chilling list of demands for the virtual creation of a workers state. It includes a threat to confront the bosses and the banks, repeal the public order laws, withdraw all troops from Ulster, the Falklands and Germany, pull out of the Common Market and open our doors to immigrants and refugees. The left want to impose punitive wealth taxes, abolish the monarchy and the Lords, and make the police, media and judges accountable to the working class.[27]

But, as Brian MacArthur points out, not one of these items was in fact in the Labour manifesto. One can go back further. Reviewing the performance of the newspapers in the 1983 election, Martin Harrop noted that the anti-Labour bias of much of the tabloid press had been increasing in virulence since 1974. He quoted the *Sun*, which had described the Labour Party as:

> a desperate, irresponsible, extremist shambles which shows the ugly face of a rampant extremism and has been torn apart and taken over by Marxists with a grotesque parody of a programme which is extreme, extravagant and nightmarish and which would virtually wipe out freedom.[28]

It was in response to this sort of treatment that New Labour's inner circle decided on a media policy that would ensure that such coverage would be neutralised, if not eliminated altogether. The overall philosophy was outlined a number of years later by Campbell, who made it clear that the modernisers were determined that Blair would not suffer the same hostility from the press as had been handed out to his predecessors:

> it's fair to say we were determined not to let Tony Blair get the same treatment as they did. So we did make a concerted effort to get a better dialogue with some parts of the media where before there had been pretty much none. This was of course about reaching their readers. It was also about preventing destruction by a hostile press. Competence with the media conveyed a general competence that was important to us in establishing ourselves as a competent Government.[29]

The approach was to create a re-branded product. Labour Party conferences began to look like sales conventions; Clause 4 was dumped, and only the most on-message media-friendly politicians (that is, those not identified with the left) were put on public display. Indeed, Minkin describes how the party conference was 'managed' – tactics included having members positioned strategically around the hall to lead the applause and ensuring that the conference Chair called only speakers from the floor who had been vetted beforehand for 'reliability'.[30] Steps were also taken to ensure that both policies, and the way they were presented, would appeal to the proprietors, editors and readers of the Conservative press – to quote a chapter heading from the autobiography of Phillip Gould, 'Reassurance, Reassurance, Reassurance'. And reassurance was the third plank of the modernisers' communications project – reassuring the press proprietors that their business interests would not only be protected by New Labour but would even be promoted. This was symbolised by the visits that Tony Blair and Gordon Brown made to Australia and the United States to meet with *Sun* proprietor Rupert Murdoch and his executives (similar meetings were held with *Daily Mail* owner Lord Rothermere) to emphasise that Labour was no longer the party of the 'loony left'. It also gave Blair a chance to assess Rupert Murdoch, and in so doing came to what was, for the leader of the Labour Party, a surprisingly positive conclusion:

> I came to have a grudging respect and even liking for him. He was hard, no doubt. He was right wing. I did not share or like his attitudes on Europe, social policy or on issues such as gay rights, but there were two points of connection: he was an outsider, and he had balls.[31]

Perhaps the moment of greatest tension between New Labour and its 'loony left' past came in 1999 when the leadership was faced with Ken Livingstone's bid to become the party's candidate to be the first elected mayor of London. For many in the Labour leadership, Livingstone personified all the worst elements of the 'loony left'. Writing in the *People*, under the headline, 'Why Red Ken is a Disaster for Labour' former leader Neil Kinnock argued:

> The Loony Left had to be beaten before the voters would treat Labour seriously again … Arthur Scargill. Derek Hatton. Ted Knight. Linda Bellos. They were the names in the headlines that made people say: 'Labour's lost it now.' And there was one name, above all, that made them say: 'Labour's lost me now.' The name was Ken Livingstone. While he led the Greater London Council the stories of high rates, public money for stunts, control by soft-headed Hard Left groups poured out of the press almost every day.[32]

Ever since the abolition of the Greater London Council (GLC) Ken Livingstone had assumed almost mythic proportions as an iconic hate figure of both the Tories and the Labour right, epitomising the 'loony left'. In reality, he was an isolated figure on Labour's back benches, an isolation enhanced by his constant criticisms of the economic policies of Gordon Brown, then Labour's Shadow Chancellor. Thus, given his GLC background, it was not surprising that when the battle for Labour's nomination for the London mayoralty began Livingstone was seen as a leading candidate. It was equally unsurprising that the antipathy of the Labour leadership towards Livingstone winning the post would be equally prominent. Both Blair and Brown had a fear that Livingstone, as Labour's candidate, would re-awaken the sleeping dragons of the 'loony left' and the 'London effect'. Tony Blair, in what must be an unprecedented attack for a leader of a mainstream political party on one of his own MPs running for high office, said:

> I was a foot soldier in the Labour Party in Battersea and in Hackney in the early 1980s. I canvassed and campaigned for Labour in London when we were at our lowest ebb. I remember knocking on doors in different parts of London only to see in the eyes of the people, time after time, that they thought the Labour Party was not for them. At that time the Labour Party was a byword for extremism. We were hopelessly divided and deeply unpopular... The leading figures in the Labour Party were people like Ken Livingstone, Tony Benn and Arthur Scargill. The policies were not just disastrous for Labour. They deprived the public of a choice that wasn't the Tories. Now, this is the issue: has Ken Livingstone really changed? If he hasn't, he would not be right for Labour or London.[33]

New Labour's hostility to Livingstone was not just a matter of public relations – their opposition was heartfelt. Liz Davies, a left-wing member of the National Executive, records that during a debate in the executive in 1999 as to whether Ken Livingstone was acceptable as Labour's candidate for the mayoralty of London, the 'loony left' agenda loomed large. One of the strongest interventions against Livingstone came because of his record of campaigning in favour of gay rights – ironically the charge was made by a prominent gay activist, Michael Cashman who accused Livingstone of having been in part responsible for Labour's defeat at the polls in 1987 and 1992. Cashman also argued that, by supporting lesbian and gay rights in the 1980s, Livingstone had been responsible for the introduction of the Conservative's Section 28, which banned the 'promotion' of homosexuality in schools (see Chapter 5). Liz Davies quotes Cashman as saying:

> I've spoken out against a particular candidate. I'm sick and tired of lesbian and gay rights being seen as the dustbin of good politics. Now we've moved, but we've taken thirteen years to get there. I will continue to be a pain in the side to anyone who is in opposition to me.[34]

New Labour's visceral hatred of Livingstone was of such an intensity that political writers had to work hard to explain the antipathy. According to an article in *The Times*:

On one level, the deep-seated desire to prevent the former GLC leader assuming power is a matter of straight politics. Blairites believe he would use the post to embarrass, challenge and wherever possible damage the Labour Government. A psychiatrist may offer a different explanation, suggesting that Labour's inability to come to terms with Mr Livingstone is more about their common roots than their differences. In the same way that family members can fall out because they are too similar, many Labour MPs see an uncomfortable reminder of their own past when they look at Mr Livingstone.[35]

*The Times'* cod psychology might, or might not be, a useful way of understanding New Labour's reaction to Ken Livingstone's re-emergence on the national political stage. What is undeniable is, as *The Times* observes, that New Labour, collectively, had a problem with coming to terms with its local government past. Many leading members of New Labour first tasted political power through their involvement with local government; throughout the 1980s, when Labour was out of power nationally and looking like it would be excluded for years to come, local government remained both the only route to achieving any sort of political power but also the best way that the public could judge what Labour in government might do. This enhanced the potency of 'loony left' stories in the media, particularly given the proximity of Fleet Street to the London councils that were controlled by Labour Left wingers.

Because of the antipathy of the Labour leadership, Livingstone eventually ran for the mayoralty as an independent and was expelled from the Party as a result. However, in his first term in office, despite surrounding himself with colleagues who had been associated with left-wing groups in and outside the Labour Party, Livingstone was seen as a success. In particular, he successfully introduced a controversial congestion charge for central London in the teeth of intense opposition from much of the media and the studied indifference of the Labour leadership. In their opposition to the congestion charge, the press reverted to the 'loony left' agenda and sought to counterpoint the notion of 'common sense' against the left's special pleading for 'the other'. When the 'loony left' was first being identified by the press, the 'other' were gays, feminists and so on. Their presumed views were contrasted with media notions of 'normality' – the views of the silent majority, or whatever formulation was being used at the time, to represent those who were not black, not gay, not disabled – in other words the classic nuclear family with its 2.4 children.[36]

If such is the norm in some parts of the UK, then it is decidedly not the case in London, a multicultural metropolis in which lifestyles, family structures and ethnicity are very different from the fabled norm. Yet, the congestion charge was portrayed as a policy designed for the minority, in contrast to the views and interests of ordinary tax-paying car-drivers. Yet, the irony was that the congestion charge was aimed at benefiting bus, tube and rail commuters who represented the vast majority of London's travelling public, at the expense of the one in ten commuters who travelled into the capital by car. Nonetheless, sections of the press lost few opportunities to construct, or re-construct, a 'loony left' agenda out of what they took to be the motivations behind, and the consequences of, the introduction of congestion charging. In the *Daily Telegraph*, columnist Barbara Amiel told us that that the charge was part of an agenda that was intended to 'coerce people on to public transport, and to eliminate the private car.'[37] Sarah Sands, writing in the same paper, claimed that it was an 'anti-family London tax' because it would drain the life out of the capital by making it difficult for families to use cars to move around.[38] On a later occasion, she accused the Mayor of 'using congestion charges as class war by other means'.[39] Simon Heffer in the *Daily Mail*, outraged by the apparent success of the scheme, turned his spleen on its supposed supporters, arguing they were the same people with the same agenda that he had been battling against over the years: 'Only six days into London's congestion charge, the usual Lefties and eco-freaks are queuing up to say what a success it is. In fact, it is yet another tax on the capital's middle classes'.[40]

The *Sun* used generalised images of inner city decay, some of which had become associated with left-wing Labour councils in the 1980s, and bracketed them with the charge: 'Families put up with graffiti, street crime and high property prices. Now they can't even drive on their own streets'[41]. But the theme of 'the loony left rides again' was best captured by *Sun* columnist Richard Littlejohn when he wrote, (perhaps with his tongue firmly in his cheek) that the charge was 'a spiteful anti-motorist measure, pure and simple, dreamed up by Red Ken and his sexually-inadequate, Lycra-clad, *Guardian*-reading, cycle-mad, control-freaks at TfL (Transport for London)'.[42]

Analysis of the use of the terms 'loony left' and 'Red Ken'[43] reveals that in the period January 2002 to the end of May 2003, the *Sun*, perhaps unsurprisingly, topped the table with twenty-nine references to 'Red Ken' and ten to the 'loony left'. But it was only just narrowly ahead of the *Daily Telegraph* which referred to 'Red Ken' thirty-one times and the 'loony left' seven times. The detailed breakdown is shown in Table 9.1.

On 11 September 2001, a Labour spin doctor – Jo Moore – tried to use the cover of the 9/11 terrorist attack on New York to blind-side the media. In an email to colleagues, she advised them that it would be 'a good day to bury bad news'.[44] It was the day when spin became a major negative factor for New Labour. In an article the following year headlined 'It's Time to Bury Spin', Alastair Campbell, after describing how he had been determined that the Blair would not suffer at the hands of the media in the same way as his predecessors, confessed:

> We appeared, and perhaps we were, over-controlling, manipulative. People stopped trusting what we had to say I think what we underestimated was the extent to which the changes we made in our relationships with the media, and in getting our media act together, would itself become an issue and a story That's in part because we carried on for too long in Government with some of the tactics of opposition.[45]

**TABLE 9.1**  References to the 'loony left' and 'Red Ken' in the
national press, January 2002–May 2003

| | | | |
|---|---|---|---|
| Sun | 29 | 10 | 39 |
| Daily Telegraph | 31 | 7 | 38 |
| Evening Standard | 23 | 14 | 37 |
| The Times | 19 | 12 | 31 |
| Daily Mail | 16 | 10 | 26 |
| Independent | 17 | 4 | 21 |
| Guardian | 10 | 9 | 19 |
| Sunday Times | 7 | 9 | 16 |
| Daily Express | 13 | 2 | 15 |
| Mail on Sunday | 10 | 5 | 15 |
| Financial Times | 9 | 2 | 11 |
| Sunday Express | 10 | 0 | 10 |
| Daily Mirror | 9 | 1 | 10 |
| Daily Star | 9 | 1 | 10 |
| News of the World | 4 | 1 | 5 |
| Independent on Sunday | 3 | 1 | 4 |
| Sunday Mirror | 1 | 3 | 4 |
| People | 2 | 1 | 3 |
| Sunday Telegraph | 2 | 1 | 3 |
| Observer | 0 | 3 | 3 |
| Metro[32] | n/a | n/a | n/a |

But if things were bad in 2002, they got even worse following the invasion of
Iraq in 2003 which had severely negative consequences for New Labour's relations with the media. In the run-up to the invasion, the media was overwhelmingly supportive of the claim by both London and Washington that Sadaam
Hussein's Iraq had strategic weapons of mass destruction that they were capable
of being launched within forty-five minutes. This claim was derived from what
came to be known as the Government's 'dodgy dossier' – most of which was
not based on intelligence reports but purloined from an American PhD thesis.
But the claim was taken up uncritically and enthusiastically by the press. The
*London Evening Standard*'s headline on its front page on the day the dossier was
released was '45 Minutes from Attack',[46] whilst the following day's *Sun* featured
a front page headline, 'He's Got 'Em' Let's Get Him' – and just in case the message was not quite clear the inside page follow-up was headlined 'Brits 45 mins
from Doom'.[47] Not only did this all prove to be totally untrue, but according to
one of his senior ministers, Blair knew these claims to be untrue.[48] And it wasn't
until well after the invasion that the press began to question their uncritical support for the invasion, but none produced the fulsome mea culpas that both the
*New York Times*[49] and the *Washington Post*[50] carried apologising for their supine
reporting. The whole affair led to Blair and Campbell's honesty in dealing with
the media being widely questioned – questioning that was exacerbated by the
death of government weapons' inspector Dr. David Kelly. The death led to the
Hutton Inquiry and the Inquiry's aftermath, which included the resignation of

the Chair and Director General of the BBC. All this came to symbolise New Labour's unhealthy obsession with image. Spin and the New Labour project became intrinsically and damagingly linked, it seemed to reinforce an image of untrustworthiness that Blair never recovered.

In 2004, 'Red Ken' was re-elected as Mayor of London, this time with the full support of the New Labour Government and the following year Blair was re-elected, on an historically low turnout with just 35% of the vote. In order to counteract the very bad publicity associated with the Iraq war and the subsequent negative ramifications that associated Labour with spin, Blair's advisors drafted a so-called 'masochism strategy' for the Labour leader in the upcoming 2005 election. The strategy would involve Blair accepting that the war had not been popular, being prepared to meet with voters to discuss it, but refusing to apologise for his support for the invasion. During the campaign, Labour adviser Phillip Gould explained how the Party was finding it very frustrating because even though, he argued, things were going well in terms of the economy and other domestic markers, voters were not prepared to give the Government credit for these achievements: 'They just don't believe us' Gould said.[51]

Blair stepped down in 2007 and was succeeded by his New Labour co-architect, Gordon Brown, but not before the toxic relationship between the two men had been exposed on an almost daily basis by the media[52] Just one example came two years before Blair made way for Brown in a *Daily Telegraph* article headlined: 'There is nothing that you could say to me now that I could ever believe'[53] based on a book – *Brown's Britain* – by journalist Robert Peston in which he put flesh and blood on the rumours about the feud between the two men, the sub-title of the book was 'this is the biggest political story in Britain today'.[54] Four years later, Blair retaliated with his autobiography, which the *Daily Telegraph* covered in a front-page story headlined: 'Gordon Brown tried to blackmail me, says Blair'.[55]

Notwithstanding, almost immediately Brown took over from Blair Labour's poll rating rose and it looked like the new Prime Minister could do no wrong as he adeptly handled a series of domestic crises over the summer – including a terrorist attack, flooding and an outbreak of foot and mouth disease. He was clearly tempted to go for a snap poll in the autumn but, following a successful Conservative Party conference, he changed his mind. He denied he had ever considered such a move and tried to convince the public that it had nothing to do with his falling poll numbers. His reputation never recovered as the spectre of Labour spin once more came into public view. A series of other PR disasters followed, including turning up late to sign the Lisbon Treaty because he did not want to be seen as a too avid supporter of the EU. Indicative of his recognition that he needed help, Brown turned to his old adversary, Peter Mandelson, and appointed him to his cabinet in the hope that he could help turn around his receding fortunes.

Gordon Brown was unfortunate in that the scandal surrounding MPs expenses in 2009, which bore no relation to his time in office, blew up in the pages of the *Daily Telegraph* under his watch. Cruelly, the very first story the paper ran was a rather weak 'revelation' that Brown was legitimately claiming expenses for a cleaner for his Westminster flat. But it didn't help and from this point on the tabloid press were in full cry against Brown. The *Sun*, unsurprisingly, announced its withdrawal of support from Brown (and Labour) on the eve of his big speech to the Labour Party conference. Perhaps surprisingly, Brown had established a good personal relationship with the editor of the *Daily Mail* Paul Dacre (some suggested it was because they shared a Calvinistic background and outlook) but this didn't stop the paper from launching a series of attacks on Brown. Throughout his time in office, Brown saw off a number of plots by colleagues to unseat him, but his media nadir came towards the end of the 2010 election campaign when a microphone caught Brown calling Labour voter Gillian Duffy, a 'bigoted woman' following a conversation with her in Rochdale. Brown lost his majority in the election, but ironically Rochdale was one of only two seats Labour gained. Although following an inconclusive general election result his political career ended in a welter of headlines accusing him of clinging to office – the *Mail*, over a picture of Brown headlined its front page 'A Squalid Day for Democracy'[56] whilst the *Sun,* on the same day, had a headline 'Squatter Holed up in No 10'.[57]

Brown resigned and was succeeded not by the crown prince apparent, David Miliband – a former Foreign Secretary, closely aligned with New Labour – but by his younger brother Ed who had campaigned on the platform that it was time to draw a line under the Blair/Brown era.

## Notes

1   *Sun*, 11 April 1992.
2   *Guardian*, 5 January 1993.
3   A. Marr, *A History of Modern Britain* (London, Pan Books, 2007), p. 487.
4   E. Shaw *The Labour Party Since 1945* (Oxford: Blackwell, 1996), p. 214.
5   Shaw op cit, p. 206.
6   Marr op cit, pp. 488–9.
7   N. Timmins 'The recall of Parliament: Smith savages 'devalued government': Labour MPs roar approval for new leader' *Independent*, 24 September 1992.
8   Personal conversation with Gaber 1996.
9   P. Hyman *One Out of Ten: From Downing Street Vision to Classroom Reality* (London: Vintage, 2005), p. 48.
10  P. Hewitt and P. Gould, in *Renewal* 1: 1 (1993), p. 47; quoted in Shaw (1994), p. 175.
11  S. Fielding *The Labour Party: continuity and change in the making of 'New' Labour* (Basingstoke: Palgrave Macmillan, 2003), p. 3.
12  L. Baston in B. Brivati and R. Heffernan *The Labour Party: A Centenary History* (Basingstoke: Palgrave Macmillan, 2000), p. 468.
13  C. Hughes and P. Wintour *Labour Rebuilt: The New Model Party* (London: Fourth Estate, 1990) p. 200.
14  *Guardian*, 12 July 1997.
15  Quoted in D. Mattison The Power of the Focus Group, *Total Politics* 20 August 2010 www.totalpolitics.com/articles/culture/power-focus-group.
16  P. Gould *The Unfinished Revolution: How the Modernisers Saved the Labour Party* (London: Orion,1998), p. 327.

17  Gould op cit, pp. 51–2.
18  E. Noelle-Neumann, *The Spiral of Silence* (Chicago: University of Chicago Press, 1974).
19  Gould op cit, p. 261.
20  T. Blair *A Journey* (London: Hutchinson, 2010), p. 298.
21  Fielding op cit, p. 78.
22  Blair op cit, p. 47.
23  Fielding op cit, p. 48.
24  T. Bale in T. Bale and B. Brivati *New Labour in Power: Precedents and Prospects* (London: Routledge, 2000), p.49.
25  Personal conversation with Gaber 1996.
26  A. Campbell, evidence to the House of Commons Select Committee on Public Administration, 23 June 1998.
27  Quoted in B. MacArthur The Press in I. Crewe and M. Harrop (eds) *Political Communications: The British General Election of 1987* (Cambridge: Cambridge University Press, 1989), p. 101.
28  MacArthur op cit, p. 102.
29  A. Campbell It's time to bury spin *British Journalism Review* 13(4) 2002, pp. 15–23.
30  L. Minkin *The Blair Supremacy: A Study in the Politics of Labour's Party Management* (Manchester: Manchester University Press, 2016), pp. 353, 355.
31  Blair op cit, p. 98.
32  N. Kinnock *People*, 21 November 1999,
33  T. Blair *Evening Standard*, 19 November 1999.
34  L. Davies *Through the Looking Glass: A dissenter inside New Labour* (London: Verso, 2001), p. 100.
35  R. Watson and T. Baldwin 'Fear and loathing for people's Ken *The Times*, 29 October 1999.
36  This issue is covered in detail in chapter 8 of the first edition of this book – J. Curran, I. Gaber and J. Petley *Culture Wars: The Media and the British Left* (Edinburgh: Edinburgh University Press, 2005).
37  B. Amiel 'Blunkett and Livingstone are planning to run our lives. If we want to keep our dignity, we must fight those who seek to interfere with our property rights, transport system and liberty *Daily Telegraph*, 8 July 2002.
38  S. Sands 'We will forgive our heroes everything except adultery' *Daily Telegraph*, 11 July 2002.
39  S. Sands, 'Livingstone takes his class war to school run mothers' *Daily Telegraph*, 23 January 2003.
40  S. Heffer, 'Treachery that's killing democracy' *Daily Mail*, 22 February 2003.
41  T. Kavanagh, 'Why we need a jam tax revolt' *Sun*, 29 November 2002.
42  R. Littlejohn, Slow, slow, quick, quick, slow *Sun*, 4 March 2003.
43  Using the LexisNexis cuttings database.
44  A. Sparrow, 'Sept 11: 'A good day to bury bad news' *Daily Telegraph*, 10 October 2001.
45  Campbell, op cit.
46  *Evening Standard*, 24 January 2002.
47  *Sun*, 25 January 2002.
48  In his memoirs, *The Point of Departure* (London: Simon & Schuster, 2004), senior cabinet minister Robin Cook wrote: 'Tony [Blair] did not try to argue me out of the view I expressed that Saddam did not have real weapons of mass destruction that were designed for strategic use against city populations and capable of being delivered with reliability over long distances', p. 312.
49  'From the editors; the *Times* and Iraq' *New York Times*, 26 May 2004.
50  'The *Post* on WMDs: An inside story' *Washington Post*, 12 August 2004.
51  Personal conversation with Gaber 2005.
52  J. Naughtie *Rivals: The Intimate Story of a Political Marriage* (London: Fourth Estate, 2002).

53 M. Kite, 'There is nothing that you could say to me now that I could ever believe' *Daily Telegraph*, 10 January 2005.
54 R. Peston *Brown's Britain* (London: Short Books, 2005).
55 *Daily Telegraph*, 1 September 2010.
56 *Daily Mail*, 'A squalid day for democracy', 10 May 2010.
57 *Sun*, 'Squatter holed up in No. 10', 8 May 2010.

# 10

## 'ENEMIES OF THE PEOPLE'

### The press, racism and Labour

*Julian Petley*

### 'Every colour is a good colour'

In its early years, New Labour sought to emphasise that it saw Britain as a diverse, plural yet unified society, and indeed wished to make it more so. But it did this in a way in which aspirational rhetoric generally played a larger role than specific policy formulations. For example, in his speech to the Labour Party conference in 1995 Tony Blair proclaimed:

> Let's build a new and young country that can lay aside the old prejudices that dominated our land for a generation. A nation for all the people, built by the people, where old divisions are cast out. A new spirit in the nation based on working together, unity, solidarity, partnership. One Britain. That is the patriotism of the future. Where never again do we fight our politics by appealing to one section of the nation at the expense of another.[1]

Or, take this characteristic remark by culture secretary Chris Smith just a few months after Labour had come to power in 1997:

> Culture – or perhaps we should talk rather of cultures – has to be seen on the widest possible canvas. Today Britain embraces cultures from all over the world, as it always has, and the diversity of our society and of our experiences is precisely what makes for the richness of our cultural environment … So when we try to understand how our national culture and sense of identity intertwine, let us remember first and foremost that diversity is one of the key ingredients of both that culture and that identity.[2]

Such sentiments also strongly imbued the 'rebranding Britain' project under-taken by the Labour-friendly Demos think tank in in the early days of the new government. The key document of this strategy, *Britain*™, argued that:

> Britain is a hybrid nation – always mixing diverse elements together into something new. Not a melting pot that moulds disparate ethnicities into a conformist whole, but a country that thrives on diversity and uses it to constantly renew and re-energise itself. Britain's royal family mixed together German, Danish and, more recently, Greek ancestry. Our most famous retailer (Marks and Spencer) was founded by Russian Jews. Some of our most successful authors, like Salman Rushdie, are drawn from for-mer colonies. Our contemporary cuisine is a fearless hybrid of elements from other nations. Our popular music began by combining American rhythm and blues with the traditions of the English music hall. But it is not just ethnicities that are mixed – Britain is also the world's capital of ways of living, the home of happily co-existing subcultures – from punks and ravers to freemasons and gentlemen's clubs. Britain is the least pure if European countries, more mongrel and better prepared for a world that is continually generating new hybrid forms.[3]

This stress on specifically *ethnic* diversity distinguishes the Demos document from many of New Labour's own pronouncements on diversity, which, as noted above, tend to be couched in very general terms. Thus, in his speech to the Labour Party conference in 1998, Blair briefly looked forward to 'a country in which every colour is a good colour, and every member of every race able to fulfil their potential' (quoted in the *Independent*, 29 September 1998), and in an interview with the *New Statesman* (19 April 1999), the Chancellor of the Exchequer Gordon Brown stated simply that 'I see Britain as being the first country in the world that can be a multicultural, multi-ethnic and multina-tional state …. We have a chance to forge a unique pluralist democracy where diversity becomes a source of strength'. Similarly, the Home Secretary David Blunkett argued that 'today, with cultural globalisation, no culture can simply be isolated from wider influences. Our society is multicultural, and it is impor-tant that our future social and political development results from a genuine cultural interaction'.[4]

## 'Bizarre issues' and 'peculiar things'

Two interconnected reasons for the Labour leadership's relative restraint on the issue of ethnicity suggest themselves. The first takes us back to Philip Gould, who features prominently elsewhere in this book. In *The Unfinished Revolution*, each time that the issues of ethnicity/minorities/immigration are mentioned, it is in order to sound a warning. Thus, for example, when discussing a presenta-tion given to Labour strategists by an advertising agency in November 1985, he notes that their research findings, which were 'the most important of any presented during the entire period I worked with the Labour Party', laid bare

> the apparent unbridgeable gap between what Labour had become and what the British electorate now wanted … The minority agenda of the emerging metropolitan left, of militant rights in welfare, race and gender was completely divorced from what the British people wanted from a government.[5]

The research showed that the key issues for the voters that Labour wanted to attract 'were those affecting their own personal and financial security: law and order, health, education, inflation, prices and taxation. Defence and the role of minorities within society, two of Labour's big preoccupations, were at the bottom of the list'.[6] He also quotes Stanley Greenberg, who had worked as a pollster for Bill Clinton in 1992 and also advised Blair from the mid-1990s, as stating that, as far as many voters were concerned: 'One of the preoccupations of Old Labour was a preoccupation with what the public often saw as "bizarre" issues: homosexuals, immigrants, feminists, lesbians, boroughs putting their money into peculiar things'.[7]

The second, and very closely related issue, concerns the absolutely ferocious campaign by Conservative politicians and newspapers to tar Labour with the 'loony left' brush during the 1980s, which is discussed elsewhere in this book. Central here were London Labour councils' alleged policies on sexuality and ethnicity, with Brent and Haringey (the former discussed in more detail in the first edition) being the main targets of the press flamethrowers as far as ethnicity was concerned. However, press hostility to minorities, immigration and anti-racist initiatives has a history that stretches back long before the 1980s, and any Labour politician who was remotely media savvy must have been well aware that New Labour would have to do a great deal more than simply distance itself from 'loony' policies on ethnicity if it was to be spared yet more onslaughts by the press. In this it singularly failed.

## Press racism

It is extremely important to stress this particular aspect of press history in order to emphasise the very considerable hurdle facing any political party which wishes to pursue policies which run counter to the racist ideology propagated daily by significant sections of the national press, an ideology which has in fact considerably intensified since Labour came to power in 1997. But this is a particular problem for Labour, which has routinely faced implacable hostility from the majority of the national press, which, as will become ever clearer as this chapter progresses, regards the party as fundamentally anti-British (and particularly anti-English) to the point of treachery, and thus as congenitally unfit to govern.

In much of Britain's national (and increasingly nationalist) press, people of colour are habitually represented as constituting a potential threat to British society, which is conceptualised as essentially white. Recent immigrants are viewed as particularly problematic, and in their case hostility frequently extends to white people as well (apart, that is, to those coming from Australia, Canada, New Zealand and other parts of the erstwhile Empire, who are regarded, however erroneously, as 'kith and kin' as opposed to 'economic migrants' and 'bogus asylum seekers'). Numbers are seen as a problem *per se* ('swamping', in Mrs. Thatcher's phrase), and the attitudes and behaviour of immigrants, whether recent or not, are seen as posing a potential threat to law and order, cultural cohesion and indeed the 'national stock'. There is now quite a substantial literature on press racism,[8] and one of the best summaries of its components is provided by Teun van Dijk, who states that:

> The very topics of news on ethnic affairs convey an overall impression that associates minorities or immigrants with problems, conflicts, deviance, or even threats. Crime, violence, drugs, and riots are usually among the most frequently covered topics on ethnic minorities, especially but not exclusively in the right-wing and popular press. Immigration is also often covered, but news reports on that issue focus on problems, large numbers, immigration rackets or 'economic' refugees who are seen as coming to live off our pockets. Cultural differences are enhanced and are often negatively interpreted as the cause of numerous social problems associated with a multicultural society ... All topics that imply a critique of the white dominant group in general, or of the authorities or other elites in particular, are seldom covered. Racism, failing legislation against discrimination, the refusal to enact Affirmative Action, the real causes of high unemployment among minority groups or the schools' lack of success in providing minority children with motivation and a good education, are among the topics that tend to be avoided.[9]

As far as the British press is concerned, this remains as accurate as when it was written, although it should be added that racism directed at people of colour has since been supplemented by a more general xenophobia and an intense hostility directed specifically at Muslims – often referred to as Islamophobia but in fact an expression of anti-Muslim racism. What also needs to be stressed is that a key component of this kind of racist discourse is the contention that British society is not itself racist – indeed compared to many other western countries it is represented as remarkably tolerant of racial differences within its midst – and that when racial tensions do arise, they are the result of agitation by sections of the non-white population and their white allies in what it is absolutely *de rigueur* in certain right-wing circles to label the 'race relations industry' and, more generally, the 'liberal establishment'. Such agitation breeds resentment in the white population, it is argued, and this provides a fertile ground in which the seeds of racism grow and flourish. Thus, racism in the 'host culture' is exonerated and explained away.

As Martin Barker noted at the time, in the late 1970s and early 1980s the notion of racial prejudice was in the process of being radically redefined by the right: 'Here it has nothing to do with disliking foreigners, or with discriminating against them. You are racially prejudiced if you refuse to adopt the characteristic life style of the country in which you have chosen to live'. Racism is thus reinterpreted as a threat *by* 'immigrants' to the 'British way of life'. A key ingredient of this way of life, so the thinking goes, is tolerance, easy-goingness and an ability to muck in together. 'Immigrants', with their demands for 'special rules' (like Sikhs not wearing crash helmets) and their complaints about such taken-for-granted toys as golliwogs and Little Black Sambo are thus 'abusing our hospitality' and generally 'rocking the boat'.[10] As Michael Billig et al. have pointed out, such complaints are key components of a deeply, if largely unconscious, nationalist ideology: 'The rules are "our" rules. This is "our" country and, if "they" want to come here, "they" must abide by "our" rules, which constrain "us". If "they" obtain special privileges, then "they" will be receiving unequal treatment'.[11] This whole 'commonsensical' edifice is, of course, founded on the notion that the 'British way of life' is self-evidently tolerant, unprejudiced and reasonable; thus, anybody who questions or criticises it is, by definition, intolerant, prejudiced and unreasonable.

## A lesson from history

However, racist attitudes in the UK long predate immigration by people of colour, and have been routinely expressed by sections of the press long before the birth of the 'race relations industry, the 'loony left' and New Labour. It is extremely important to understand this, as so much of the right-wing hostility to all three is predicated on the entirely erroneous assertion that Britain was largely free of racism until the actions of anti-racist 'agitators' in the second half of the twentieth century provoked resentment in the white population against people of colour.

The early targets of racism in Britain were not people of colour, but Jews fleeing first from pogroms in Eastern Europe in the nineteenth and early twentieth centuries, and then the Third Reich.[12] To take but two of many possible examples of articles critical of the first cohort of refugees, an editorial from the *East London Advertiser* (6 May 1899) argued, like so many articles about Muslims in today's papers, that members of certain groups either cannot or will not assimilate to the 'host nation':

> People of any other nation, after being in England for a short time, assimilate themselves with the native race and by and by lose nearly all their foreign trace. But the Jews never do. A Jew is always a Jew. No doubt this is due to their desire for the formation of a new Hebrew nation, a fact which inclines them to look upon themselves as pilgrims in a strange land.

Meanwhile the *Mail* (3 February 1900), in an article headed 'So-called refugees', deployed a veritable battery of anti-Semitic clichés, and prefigured much modern 'reporting' by casting doubt on the refugees' status; it also draws an all-too-familiar distinction between deserving (English) and undeserving (Jewish) refugees:

> There landed yesterday at Southampton from the transport Cheshire over 600 so-called refugees, their passages having been paid out of the Lord Mayor's Fund … There was scarce a hundred of them that had, by right, deserved such help, and these were the Englishmen of the party. The rest were Jews… They fought and jostled for the foremost places at the gang-ways … When the Relief Committee passed by they hid their gold and fawned and whined, and, in broken English, asked for money for their train fare.

Moving on to the influx of Jewish refugees in the 1930s, we find prefigured another present-day obsession, namely numbers. Here it's extremely important to provide a degree of historical and political context.

By the end of 1938, the year of both the *Anschluss* and *Kristallnacht*, the number of Jews fleeing Germany and Austria was growing rapidly, and although the British government liberalised its immigration policy to some extent after the latter, it actually tightened entry requirements for Austrian Jews in the wake of the former.[13] The most famous example of mercy shown towards refugees – the *Kindertransport* – was not a government initiative at all, but one proposed by a loose grouping of Jewish and Quaker organisations, in particular the British Committee for the Jews of Germany and the Movement for the Care of Children from Germany. As a result of their pressure, the British government agreed to allow unaccompanied refugee children, up to the age of seventeen, to enter the country on temporary travel visas, on the understanding that, when conditions permitted, the children would return to their families. The bodies which had originated the scheme promised to fund the entire operation, find homes for all the children and ensure that none of them would become a financial 'burden' on the public purse. In 1940, the British government ordered the internment of all male sixteen- to seventy-year-old refugees from enemy countries, and those refugee children who had reached the age of sixteen were rounded up and placed camps, whilst around 400 were transported overseas to Canada and Australia.[14] Many of those who sailed to the former died when the Arandora Star was torpedoed, and those headed to the latter on the Dunera were treated so abominably that they were later awarded compensation by the British government.[15]

As the numbers of Jewish refugees began to grow in 1938, so did the increasingly shrill demands for tighter immigration controls in sections of the press (and indeed of the population), which goes a considerable way to explaining why the government was loathe to take a more humanitarian stance. So, for example, the *Mail* (23 March 1938) argued that 'once it was known that Britain offered sanctuary to all who cared to come, the floodgates would be opened, and we should be inundated by thousands seeking a home', whilst the *Express* (24 March 1938) ran the argument that immigration breeds racism (as opposed to racism breeding hostility to immigrants), which we will be discussed below:

> There is powerful agitation here to admit all Jewish refugees without question or discrimination. It would be unwise to overload the basket like that. It would stir up the elements here that fatten on anti-Semitic propaganda ... Because we DON'T want anti-Jewish uproar we DO need to show common sense in not admitting all applicants.

That there was indeed an anti-immigration campaign being waged by sections of the press is confirmed by an article in the *Mail* (20 August 1938), which stated:

> 'The way stateless Jews from Germany are pouring in from every port of this country is becoming an outrage'. In these words, Mr Herbert Metcalfe, the Old Street magistrate, yesterday referred to the number of aliens entering the country through the 'back door' – a problem to which the *Daily Mail* has repeatedly pointed.[16]

The story of the 1930s Jewish refugees, and especially of the *Kindertransport*, is an extremely important one in the present context for two reasons. First, it shows that there is nothing new about the racism expressed by sections of the press nor about government sensitivity to it. That this undoubtedly reflected concerns in sections of the population as a whole brings us on to the second point – namely, the existence of racism in British society. This gives the lie to the endlessly repeated claims by politicians and most of the press that Britain is an open society which is tolerant of ethnic differences and has always welcomed those in need of refuge and succour – that is, as long as they're prepared to abide by the 'British way of life' and adopt 'British values'. In this narrative, the *Kindertransport* has come to play an ever more important role[17]. But perhaps one of the most significant aspects of most present day press articles on the subject is that they remain entirely silent on the reasons *why* these poor wretched children arrived on their own, separated by government policy from their parents, the majority of whom would perish in the Holocaust. As Louise London has observed:

> We remember the touching photographs and newsreel footage of unaccompanied Jewish children arriving on the Kindertransports. There are no such photographs of the Jewish parents left behind in Nazi Europe, and their fate has made a minimal impact ... The Jews excluded from entry to the United Kingdom are not part of the British experience because Britain never saw them.[18]

London recalls watching the then Home Office immigration minister Barbara Roche on television in 2000 defending the UK's latest round of harsh policies towards asylum seekers and hearing her intone the usual mantra that 'this country has a proud tradition of taking in refugees over many centuries', which caused her to wonder

> what adjective Roche would propose, then, to describe Britain's history of *not* taking in refugees: would that be proud too? Or would it be the opposite? Shamefaced? Hidden? Denied? Suppressed? Because, even if it isn't proud, even if it doesn't fit the political message, this country also has a history of not taking in refugees. It is not true that whatever Britain may do to hamper asylum seekers, it will always take in the genuine refugee. This is a myth. And one of the cornerstones of the myth is the remarkably persistent claim that this country did all it could to aid Jews trying to escape Nazi persecution.[19]

Hence the ever-lengthening list of legislation designed specifically to keep as many immigrants as possible, of all kinds, out of the country: for example, the Commonwealth Immigrants Act 1962, the Commonwealth Immigrants Act 1968, the Immigration Act 1971, the Immigration Act 1988, the Asylum and Immigration Appeals Act 1993, the Asylum and Immigration Act 1996, the Immigration and Asylum Act 1999, the Nationality, Immigration and Asylum Act 2002, and the Immigration, Asylum and Nationality Act 2006. These were passed by Labour and Conservative governments alike and vociferously supported by significant sections of the press. Absolutely invariably their enactment was accompanied by politicians and journalists hymning the UK's 'proud tradition' of taking in refugees and asylum seekers.

In the rest of this chapter, I want to show in some detail how the ideological forces outlined above were brought into play against three initiatives concerning racism, the first by 'loony left' councils in the 1980s, the second by the newly elected Labour government in 1997 and the third by Commission on the Future of Multi-Ethnic Britain at the turn of the millennium.

## Anti-anti-racism

During the 1980s, Conservative politicians and newspapers routinely argued that black unrest was stirred up by 'agitation', rather than fuelled by justified grievances. Such a position was anchored in the premise that racism was not systemic in the UK, and came into being only when white people were antagonised by the behaviour of people of colour. Crucial here were organisations such as the Centre for Policy Studies, the Social Affairs Unit, the Hillgate Group, the Conservative Philosophy Group and the Salisbury Group, whose ideas were routinely pedalled in the press in more populist terms by pundits such as Ronald Butt, Peregrine Worsthorne, Paul Johnson, George Gale, John Vincent, Andrew Alexander, Ray Mills and Roger Scruton.[20] Chief amongst the sources of this alleged 'agitation' was the 'race relations industry', and, in particular, the philosophy of anti-racism.

What emerged from their writings, as Paul Gordon has argued, was 'not just a campaign against anti-racism, but a campaign which used as its means a fertile mixture of intellectual dishonesty, fabrication, smear, innuendo, half-truth and selection'.[21] Indeed, at its most extreme, anti-anti-racism did not simply imply that racism did not matter, but, rather, that it did not actually exist. And in more directly political terms, the attractions of anti-anti-racism for the political right are not exactly hard to fathom. As David Edgar has put it:

> Anti-anti-racism provides a means to transfer responsibility for the most visible and threatening sector of the young unemployed (and thereby responsibility for the problems, including civil unrest, connected in the public mind with that unemployment) away from the state and toward the black community itself, aided and abetted by the sinister forces manipulating it.[22]
>
> *(1988: 133)*

By the early eighties, anti-racist initiatives had come to occupy a significant place on the left's political agenda, particularly at the local level, not least as a result of urban unrest in black communities such as Tottenham, Brixton, Bristol and Handsworth, and such initiatives were regularly lambasted as 'loony' by right-wing papers and politicians, as noted in the chapter in this book on urban myths, and also the chapter on Brent in the previous edition. However, alarm bells had long been ringing on the right at any sign of anti-racist activity in black and Asian communities. Thus, in his famous 'Rivers of Blood' speech of 20 April 1968, Enoch Powell had specifically targeted those 'immigrants' and their sympathisers who, as he saw it, were determined to 'agitate and campaign against their fellow citizens, to overawe and dominate the rest with legal weapons which the ignorant and ill-informed have provided'.[23] For the right, then, the urban unrest proved conclusively that Powell had been entirely correct; in their view, what was needed, above all, was law, order, discipline and, if necessary, *force majeure*. Anti-racist measures were, for the right, part of the problem, not part of the solution, as they were seen by social conservatives as a form of left-wing propaganda, both un- and anti-British, fostering divisions along racial lines. Meanwhile, for economic liberals they were a waste of public money and an interference with both individual and corporate freedoms.

Thus, for example, after the Brixton events of 1981, the *Express* (20 April) argued that race relations law was giving black people 'special status' and so 'dividing the two communities, instead of uniting them', whilst in *The Times* (10 July 1981) Ronald Butt complained that young blacks 'are *instructed* that they are discriminated against, oppressed and denied work by a racialist society, and are misused and persecuted by the police'. A *Telegraph* editorial (8 January 1982) attacked a Commission for Racial Equality (CRE) code of practice on equal opportunities as 'bossy nonsense' and the *Mail* (30 July 1982) denounced it as an 'agent for discord'. Similarly, on 24 October 1983, Andrew Alexander in the *Mail* dubbed the CRE 'the equivalent of the Holy Inquisition', and the *Express*

(16 May 1984) referred to the 'thought police of the Commission for Racial Equality'. In the wake of the Broadwater Farm disturbances in 1985, Ronald Butt in *The Times* (17 October 1985) claimed that race had become a weapon in a 'new class war' in which 'class warriors' manipulated blacks, seeing in them a class politics which had otherwise disappeared from Britain. Meanwhile the *Mail* (8 October 1985) linked the unrest with a video on policing produced by the GLC and a cartoon book on racism produced by the CRE as 'evidence of the torrent of lies and twisted truths that is indoctrinating our society today'.

Hardly surprisingly, then, the anti-racist policies of the GLC, the Inner London Education Authority (ILEA) and the Labour London boroughs reduced the anti-anti-racists of the right-wing press to a state of apoplexy. Thus, when in 1983 ILEA set out its anti-racist policy for London schools, which merely stressed its commitment to equality for all pupils and called for the removal of all forms of discrimination in schools, the *Mail* (30 September) called this 'reverse discrimination' and the *Express* (2 October) 'school apartheid' and 'racist, patronising, divisive'. The offensive was significantly stepped up when the GLC named 1984–5 as Anti-Racist Year; this was also the moment when certain Labour boroughs decided to make anti-racism a political priority. At the Conservative Party conference in 1985, the Party chairman Norman Tebbit attacked 'the divisive racism preached by the black power merchants of the extreme left' which he described as 'as objectionable and destructive as that preached by the white racists of the National Front'.[24]

By the time of the events dealt with in the rest of this chapter, then, the notion that anti-racism is itself a form of racism had become firmly established on the right. A good example of this form of thinking is offered by the *Mail* (3 May 1984) in an editorial which declared that: 'Nowadays racial strife is less likely to be caused by ordinary folk [sic] than by the professionals of the race relations industry who in effect go round looking for ways of stirring it up'. Roger Scruton helped to give such ideas an 'intellectual' gloss, arguing in *The Times* (30 October 1984) that it was the anti-racists who are 'the real racists'. In similar vein, in the *Sunday Telegraph* (30 June 1985) Peregrine Worsthorne stated that: 'Much more effective than the National Front in stirring up racial hatred today are those ostensibly dedicated to anti-racism'. Likewise Paul Johnson, in the *Mail* (17 June 1985) compared the 'primary racism ... preached by the brutish bigots of the National Front' with the 'secondary racism' of the 'race relations fanatics'. For Johnson, the latter were the 'more insidious phenomenon'. He continued: 'I can think of nothing more likely to stir up race trouble in Britain than the activities of these secondary racists .... The National Front and the race relations doctrinaires are in unconscious alliance'. Another doughty fighter in this particular cause was Roy Kerridge, who argued in the *Mail* (15 October 1984) that those who argued that black children should be fostered by black people were demanding a form of apartheid and claimed that:

The new guerrilla fighters are ... the black equivalent of those Trotskyites who falsely claim to represent the working man ... Anti-Racist year, an encouragement to those whose interests lie in a racial power structure, seems to have set the seal of officialdom on a black movement that is essentially no different from the National Front.

The publication of the Swann report, *Education for All*, in 1985, provided the anti-anti-racists with yet another field day. In March 1979 Labour education secretary Shirley Williams had established the Committee of Inquiry into the Education of Children from Ethnic Minority Groups. This was a result of the Commons Select Committee on Race Relations and Immigration highlighting in 1977 widespread concerns about the poor performance of West Indian children in schools. Under the chairmanship of Anthony Rampton, the committee published its interim report *West Indian Children in Our Schools* in 1981. This concluded that the main problems were low teacher expectations and racial prejudice among white teachers and society as a whole. Inevitably, the press rubbished the report even before it was published, and Mark Carlisle, then education secretary under the Tories, sacked Rampton and appointed Lord Michael Swann in his place. His report,[25] which argued, *inter alia*, that poor performance by minority ethnic children in schools was partly the result of racial prejudice and discrimination in the wider society, that multicultural understanding must permeate all aspects of a school's work and that all schools should adopt clear policies to combat racism, was largely ignored by the government, but it did underpin many of the educational policies pursued by the councils stigmatised as 'loony' by the press, such as those contained in Brent's *Two Kingdoms* initiative as outlined in the first edition of this book. Even before it was published, Swann's report was met by sections of the press with as much hostility as the interim one, thanks to judicious leaks. The free market guru Alfred Sherman prophesised in the *Telegraph* (19 January 1985) that the report would recommend 'a procrustean pidgin culture to be imposed on majority and minorities alike', a recipe for 'cultural genocide' which 'in effect outlawed the concept of the English nation'. Meanwhile, Mary Kenny in the *Mail* (13 September 1984), under the headline 'Race madness', warned that its proposals would turn 'mild British people into resentful misanthropes … as they see everything native to their own tradition scuttled', a sentiment which was echoed by the *Telegraph* (14 March 1985) which argued that the report would 'lead only to great racial bitterness among the white population'. On 22 November 1984, the same paper had also run a piece by regular columnist Honor Tracy, who asserted that 'our own new role will be that of native freedom fighters. We are not merely the people of the land, but trustees for those who come after us'.[26]

The real hero, or rather, martyr, of the anti-anti-racists was, and indeed continues to be, Ray Honeyford, the Bradford headmaster who, amidst howls of outrage from the right-wing press, was forced to resign after publishing articles highly critical of multicultural education in the *Times Educational Supplement* and the ultra-right-wing journal *The Salisbury Review*, then edited by Roger Scruton, thereby alienating both his local education authority and many parents of children at his school. The *Mail* (30 October 1984) gave him a considerable amount of uncontested space to denounce multicultural education as 'the most dangerous force in Britain today', whilst the same paper (3 April 1985) alleged that the campaign against Honeyford was the work of extremists who 'prate of the evils of racism' but themselves 'personify fascism'. Absolutely nothing has changed since these words were written. For example, on 5 July 2014, the *Telegraph*, always one of Honeyford's most fervent admirers, published an article by Scruton headed 'Let's face it – Ray Honeyford got it right on Islam and education', in which he argued that:

> The anti-white and anti-British pronouncements of the people who were trying to undermine his attempts to provide an equal education to all the children in his school were, to his mind, far more evidently racist than any feature of the curriculum that he was striving to impart.

Foremost amongst these people, absolutely inevitably, were the Commission for Racial Equality, 'a quango run by the leftist militants of the day'.

## Institutional racism

In July 1997, the new Labour home secretary Jack Straw announced an inquiry into matters arising from the murder of Stephen Lawrence. This had been refused point blank by the Tories. The inquiry report, which was published in February 1999, found that the investigation was marked by a 'combination of professional incompetence, institutional racism and a failure of leadership by professional officers'.[27] Indeed, it argued that all major organisations in British society, and not simply the police, were characterised by institutional racism, which it defined as:

> The collective failure of an organisation to provide appropriate and professional services to people because of their colour, culture or ethnic origin. It can be seen or detected in processes, attitudes and behaviour which amount to discrimination through unwitting prejudice, ignorance, thoughtlessness and racist stereotyping which disadvantage minority ethnic people.[28]

Speaking in the House of Commons, 24 February 1999, Straw welcomed the report, and stated that:

> The Macpherson inquiry has demonstrated the failings of one very important public institution, the police service. The police do have a special responsibility in our society because day by day they are the immediate guardians of fairness and justice. But we would all be deluding ourselves if we believe that the issues thrown up by this inquiry reflect only on the police. Indeed the implications of this report go much, much wider and the

very process of the inquiry has opened all our eyes to what it is like to be black or Asian in Britain today. And the inquiry process has revealed some fundamental truths about the nature of our society, about our relationships one with another. Some of these truths are uncomfortable but we have to confront them.

So I want this report to serve as a watershed in our attitudes to racism. I want it to act as a catalyst to permanent and irrevocable change, not just across our public services, but across the whole of our society. This report does not place a responsibility on someone else. It places a responsibility on each one of us.

We have to make racial equality a reality. The vision, I believe is clear, to create a society where every individual, regardless of colour, of creed, or race, has the same opportunities and respect as his or her neighbour. On race equality let us make Britain a beacon to the world.[29]

The concept of institutional racism was originally coined by Black Power activists Stokely Carmichael and Charles V. Hamilton in their 1967 book *Black Power: The Politics of Liberation*, and subsequently embraced in Britain by the Institute of Race Relations. As Gary Younge pointed out at the time,[30] the importance of Macpherson's invocation of the notion of institutional racism was that:

It charted a path from the crudest forms of racism to the most well-concealed; from Stephen's violent death to the Metropolitan Police's wilful negligence; from the failure of the Met to recruit ethnic minorities to the need for greater racial and cultural awareness in the national curriculum. In short, it exposed the way in which racism affects all areas of black people's lives. It shifted the focus of debate from individual prejudice to institutional discrimination; to include not just obvious racism but the obtuse as well. It showed that racism does not have one face but both many faces and no face at all.

In Younge's view, it also helped to correct 'the very unsophisticated concept of race and discrimination under which most of Britain still labours', which consisted largely of the idea of yobs being unpleasant to black people and overt colour bars in the housing market[31]. Younge also argued that the report marked

a seminal moment in British race relations. This was no longer a debate about how to contain the problems that black people cause by their very presence. This was white people talking to other white people about the problems engendered by their racism. This very fact alone shifted the burden of responsibility off the weary shoulders of those within the black community who are wheeled out after a disturbance and asked to account for and explain the behaviour and grievances of their peers. Instead, white people had to explain themselves to each other.[32]

In his view, 'the report represented a significant shift away from the question: "What are we going to do about these blacks?"' and towards: '"What are we going to do about the racism in our institutions?"'. However, although it 'advanced the debate about race in Britain; nudging it from talk of muggers and immigrants to issues of disadvantage and affirmative action',[33] very little actually happened as a result, at least in the short term. Given the absolutely ferocious press response to the report's findings on institutional racism, this is not altogether surprising.

## 'A flawed and dangerous concept'

That the report was going to find the Metropolitan Police guilty of 'institutional racism' was widely predicted by papers across the political spectrum in the weeks prior to its publication, and certain ones were keen to set the anti-institutional racism hare running as soon as possible. Thus, the *Telegraph* (8 February) opined that a more serious problem for the police was

> the growing culture of paperwork and political correctness. This condition, unlike racism, really is 'institutional' ... The number of people who have actually experienced police racism is almost certainly smaller than the number who have suffered from crimes while local policemen were attending racism awareness courses.

On 16 February, in an 'Exclusive' headlined 'Judge accuses "racist" police', with the strap 'Lawrence inquiry chairman points the finger of blame for discrimination at Britain's entire police force', the *Mail* laid down a set of tramlines along which numerous subsequent reports would run, reporting that 'senior officers fear Leftwing agitators will make political capital out of it, which in turn could deter some officers from tackling black crime'.

Straw had intended to make a speech to Parliament about the report on the day of its publication, during which he would announce a number of police reforms drawn from the report's seventy recommendations. But on 21 February the *Sunday Telegraph* published leaked extracts from the penultimate draft of the report (Version 7). The leaks were published on the front page under the headline 'Condon must admit Met racism or face sack', and inside there were two more articles, and a comment piece which argued that institutional racism 'is an ominous phrase, one that automatically damns everyone in the "institution", irrespective of their individual attitude' (that it does no such thing didn't stop other papers taking precisely the same line, as we shall see) and that it was 'a flawed and dangerous concept'. This well and truly set the press agenda. Straw injuncted the paper, but, following a media furore, backed down and allowed other papers to reprint what had already been published. A mole hunt in the Home Office was swiftly commenced, but drew a blank. Another possibility, however, is that Scotland Yard officers had stolen the penultimate draft, either by bugging or burglary, and had shown this to the *Sunday Telegraph*'s political editor, Tom Baldwin.[34]

The question inevitably arises: *cui bono*? Liberal papers' stress on the issue of institutional racism was almost certainly related to the Home Office's determination to force Sir Paul Condon, the Metropolitan Police Commissioner, to accept publicly that the force was institutionally racist, something which he had repeatedly refused to do, in spite of it being made abundantly clear that his job depended on it. But for right-wing papers, it very usefully distracted attention from the report's revelations of appalling police incompetence and failure, and provided an opportunity to attack 'political correctness' and Labour policies. As Brian Cathcart argued, the Conservative press

> was of one mind: the report was flawed and unbalanced and the idea that all police officers or all white British people were racist was wrong and unjust. Many critics portrayed it as an exercise in political correctness which would make it impossible for the police to uphold the law where black people were concerned.[35]

Arun Kundnani, in a seminal piece focussed on the themes which are central to this chapter – press hatred of liberal values (albeit at this time still dressed up as an attack on 'political correctness'), New Labour represented as unpatriotic to the point of treachery, and an absolute refusal to countenance the idea of racism as systemic in British society – argued:

> The Macpherson report was represented in much of the press as an attack on Englishness and as a capitulation by a cosmopolitan anti-English ruling elite to the foreign concept of political correctness. For a few weeks, newspaper readers bore witness to this staged skirmish between a top-down, liberal anti-racism represented by Macpherson and the common-sense tolerance and moderation of the ordinary Englishman, for whom the papers claimed to speak.[36]

He concluded that 'with the political parties of the Right having lost their way, a newspaper-led English nationalism, which recognises the anxieties of economic globalisation and offers cultural protectionism in response, has become the main opposition to Blair's government'.[37] And as Gary Younge put it, 'the consequent debate revealed just how little had changed, and intimated how grudging even that change had been, among certain vocal and powerful sections of the white community'.[38]

## 'Political correctness gone mad'

Let us now examine the hostile press reaction to the report, focussing in particular on how it was used to attack New Labour and deny the existence of systemic racism in the UK. The *Telegraph* (23 February) claimed that 'the idea of institutional racism makes policing unworkable' and rejected it as unprovable.

Peter Hitchens in the *Express* (23 February) stated that the idea of institutional racism was 'a wild over-reaction' and raised fears of a 'politically correct purge'. Such papers vociferously argued that the real problem with British society was not racism, but the political correctness infecting the liberal establishment. The *Mail* (24 February 1999) warned of 'an hysterical witch-hunt that will damage the cause of race relations' and of the Lawrence's cause being 'overtaken by a kind of politically correct McCarthyism'. In its view, the words 'institutional racism' could 'hardly be more chilling' and 'they must damn every member of the Force, irrespective of personal beliefs and behaviour. It is precisely the kind of prejudiced blanket condemnation in which genuine racists like to indulge'. It continues: 'If the police are institutionally racist, must not the same be true of the Home Office, which controls the Force? And of the Government, which controls the Home Office? And indeed of the British people, who elect the Government? The logic of Sir William's assessment is that the whole country is institutionally racist'. It condemns such a view as 'political correctness gone mad' and 'rampant political correctness', and accuses the 'race relations lobby' (personified here by Sir Herman Ouseley of the hated Commission for Racial Equality) of trying 'to find a grievance – real or imagined – and exploit it for all it's worth'. It worries that 'there is the very real danger that the burgeoning race relations industry will now be encouraged to exert even more influence over every area of British life'. In the same issue, Lynda Lee Potter calls institutional racism 'an inept, woolly and dangerous phrase which everyone ought to stop using'.[39]

In the *Mail*, 26 February, Stephen Glover, in an article headed 'As the Prime Minister damns the entire nation', argued that 'following the publication of the Stephen Lawrence report, Tony Blair and Jack Straw have effectively said that white Britons are a nation of racists', and condemned what he called 'this post-Macpherson hysterical climate'. He also stated that the government's reaction to the report and some of its conclusions 'verge on the lunatic', and noted that 'as a retired High Court judge, Sir William has not officially signed up to New Labour. But several of his recommendations have that smack of authoritarianism and obsession with control that we associate with this Government.' In his view, many of Macpherson's proposals

> would enhance the power of the State and the police, and cause bitter resentment. Some will also take issue with the cradle to grave indoctrination envisaged by Sir William. 'If racism is to be eradicated,' he writes in a particularly preposterous passage, 'there must be specific and co-ordinated action, both with the agencies themselves and by society at large, particularly through the educational system, from pre-primary school upwards and onwards.' This is the language of Soviet Russia, not a fuddy-duddy retired High Court judge.

In an editorial published on 25 February and headed 'A misguided and unfair report', the paper invoked the spectre of the 'loony left' by arguing that

Macpherson's analysis represented 'the wild dreams of the left, kept down, just, in the 1980s, and now reaching for power'. Similarly, Leo McKinstry in the *Sunday Telegraph* (28 February), under the heading 'Final triumph for town hall political correctness', warned that Macpherson had given a 'sub-marxist analysis of the institutions of contemporary ... Britain like a lecturer in sociology from the sixties' in a report written in the language of 'the inner-city council chamber'. Similarly, in the *Mail on Sunday* (28 February), Stewart Steven expressed his disgust at the fact that in America 'half-baked so-called academics in so-called disciplines like sociology have produced definition after definition [of racism] owing a good deal to Marxist theory and very little to real people's lives' and complained that the Macpherson report had 'produced a definition of institutional racism which has flown to us from across the Atlantic and the wilder fringes of the race industry there'.

In *The Sunday Times* (28 February), Melanie Phillips pursued the anti-anti-racist line, complaining that attempts

> to purify thought are as sinister as they are useless. White people are subjected to managerial McCarthyism; the real needs of black people, meanwhile, are trampled down in the stampede to claim moral virtue. We've seen all this played out hideously in 'anti-racist' social work and probation .... Similarly, he recommends anti-racist and multicultural education in schools. But we've had all that since the 1980s. Teachers have been censoring 'offensive' fiction; they won't teach British political history on the grounds that it is 'colonialist' and 'racist'; we've even had multicultural maths. The result has been that white children have been abandoned to an ignorance which breeds prejudice, while black children have been effectively excluded from mainstream culture.

In her view, 'anti-racist activists aren't interested in preventing such tragedies by tackling the real roots of white bigotry. They want instead to prove white society is endemically racist so they can build their empires and wield power over others. The poor Lawrences, who only want justice for their murdered son, have been used'. Macpherson had played the role of 'useful idiot' and 'the age of political correctness has officially arrived'. In the *Mail* (5 March), Andrew Alexander worried that 'beneath the benign face of do-gooders may lurk sinister totalitarian instincts of the sort normally associated with Stalin and Hitler'.

## 'Something terrible is happening'

In the *Sun* (23 February), Richard Littlejohn presented the report as evidence of a new establishment which despised England and hated all its institutions. And in the *Sun* (2 March 1999) he asked whether Tony Blair's attacks on racism in Britain meant that Tony Blair had 'become our first black Prime Minister'. In Littlejohn's view, for all Blair's talk of 'the people', he actually 'loathes the English

... It has become clear that Blair's mission is to eradicate, denigrate or undermine every quintessentially English institution from the Metropolitan Police downwards'. Responding to this press onslaught Polly Toynbee published an article in the *Guardian* (3 March) article headed 'The white backlash: Macpherson is now a rallying cry for a vision of nation and race that is vile'. In it she argues:

> If you want a perfect model of institutional racism, buy the *Telegraph* for a whiff of Britain's conservative establishment. In its leaders and columns the racism is witting and unremitting, proud and disgraceful. It revels in it, rolls in it, abominating politically correct non-racists. Its letters page is the noticeboard for racists .... No, this is not institutional racism – Macpherson describes that as 'unwitting' – this is just plain old-fashioned racism.

Littlejohn renewed his attack in the *Sun* (5 March) in a piece headed 'Enemies of the people', asserting that 'Toynbee represents an entire class of people who run this country from day to day', who have 'a hatred of all British institutions, especially the police', and are 'ashamed of [their] own nationality'. Similarly, in the *Sunday Telegraph* (7 March), Minette Marrin called Toynbee 'extremely well-connected and influential in Centre and Left of Centre circles and is, generally speaking, a powerful Establishment figure'. In her view, 'Toynbee's attitude is typical of the views of a large class of important and influential people in this country. It is typical of the instinctive response of the new Establishment' who seem 'positively to enjoy despising the police, and British institutions generally' and have a dismissive attitude to their own British heritage. She complains that 'something terrible is happening to public debate if such a person can make such serious public denunciations without any evidence' (which is demonstrably not the case) and attributes this to a climate encouraged by the report in which 'something is now racist if someone thinks it is'.

The Macpherson report had clearly touched a very raw nerve in right-wing circles, and particularly in the press. But beneath the rhetoric about 'political correctness gone mad' and the customary attacks on anti-racism, there is clearly something else that is being expressed here, albeit somewhat inchoately, namely that the Labour government is quite simply illegitimate and not fit to be in power. This, of course, is the other side of the coin to the deeply held conviction that the Conservatives are not only the natural but the rightful party of government. What we hear in the pages of these newspapers are the outraged roars of those who feel that they have been politically dispossessed, and that the politicians to whom they have traditionally paid allegiance have been ousted by an interloper, and an illegitimate one at that. This is revenge for the aspirations set out at the start of this chapter, encapsulated in the term 'Cool Britannia', which was not coined by New Labour but was routinely employed by the right-wing press in order to denigrate its cultural policies. For these people, the sight of Noel Gallagher drinking champagne with Tony Blair at No. 10

seems to have been utterly traumatic, and to have epitomised an out-of-joint state of affairs which gave rise to a rancid sense of grievance and boiling resentment which found its first major expression in press reaction to the Macpherson report. But much more, and much worse, was to come, as outlined in the following sections.

What effect the press onslaught actually had on the government and ensuing policy is hard to judge. Alastair Campbell's diaries record that at this moment Blair was 'losing his nerve a bit', 'feeling a bit scarred',[40] was worried that 'the whole thing would be used as a stick to beat all the police',[41] 'that we would lose the support of the police if we weren't careful'[42] and that the report 'should not lead to an over-the-top mass of new laws and procedures'. He also felt that the government was 'veering towards the politically correct',[43] which certainly suggests an affinity with some of the ideas expressed by the press.

To begin with, Straw agreed to Macpherson's recommendation that the provisions of the Race Relations Act 1976, which covers direct (overt) discrimination as well as indirect (institutional) discrimination, should be extended to the police, who had hitherto been exempted. But in the Queen's speech in November it was announced that the Act would be amended to extend it to the police and other public bodies only in relation to direct discrimination. This was reversed after an outcry. Under the amended Act:

- Racial discrimination is 'unacceptable' and is outlawed in all public authorities, and in those functions of public authorities run by the private sector.
- Public bodies have a general duty to promote race equality – they have no discretion to decide 'whether the promotion of race equality is an "appropriate activity"'.
- They must promote equality of opportunity and 'good relations' between people of different racial groups.
- The general duty to promote race equality is a 'positive one' requiring public authorities to be pro-active in seeking to avoid unlawful discrimination before it occurs.[44]

This was a relatively modest response to Macpherson's seventy recommendations, although, in subsequent years, sixty-seven of these led to various specific changes in practice or the law.[45] But it can also be argued that the negative and destructive press campaign against the report meant that, even if it did manage to bring the notion of institutional racism into public debate, it failed to open up the issue of systemic and endemic racism as fully as it had intended to do. Furthermore, it should be noted that, not long after it had welcomed the Macpherson report, Labour introduced what would become the Nationality, Immigration and Asylum Act 2002, which its critics regarded as representing institutional racism writ large. This followed on from the 2002 white paper *Secure Borders, Safe Havens: Integration with Diversity in Modern Britain* (in which there was considerably more stress on integration than diversity), and amended existing nationality legislation, already highly restrictive, by:

- Extending the power to detain asylum seekers;
- Creating a 'white list' of safe countries, whose citizens who have their asylum applications rejected cannot remain in the UK while they mount an appeal;
- Establishing accommodation (i.e. detention) centres to house asylum seekers for up to six months while their applications were considered;
- Removing access to support for asylum seekers who were destitute but who did not claim asylum immediately upon arrival.

For critics of the Act, these measures represented institutional racism writ large. In 2004 the court of appeal found that the final provision breached Article 3 of the European Convention on Human Rights and in October 2004 the home secretary was forced to abandon this policy.

## The future of multi-ethnic Britain

On 27 January 1998, the Commission on the Future of Multi-Ethnic Britain was launched by the Runnymede Trust, an independent think-tank dedicated to promoting racial justice. Although formally independent of government, it had close ties to Labour, and Jack Straw accepted an invitation to launch the Commission. Its remit was to 'analyse the current state of multi-ethnic Britain and propose ways of countering racial discrimination and disadvantage ... making Britain a confident and vibrant multicultural society at ease with its rich diversity'.[46] The ensuing report argued that Britain was 'both a community of citizens' and a 'community of communities, both a liberal and a multicultural society'. Since citizens had 'differing needs', equal treatment required 'full account to be taken of their differences'.[47] It argued that building and sustaining a community of citizens and communities would involve:

- Rethinking the national story and national identity;
- Understanding that all identities are in a process of transition;
- Developing a balance between cohesion, equality and difference;
- Addressing and eliminating all forms of racism;
- Reducing material inequalities;
- Building a pluralistic human rights culture.[48]

On 10 October 2000, a day before the official launch of the report, and when it was still embargoed, the *Telegraph* ran a front-page article by its Home Affairs editor, Philip Johnston, headed 'Straw wants to rewrite our history', with the strap line '"British" is a racist word, says report'. The article opens with the words: 'Britain should be formally recognised as a multi-cultural society whose history needs to be "revised, rethought or jettisoned", says a report that has been welcomed by ministers', and continues:

> The inquiry was set up three years ago by the Runnymede Trust, a race equality think tank, and launched by Jack Straw, Home Secretary. Its report, to be published tomorrow, defines the UK as 'a community of communities' rather than a nation. It says the description of its inhabitants as British 'will never do on its own', largely because the term has 'racist connotations'.

Inside, an article by Johnston entitled 'Thinkers who want to consign our island story to history' refers to 'the campaign to turn Britain officially into a multicultural nation' and calls the report 'a cauldron of political correctness'. An editorial entitled 'The British race' complains that 'it is astonishing that ministers should have welcomed the sub-Marxist gibberish' contained in the report, condemns its findings as 'extreme and tendentious', alleges that almost all of its authors 'are directly or indirectly supported by the taxpayer' and concludes that 'under the guise of "multiculturalism", they are advancing their old Marxist dislike of *any* national culture. It is shameful that the Government should have been cowed into going along with this rubbish'.

The front-page article contains no less than five major errors in a few lines, but they were absolutely to determine the way in which not only the *Telegraph* but other papers were to cover the report over subsequent days. The parallel with the *Sunday Telegraph*'s jumping the gun with the Macpherson report is inescapable.

First, and most seriously, the report nowhere says that the term 'British' has 'racist connotations', as the *Telegraph*'s use of quotation marks clearly suggests. What it actually says is: 'Britishness, as much as Englishness, has systematic, largely unspoken, racial connotations. Whiteness nowhere features as an explicit condition of being British, but it is widely understood that Englishness, and therefore Britishness, is racially coded'. It notes that, for Asians, African-Caribbeans and Africans, 'Britishness is a reminder of colonisation and empire, and to that extent is not attractive' but adds that, although 'Britishness is not ideal ... at least it appears acceptable, particularly when suitably qualified – Black British, Indian British, British Muslim, and so on'[49]. However, since the *Telegraph* article, and subsequent ones in the same paper, repeatedly substitute the word 'racist' for 'racial' one can only assume that the editor took them to mean the same thing, in which case he would also have been bound to agree that the statement of fact: 'The *Telegraph* is a national newspaper' is the same as the judgement: 'The *Telegraph* is a nationalist newspaper'.

Second, the report does not define the UK as a community of communities rather than a nation but simply uses the phrase as a means of picturing how Britain could, and in its opinion, should, develop. It does this as a way of trying to displace a different picture: Britain as consisting of one large homogenous majority plus various small minorities. But nowhere is it suggested that this is how Britain should be re-named. This is what the report actually says:

> It would be consistent with the dictionary definition [of community] to envisage Britain as a community whose three principal constituent parts are England, Scotland and Wales, and to envisage each of the constituent parts as a community, as also each separate region, city, town or borough. Any one individual belongs to several different communities.[50]

Third, like so much of the myopically London-based national press, the *Telegraph* makes the elementary mistake of conflating the United Kingdom and the British Isles. What the report actually says is this:

> Many acknowledge that ideally there needs to be a way of referring to the larger whole of which Scotland, Wales and England are constituent parts. But the nation state to which they belong is the United Kingdom not Britain ... The Good Friday Agreement of 1999 implies that there should be a sense of affiliation to the supranational identity known as 'these islands' [that is, including the Republic of Ireland]. Perhaps one day there will be an adjective to refer to this entity, similar in power perhaps to the unifying word 'Nordic' in Denmark, Finland, Norway and Sweden. But for the present no such adjective is in sight. It is entirely plain, however, that the word 'British' will never do on its own.[51]

This is self-evidently true as applied to the British Isles, as in the report, and as Philip Johnston would have discovered if he had dropped into a bar in, say, a nationalist part of Derry and informed the assembled company that they were all British. Applied to the United Kingdom, however, it becomes quite a different proposition, and one which the report never puts forward.

Fourth, to state that the report argues that British history needs to be rewritten, revised, rethought or jettisoned is selective to the point of serious distortion. The passage to which this charge refers merely argues that if Britain is to acquire 'a broad framework of common belonging' in which 'cultural diversity is cherished and celebrated', then

> one critical prerequisite is to examine Britain's understanding of itself. How are the histories of England, Scotland and Wales understood by their people? What do the separate countries stand for, and what does Britain stand for? Of what may citizens be justly proud? How has the imagined nation stood the test of time? What should be preserved, what jettisoned, what revised or reworked? How can everyone have a recognised place within the larger picture?[52]

Thus, what the *Telegraph* presents as a bald statement is actually a series of questions for discussion, and the report's remarks about pride in and preservation of aspects of British history are conveniently ignored.

Finally, and perhaps most importantly, is the role which the paper allots to Jack Straw in the publication of the report. The headline is unequivocal – 'Straw wants to rewrite our history' – and unequivocally wrong, as there is nothing in the article that remotely substantiates such a wild accusation. In fact, Straw's role in the report was limited to launching it. However, it is abundantly clear, and becomes ever more so as the controversy develops, that it is Straw in particular and Labour in general which are the *Telegraph's* (and other Conservative papers') real target. Thus, the article states that 'although the Government finds some of the report's recommendations unwelcome, particularly on asylum and immigration policy, it apparently accepts the thrust of its conclusions', and Home Office minister Mike O'Brien is quoted to the effect that: 'This is a timely report which adds much to the current debate on multi-ethnic Britain. The Government is profoundly committed to racial equality and the celebration of diversity. We are a multi-cultural society'. Similarly, the editorial, headed 'The British race', begins: 'It is astonishing that ministers should have welcomed the sub-Marxist gibberish' contained in the report, and concludes that: 'Under the guise of "multi-culturalism", they are advancing their old Marxist dislike of *any* national culture. It is shameful that the Government should have been cowed into going along with this rubbish'.

## A galvanic reaction

It is extremely important to realise that the passages of the report which so enraged the *Telegraph* occupy just over three pages of its total of 417. Nonetheless, the effect of its reporting on much of the rest of the press was nothing less than galvanic. In spite of the fact that they had review copies of the report, and could have contacted Runnymede to ascertain if the *Telegraph* report was accurate, journalists on most other papers simply repeated what that *Telegraph* had said. Thus, that day's *Standard* carried an article headed 'The word "British" is racist – report', and the late edition of the *Sun* ran a short piece headlined '"British" is race slur'. The next day, the *Mail* ditched the front page article it had intended running and replaced it with one headed 'Racism slur on the word "British"'; the inside pages were also changed to include a typically partisan run-down of members of the commission which produced the report (similar 'rogues galleries' would appear in the *Sun* (11 October) and the *Telegraph* (12 October), which resulted in commissioners receiving hate mail and other forms of abuse), a lengthy editorial ('What an insult to our history and intelligence'), an essay by Paul Johnson, and a hostile commentary by Raj Chandran of the Commission for Racial Equality ('An insult to all our countrymen'). Similarly, the same day's *Sun* ran an article headlined 'Ministers welcome report which says "British" is racist and all our history must be re-written', a lengthy piece by its political editor

Trevor Kavanagh headed 'Ministers welcome report which says "British" is a racist word', an indignant editorial ('Proud history') which urged Straw to 'stick this report in the bin', and a comment piece ('It's ridiculous') by the athlete Daley Thompson. *The Times* headed its report 'Drop the word "British" says race trust' and the *Mirror* ran with 'British is "just another word for prejudice"'.

Indeed, such was the pack mentality of the press on this issue that even the liberal *Guardian* intermittently joined the fray. Thus, the headline of its main article on 11 October reads: 'British tag is "coded racism"', even though the term 'coded racism', quotes notwithstanding, appears neither in the report nor in the article itself, which is a characteristically well-informed piece by home affairs editor Alan Travis. The paper did run a broadly welcoming editorial entitled 'Prescription for harmony', although this carried the strap 'But race report is spoilt by bad idea': this appears to be 'dropping Britain' and suggesting that 'Britain is a racially coded word that should be replaced with the term "community of communities"', neither of which is recommended by the report. The paper does, however, redeem itself to some extent with an article by Parekh himself, and also one by Gary Younge, which opens with the most pertinent words written during the whole furore: 'If you really want to take the racial temperature in Britain, you would be better off examining the reactions to the report on multi-ethnic Britain than the report itself'. Only the *Independent* and the *Express* succeeded in dealing with the report largely in their own terms, as opposed to following the *Telegraph*'s tramlines. At that point, the *Express* was a Labour-supporting paper and owned by the husband of one of the commissioners, Lady Gavron. Its editorial on 12 October observed 'that a single phrase in a 400-page report into the future of a multiracial Britain has been pounced upon by those determined to suggest that the Government is undermining the identity of this country with mad political correctness'.

It should be pointed out that in a leader on 12 October, headed 'Don't diss Britannia' (which must surely have baffled many of its elderly middle-class readers), the *Telegraph* slightly modified its original line by stating that 'the report appeared to suggest' that Britishness and Englishness were 'racist' terms, although in point of fact it appeared to do no such thing. However, this was mentioned merely *en passant*, and did not affect coverage of the affair either in that paper or elsewhere in the national press. It did publish an article by Parekh on 18 October, which belatedly set the record straight, but the following day ran a letter which misquoted the report and wrongly claimed that Parekh had misrepresented his own report.

Over the next few days, the commissioners were to find themselves described as 'worthy idiots', 'of foreign extraction' and 'purblind, self-indulgent and insensitive' in *The Times*; 'middle-class twits' in the *Star*; 'crack-brained', 'Left wing cronies' and 'a bunch of cranks and losers' in the *Telegraph*; 'left-wing wafflers' in the *Evening Standard*; and a 'second-rate unrepresentative clique' composed of 'disconnected, whining liberals' and 'self-satisfied champions of liberal orthodoxy' in the *Mail*. The report itself was condemned variously as 'sub-Marxist gibberish', 'balderdash', 'ridiculous', 'burblings', 'rhubarb', 'an aberrant piece of politically correct lunacy', 'potty and sinister', 'ignorant clap-trap' and 'thoroughly nasty' in the *Telegraph*; 'right-on trendy tosh' and a 'pile of cack' in the *Star*; 'tendentious rubbish', 'ignorant and dishonest' and 'insulting trash' in the *Mail*; 'egregious', 'destructive', displaying 'ahistorical ignorance', 'just plain idiotic' and 'wrong in almost every possible way' in *The Sunday Times*; and 'tosh', 'dreadful rubbish' and 'ludicrous' in the *Sun*, whose columnist Richard Littlejohn alleged that if the report's recommendations were implemented, 'children will be told lies about their history and encouraged to feel ashamed of their country' (13 October). Meanwhile, exactly as in the case of the Macpherson report, the *Telegraph* gave over its letters pages to correspondence much of which would not have been in the least out of place in the official publications of the British National Party or the National Front, in which racism, rage and bile were relieved only by galumphing attempts at 'humour' which made *Private Eye*'s spoof e-mails from 'Mike Giggler' side-splitting by comparison.

## Targeting Labour

The immediate purpose of all this fury and vituperation was, quite clearly, to force Jack Straw to distance himself from the report, which, just like the Macpherson report, was used by sections of the press as a pretext to attack everything about the Labour government which the Right detests, and in particular what it takes to be its attitudes to ethnicity and national identity. It is also important to bear in mind that a general election was widely expected in the next six months. Thus, for example, the *Mail* editorial (11 October) argued that:

> In ordinary circumstances, the report's clunking prose, flawed argument and lamentable ignorance of history would be risible. But this exercise was launched by Home Secretary Jack Straw. Its conclusions have been welcomed by the Home Office. If not yet official policy, the report reflects New Labour attitudes. Why should anyone be surprised? New Labour has never shown the slightest understanding of this nation's past, or sympathy with its traditions.

It concluded: 'The tragedy is that this self-serving exercise by a second-rate, unrepresentative clique is being embraced by Ministers who claim to represent Britain and the British people, but have plainly lost confidence in both'. Similarly, the essay in the same day's paper by Paul Johnson argued that 'the Runnymede Trust report, calling for a total re-write of our history and the banning of such terms as "English" and "Britain" as racist, looks like the first move in a New Labour brainwashing exercise designed to destroy our sense of nationhood'.

Further proof of the political motivation of this story, if any was needed, was provided by the *Telegraph* (12 October), which devoted no less than six self-congratulatory pieces to the conflagration which it had so successfully ignited. A column by Boris Johnson, headed 'Why I give way to righteous paranoia about

Britain', warns that 'this is a war over culture, which our side could lose'. One of the major points at issue in this 'war' is, of course, the Macpherson report which, as demonstrated above, earned Straw the undying hatred of papers such as the *Telegraph*. And, inevitably, this hoves into view in its editorial 'Don't diss Britannia', which argues that 'Mr Straw is unconvincing when he dons the mantle of John Bull. He has pulled a similar stunt before – making much of rowing back from some of the wilder shores of the Macpherson report on "institutionalised racism" in the Metropolitan Police'. Of that report, the editorial alleges that 'Mr Straw was able to smuggle it past the public by playing the role of commonsense watchdog. So it is with this commission. Mr Straw and Number 10 have distanced themselves from the report's most offensive comments, but they have not distanced themselves from its substantive proposals'. The editorial concludes that 'the Conservatives now have an excellent chance to make good their past silence on Macpherson. They must expose the Government's collusion in this attempt to destroy a thousand years of British history'.

Similarly, the same day's *Sun*, in an editorial headed 'A disgrace', used the report to lambast one of its favourite Labour targets: the 'metropolitan elite':

> We cannot tolerate an officially sanctioned Government report that says these things. The fact that the Home Secretary hasn't binned the ludicrous 'British is racist' report is a disgrace. What on earth is going on? Too many in the Government don't seem to like Britain ... The new Establishment – the metropolitan elite – have no confidence in the British. *They simply do not understand that patriotism is a good thing.* In America, many homes have flags outside. Here, we have a government that appears to think its own people are racists. What a scandal. What a state of affairs.

The overtly party-political thrust of the *Telegraph*'s campaign was further emphasised on 13 October when it ran a lengthy piece by William Hague entitled 'Why I am sick of the anti-British disease'. This began:

> In the 1970s, the threat from the Left was an economic one and came in the form of militant unions, punitive taxes and picket lines. We called it the British disease. In 2000, the threat from the Left is as much a cultural one, and manifests itself in the tyranny of political correctness and the assault on British culture and history. We should call it the anti-British disease. Never has this cultural threat been more clearly expressed than in the report by the Runnymede commission.

According to Hague:

> The report's recommendations may range from the potty to the sinister, but it is the overall thinking that gave rise to creating the commission in the first place that represents the real threat. For when the commission says

that 'Britishness has systematic racial connotations', it is betraying a wider agenda of the New Labour elite. These people believe that the very idea of 'Britain' is irredeemably tainted by the combination of our imperial history, a concept of nationality that is past its sell-by date and public institutions that are 'institutionally racist' In short, they hate who we are, where we have come from, and where we are going.

The report is then lumped together with 'Cool Britannia', devolution, 'Europe' and every other hate object in Tory demonology to argue that we have a government 'led by a Prime Minister embarrassed about the country he lives in and the people who elected him'.

The paper also carried an editorial, headed 'Turning point at Runnymede'. This again explicitly links the Runnymede document with the Macpherson report, of which it states that 'no more disgracefully unfair document has ever been produced by a judge in modern British history'. However, it argued:

> Its bigoted conclusions were accepted with only a whimper of protest by the institutions it criticised. The bullying of the 'anti-racists' had won. At last, though, something is changing. To the obvious shock of the comfortable peers, millionaires' wives and public sector grandeees who lent their names to the report, people are starting to say that they will not take any more. The report's suggestion that the word 'British' is racist has finally frightened even those ministers who thought that they could never go wrong by appeasing such doctrines. Jack Straw and Tony Blair have suddenly changed from their usual approval, and have reached instead for a Union flag in which to wrap themselves. It doesn't fit very well, but it is interesting that it has happened at all.

Similarly, in the *Sun* (13 October), Richard Littlejohn claimed that the report

> only addresses the agenda of the tiny, self-obsessed, unrepresentative New Labour elite. They're not so much anti-British, as anti-English. They don't seem to have a problem with Welsh, Irish or Scottish identity. In fact, they encourage it. That's because top of their wish list is destroying the United Kingdom and splitting it into its component parts, subordinate to Brussels ... A nation in which is nothing but a 'community of communities' can not survive as a nation, which is what many in New Labour actually crave.

Anti-Labour sentiment was also very much to the fore in the *Sun* (18 October) in an attack on the vice chair of the Runnymede Trust, Lady Gavron. She is described as 'the poetry-loving wife of a millionaire' and

> a quintessential member of the London-based elite that we keep warning you about. Her husband is the ex-chairman of the Guardian Media Group – which owns the *Guardian* newspaper – the very essence of the

commanding heights of metropolitan elitism. Don't forget that Kate Gavron is only called Lady because her husband got a peerage after donating £500,000 to Labour. She has an agenda of her own which denigrates history, deplores nationhood and dedicates itself to intellectual revolution. She is privileged, moneyed and benefits from the system which she chooses to attack.

## Spin and wishful thinking

However, to read most of the press reports of what Jack Straw said at the launch of the report and then to read the entire speech[53] is to read about two apparently different events. The tone of the reports can be gathered from headlines such as 'Straw beats very British retreat over race report' (*Telegraph*) and '"Proud to be British" Straw raps race report' (*The Times*), with even the more friendly papers appearing to join in the fray with 'Race report angers "proud Briton" Straw' (*Express*) and 'Straw launches scathing attack on "unpatriotic" political left' (*Independent*), although in the case of the last two the articles themselves gave a much more balanced account of the event than the headlines would have led the reader to expect.

Most of the lengthy speech by Straw (who had earlier seen a first draft of the report) is actually taken up with fulsome and clearly heartfelt praise for Runnymede's work over the years. Given the sheer amount of criticism directed at the report by the press, Straw was clearly left with absolutely no option but to respond to it. What he in fact did was to re-write at least parts of the speech which he had intended to deliver, and to delay publication of the Home Office's official forty-page response. Equally importantly, as Robin Richardson points out[54], and as is clear from two articles in the *Independent* (12 October) by its home affairs correspondent Ian Burrell, key journalists were briefed by the Home Office in such a way as to accentuate the more critical aspects of the speech, and much of the resulting coverage shows just how readily they accepted the officially spun line.

However, the positive parts of his speech (which also repeatedly praise the Macpherson Report) massively outnumber the few negative comments, which could be taken as its main point only by papers absolutely determined to spin a particular editorial line, or by journalists who believe and then parrot every word that they are told by spin doctors. Straw's criticisms are actually pretty mild by comparison with his positive remarks, and occur near the end of his speech. What he actually said was that he felt that 'the Commission were a little grudging in recognising what's been achieved already', that 'I frankly don't agree with the Commission' over its views on Britishness (which he quite explicitly contrasted with what the *Telegraph* alleged its views were), and, via a reference to George Orwell's famous remark that 'almost any English intellectual would feel more ashamed of standing to attention during God Save the King than of stealing from the poor box', that the task of moulding Britishness into a 'single shared identity was always going to be a challenge, but it was in my judgement made more difficult by those on the left who turned their backs on concepts of patriotism and who left the field to those on the far right'. And that was it. Indeed, Straw's strongest criticisms were actually reserved for the *Telegraph* itself: the *Independent* (but no other paper) quoted him as being 'astonished' at its 'extraordinary intervention', but nowhere was reported his remark that it '*has had* [emphasis added] a record of separating its news coverage which, on the whole, has broadly subscribed to the facts, from its opinion which is its business' – which last remark could be taken as implying that the *Telegraph* is more of a viewspaper than a newspaper. Nor did any paper see fit to print the unqualified praise for the report voiced on the same day by Baroness Amos, a government Whip in the Lords. In this respect, funeral orations such as those read by *The Times* (12 October) – 'the sheer force with which Jack Straw, the Home Secretary, distanced himself from the most controversial aspects of the *Future of Multi-Ethnic Britain* report yesterday shows that this document will not influence official thinking in the future' – come across as decidedly premature and the product of wishful thinking.

## 'Commissars of the new order'

Another target of the newspapers' wrath was, inevitably, the 'race relations industry'. Thus, the original *Telegraph* editorial (10 October), complains that there is no evidence that the authors of the report 'consulted anyone outside the race industry'; the *Sun* (12 October) condemns the authors as a 'bunch of left-wing academics and race relations "experts"'; the *Telegraph* (12 October) attacks the 'members of the monocultural race relations industry who staffed the commission [who] have written themselves a meal ticket for life as commissars of the new order – all at the expense of our freedoms and traditions'; the *Standard* (12 October) talks of 'a committee composed of Left-wing wafflers and professional pillars of the race relations industry'; Richard Littlejohn in the *Sun* (13 October) derides people 'who make a good living out of promoting racial division'; and Norman Tebbit in the *Mail on Sunday* (15 October) argues that 'racism is not widespread among most of British society, but it permeates every nook and cranny of the race relations industry', staffed as it is by 'race relations warriors'.

In the wake of the disturbances in Oldham in May 2001, Minette Marrin wrote a column, in the *Guardian* (29 May 2001) in which she claimed that:

> One of the greatest obstacles in the way of good race relations here is multiculturalism. Multiculturalism actually promotes racism. It engenders confusion, resentment and bullying; it encourages division and prevents people developing a shared British identity ... Multiculturalism is the idea that all cultures are of equal value, and deserve equal respect – an understandable response to the confusions of mass mobility. Unfortunately it has become overloaded with anxieties about race; in fact to say you are against multiculturalism is pretty much to confess to racism.

She continued:

> What we must have to live together in harmony is a tolerant, over-arching common culture. We already have one, in what one might call our host culture, but the very idea of a host culture is denounced by multiculturalists as supremacist and racist; people have begun to feel confused by the fear of being thought racist into being ashamed of their own culture. Multiculturalism is always celebrating difference. Of course it is right that everyone should be free to remember their traditions and practise their faith, within the limits of the laws and traditions of this country. Of course all these differences can enrich the common culture ... But what we've seen too often is a vociferous insistence on ethnic differences, which constantly remind people of their otherness. Worse still, this celebration of ethnic diversity has tended, pointedly, to exclude only one ethnic tradition – Englishness (or sometimes, more loosely, Britishness).

In Marrin's view, 'most astonishing was the Parekh report's condemnation of the word British. This was truly inflammatory'. According to her 'that report actually stated "immigrants owe loyalty to the British state, but not to its values, customs and way of life"'. She then asks:

> What could be more destructive of any aspirations to a mixed community? What could be more destructive of the ideal of a multiracial Britain? What can be the point of coming here as an immigrant, if one feels no respect for our way of life? How could anyone truly welcome an immigrant with such a view? How can any minorities already loyal to the British way of life fail to be deeply offended or confused?

The only problem is, however, that the account that she presents of multiculturalism is a barely recognisable caricature, and, more seriously still, the report did not condemn the word British nor does it contain the words she attributes to it, her use of quotation marks notwithstanding.

Thus, we return to our starting point in this study of press reaction to the Parekh report: the generation of outrage and controversy based on misquotation and false premises – unfortunately an all too familiar tactic on the part of right-wing newspapers in the UK (and not simply tabloid ones either). Whether this was deliberate on the part of the *Telegraph* in the first place is impossible to ascertain, but it does not really matter. It did what it did, and most other papers immediately followed suit, without bothering to check the facts, because it suited their ideological agenda to do so. It has been suggested[55] that, disappointed that the report was failing to garner much press coverage prior to its publication, certain commissioners, or employees of the PR company hired by Runnymede to promote the report, may have drawn the attention of the *Telegraph* to what the report said about the connotations of the word 'Britishness', hoping thus to generate more column inches. If so, given that paper's reaction to the Macpherson report, and its immediate effect on subsequent coverage of the report by other right-wing newspapers, they were really quite extraordinarily naïve and fool-hardy. *Pace* Sarah Neal and Eugene McLaughlin,[56] there was nothing remotely unpredictable about the press coverage of the report, whose conclusions, even if reported accurately, would have been like waving a red rag at a furiously charging bull, one which had already gored the Macpherson report and was eagerly sniffing out its next victim.

## Conclusion

The press reaction to the Macpherson and Parekh reports clearly demonstrates that even though Labour had finally managed to ditch the 'loony' label, it had by no means assuaged the customary and intense right-wing hostility towards it on the part of both politicians and the press. Its policies on ethnicity would continue to be its Achilles heel, not least because sections of the press have, as we have seen, a long history of hostility to ethnic 'others' of one kind or another. What would follow the assaults on the Macpherson and Parekh reports would be a long series of attacks by these papers on 'multiculturalism', which they rarely defined and which simply became a boo word for everything which the right loathed about a government which it clearly regarded as treacherous and illegitimate. These attacks became all the more intense in the wake of the urban disturbances in Burnley, Oldham and Bradford in summer 2001. With the attack on the Twin Towers in September 2001 and the London bombings of July 2005 the press began to focus increasingly on Britain's Muslim communities and to blame Islamic extremism on the consequences of Labour's 'multicultural' policies, which the right repeatedly and consistently represented as having created ethnic ghettos and caused 'white flight', with the consequence that the country was 'sleepwalking to segregation'. This was the phrase coined by Trevor Phillips, then chairman of the Commission for Racial Equality, in a speech in September 2005 which received vast amounts of adulatory (if not always accurate) press coverage in Conservative papers.

What the consequences of these press attacks were for Labour's actual policies is extremely hard to gauge. They clearly made it very defensive, and desperate to display its patriotic credentials (witness the numerous speeches by the likes of Robin Cook, Gordon Brown and David Blunkett about Britishness). Various newspapers regularly claimed that Blair, Blunkett, Straw and other leading Labour figures had repudiated 'multiculturalism', but such was the selectivity of their reporting, and so unclear was what the papers actually meant by 'multiculturalism' (which is an extremely slippery term even in less partisan and ideologically driven hands), that it's extremely difficult to judge what substance, if any, these reports actually had. Much more to the point is Keenan Malik's observation that 'much of the contemporary criticism of multiculturalism is driven by racism, bigotry and sheer hatred for the other'[57], which points to the fact that today, opposition to immigrants, immigration and indeed people of colour in general is often expressed indirectly, through opposition to 'multiculturalism'. In other words, it is frequently a coded form of racism.

Whatever the case, it would be far too easy to claim that, had it not been for the press onslaught on institutional racism and 'multiculturalism', Labour would have pursued policies more in keeping with Macpherson's and Parekh's conclusions and recommendations. In particular, the alacrity and zeal with which it set about drastically tightening up on immigration and asylum via the legislation listed above suggests otherwise. As argued elsewhere in this book, Labour's more right-wing tendencies cannot simply be explained away by its fear of and subservience to the Conservative press.

I have concentrated on the Parekh and Macpherson reports in this chapter partly because they were so clearly employed by the press to put Labour on notice during its early years in power. But I have also done so because the bitter assaults on the 'liberal elite' have a remarkably contemporary ring to them in the wake of Brexit, and point to much deeper ideological forces at work here. As Andrew Pilkington has argued in respect of the Parekh Report:

> [It] clearly touched a nerve. The hostile media coverage indicated the existence of considerable anger towards the idea that Britain needed to change in fundamental ways. The selective attention paid to national identity and the need to rethink the national story arguably points to anxiety over who we are in a postcolonial world (and it should be noted devolved/ European world). Who are we, Brits any longer? Who are we in a world where we seem threatened from below by migrants from other countries that we used to rule and from above by our membership of an organisation dominated by countries who have been our traditional enemies. And who are we when the UK seems to be fragmenting with the restoration of national assembles and parliaments? The hysteria manifest in the media reaction signals the depth of the anxiety.[58]

The problem is, however, that the prevalence in so much of the national press of the kinds of views outlined above makes it extremely difficult to conduct public discussion of these kinds of extremely urgent issues. It is clearly highly unpleasant for any government to live with the daily diatribe which is liable at any time, as in the case of the two reports discussed here, to mushroom into a full-blown assault in which truth is the first casualty, and it is also far too tempting for Conservatives, whether in government or opposition to play to the populist press gallery when it suits their cause. Liberal *bien pensants* who read only the *Guardian*, *Independent*, *Financial Times* or no national newspaper at all can have little idea of the sheer amount of rabid, raging reaction that daily erupts from much of our national press.

However, discussion of the future direction of Britain is far too important for its terms to be dictated by unelected, unrepresentative and unaccountable newspaper owners, editors and pundits[59], whose daily outpourings have significantly contributed to Britain leaving the EU and to the growth of a particularly toxic and *enragé* form of English nationalism. But such discussion cannot simply be avoided as too awkward. As Stuart Hall, one of the members of the Commission on the Future of Multi–Ethnic Britain, put it at the time of the report's publication:

> Britain always was and really is now a nation of nations. It cannot continue to conflate 'Englishness' with 'Britishness'. Some commentators really do suppose that Britain will obliterate all trace of its imperial history, devolve government, integrate with the global economy, play an active role in Europe, treat all minority peoples as equal citizens – and retain its self-understanding intact since Magna Carta! This is not serious analysis, it is cloud cuckoo land. The question of Britishness is a timebomb which is ticking away at the centre of this society and it is either faced and confronted or it will explode in our face in ways which we do not wish.[60]

This was a quite remarkably prescient remark, but at the time of writing the omens are not at all hopeful, and this is a situation for which the British national press must take a very considerable share of the blame.

## Notes

1  T. Blair, *New Britain: My Vision of a Young Country* (London: Fourth Estate, 1996), p. 71.
2  C. Smith, *Creative Britain* (London: Faber and Faber, 1998), p. 36.
3  M. Leonard, *Britain*™ (London: Demos, 1997), p. 56.
4  D. Blunkett, *Politics and Progress: Renewing Democracy and Civil Society* (London: Politico's Publishing, 2001), p. 128.
5  B. Gould, *The Unfinished Revolution: How Labour Changed British Politics for Ever* (London: Abacus,2011), pp. 46–7.
6  Ibid., p. 48.
7  Ibid., p. 253.
8  See in particular N. Murray, 'Anti-racists and other demons: the press and ideology in Thatcher's Britain', *Race & Class*, 27(3), 1986, pp. 1–19; P. Gordon and D. Rosenberg, *Daily Racism: the Press and Black People in Britain* (London: The Runnymede Trust 1989); T. van Dijk, *Racism and the Press* (London: Routledge, 1991); the SubScribe website (www.sub-scribe.co.uk/).
9  T. van Dijk, *Elite Discourse and Racism* (London: Sage, 1993), p. 278.
10  M. Barker, *The New Racism* (London: Junction Books, 1981), p. 17.
11  M. Billig, S. Condor, D. Edwards, M. Gane, *Ideological Dilemmas: A Social Psychology of Everyday Thinking* (London: Sage, 1988), p. 120.
12  C. Holmes, *Anti-Semitism in British Society, 1876–1939* (London: Routledge, 1979); T. Kushner and K. Knox, *Refugees in an Age of Genocide* (London: Routledge, 1999), pp. 19–63.
13  The best accounts of British policy towards Jewish refugees in the 1930s are L. London, *Whitehall and the Jews: British Immigration Policy and the Holocaust* (Cambridge: Cambridge University Press, 2000); A.J. Sherman, *Island Refuge: Britain and Refugees*

*from the Third Reich* (London: Frank Cass, 1994); Kushner and Knox, *Refugees*, pp. 126–214).

14  S. Cohen, *From the Jews to the Tamils: Britain's Mistreatment of Refugees* (Manchester: South Manchester Law Centre, 1988).

15  www.bbc.co.uk/news/10409026; http://judeninthemar.org/the-voyage/.

16  For an excellent account of the parallels between the hostility shown by sections of the press to Jewish refugees and to their contemporary counterparts see A. Karpf, 'We've been here before', *Guardian*, 8 June 2002.

17  T. Kushner, *The Battle of Britishness: Immigrant Journeys, 1685 to the Present* (Manchester: Manchester University Press, 2012), pp. 119–38; London, *Whitehall*; L. London, 'Whitehall and the refugees: the 1930s and the 1990s', *Patterns of Prejudice*, 34(3), 2000, pp. 17–26.

18  London, *Whitehall*, p. 13.

19  London, 'Whitehall', p. 18.

20  For numerous examples of this kind of thinking, see F. Palmer (ed.), *Anti-racism: An Assault on Education and Value* (London: The Sherwood Press, 1986).

21  P. Gordon, 'A dirty war: The New Right and local authority anti-racism', in W. Ball and J. Solomos (eds), *Race and Local Politics*, (Basingstoke: Macmillan, 1990), p. 176. For further discussion of anti-anti-racism see Murray, 'Anti-racists'; Gordon and Rosenberg, *Daily Racism*, pp. 39–51; P. Bonnett, *Anti-racism* (London: Routledge, 2000), pp. 147–68; J. Burnett, 'Anti-racism: totem and taboo – a review article', *Race & Class*, 57:1, 2015, pp. 78–87.

22  D. Edgar, *The Second Time as Farce: Reflections on the Drama of Mean Times* (London: Lawrence and Wishart, 1988), p. 133.

23  B. MacArthur, *The Penguin Book of Modern Speeches* (London; Penguin, 2017), p. 392.

24  Quoted in Gordon 1990: 178.

25  Summarised at www.s-cool.co.uk/a-level/sociology/inequalities/revise-it/the-swann-report-racism.

26  Tracy was a British travel writer and novelist who regularly wrote for the *Telegraph*. On occasion her columns defended South Africa, and also WISE (Welsh, Irish, Scottish, English), an anti-immigration organisation founded in 1947 which had links to the National Front and the Monday Club. On 24 December 1977 her column suggested a Christmas present for David Lane, the chair of the CRE, 'who has just broken a long and welcome silence … with a string a clichés remarkable even for him'. This was 'a terrace house in Southall, with an ethnic slaughteryard on one side and on the other a temple, with chanting kept up merrily day and night; and a little pied a terre in Notting Hill for the August weekend'.

27  *The Stephen Lawrence Inquiry: Report of an Inquiry by Sir William MacPherson of Cluny* (London: HMSO, 1999), para. 46.1.

28  Ibid., para. 6.34.

29  www.theguardian.com/uk/1999/feb/24/lawrence.ukcrime1

30  Gary Younge, 'The death of Stephen Lawrence: the Macpherson Report', *Political Quarterly*, 70(3), 1999, p. 330. For a useful discussion of the concept of institutional racism, see J. Bourne, 'The life and times of institutional racism', *Race & Class*, 43(2), pp. 7–22.

31  Ibid., p. 331.

32  Ibid., p. 332.

33  Ibid., p. 333.

34  M. Gillard and L. Flynn, *Untouchables: Dirty Cops, Bent Justice and Racism in Scotland Yard* (London: Bloomsbury 2012), pp. 394–405. These suggestions, which first appeared in the *Independent*, 2 April 2001, tended to be dismissed at the time as conspiracy theorising. However, the substantial evidence of press/police collusion which emerged at the Leveson Inquiry, much more of which would doubtless come to light if the second part of the Inquiry took place, lends them weight.

35  B. Cathcart, *The Case of Stephen Lawrence* (London: Penguin 2000), p. 416.
36  Arun Kundnani, '"Stumbling on": race, class and England', *Race & Class*, 41(4), 2000, p. 2.
37  Ibid., p. 16.
38  Younge, 'Death', p. 332.
39  It needs to be pointed out here that the endlessly rehearsed argument that, without the *Mail* calling the five men accused of killing Stephen Lawrence murderers on its front page on 14 February 1997, the Inquiry would never have taken place, simply will not wash. As Brian Cathcart notes in 'The *Daily Mail* and the Stephen Lawrence murder', *Political Quarterly*, 88(4), 2017:

> The front page was intended as a challenge to an outrage against justice, but the scandal was not about the police or about race and the Lawrences were wrong to believe that it was. The paper's wrath was directed at five white men who it complained had terrorised their white neighbours into silence and then raised two fingers to the white establishment.
>
> *(644)*

In spite of what the *Mail* has claimed, the published record shows that

> the *Mail* never sought a public inquiry. From the day of the famous front page in February 1997 to the day the inquiry was announced five months later, the *Daily Mail* did not once call for an inquiry in its pages. Even when the Lawrences publicly demanded an inquiry, the paper remained silent on the subject. More than that, it explicitly opposed an inquiry of the kind that came about.
>
> *(645)*

Thus in an editorial on 25 June 1997, when it became clear that an inquiry of some sort would be held, the *Mail* made its view on what kind of inquiry very clear:

> Of course police methods are open to criticism and claims of racism within the force will have to be investigated. But it would be tragic if such an inquiry were to turn into a witch-hunt against the police. It is not the police who should be on trial. The truth that cries out to be told is about a monstrous wall of silence which continues to shield the guilty.
>
> *(645)*

It was personal pressure by Doreen Lawrence on Straw that ensured that the police investigation would be at the centre of the inquiry.
40  A. Campbell, *Power & the People: 1997–1999: The Alastair Campbell Diaries: Volume Two* (London: Arrow Books, 2011), p. 663.
41  Ibid., p. 664.
42  Ibid., p. 666.
43  Ibid., p. 667.
44  For further details see 'Key points of the Race Relations Amendment Act implementation report', *Guardian*, 22 February 2001, (www.theguardian.com/society/2001/feb/22/policy.raceequality)
45  A. Travis, 'Stephen Lawrence: how his murder changed the legal landscape', *Guardian*, 22 April 2013 (www.theguardian.com/uk/2013/apr/22/stephen-lawrence-murder-changed-legal-landscape).
46  *The Future of Multi-Ethnic Britain: The Parekh Report* (London: Profile Books, 2000), p. viii.
47  Ibid., p. ix
48  Ibid., p. xiii.

49  Ibid., p. 38.
50  Ibid., p. 47.
51  Ibid., p. 38.
52  Ibid., p. 15.
53  'Launching the report: responses from government', *Runnymede's Quarterly Bulletin*, 324, December 2000, pp. 2–4.
54  R. Richardson, 'Children will be told lies', *Runnymede's Quarterly Bulletin*, 324, December 2000, p. 16.
55  E. McLaughlin and S. Neal, 'Misrepresenting the multicultural nation', *Policy Studies*, 25(3), 2004, pp. 165–6.
56  E. McLaughlin and S. Neal, 'Assumptions of power subverted: media and emotions in the wake of the Parekh Report', in S. Lefebvre and P. Brodeur (eds), *Public Commissions on Cultural and Religious Diversity* (London: Routledge, 2017), p. 53.
57  K. Malik, *Multiculturalism and its Discontents* (London: Seagull Books, 2013), p. 79.
58  A. Pilkington, 'From institutional racism to community cohesion: the changing nature of racial discourse in Britain', in Sociological Research Online, 13(3)6, May 2008, (www.socresonline.org.uk/13/3/6.html).
59  A point made at considerable length and great detail in M. Dean, *Democracy under Attack: How the Media Distort Policy and Politics* (Bristol: The Policy Press, 2012).
60  S. Hall, 'Occupying Britishness and entrenching change', *Runnymede's Quarterly Bulletin*, March 2001, pp. 17–8; 'A question of identity', *Observer*, 15 October 2000.

# 11

## ALL CHANGE AT THE TOP

*Ivor Gaber*

On 27 September 2013, the *Daily Mail* published a 2,000-word article about a left-wing academic at the London School of Economics who had died twenty years previously. The article was headlined 'The Man Who Hated Britain', and the reason why the newspaper devoted so much space to a relatively obscure academic was explained in the sub-heading – 'Red Ed's Pledge to Bring Back Socialism is a Homage to his Marxist Father. So what Did Miliband Senior Really Believe in? The Answer Should Disturb Everyone Who Loves This Country'.[1] But was it patriotic fervour, or an attempt to resurrect a crude political (and some would argue ethnic) stereotype that really lay behind, not just this article, but the newspaper's campaign that preceded it, and followed in its wake?[2]

Two days prior, the then Labour leader Ed Miliband had told the annual Labour Party conference that an incoming Labour Government would impose a price freeze on the energy companies (a policy later enthusiastically adopted by a subsequent Conservative Government). This, according to most commentators, appeared to turn the political tide and what looked like it was going to be a summer of warm triumph for the Conservatives (with the British economy seemingly in recovery mode) instantly became an autumn of uncertainty as Miliband's initiative seemed to put new wind into the Labour Party sails.[3] But the *Daily Mail*, unlike the Conservative Party, appeared ready for the Labour assault. It had manifestly prepared its counter-blast in advance and that counter-blast was named Ralph Miliband – father of the Labour leader.

On the day of Ed Miliband's address to the Labour conference, the newspaper's 'star' political columnist, Richard Littlejohn, wrote 'clearly some of his [Ralph Miliband's] discredited ideas have rubbed off on his youngest son.' In the article, Littlejohn reprises his own days as an industrial correspondent in the 1970s; painting a highly contentious picture of a Britain hobbled by high taxes, failing industries and dominated by 'union barons'. And he warned that

Miliband was planning 'a re-run of the tax and spend disaster movie which got us into this mess in the first place. The modern face of socialism manifests itself in the shape of the same old "bash the rich" politics of resentment, a war on wealth creation and a shopping list of generous "giveaways" funded by reckless borrowing and higher taxes'.[4]

The day after Miliband's speech, the *Mail* published a lengthy article by the historian Dominic Sandbrook, headlined 'Miliband's Marxist Father and the Real Reason He Wants To Drag Us Back To The Nightmare 70s'. Sandbrook's article, running to more than 1300 words, began: 'At his peak in the Sixties and Seventies, Ed Miliband's father was one of the best-known intellectuals in Britain' – something of an exaggeration to put it at its kindest when comparing his obituary in *The Times*, which ran at 753 words,[5] compared with the 2,532 words the paper devoted to his fellow left-wing intellectual, Eric Hobsbawm.[6] Sandbrook concluded by re-playing Littlejohn's theme of 'Beware the Seventies:

> What really matters to ordinary families, though, is not where Mr Miliband is coming from, but where he wants to take us. And on this evidence, his ideal society looks worryingly like the seedy, shabby, downbeat world of Britain in the mid-1970s.[7]

On the following day came the real offensive (in both senses of the word) – an article headlined 'The Man Who Hated Britain'. Running across two pages, journalist Geoffrey Levy fulminated, no other word quite captures the tone, against Red Ed and his 'revolutionary' father. Levy painted a picture of a bitter Marxist revolutionary who 'hated Britain'. In the 2,000 words of the article, a mere ten are devoted to the fact that Ralph Miliband spent three years in the Royal Navy fighting for Britain, and the fact that he was a volunteer is entirely omitted. Instead, the reader is presented with a Svengali-like figure exercising an influence from beyond the grave over his son 'Red Ed'; as Levy wrote 'how passionately he would have approved today of his son's sinister warning about some of the policies he plans to follow if he ever becomes Prime Minister'.[8]

The article caused a furore with both the leaders of the Conservative and Liberal Democrat parties distancing themselves from it, as did most other newspapers – with the notable exception of the *Sun*. But the disapproval only seemed to encourage the *Daily Mail* to new heights of vituperation. They did allow Ed Miliband a half-page response, but accompanied it with an editorial describing Miliband's response to the attacks on his father as 'tetchy and menacing'.[9] As the weight of political and public opinion gathered momentum the *Mail* started thrashing around for justifications for their attacks on Miliband's father. At one point they linked their Miliband campaign to the proposals to reform press regulation that the Labour leader had supported, opining that, 'If he (Miliband) crushes the freedom of the Press, no doubt his father will be proud of him from beyond the grave'.[10]

The *Mail*'s fury around Miliband's father continued for a number of weeks, involving the paper in some odd contortions. These contortions included reprinting the 'Man Who Hated Britain' article a few days later and also re-publishing their own editorial in support of their own stance – on consecutive days. The stream of abuse aimed at both Ed and Ralph Miliband was unceasing and, to most political observers, wildly out of touch with the reality. For example, under a leader article headlined 'An Evil Legacy And Why We Won't Apologise' the paper wrote:

> Indeed, his son's own Marxist values can be seen all too clearly in his plans for state seizures of private land held by builders and for fixing energy prices by government diktat. More chillingly, the father's disdain for freedom of expression can be seen in his son's determination to place the British Press under statutory control'.[11]

All of which begs the question: why did the *Mail* launch such a tirade? The obvious answer is that in terms of political positioning, the paper, always on the right of the political spectrum, was intent on doing 'whatever was necessary' to prevent Labour from winning the 2015 General Election. But there was another aspect of the campaign, a campaign largely driven by the *Mail* but with enthusiastic support from other sections of the press (the *Sun* in particular) whose principle narrative was to characterise Miliband Junior and the Labour Party, as having moved to the far left after the years of New Labour, which they sought to encapsulate in their constant repetition of the moniker 'Red Ed'.

How successful it was is debateable. In calendar year 2013, the number of individual articles containing the phrase 'Red Ed' occurred as shown in Table 11.1.

In 2013, the *Mail* featured an article referring to 'Red Ed', on average, five times a week, this compares to its sister mid-market tabloid the *Daily Express*, which ran just one such article every two weeks. Despite the ongoing decline in newspaper circulations the *Daily Mail* remains a hugely important newspaper. It has the largest readership of any newspaper in the UK with a combined print and

**TABLE 11.1** Articles referencing 'Red Ed', by newspaper groups, 2013

| Newspaper Groups (All Sources) | Articles Referencing 'Red Ed' 2013 |
| --- | --- |
| Daily Mail/Mail on Sunday | 245 |
| Sun | 134 |
| Daily Telegraph | 113 |
| Independent | 91 |
| The Times/Sunday Times | 84 |
| Guardian/Observer | 53 |
| Daily Express/Star | 26 |
| Financial Times | 25 |
| Daily Mirror/Sunday Mirror | 23 |

Source: Factiva.

online readership of over 31 million a month – in other words more than half the British adult population sees the newspaper at least once a month.[12] Perhaps more importantly, the *Mail* has an influence that outweighs even its impressive readership numbers; this is because it has come to occupy a unique space in the political and media landscapes of the UK. It has managed to convince journalists and politicians alike that somehow it represents the authentic voice of 'middle England'. Former BBC news presenter, Robin Lustig, asked 'Who cares what the *Daily Mail* thinks and does?' and answered his own question thus:

> Just about the entire political leadership of Britain, that's who – because they believe that the paper somehow has a mystical insight into the deepest thoughts of British voters, that it taps into the veins of the national psyche, and that to ignore it is to ignore the instincts of the British people'.[13]

However, the *Mail's* 'Red Ed' campaign – which in fact preceded the attack on Ralph Miliband – never really gathered momentum in the British press (with the 'honourable' exception of the *Sun)*. For, despite the *Mail's* almost mantra-like repetition of the moniker, as the table below illustrates, the 2013 monthly usage figures, prior to the Ralph Miliband articles, would have made depressing reading for them (Table 11.2).

What the Red Ed campaign had in comment with the 'loony left' campaign was that they both represented attempts by sections of the press to frame both Miliband and the 'loony left' as the 'other'. In the case of the 'loony left', this was based on their support for policies and groups that the right-wing press regarded as beyond the pale. Miliband's othering framing was more personal. Primarily the *Mail* framed Miliband as the 'other' by seeking to represent him as 'alien', not quite British – as most dramatically illustrated by the paper's 'Ralph Miliband' offensive. In the immediate weeks following publication of the article

**TABLE 11.2** Articles in national press mentioning 'Red Ed', by month, 2013

| Month | Articles in national press mentioning 'Red Ed' |
| --- | --- |
| January | 12 |
| February | 6 |
| March | 23 |
| April | 30 |
| May | 17 |
| June | 13 |
| July | 49 |
| August | 33 |
| September | 190 |
| October | 160 |
| November | 38 |
| December | 72 |

*Source*: Factiva.

the *Daily Mail* carried seven articles that reminded readers that Ed Miliband was Jewish – echoing the newspaper's historic anti-Semitism, which had included opposing the entry of Jewish refugees at the start of the last century and support for Hitler and his British acolyte Oswald Mosley in the 1930s.

As journalist Jonathan Freedland pointed out in an article in the *Guardian*, there was more than 'a whiff of antisemitism' about the *Mail's* coverage. He wrote:

> there are familiar tunes, some centuries old, which are played again and again. An especially hoary trope is the notion of divided allegiances or plain disloyalty, as if, whatever their outward presence, Jews really serve another master besides their country. Under Stalin, Jews, especially Jewish intellectuals, were condemned as 'rootless cosmopolitans' (another euphemism) lacking in sufficient patriotism. The *Mail's* insistence that Miliband Sr. was not only disloyal but actively hated his country fits comfortably in that tradition.[14]

Of course, the *Daily Mail* was careful to avoid this obvious bear trap – the article was written by a Jewish journalist and one of their senior Jewish executives was wheeled out on television to protest that he had found more anti-Semitism (albeit masquerading as criticism of Israel) when he worked at the *Guardian* than he ever had experienced at the *Mail*. Nonetheless, with the *Mail* identifying Harold Laski and Eric Hobsbawm – both Jewish – as particular friends and influencers of Ralph Miliband (and both described as defenders of Stalinism), it is not difficult to make the case that father and son were being framed as 'alien'. And, as if to underline the point, in a leader column headlined 'An Evil Legacy And Why We Won't Apologise', the *Mail,* commented, 'We do not maintain, like the jealous God of Deuteronomy, that the iniquity of the fathers should be visited on the sons'[15] – wording worryingly redolent of the ancient accusations of the blood libels that have been levelled against Jews over the centuries

A related way that the *Mail* framed Miliband's 'otherness' was to emphasise his background as the son of a Hampstead intellectual who lived a life very different from that enjoyed by the average Labour voter. In the weeks following the Ralph Miliband article, there were no fewer than seven references to the fact that Miliband grew up in Hampstead; emphasising that Miliband's background was that of an intellectual and elitist. Even the fact that he went to the local comprehensive school (which incidentally was not in Hampstead but in far less fashionable Chalk Farm) was put into the mix with headlines such as 'The Finishing School For Left-Wing Politicians'[16] and 'Hardly Bog Standard … Ed's Days At The Eton For Lefties'[17] But the *Mail* headline that captured both senses of the Ed Miliband 'other' was under a story written by historian Michael Burleigh that read: 'In Hampstead Parlours, Intellectual Apologists For Stalin Like Ralph Miliband's Great Friend Eric Hobsbawm And His Tutor Harold Laski Loved Talking In Abstractions As Millions Died In Horror'.[18]

The second aspect of 'otherness' employed by the *Mail* was that of characterising Ed Miliband as a 'Marxist' throwback to the 1970s, wedded to a doctrine of state intervention and in hock to the 'union barons' who had helped get him elected. This frame was facilitated by the electoral arithmetic that saw Miliband winning the leadership of the Labour Party largely on the basis of the greater number of trade union votes he had secured against his brother, David. Hence. It was not difficult to characterise him as one who owed his position to the votes of the trade unions and this in turn provided an umbilical link to the notion that Ed Miliband was a left-winger who symbolised a return to the 'bad old days of the seventies'; in the words of the *Mail's* headline writers, 'Revealed: How The Unions Got Red Ed In A Headlock,[19] The Spectre Of Red Ed's Thought Police'[20] and 'Back To The Bad Old Days: Fixing Energy Prices. Grabbing Land From Property Firms. Boosting Minimum Wage ... Red Ed Revives 70s Socialism'.[21]

The third aspect of the *Mail's* 'othering' of Miliband was to portray him as representing a 'rejection' of traditional family values (something the *Daily Mail* sees itself as championing). This can be found in two separate, but linked, narratives. First, in Ed Miliband's decision to challenge his older brother, David, for the leadership of the Labour Party, despite the fact that, in terms of political prominence, Ed was clearly the junior partner. The *Mail* emphasised Ed Miliband's supposed fraternal 'betrayal' with headlines such as: 'Wife Who Still Can't Forgive Brother-In-Law Ed's Betrayal'.[22] From the other side of the fraternal trenches was a piece headlined: 'Treachery And A Very Bitter Wife' recounted a 'dirty tricks campaigns of smears and name-calling both brothers fought against each other'.[23]

The other way in which Miliband supposedly represented a rejection of the *Mail's* notion of traditional family life was in his apparent reluctance to marry the mother of his children, encapsulated in an article headlined: 'So Will He Now Marry The Mother Of His Son?' and 'Why Isn't He On The Birth Certificate' which carried the stark statement that 'Ed Miliband is the first major political leader in British history not to be married to the mother of his children'.[24]

An additional aspect of the Labour leader's 'othering' was his supposed 'oddness' – indeed, this was a theme that had greater resonance for voters than did Miliband's characterisation as being a left-winger. This was alluded to, not so much in headlines, but in asides and pictures. Andrew Pierce, one of the most constant 'Red Ed' chirrupers, notes that Miliband 'could solve the Rubik's Cube in one minute 20 seconds, one-handed, as a young boy.' Or that while the mildly less geeky David was playing football with friends, 'Ed honed his social skills alone in his room, mastering computer games'.[25] In an article headlined 'The Week That Proved Red Ed Is Totally Out Of Touch With The British People', Miliband was castigated for reportedly ordering a 'Britvic orange' when drinking in Strangers' Bar with his fellow Labour MPs which, according to the paper, 'elicited groans all round'[26]; or in a diary item that noted how Miliband 'has an increasing habit of wagging his (remarkably long) forefingers at the Government benches. He could almost conduct an orchestra with those digits'.[27]

So how successful was this 'othering' campaign? On the attempt to 'other' Miliband for his left-wing politics there is some evidence that this failed to catch hold with the British public. When, in September 2013, the pollsters YouGov put a number of statements to voters about how they saw Ed Miliband, the one that secured the lowest level of agreement – just 26% – was 'He is too left wing' (Figure 11.1).

And when, a month later, voters were asked by pollsters Ipsos Mori, to place Miliband and Cameron on a left/right scale it was clear that, if anything, Cameron was seen to be further to the right than Miliband was to the left. Cameron was placed as 'right of centre' or 'right wing' by 57% of those questioned by Ipsos Mori, whilst Miliband was categorised as 'left of centre' or 'left wing' by 54% of respondents (Figure 11.2).

So why did the 'Red Ed' campaign apparently fail to capture the public's imagination?

First, because we are now almost thirty years on from the collapse of the Soviet Union and the 'red scare' clearly does not have the potency it once possessed. This is not just because the 'communist menace' is no longer a realistic threat, but also because many of today's voters were not politically conscious during the period of the Cold War – communism is something they may have read about in their history books, not something they fear as a realistic and ongoing threat to Britain. In the same vein, the picture of the seventies that the *Mail*, and other newspapers, have sought to reprise – the three-day week, the winter of discontent and so forth – is equally distant to anyone under the age of fifty. And

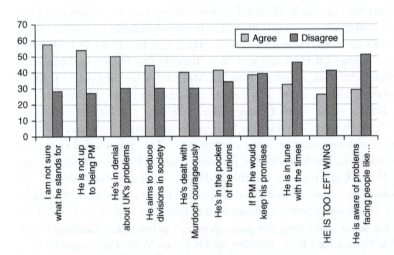

**FIGURE 11.1** Statements about Ed Miliband. 'Agree' is shaded light grey and 'Disagree' is shaded dark grey.

*Source*: YouGov/September 2013. YouGov/*Sunday Times* Survey Results 26th–27th September 2013. http://d25d2506sfb94s.cloudfront.net/cumulus_uploads/document/zxldrzv2x9/YG-Archive-Pol-Sunday-Times-results-270913.pdf. Accessed 8 August 2017.

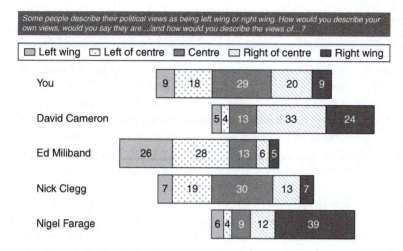

**FIGURE 11.2**  Political views of party leaders.

*Source*: Ipsos Mori/October 2013. Ipsos Mori Survey October 2013. www.ipsos-mori.com/research publications/researcharchive/3282/Public-sees-both-Miliband-and-Cameron-drifting-further-to-theleft-and-right.aspx. Accessed 21 January 2014.

the fear of 'trade union barons', very much part of this 1970s image, is equally distant for many of today's voters.

However, that did not stop the Conservative party and its supporters in the press seeking to paint Miliband's successor, Jeremy Corbyn, in the same light from the time he took over leadership of the Labour Party through to the 2017 election. Still, just as with Miliband, the left-wing bogeyman threat no longer seemed as potent. But there are other explanations why the Red Ed campaign, and the subsequent campaigns against Corbyn, did not appear to capture the popular imagination to the extent to which similar campaigns appeared to do so in the 1980s and 1990s.

First, because television news has far larger audiences and greater credibility than the *Daily Mail*, indeed than of the entire press; broadcasters have, by and large, signally failed to respond to the 'Red Ed' or the Corbyn 2017 campaigns, or the other aspects of the 'othering' framing of Miliband. But the rise of social media has also been another important countervailing force. Social media – Twitter and Facebook in particular – are now able to offer both alternative views and, at times, robust challenges to the political narrative of the mainstream media. Indeed, one of the major drivers of social media conversations is what the mainstream media is reporting, and whether or not it should be trusted. Former BBC Political Correspondent Nick Jones recently wrote:

> While the *Daily Mail's* editor Paul Dacre continues to lick his wounds after a mauling at the hands of what he derides as the 'Twitter mob', his headline writers have had no alternative but to accept the power of social media. Britain's national newspapers are finding that the tone and direction of

their news content is being influenced increasingly by online insurgencies which instantly reveal a level of public reaction which cannot be ignored'.[28]

But perhaps the most important reason why the 'Red Ed' tag failed to resonate is that it did not contain the essential ingredient that a nickname requires for it to have any sort of political potency, which is that it must contain an element of truth – an observation that reflects wider public perceptions or anxieties. The tag 'loony left' worked, and became part of the national conversation, because for some, it did reflect what they perceived (or believed) to be a reality and possibly a threat. Ever since Stanley Cohen revealed in his ground-breaking study how the popular media thrived on the fear engendered by narratives of outside forces threatening society – whether it be Mods and Rockers, extreme weather conditions, the latest infectious disease or anxieties about a supposed 'invasion' of foreign immigrants – fear is a prime media motivator.[29] Ed Miliband no doubt provoked many reactions among British voters, but fear was probably not one of them. Though fear of Miliband forming a coalition government with the Scottish Nationalist Party after the 2015 election did appear to worry some, no doubt fuelled by the extensive coverage this issue received in the media – according to the media content analysis by Loughborough University, it was the second most covered campaign issue.[30]

The abuse against Ed Miliband heightened during the 2015 election. A photograph of Miliband struggling to eat a bacon sandwich, with Scottish Nationalist leader, Nicola Sturgeon, peering over his shoulder, featured prominently during the campaign and formed the *Sun*'s front page two days before the election with the headline 'Save Our Bacon' and a sub-head that read 'This is the Pig's ear Ed made of a helpless sarnie. In 48 hours he could be doing the same to Britain. Don't swallow his porkies and keep him out'.[31] There is no evidence that this was a deliberate attempt to replay the anti-Semitic theme reminiscent of the earlier *Daily Mail* campaign, but inevitably some made that connection, especially as the same picture had first been used in the *Sun* a year before (Figure 11.3). Keith Kahn Harris writing in the *Guardian* observed:

> It's fair game to use an unflattering picture of Miliband – and the picture certainly is unflattering – but why this one? And why use it again, a year after its first use? After all, Miliband's geekiness provides an embarrassment of riches to those seeking his ridicule. And why point out that this is a bacon sandwich? And then emphasise it with jibes about 'pig's ears', 'porkies' and 'saving our bacon'? It's hard to avoid sensing a whiff of antisemitism here. Miliband, after all, could be the first Jewish-born prime minister since Disraeli.[32]

The *Daily Mail* and the other newspapers involved in this campaign of denigration, could point to one other 'success' – that was, as ongoing polling figures demonstrated, in terms of leadership characteristics, the 'othering' of Ed Miliband reflected, or even heightened, widespread public doubts Miliband's

**FIGURE 11.3**   The *Sun* front page, Wednesday 5 May 2016. Courtesy of the *Sun*/News Licensing.

'prime ministerial' qualities. Since being elected to the Labour leadership in 2010, Miliband consistently trailed Prime Minister David Cameron on the crucial personal trait measures – 'He is a natural leader' and 'He is charismatic'. Miliband remained doggedly in single figures on these characteristics throughout his time as Labour leader, whilst David Cameron, and even Nick Clegg, then leader of the Liberal Democrats, were comfortably ahead of Miliband. The 'othering' of Miliband was a clear attempt to keep these negative perceptions in the public eye. Given that post-election polling by the British Election Study appeared to show that Miliband's personal ratings had been a drag on Labour's electoral performance, it is possible to suggest that the *Daily Mail*-led campaign of personal denigration of the Labour leader, could claim to have been successful.[33]

So overall what, if anything, was the significance of the 'Red Ed' phenomenon? First, that even before the rise of Jeremy Corbyn the power of the 'red scare' appeared to be if not over, then significantly diminished in the public mind – even if some sections of the media still see it as a potentially useful weapon to deploy against the Labour Party. This conclusion is reinforced by the failure of similar tactics to dent Jeremy Corbyn's personal popularity during the 2017 election campaign. Indeed, they could well have been decidedly counter-productive.

Second, that the proclivity among some sections of the British press, to seek to undermine Labour support by personal attacks on its leadership is alive and well. One thinks of the personal opprobrium poured on the heads of Neil Kinnock and Michael Foot – that appeared to have vanished under Tony Blair's leadership – re-emerged during the premiership of Gordon Brown, continued under the leadership of Ed Miliband and greatly intensified when Jeremy Corbyn took over.

Having said that and, despite the continuing perception that the right-wing press – particular the *Daily Mail* and the *Sun* – are all-powerful in terms of their influence on the politicians, that power does appear to be diminishing. It is diminishing because there is some evidence, albeit anecdotal that the broadcasters, whose reach and levels of trust among the public far outstrip that of the press, are now aware about, and seek to avoid, being seen as slavishly following the agendas of the *Mail* and the *Sun*.[34] But also, because the political blogs and the social media now see it almost as a badge of honour, to trumpet attempts by the press to abuse their position as the 'fourth estate'.

Following defeat in the 2015 election, Ed Miliband stood down and what followed was a campaign for the Labour leadership unlike any seen before. With four candidates in the mix it attracted a great deal of national media interest, most of which appeared to be focused on either ridiculing the left's candidate, Jeremy Corbyn or trying to ensure that he was not elected. When Corbyn first scraped enough nominations to stand (helped by political opponents who nominated him, secure in the knowledge that he could not win) the media, like most of his parliamentary colleagues, gave him little real chance of success and the initial coverage of his campaign ranged from a complete lack of interest to mockery. Corbyn was described as 'scruffy' and mocked for his apparent Lotharian background – three wives plus a well-documented affair with fellow left-winger Dianne Abbott – which led to him being dubbed by the *Mail* the 'sexpot Trot'; not a moniker that was picked up by any other publication. He was also taken to task for his vegetarianism, his devotion of cycling, his allotment and his fascination with studying manhole covers (not dissimilar to Ken Livingstone's devotion to newts). This mockery soon morphed into a reminder of his 'loony left' associations, current and past. As in previous incarnations of the 'loony left' phenomenon, journalists ascribed to left-wing politicians words associated with lunacy or madness, indicative of the journalists' inability to either understand the rationale behind their politics or their appeal to the public.

As Corbyn's campaign gathered momentum (when spelt with a capital M, this was the clever name that his support group adopted) the *Sun*, almost admiringly, described him as 'A true torch-bearer of what was called the "loony left"'.[35] But in a less charitable mood *Sunday Telegraph* columnist Janet Daley furiously denounced Corbyn and all his works in a piece headlined: 'I've lived under Jeremy Corbyn's rule – it was what turned me into a Tory; the views of this 'loony left'-winger resulted in class hatred and Soviet-style stagnation in the Seventies.'[36] Accusations of lunacy extended to those beyond Corbyn, his number two John McDonnell was described by Jeremy Warner in the *Daily Telegraph* as a 'nutjob'[37] – a jibe for which Warner subsequently apologised. Two days later Matthew Lynn also in the *Telegraph* tastelessly wrote: 'to describe "Corbyn-omics" – to coin a phrase that we may unfortunately have to get used to – as "loony left" would be unfair to the mentally unstable'.[38] Nervousness about what was perceived as 'loony' soon led to fear and anger. Tom Utley, in the *Daily Mail* wrote a gloves-off attack of the Labour leadership candidate headlined: 'What's Labour Come to When the Scumbag Who Applauded My Friend's Ira Murderers Is Shadow Chancellor'.[39] But in a familiar trope, it didn't take the press long to decide that there must be a conspiracy afoot. The *Sunday Times* claimed: 'The Communist party of Great Britain has called on supporters to join and back Corbyn as part of its revolutionary 'strategy'[40] (one is tempted to suggest that 'called on both its supporters' might have given a more accurate picture of the size and relevance of the organisation).

But the *Sunday Times* also carried some of the more intelligent reporting of the Corbyn phenomenon. On the same day that they were discovering 'reds under the bed', there were excellent analysis articles by Sky's Political Editor Adam Boulton, who described Corbyn as 'charming and articulate'[41] and Gordon Brown's former spin doctor, Damian McBride, talked of Corbyn as someone 'with great authenticity, intelligence and principle, and with solid and interesting policies to back it up'.[42] As Corbyn's chances of winning the party leadership began to look more and more like a racing certainty the right-wing press's coverage became ever-more oppositional. Corbyn was portrayed as an angry representative of the hard left with sinister men in the shadows behind him and readers were frequently reminded of Corbyn's previous apparent support for the IRA, Hamas and Hezbollah.

It is hardly surprising that the right-wing media's coverage of Corbyn, the most left-wing leader Labour has had in the post-war period, would be hostile; but what was significant about Corbyn's first leadership campaign was that this hostility was also perceived by many to be found in the BBC's coverage as well. It is frequently claimed that the broadcasters all too often follow the news agenda set by the national newspapers, with their decidedly right-wing take on the news. Indeed, the BBC's former Economics Editor Robert Peston has said the broadcaster had grown 'completely obsessed' with following the news agenda set by coverage of the right-wing papers such as the *Daily Telegraph* and *Daily Mail*. 'There's a slightly "safety first" thing at the BBC – that if we think the *Mail* or the *Telegraph* is gonna lead with it, then we should lead with it,' he said. 'I happen to think that's mad,' he added.[43]

During the discussions about the coverage of Corbyn, Paul Myerscough in the *London Review of Books* observed that the media play a large role in deciding what criteria should be used for judging a political leader's 'electability'. He wrote: 'The hegemon in this respect ... is not the *Guardian*, or even the *Daily Mail*, but the BBC'.[44] But it is not the case that the BBC is simply biased to the right (or to the left for that matter) but that they in fact have a bias towards the status quo, as represented by what they perceive to be a consensual centre, though it's a 'centre' as seen by elite opinion rather than the public at large.[45] In other words, broadcast journalists in general, and particularly those based at Parliament, have been so suffused with a culture of a politics that is orientated around some mythical centre-ground that they are unable to treat fairly politicians (and parties) that are seen to lie outside this consensus.

The BBC's coverage of the first Corbyn leadership campaign in 2015 (he faced a second a year later) was criticised by both those in and outside the Corporation. The former BBC Political Editor, and now presenter of BBC radio's influential 'Today' programme, Nick Robinson, was moved to say publicly how unimpressed he had been with the Corporation's reporting of Corbyn's leadership bid.[46] He was not alone. Sir Michael Lyons, a former Chair of the BBC Trust, claimed that there had been 'some quite extraordinary attacks on the elected leader of the Labour party. I can understand why people are worried about whether some of the most senior editorial voices in the BBC have lost their impartiality on this'[47] and similar concern was expressed by the BBC's former Editorial Director, Roger Mosey who commented:

> My impression is that political correspondents struggle with leaders who are not towards the centre of their parties. There was an incomprehension about Iain Duncan Smith that we now see displayed towards Jeremy Corbyn. Having failed to predict his nomination and then his landslide leadership victory, viewers would now be entitled to be sceptical about pundits' predictions about Corbyn's wider electability.[48]

Much of the criticism of the BBC's coverage was aimed at their Political Editor, Laura Kuenssberg. How much of it was deserved is a moot point, though none of it justified the vilification that Kuenssberg subsequently received. The widely perceived bias was probably being more attributable to the innate 'pro-Westminster bias' discussed earlier than any anti-Corbyn one. One BBC correspondent admitted that initially the would-be Labour leader was seen through a prism that labelled him as either, or both, a hopeless outsider and an extreme left-winger.[49] It probably took the BBC longer than other broadcasters to recognise their own limitations. The BBC's Political News Editor, Katy Searle, appeared to accept the Corporation's 'Westminster bias', telling the BBC Radio 4's Feedback programme 'that traditionally our focus here at BBC Westminster has been across the road the House of Common and House of Lords, Jeremy has forced us to look beyond that'.[50]

There was one particular report by Kuenssberg, in November 2015, that following a complaint from a viewer, was found by the BBC's regulators (at the time the BBC Trust) to have failed to meet the Corporation's standards of accuracy and impartiality. It involved an interview with Corbyn following a horrific terrorist attack in Paris. In the edited interview, Corbyn appeared to suggest that he would have opposed a 'shoot-to-kill' policy being enacted by the French security forces. However, a viewing of the unedited interview showed that Corbyn said he was against such a policy in general, but supported the decision taken by the French authorities in Paris in the particular circumstances of the recent terrorist outrage.

Negative coverage of Corbyn persisted long after he had convincingly won the Labour leadership, indeed, to some extent, it intensified. Researchers for the Media Reform Trust analysed press coverage of Corbyn's first week as leader. Out of a total of 494 news, comment and editorial articles, in the eight daily and Sunday papers they monitored, they found that 60% of articles were mainly negative with only 13% mainly positive and 27% taking a more neutral stand.[51] These findings appeared to be substantiated by research conducted at the same time at London School of Economics, which looked at the coverage in the month of Corbyn's election in September 2015 and the subsequent two months of his leadership. They observed that scorn and ridicule had been key components in the coverage and concluded:

> The results of this study show that Jeremy Corbyn was represented unfairly by the British press through a process of vilification that went well beyond the normal limits of fair debate and disagreement in a democracy. Corbyn was often denied his own voice in the reporting on him and sources that were anti-Corbyn tended to outweigh those that support him and his positions. He was also systematically treated with scorn and ridicule in both the broadsheet and tabloid press in a way that no other political leader is or has been. Even more problematic, the British press has repeatedly associated Corbyn with terrorism and positioned him as a friend of the enemies of the UK. The result has been a failure to give the newspaper reading public a fair opportunity to form their own judgements about the leader of the country's main opposition.[52]

In terms of associating Corbyn with the 'loony left' the LSE Report found that the press came to the view that ridicule was a more effective way of denigrating Corbyn than fear:

> Corbyn is systematically ridiculed, scorned and the object of personal attacks by most newspapers. Even more problematic were a set of

associations which delegitimised Corbyn as a politician, calling him loony, unpatriotic, a terrorist friend and a dangerous individual. It has to be noted though that whereas ridicule and scorn increased in time, the more hard-hitting and emotive frames such as calling him a communist or a terrorist friend diminished over time.[53]

In 2016, a year after his election as party leader, Corbyn faced a second challenge: the coverage of which was monitored by the Media Reform Coalition which, this time, looked at both the press, the broadcasters' and some online coverage of Corbyn's campaign. They analysed a total of 465 articles and reports, drawn from eight online news sites, as well as forty television news bulletins on BBC and ITV. Their sample also covered four national newspapers and three online-only news sites. They found that:

> ...a marked and persistent imbalance in favour of sources critical of Jeremy Corbyn, the issues that they sought to highlight, and the arguments they advanced. This was the case across both the online and television sample. Online news stories overall were almost twice as likely to be written by, or focus on sources critical of Corbyn compared to those that were supportive. The BBC evening news bulletins gave nearly twice as much unchallenged airtime to sources critical of Corbyn compared to those that supported him (an imbalance that was not matched by ITV which gave considerably more equal attention to opposing voices.[54]

The following year, Corbyn suddenly faced the test of a General Election when Conservative Prime Minister, Theresa May, called a snap election in June 2017. The campaign has been described by ITV's Political Editor Robert Peston as: 'The most relentlessly negative campaign that any of us have ever seen'.[55] Media monitoring undertaken by Cardiff and Loughborough universities (which has been a regular feature of past election campaigns) demonstrated that whilst the BBC's coverage was less biased against Corbyn than it had been, there was still some way to go. Cardiff researchers reported that:

> In the run up to election day, Corbyn's popularity was improving according to the polls – and now exceeds May's – but this was not reflected in the editorial construction of public opinion. BBC presenter Jonny Dymond expressed regret about his use of vox pops after the campaign, acknowledging they had failed to accurately reflect the public's changing mood towards Corbyn.[56]

And Loughborough University's monitoring of press coverage of the 2017 campaign revealed:

> the Labour Party received the overwhelming majority of negative evaluations published by the press, largely due to the hostile coverage provided

by higher circulation papers such as the *Sun*, the *Daily Telegraph* and the *Daily Mail*. Newspaper treatment of the Conservatives was broadly more sympathetic.[57]

The election, which many had forecast would be Corbyn and Labour's nemesis, proved not to be the case at all. Whilst the Conservatives were returned as the largest single party they lost their parliamentary majority and were forced to rely on the Democratic Unionist Party of Northern Ireland to stay in power. Meanwhile Labour, far from experiencing an election meltdown as had been predicted, in fact captured thirty seats from the Conservatives. The right-wing press had campaigned against Labour, and Corbyn in particular, with as much venom as they had against Ed Miliband but with, apparently less effect. Many believed that it was a combination of the waning power of the press combined with the rise of social media (Figure 11.4).

But to what extent did the 2017 General Election campaign represent the start of a process in which the influence of the Conservative-supporting press could be seen to be on the wane? They were no less voracious in their attacks on Labour than they had been in the past, indeed on election day under a headline 'Apologists for Terror' they featured pictures of Corbyn, John McDonnell and Diane Abbott (all associated with 'loony left' campaigns in the past), followed by thirteen pages of anti-Labour propaganda[58]. Throughout the election, there was a degree of bile and disdain adopted towards Corbyn by the *Sun*, the *Daily Mail*, the *Daily Express* and the *Daily Telegraph* which outstripped even the hostility they had shown to Miliband. But public opinion was unmoved, indeed throughout the campaign the polls showed growing support for both Labour and Corbyn. At the start of the election campaign, incumbent Prime Minister Theresa May enjoyed a 38% lead over Jeremy Corbyn when the pollsters asked, 'Who would make the better Prime Minister'; by polling day that lead had shrunk to just 11% – an unprecedented narrowing for an election campaign.[59]

A new feature of the campaign that clearly reached a younger audience were the hyper-partisan left-wing news blogs – Skwawkbox, Another Angry Voice, The Canary and Evolve Politics, being the main ones.[60] Despite their relative novelty, often more than matched the traditional media in terms of their social media reach, succeeding in getting articles and videos shared many millions of times across social media platforms. According to the *BuzzFeed News* website, which has developed its own social barometer for measuring online news impacts, 'Nine out of the top 20 most-shared articles came from non-traditional news outlets'.[61]

In terms of influencing the result – to the extent that any media can be said to influence the result – it is this ability to spread the online message virally that appears most potent. *BuzzFeed* found that Labour (and Momentum and the left partisan news blogs) were far more successful at sharing material across social media in general and on Facebook in particular, than were the Conservatives. *BuzzFeed*'s social barometer analytical tool tracked hardly any pro-Conservative material being shared on Facebook as widely as was the case with Labour

# Daily Mail

WEDNESDAY, JUNE 7, 2017          www.dailymail.co.uk          NEWSPAPER OF THE YEAR          65p

VOTE TO SAVE BRITAIN!

# APOLOGISTS FOR TERROR

Jeremy Corbyn

John McDonnell

Diane Abbott

## The Mail accuses this troika of befriending Britain's enemies and scorning the institutions that keep us safe

TODAY, the Daily Mail accuses Jeremy Corbyn, John McDonnell and Diane Abbott — the troika who could run the next government — of being unashamed apologists for terror, who have devoted their lives to befriending the enemies of Britain while undermining the very institutions that keep us safe in our beds.

Let us be clear. We have no doubt that Mr Corbyn's expressions of horror over the atrocities in

### Daily Mail COMMENT

Manchester and at London Bridge, and his sympathy for the victims and their families, were sincere.

But the ineluctable truth is that the Labour leader and his closest associates have spent their careers cosying up to those who hate our

country, while pouring scorn on the police and security services and opposing anti-terror legislation over and over and over again.

Yes, Mr Corbyn has impressed some with his quiet composure under hostile questioning. But he

personally has spent a political lifetime courting mass murderers in the Middle East, Ireland and elsewhere in the world, affronting his party and its decent traditional supporters, while voting on 56 occasions against measures aimed at containing the terrorist threat.

Meanwhile, his closest ally, the Marxist shadow chancellor John McDonnell, has called for MI5 and **Turn to Page 2**

FIGURE 11.4   The *Daily Mail* front page, Wednesday 7 June 2017. Courtesy of Solo Syndication.

material. The most popular article of the entire campaign, that they tracked, was a pro-Labour post on a site called Films for Action which was shared 177,000 times and was read by four million people – it was simply entitled 'This Facebook Comment About the UK Election Is Going Viral'.[62]

A particularly potent example of the effectiveness of Labour's activity on social media was when the left news website *Evolve Politics* picked up a story from a specialist animal rights magazine which they headlined: 'Theresa May's Tory manifesto Scraps the Ban on Elephant Ivory Sales After Bowing to Millionaire Antique Lobbyists'.[63] The original story was completely ignored by the mainstream media, but the Evolve story was shared more than 70,000 times on social media; it was then picked up by the *Independent* website and the *Daily Mirror*. *BuzzFeed* commissioned a YouGov poll to try and ascertain the extent to which this story had reached the public. They found that 14% of the public said they recalled the issue but in the eighteen to twenty-four group that figure rose to 30%. The poll found that of those who knew about the ivory ban, half had encountered it via social media. In the original Evolve story, prime responsibility for getting the ban lifted was attributed to the then Conservative MP Victoria Borwick; she subsequently went on to lose her Kensington seat by just twenty votes.

Following Labour's better than expected election result in 2017, the hostility of the right-wing press to Corbyn briefly died down, only to suddenly fare up again in February 2018 with an almost nostalgic theme, summed up in the *Sun's* front page – 'Corbyn and the Commie Spy'. The *Sun's* story was enthusiastically taken up by the press, despite overwhelming evidence refuting the claim. The smearing of Labour and its leaders has a long and dishonourable history going back to the *Daily Mail's* notorious Zinoviev letter in 1924 – a forgery which painted Labour leaders as secret agents of Moscow. In 1995, Labour leader Michael Foot won a large libel settlement from the *Sunday Times* when it wrongly suggested that he was a KGB 'agent of influence' and; as documented in this chapter, the *Daily Mail* (again) made a sustained and unsuccessful attempt to paint Ed Miliband – Red Ed as they (and virtually they alone) dubbed him – as a far leftist with a communist father "who hated Britain". Now it was Jeremy Corbyn's turn – a far easier target in many ways because of his long and public record campaigning for left-wing causes.

But the attack on Corbyn was, unlike the generalised smears against Miliband; they were based on apparently detailed evidence from a former Czech spy backed up by files found in the archives of the Czech secret police. Following the *Sun's* revelations, the rest of the right-wing press weighed in. Dominic Sandbrook (who played a role in the earlier smearing of the Milibands), denounced Corbyn in the *Mail* under a headline: 'The useful idiot: Jeremy Corbyn's assignations with a secret agent were part of the gullible British Left's love affair with a totalitarian Russian regime that murdered millions'. But in fact, Corbyn had no love for the Soviet Union nor its Eastern bloc allies. Corbyn's politics grew out of the 'new left', which was determinedly opposed to the Soviet brand of Communism. As Robert Colville, Director of the right-wing Centre for Policy Studies think-tank, noted in the *Daily Telegraph* 'he (Corbyn) was a socialist not a Communist; Team Trotsky not Team Stalin'.[64] *Times* columnist, Daniel Finklestein, couldn't make up his mind if Corbyn was for or against the Soviet Union, writing: 'the Labour leader was always plain about his attachment to the Soviet Union' but then going on to remind us that in 1988, when Corbyn was supposed to be acting in the interests of the Soviet Union and its allies, he was publicly calling on Moscow to rehabilitate Trotsky.[65]

Shortly after the stories alleging Corbyn's links with Eastern bloc spies appeared, his close colleagues on the Labour left Ken Livingstone and John McDonnell were also drawn into the conspiratorial net with the *Daily Mail* claiming that they too 'were ALL spying for the Russians along with 12 other senior Labour figures' (original emphasis).[66] The hue and cry should have died down as authoritative secret service sources in both Prague and London denounced the Czech informant as a liar and fantasist – at one stage, he claimed to have organised either, or both, the Live Aid concert and the Free Mandela concerts in the UK. Even more definitive refutations came from officials working in the Czech and German archives (German, because it wasn't long before the Stasi were brought into the picture) – both categorically denying that there was any evidence in their files that Corbyn was either a spy or even an 'asset' (in the parlance of the espionage industry).

One might have thought that that would have been the end of the matter, but the squashing of the original story only succeeded in diverting the press to pursue their earlier vendetta against Corbyn for his support for the reforms to press regulation recommended by the 2012 Leveson Inquiry.[67] In refuting the allegations made by the right-wing press, Corbyn hit back in an online video, saying:

> A free press is essential for democracy and we don't want to close it down, we want to open it up … The general election showed the media barons are losing their influence and social media means their bad old habits are becoming less and less relevant. But instead of learning these lessons they're continuing to resort to lies and smears. Their readers – you, all of us – deserve so much better. Well, we've got news for them: change is coming.[68]

The words 'change is coming' acted like the proverbial red rag to a bull. Corbyn's supposed past support for the Soviet Union was linked to his alleged desire to control the British media. The *Mail* ran an article by John Stevens linking the two, under the headline: 'Corbyn's Response To Spy Row: No Answers And A Chilling Threat To Britain's Free Press'.[69] The *Sun*, in its editorial column, warned: 'Controlling the press is a first step towards the one-party state Corbyn's hard-left extremist's dream of'.[70] The *Mail* offered its 'assistance' to BBC journalists, advising them that the purge wouldn't stop at the press: 'The Corporations' staff should watch out. If this Marxist comes to power he'll be gagging them too'[71] it fulminated.

## Notes

1 G. Levy 'The man who hated Britain' *Daily Mail* 28 September 2013.
2 For an extended discussion of the targeting of Ed Miliband see I. Gaber 'The Tory targeting of Miliband' in D. Wring, S. Atkinson and R. Mortimore (eds) *Political Communications: the 2015 Election* (Basingstoke: Palgrave-Macmillan, 2017) pp. 273–91.

3 ICM for the *Guardian* recorded a doubling in Labour's lead over the Conservatives from 4% to 8% in the period before and after the speech www.theguardian.com/news/datablog/2009/0ct/21/icm-poll-data-labour-conservatives accessed 22 January 2014.

4 R. Littlejohn 'Back to the future with Marxist Miliband' *Daily Mail* 24 September 2013.

5 'Obituary Ralph Miliband' *The Times* 10 June 1994.

6 'Obituary Eric Hobsbawm' *The Times* 2 October 2012.

7 D. Sandbrook 'Miliband's Marxist father and the real reason he wants to drag us back to the nightmare' *Daily Mail* 26 September 2013.

8 Levy op cit.

9 *Daily Mail* 'An evil legacy and why we won't apologise' 1 October 2013.

10 Ibid.

11 Ibid.

12 *Press Gazette* 26 June 2017. www.pressgazette.co.uk/nrs-national-press-readership-data-telegraph-overtakes-guardian-as-most-read-quality-title-in-printonline/.

13 R. Lustig 'The newspaper that really hates Britain' 4 October 2013.

14 J. Freedland 'Antisemitism doesn't always come doing a Hitler salute' *Guardian* 5 October 2013.

15 *Daily Mail* Comment 11 April 2013.

16 A. Rawstorne 'Hardly bog standard … Ed's days at the Eton for Lefties' *Daily Mail* 2 October 2012.

17 Ibid.

18 M. Burleigh In Hampstead parlours, intellectual apologists for Stalin like Ralph Miliband's great friend Eric Hobsbawm and his tutor Harold Laski loved talking in abstractions as millions died in horror' *Daily Mail* 2 October 2013.

19 A. Pierce 'Revealed: how the unions got Red Ed in a headlock' *Daily Mail* Comment 4 July 2013.

20 *Daily Mail* 'The spectre Of Red Ed's thought police' 22 March 2013.

21 Littlejohn op cit.

22 R. Pendlebury 'Wife who still can't forgive brother-in-law Ed's betrayal' *Daily Mail* 27 March 2013.

23 A. Pierce and R. Pendlebury 'Treachery and a very bitter wife' *Daily Mail* 13 June 2011.

24 R. Pendlebury 'Will he now marry the mother of his son? And why isn't he on the birth certificate?' *Daily Mail* September 27, 2010.

25 Pierce and Pendlebury op cit.

26 Black Dog 'Now it's Orange Ed' *Mail on Sunday* 3 February 2013.

27 Letts, Q "Red Ed points the finger" *Daily Mail* 14 December 2012.

28 N. Jones, 'Is the "Twitter mob" taming the *Daily Mail*? How online reaction influences mainstream news' 2013 www.nicholasjones.org.uk/articles/34-media-trends/271-is-the-twitter-mob-taming-the-daily-mail-how-online-reaction-influences-mainstream-news.

29 S. Cohen *Folk Devils and Moral Panics* (London, Routledge 2011).

30 Media Coverage of the 2015 General Election, Centre for Research in Communication and Culture, University of Loughborough. http://blog.lboro.ac.uk/crcc/general-election/media-coverage-of-the-2015-campaign-report-5/.

31 *Sun* 6 May 2015.

32 K. Kahn-Harris 'Is the *Sun's* "save our bacon" election front page antisemitic? *Guardian* 6 May 2015.

33 British Election Study 2015. www.britishelectionstudy.com/news-category/2015-general-election/.

34 Broadcast journalists tend to deny that they give undue prominence to the news agendas of the right-wing press but private conversations between the author and

current broadcast journalists suggests that recognition of this 'bias' is now accepted and is consciously being combatted, see later in this chapter for further discussion of this issue.

35 'Are you Michael Foot in disguise? We ask as Corbyn vies to lead Labour' 24 July 2015.

36 J. Daley 'I've lived under Jeremy Corbyn's rule – it was what turned me into a Tory; the views of this "loony left"-winger resulted in class hatred and Soviet-style stagnation in the Seventies' *Sunday Telegraph* 26 July 2015.

37 J. Warner 'Corbyn has just appointed a nutjob as Shadow Chancellor' *Daily Telegraph* 14 September 2015.

38 M. Lynn 'Why we should all start feeling nervous about Corbyn-omics' *Daily Telegraph 31* July 2015.

39 T. Utley 'What's Labour come to when the scumbag who applauded my friend's IRA murderers is Shadow Chancellor?' *Daily Mail* 18 September 2015.

40 J. Lyons and R. Henry 'Hard left plot to infiltrate Labour race; Harman urged to halt leadership vote' *Sunday Times* 26 July 2015.

41 A. Boulton 'No beard, no loony leanings: meet Labour's real next leader' *Sunday Times* 26 July 2015.

42 D. McBride 'Labour must use Cameron's pin to pop the Corbyn bubble' *Sunday Times* 26 July 2015.

43 M. Brown & J. Deans 'Robert Peston: BBC follows the *Daily Mail*'s lead too much' *Guardian* 6 June 2014.

44 P. Myerscough, 'Corbyn in the media'. *London Review of Books* 37(20) 2015 pp. 8–9. Available from www.lrb.co.uk/v37/n20/paul-myerscough/corbyn-in-the-media.

45 See I. Gaber 'Bending over backwards: the BBC and the Brexit campaign' in *EU Referendum Analysis 2016: Media, Voters and the Campaign* by D. Jackson, E. Thorsen, and D. Wring (eds), (Bournemouth: Political Studies Association and Bournemouth University 2016).

46 L. Barber 'Here's to you, Mr Robinson' *Sunday Times* 15 November 2016.

47 R. Mason 'BBC may have shown bias against Corbyn' *Guardian* 12 May 2016.

48 Roger Mosey private correspondence with author 8 June 2016.

49 Private conversation with author.

50 *Feedback* BBC Radio 4 16 September 2016.

51 'Media reform trust Corbyn's first week: negative agenda setting in the press' www.mediareform.org.uk/wp-content/uploads/2015/11/Corbyns_First_Week-Negative_Agenda_Setting_in_the_Press.pdf.

52 'Journalistic representations of Jeremy Corbyn in the British press: from watchdog to attack dog' Media@LSE Report p. 1. www.lse.ac.uk/media-and-communications/research/research-projects/representations-of-jeremy-corbyn.

53 Op cit, p.12.

54 'Should he stay or should he go?' Television and Online News Coverage of the Labour Party in Crisis Media Reform Coalition op cit, p. 4.

55 Robert Peston speaking on *The Media Show*, BBC Radio 4 20 December 2017.

56 S. Cushion 'Were broadcasters biased against Jeremy Corbyn? It's the details that count' *New Statesman* 21 June 2016.

57 Loughborough University Centre for Research in Communication and Culture 'A tale of two leaders: news media coverage of the 2017 General Election' 19 June 2017. http://blog.lboro.ac.uk/crcc/general-election/tale-two-leaders-news-media-coverage-2017-general-election/.

58 *Daily Mail* 'Labour's apologists for terror: The *Mail* accuses Corbyn troika of befriending Britain's enemies and scorning the institutions that keep us safe' 8 June 2017.

59 Ipsos Mori www.ipsos.com/ipsos-mori/en-uk/most-capable-prime-minister-trends.

60 The challenge to the mainstream media that began with Corbyn's Labour leadership campaign and extended to the 2017 election is discussed in more detail in Chapter 12.

61 J. Waterson 'This was the Election where the newspapers lost their monopoly on the political news agenda' *Buzzfeed* 18 June 2017. www.*Buzzfeed*.com/jimwaterson/how-newspapers-lost-their-monopoly-on-the-political-agenda?utm_term=.ywrm-rqrRE4#.qevJdodNjw.

62 www.filmsforaction.org/articles/this-facebook-comment-about-the-uk-election-is-going-viral/.

63 S. Winterbottom 'Theresa May's Tory manifesto SCRAPS THE BAN on elephant ivory sales after bowing to millionaire antique lobbyists' *Evolve Politics* 20 May 2017. http://evolvepolitics.com/theresa-mays-tory-manifesto-scraps-ban-elephant-ivory-sales-bowing-millionaire-antique-lobbyist/.

64 R. Colville 'The truth about Jeremy Corbyn: not a spy but a fool who hates capitalism and the West' *Daily Telegraph* 22 February 2018.

65 D. Finklestein 'Communism Explains a Lot About Corbyn' *The Times* 21 February 2018.

66 K. Ferguson and K. Southern 'Czech agent claims Ken Livingstone, John McDonnell and Jeremy Corbyn were ALL spying for the Russians along with 12 other senior Labour figures' *Daily Mail* 18 Feb 2018.

67 Department for Digital, Culture, Media & Sport 'Leveson Inquiry – Report into the culture, practices and ethics of the press' 2012. www.gov.uk/government/publications/leveson-inquiry-report-into-the-culture-practices-and-ethics-of-the-press.

68 D. Sabbagh 'Spying row: how Corbyn seized chance to take on the Sun; Labour used to woo the right-wing press; the age of social media has changed all that' *Guardian* 21 February 2018.

69 J. Stevens 'Corbyn's response to Spy Row: no answers and a chilling threat to Britain's free press' *Daily Mail* 21 February 2018.

70 The *Sun* 'The *Sun* Says Jeremy Corbyn's war on press is a hostile attempt to silence negative stories about him' 22 February 2018.

71 Mail Editorial 'Memo to the BBC: he will come for you too' *Daily Mail* 22 February 2018.

# 12

# RETURN OF THE REPRESSED

*James Curran*

During the 1980s, the new urban left was rendered toxic. It was reviled by the press, demonised by Conservative government minsters, denounced by Labour's leadership and viewed as a liability by a large part of the Labour movement. Its project was widely dismissed by the end of the 1980s as a failed experiment – a view that solidified in the 1990s.[1] The phrase 'loony left' entered the English language to denote a deluded socialism that warranted only ridicule. Nothing more needed to be said, no additional arguments needed to be mustered: the 'loony left' stood for all that was absurd about an unhinged, zealous, politically correct strand of social radicalism.

Yet, quietly and unobtrusively, the new urban left's political agenda was incorporated into mainstream politics. Their once derided policies gave rise to new laws, new business practices and revised social norms. This shift came about because the new urban left, dominated by people born in the late 1940s and shaped by the cultural ferment of the 1960s, were the outriders of change. They controlled some London town halls, the foothills of power, in the 1980s. But by the 2000s, members of this baby boomer generation, and their successors, were heading the government, opposition parties, leading public institutions and large business corporations, and advanced the derided politics of the 'loony left'.

Of course, this account contains an element of simplification. Generations are not homogenous: there were ardent social liberals in the pre-1945 generation, and zealous social conservatives in the next. Furthermore, the new urban left was not the principal authors of political innovation: they were responding primarily to external pressures generated by new dynamic forces within the wider community.[2] But while not implying a monistic explanation of change, a generational shift was an important factor in making acceptable attitudes and policies that had been scorned by middle-aged Conservative politicians and journalists in the 1980s.

## Gay liberation

The issue that generated the greatest hostility towards the new urban left was sexuality. The AIDS panic began in 1983, and reached its peak in the mid-1980s, exacerbating already widespread animosity towards gays and lesbians. The stance of the new urban left, that no social stigma should attach to being gay and lesbian, that the Gay Liberation movement should be supported and that homophobia should be actively confronted, was viewed by much of the press as dangerous and irresponsible. It 'pretended' that unnatural sex, proscribed by religion and social convention, was natural. It promoted, it was argued, sexual activity which spread the 'gay plague', AIDS, and endangered 'innocent' people. It 'encouraged' suggestible teenagers into abhorrent behaviour. It supposedly placed children at risk since, it was then believed, homosexuals were especially prone to be paedophiles.

The new urban left's support of Gay Liberation in the 1980s challenged the liberal political bargain that had been struck in the 1960s. Although sex between gay men aged over twenty had been decriminalised in 1967, gays and lesbians had been denied the same legal entitlements as heterosexuals. By attacking this compromise, the new urban left was waging war on two fronts: against social conservatives who thought that gay sex should never have been legalised in the first place, and against traditional liberals who, while not wanting gay men to be jailed, did not think that the state should approve (and 'encourage') their way of life.

The new urban left paid a heavy price for flouting prevailing views in both the press and public life. So ardent was the Sun's hostility towards homosexuals during the AIDS panic that it even offered British gay men a one-way air ticket to Norway, under the headline, 'Fly Away Gays – and We Will Pay!'[3] Britain's best-selling daily regularly denounced what it called 'the lunatic fringe of the Labour Party, which has adopted homosexuality as a political cause'.[4] Along with other popular papers, it fuelled animosity both towards gays and to the political movement that spoke up for them.

However, the prejudices that fed this newspaper bigotry receded. Whereas 74% said that same sex relationships were always or mostly wrong in 1987, only 16% took this view in 2016.[5] In 1983, only 41% thought it was right for a homosexual person to be teacher at a school, compared with 83% in 2012. Similarly, a bare majority (53%) in 1983 thought that it was acceptable for a homosexual 'to hold a responsible position in public life' whereas nearly everyone (90%) was comfortable with this position in 2012.[6] While social disapproval of gays and lesbians did not disappear, the proportion of people opposing the adoption of children by gay couples more than halved between 1983 and 2012.[7]

This remarkable shift was mainly a product of generational change. As Alison Park and Rebecca Rhead conclude on the basis of three decades of survey data, 'each successive generation has more liberal views on homosexuality than the one before'.[8] In addition, 'all generations have become more liberal [on the issue of homosexuality] over time'.[9] In brief, the municipal left of the 1980s were reviled for holding opinions that became commonplace by 2012.

In line with this shift of public opinion, state discrimination against gays and lesbians was overturned through successive reforms. In 2000, the policy of banning homosexuals from the armed forces was dropped. In 2001, the age of consent for gay sex was lowered from twenty-one to sixteen (same as for straight sex). In 2002, same sex adoption was legalised. In 2003, the notorious section 28 was repealed, and discrimination against gays and lesbians was made illegal. In 2004, gay couples were given the same rights as heterosexual couples through the Civil Partnership Act. In 2007, discrimination against gays and lesbians in the provision of goods and services was outlawed through strengthened legislation. In 2013, gay and lesbian marriage was legalised by the Marriage (Same Sex Couples) Act.

The position adopted by the new urban left in the 1980s that gay and lesbian relationships should be 'normalised' thus became part of mainstream politics. The derided margins became the centre ground of British politics. The extent of this change is illustrated by the different political responses that occurred over time. In 1986, Labour Leader Neil Kinnock, and his team, rebuked the new urban left for championing gays and lesbians because they feared that this was alienating Labour's core support.[10] In 2004, Tony Blair broke with this caution by establishing same-sex civil partnerships. And in 2013, Prime Minister David Cameron faced down opposition in his own party to introduce gay marriage. Where a Labour leader had feared to tread in the 1980s, a modernising Conservative leader marched confidently forward and introduced historic legislation.

## Feminism

Something not dissimilar happened in relation to women's rights. The second wave of feminism had helped to secure major gender equality legislation in the 1970s. However, feminism still attracted widespread derision and hostility during the early 1980s. It was attacked as 'man-hating', and associated with lesbianism and the militant left.[11] When the new urban left championed women's liberation, it was castigated by popular national papers for questioning 'the traditional values of the sexes'[12] and 'turning all accepted ideas upside down'.[13]

But, as with homosexuality, a sea-change occurred in public attitudes. Whereas in 1987 48% of the population agreed that 'a man's job is to earn money' and 'the woman's job is to look after the home and family', only 13% took this view in 2012.[14] This reflected a generational shift. In 2012, support for a gendered division of labour between the male breadwinner and the female homemaker was much more pronounced among old people (those aged sixty-six years and over) than among the young.[15] In particular, younger people were much more inclined than the older generation to say that it was acceptable for women with young children to go out to work.[16]

Attitudes towards opposing gender inequality also changed, although in a qualified way. The traditional stigma attached to feminism lingered on. In 2015, only 7% of British adults (and 9% of women) defined themselves as feminists,[17] principally because feminism was associated with being extreme, polarising and political.[18] But the woman's movement became stronger from the 1980s onwards partly as a consequence of gaining increased support from the right, and also from men. By 2015, large majorities in Britain agreed that gender equality was desirable, that it had not been achieved and that more needed to be done to rectify this.[19] Indeed, 67% said that they were sympathetic to feminism.[20] Feminism-lite became mainstream.

Gender inequality lessened[21] but still remained pervasive. In 2015–6, women made up 39% of senior civil servants, 14% of police commissioners, 21% of high court judges, 17% of university vice-chancellors and 26% of FSTE 100 board directors.[22] In 2012, men spent an average of eight hours per week on housework compared to thirteen hours spent by women.[23] This prompted six out of ten women to complain that they did more than their fair share of household work.[24]

Continuing inequality generated pressure for reform. In 2017, the 'Me Too' hashtag campaign targeted powerful men who sexually harassed younger women. As a result, a number of prominent figures in politics and the media in both Britain and the United States were forced to resign. Public debate is now causing what is acceptable and unacceptable to be redefined.

Changing times made the feminist politics espoused by the new urban left seem less contentious. Thus, the women's committees set up by radical councils in order to offset the male dominance of local politics, and strengthen the voice of women in local government decision-making, had been attacked in the right-wing press in the early 1980s. Yet, this affirmative action approach was later adopted in a new form that changed national politics. After the 1992 general election, the Labour Party introduced, in some constituencies, women-only shortlists for the selection of parliamentary candidates. This was largely responsible for the number of women MPs doubling between 1992 and 1997 general elections.[25] The selective adoption of women-only shortlists continued during the New Labour era, and beyond, helping to change the composition of the Commons. The number of women MPs increased from just twenty-three in 1983 to 208 in 2017.[26]

Women-only shortlists were not adopted by the Conservative and Liberal parties, and were denounced in right-wing newspapers. However, a softer version of this 'positive action' approach – affirmative *targeting* – became part of the new consensus both in business and politics. Thus, in response to pressure from a Conservative government, the FSTE 350 companies set a target of securing 33% of women on their boards by 2020.[27]

In addition to creating women's committees, radical councils in the early 1980s funded more nurseries; adopted working practices that encouraged the retention and promotion of female council staff; and supported women's groups in order to strengthen the voice of women in the local community. None of these policies appeared controversial in the twenty-first century. The expansion of nursery provision accelerated during the early 2000s. The women-friendly employment policies of left-wing councils in the 1980s – such as crèches, flexible working hours, job-share posts, in-service training, multiple points of entry and new routes for career progression – were later adopted in numerous large organisations from Goldman Sachs to the National Health Service. The funding of women's groups – whether by the government, the Arts Council or charitable bodies – no longer causes eyebrows to be raised. Once again the passage of time resulted in policies championed by the new urban left becoming part of the mainstream of public life.

## Environmentalism

The environmentalism of the new urban left was less controversial than its feminism because green politics had significant minority right-wing as well as left-wing support in the 1980s. But it was widely viewed as a fringe interest, part of the eccentricity of the 'newt-loving' leader of the GLC, Ken Livingstone. This tolerance evaporated, however, when Livingstone – elected as Mayor of London in 2000 – introduced in 2003 a congestion charge for cars entering the centre of London in order to reduce both traffic congestion and pollution. The *Daily Telegraph* (25 January 2003) denounced 'Ken Livingstone's mad-cap plans for London Traffic control', while the *Sunday Times* (29 January 2003) attacked the 'madness' imposed by a 'barmy' dictator. The *Sun*, in a succession of articles, called Livingstone variously the 'madcap mayor', 'crazy', 'loopy', 'crackpot', 'potty' and 'barmy'.[28] The *Sunday Mirror* (14 July 2002) joined in, calling Livingstone 'barmy', and the congestion charge a 'farce' created by a 'power-crazed and authoritarian politician', while a feature article in the *Daily Mirror* (24 January 2003) denounced the congestion charge as 'nothing short of legalised mugging'.

Yet, despite this press excoriation, the congestion charge proved a success in reducing traffic in central London, and addressing the growing problem of pollution. No attempt was made to abolish the congestion charge when a Conservative London Mayor was elected in 2008. Indeed, congestion charge schemes were introduced in numerous other cities (such as Milan and Singapore).

The green politics of the new urban left – its desire to prevent the destruction of the environment, its drive to preserve wildlife in the capital and crusade to support public transport – no longer seemed so marginal due to a change in the zeitgeist. In the new millennium, there was a growing realisation that the world faced a catastrophe unless accelerating climate change was arrested. Indeed, climate change sceptics were increasingly confined to free market fundamentalists, like former Conservative Ministers Nigel Lawson and Peter Lilley, whose voices were amplified by the right-wing press. But only a handful of MPs opposed the Labour government when it introduced the Climate Change Act in 2008 setting out a detailed plan for reducing carbon admissions. Britain's support for the Paris Agreement on Climate Change in 2016, under the aegis of a Conservative government, had all-party backing. Public opinion also turned strongly against climate change deniers. In 2014, a mere 6% disputed that the planet was warming; and a further 6% disagreed that human activity was contributing to climate change.[29]

In short, the climate warming crisis cast the new urban left's green politics in a new light. It made the desire to protect the environment less of a minority concern.

## Anti-racism

The new urban left had argued in the 1980s that an abstract commitment to equal opportunities was not enough, and that ethnic monitoring of employees, targets for increased ethnic minority recruitment, anti-racism training courses and the funding of ethnic minority organisations were needed to overcome the cumulative effects of racial disadvantage and discrimination.[30]

The right-wing press had angrily denounced this at the time as 'inverted racism'. Yet, when the baby boomer generation took control in the Blair years, the new urban left's 'positive action' race agenda became mainstream policy. In 1999, the Home Secretary, Jack Straw (born in 1946) established targets for increased recruitment of Black and Asian officers in the fire, immigration, probation and prison services.[31] In 2001, the BBC's new Director General, Greg Dyke (born in 1947) called the corporation 'hideously white' and introduced targets for ethnic minority recruitment.[32] The Metropolitan Police, troubled by how unrepresentative it was of multi-ethnic London and disconcerted by the damning criticisms of police failings in the Macpherson Inquiry Report, had done the same thing two years before.[33] Large numbers of commercial organisations, with a social responsibility orientation, also adopted 'positive action' policies on race. For example, the great majority of premiership and first division football clubs in the early 2000s ethnically monitored their staff, sought to recruit from minority communities, and opposed with growing success racism in football.[34] In 2004, the Football Association decided to 'fast-track' ethnic minorities on its decision-making bodies at both national and local level.[35] By 2016, the promotion of greater ethnic diversity in the recruitment of the police, teaching and other public services had become part of the new consensus. The issue had become not whether to pursue an ethnic diversity programme but how to do it more effectively, particularly in the higher reaches of management.[36]

The legacy of the new urban left thus appeared to be reshaping the politics of race relations. This was seemingly in tune with a wider change in society. When Labour governments had passed the historic Race Relations Acts of 1965 and 1968 outlawing racial discrimination, they had faced fierce opposition. But whereas only an average of 45% had supported national legislation against race discrimination in the period 1967–8, this rose to 69% by 1983.[37] This was in a context where most people recognised that racism was widespread, and thought that something should be done about it. In 1983, nine out of ten people thought that British society was racially prejudiced against its black and Asian members.[38]

Two-thirds also believed that these minorities suffered discrimination in terms of getting jobs.[39]

After the 1980s, the progressive tide seemingly continued to rise. The British Social Attitudes Survey asked at periodic intervals whether respondents would mind if a close relative married someone who was black or Asian. Whereas over 50% expressed hostility to inter-racial marriage in their family in the late 1980s, this dropped to 35% in 1996 and to 20% in 2013.[40] This shift was related to generational change: young people growing up in multiracial Britain were much more accepting of ethnic inter-marriage than elderly people growing up in a largely white society.[41] It was also linked to the rapid expansion of universities: graduates were more accepting than school leavers.[42]

But if one part of society became less racist, another part dug in its heels. Between 1983 and 2017, the percentage of people saying that they were prejudiced against other races fell from 36% to 26%. But this decline was not linear. Setting aside temporary fluctuations, explicit racism moved downwards until 2001, then increased reaching a peak in 2012 (38%), before falling back again. Even though the overall trend was downwards, those saying that they were racially prejudiced never dropped below a quarter of the population for over thirty years.[43]

One explanation for the resilience of this racism is that it was anchored by beliefs about racial inferiority. In 2014, 44% said that some races or ethnic groups were born harder-working than others, while 18% said that that some were born less intelligent.[44]

Racism was further fuelled by the rise of Islamophobia, in the context of terrorist attacks after 2001 and sustained newspaper criticism of Muslim communities accused of incubating home-grown jihadis.[45] In 2013, twice as many people said that they would mind a family member marrying a Muslim as said the same of a black person.[46]

A third reason is that racism was boosted by growing opposition to high migration into the United Kingdom. By 2013, 77% of people wanted immigration reduced, with 56% saying that they wanted a large reduction. This was a significant jump compared with 1995 when 39% wanted immigration reduced by a large amount.[47] Growing resentment was reinforced by a right-wing popular press campaign against migrants that began in 2002 and persisted up to the 2016 Brexit referendum. Popular papers exaggerated the number of migrants, attacked them for importing crime and terrorism, criticised them for their alien ways and lambasted them for imposing a heavy burden on already strained public services. Popular newspaper articles about migrants rarely quoted them or offered perspectives from their point of view.[48]

There were further indications that the progressive tide in relation to race was receding. In keeping with the symbolic proselytising of the new urban left, the Blair government initially promoted a multicultural, plural definition of what it is to be British in opposition to a traditionalist understanding emphasising Britain's historic national heritage. But, as we have seen, when New Labour encountered strong headwinds on this issue, it backed down.[49]

So what emerges is a mixed picture. A rising tide of social liberalisation gave rise to more tolerant attitudes in relation to sexuality, gender and race (among other issues).[50] This caused the policies of the municipal left – which had been reviled in the 1980s – to become more politically acceptable. However, race was the one area where the advance of social liberalism encountered entrenched resistance. It was an early indication that the pendulum could swing back.

## Brexit revolt

In 2016, Britain voted by a narrow majority (52–48%) to leave the European Union. The level of turnout (72%) was relatively high, significantly higher than in recent general elections. Numerous people, who tended not to vote, participated in this historic poll.

The referendum result did not reflect a conventional left-right split. Thus, Conservative supporters divided 54/46% in favour of Leave. A third of Labour supporters, and over a quarter of Liberal supporters, joined the Conservative Brexiters.[51] The referendum registered a deep-seated cleavage not so much on party as on educational, generational and class lines. Only 22% of graduates voted to Leave, compared with 72% of those without educational qualifications. Just 28% of those aged eighteen to twenty-four voted Leave, compared with 63% aged sixty-five or over. And only 36% of voters in the managerial and professional groups opted for Leave, compared with 60% in routine or semi-routine occupations.[52] What gave rise to this new political geography?

First, the Leave vote was, in part, a protest against migration. Of those who cited immigration as a concern, 73% voted Leave.[53] In another survey, 80% of those who thought that immigration is 'a force for ill' voted Leave.[54]

Net migration had risen sharply between 1998 and 2015, provoking growing opposition which had been ignored or been met with misleading reassurances. The free movement rules of the European Union ultimately made it very difficult for any party in power to prevent migration to relatively prosperous Britain.

However, it was not just the openly racist minority who were opposed to increased migrant numbers. Most new migrants in the recent period came in fact from Eastern Europe and were not ethnically different from the majority in the UK. Something more lay behind this opposition. People in unskilled and semi-skilled jobs tended to view migration negatively, whereas those in managerial and professional grades tended to view migration positively.[55] While this divergence could reflect differences of outlook between those anchored in local communities ('somewheres') and geographically mobile graduates open to new people and experiences ('anywheres'),[56] it also stemmed from a basic economic fact. The unskilled and semi-skilled faced the brunt of competition from cheap migrant labour.

Second, the key driver of the Brexit vote was the 'lure of greatness'.[57] Leaving Europe offered the promise of national renewal. Leave campaigners argued that the British people would be able to take back control from stifling European bureaucracy and regain the vigour and dynamism that had made Britain great. This vision of national renewal was evoked by Foreign Secretary Boris Johnson when he spoke in Manchester in 2017:

> Two hundred years ago people used to come to this city to see something revolutionary – the beginning of the modern world. And once again this country has had the guts to try to do something new and different: to challenge received wisdom with a democratic revolution that we can turn into a cultural and technological and commercial renaissance. ... We [the government] have been privileged collectively to be placed in charge of this amazing country at a critical moment in our history. We are not the lion. We do not claim to be the lion. That role is played by the people of this country. But it is up to us now – in the traditional non-threatening, genial and self-deprecating way of the British – to let that lion roar.[58]

This vision of 'Brexitannia' resonated more with older people, who had a stronger sense of Britain's national decline and of a connection to a glorious past, than to the younger generation. It also appealed more to people with a strong English rather than more inclusive British identity,[59] reflecting in part differences of national identity and outlook in divergent parts of a conglomerate country.[60]

'Taking back control' also chimed with what the British press had been publishing for two decades. For example European bureaucrats, it was reported, were about to ban barmaids from wearing low cut tops ('Hands off our barmaids' boobs') (*Sun* 4 August 2005); instruct 'women to hand in worn-out sex toys' (*Sun* 4 February 2004); outlaw corgis ('the Queen's favourite dog') (*Daily Mail* 30 April 2002); stop the weekday sale of booze by off-licences (*Sun* 21 February 2005); insist on the relabelling of yoghurt as 'fermented milk pudding' (*Sunday Mirror* 5 March 2006); 'rename Trafalgar Square and Waterloo Station' (*Daily Express* 16 October 2003); and impose a quota of gypsy MPS on the UK (Daily Express 30 September 2013). Not one of these stories was true.[61] Yet, they conveyed the impression that the British people were being bossed about by Brussels in pettifogging and absurd ways.

During the campaign itself, only 27% of articles concerned with the Referendum in nine national papers were pro-Remain, whereas 41% were in favour of Brexit.[62] The imbalance was even greater due to the circulation dominance of the Leave press. Over 80% of consumers who bought a daily newspaper read a title favouring British withdrawal from the EU.[63]

Third, the Brexit vote was an anti-establishment protest. The neo-liberal consensus at Westminster was not shared by the majority of British public which clung, as successive surveys over more than thirty years demonstrate, to key aspects of the post-war social democratic settlement.[64] In addition, the 2008 crash led to a long period of stagnant wages, and gave rise to increased resentment of an unrepresentative political class. In 2015, 72 % agreed that politics 'is dominated by self-seeking politicians protecting the interests of the already rich and powerful', with just 8% disagreeing.[65] Reluctant public consent for austerity measures as being necessary ebbed in 2015.[66] Above all, there was a backlog of resentment in the declining parts of Britain. This is why areas with long term declines in manufacturing (but also in agriculture and public employment) were more inclined to vote Leave.[67] Those thinking that 'life in Britain today is worse than 30 years ago' were disposed to vote Leave, while those thinking that life is better were strongly in favour of Remain.[68] The Brexit vote was thus partly an expression of anger and disappointment by people who felt that they had been left behind and disregarded.

Fourth, Brexit reflected a resurgent social conservatism. The referendum was a mobilising moment for an anti-liberal reaction. 81% of those who thought multiculturalism is a force for ill voted Leave. By contrast, 71% of those who viewed multiculturalism as a force for good voted Remain. 74% of people with a negative view of feminism voted Leave, whereas 62% with a positive view voted Remain. In line with this, 80% with a negative view of social liberalism voted Leave, whereas 68% of those with a positive view voted Remain. This cultural schism extended into other areas. Thus, 69% of those with a negative image of the green movement voted Leave, in contrast to the 62% of those with a positive image who opted for Remain.[69]

John Curtice also found that the Referendum triggered an analogous clash between what he termed 'authoritarians' and 'libertarians'. 'Authoritarians' who feel that everybody in society should adhere to a common set of social mores and cultural practices, making for a more cohesive society (about a third of the country), voted overwhelmingly to vote Leave. By contrast, 'social libertarians' (another third of the nation) who emphasise the value of personal freedom and social diversity overwhelmingly voted Remain.[70]

The European Union referendum was thus a veiled culture war between social liberals and social conservatives. However, social conservatives had the wind behind them. The global re-division of labour, and consequent de-industrialisation in Britain, had created huge resentment. Indeed, 71% of those who said that glo-balisation was a force for ill voted Leave.[71] But this bottled up sense of anger and impotence found a focus in opposition to rapid immigration, and hope in the vision of national renewal. Economic resentments were channelled in a conserva-tive direction: into hostility towards foreigners and resurgent nationalism.

This brought into focus the uneven nature of the supposed 'success' of the new urban left. In its 1980s incarnation, the new urban left was both economi-cally interventionist and socially radical. It believed that an activist state should generate jobs and redistribute resources from rich to poor. Its social radicalism in promoting greater tolerance and embracing diversity was only one part of its programme.

But while the social radicalism of the new urban left won increasing support, its economic activism was rejected. The period between 1979 and 2015 marked the political ascendancy of neo-liberalism – in the sense of support for privati-sation, deregulation, a more open market and the legal emasculation of trade unions. Measures that could have been taken to support failing, de-industrialising regions by an activist state were rejected because they were deemed to be misconceived within the prevailing economic orthodoxy. This fuelled the anger and despair that contributed to the Brexit vote, and the reinvigoration of a nationalist conservatism.

The new urban left was thus influential in the cultural sphere but was decisively defeated in the economic sphere. The Brexit result is a warning that failure in one area may undo success in the other.

## Notes

1　See Chapter 7.
2　See Chapter 2.
3　Cited in S. Watney, *Policing Desire* (London: Commedia, 1987), p. 147.
4　*Sun*, 6 March 1987.
5　K. Swales and E. Taylor, 'Moral issues: Sex, gender identity and euthanasia' in E. Clery, J. Curtice and R. Harding (eds.) *British Social Attitudes 34* (London: National Centre for Social Research, 2017), p. 88. Available at: www.bsa.natcen.ac.uk/latest-report/british-social-attitudes-34/moral-issues.aspx (accessed January 3, 2018).
6　'Key findings' in A. Park, C. Bryson, E. Clery, J. Curtice, and M. Phillips (eds.) *British Social Attitudes: the 30th Report* (London: NatCen Social Research, 2013), p. ix.
7　Ibid, p. x.
8　A. Park and R. Rhead, 'Personal relationships: Changing attitudes towards sex, marriage and parenthood' in A. Park, C. Bryson, E. Clery, J. Curtice, and M. Phillips (eds.) (2013), *British Social Attitudes: the 30th Report* (London: NatCen Social Research, 2013), p. 17. Available online at: www.bsa-30.natcen.ac.uk (accessed 4 December 2018).
9　Ibid.
10　See Chapter 7.
11　See Figure 5.1.
12　*Daily Mail* 2 November 1984.
13　*Daily Telegraph* 23 January 1985.
14　J. Scott and E. Clery, 'Gender roles: An incomplete revolution?' in Park et al. (eds.) *British Social Attitudes: the 30th Report* (London: NatCen Social Research, 2013), p. 119.
15　Ibid, p. 122.
16　Ibid, p. 125.
17　J. Olchawski, *Sex Equality: State of the Nation 2016* (London: Fawcett Society, 2016), p. 10
18　Ibid, p. 12.
19　Ibid, pp. 8–9.
20　Ibid, p. 10.
21　S. Rowbotham, *A Century of Women* (New York, Viking, 1997).
22　*Equality: Timeline of women's rights 1866–2016* (London: Fawcett Society, 2016), p. 8. Available at https://www.fawcettsociety.org.uk/equality-its-about-time-timeline-of-womens-rights-1866-2016 (accessed 3 January 2018).
23　Scott and Clery, 'Gender roles', p. 126.
24　Ibid, p. 129.
25　D. Butler and G. Butler, *Twentieth-Century British Political Facts 1900–2000* (Basingstoke: Macmillan, 2000), pp 256–267.
26　Ibid; 'Election 2017: Record number of female MPs', BBC News Online, 10 June 2017. Available at www.bbc.co.uk/news/election-2017-40192060 (accessed 5 January 2018).

27  *Equality*, p. 8.
28  *Sun*, July 2002–May 2003 cited in *Culture Wars*, first edition, p. 230.
29  'Energy and climate change public attitudes tracker: wave 21' (2014) *Gov.uk*. Available at   https://www.gov.uk/government/statistics/energy-and-climate-change-public-attitude-tracking-survey-wave-21 (accessed 16 December 2017).
30  See Chapter 2.
31  'Ethnic targets for public services', BBC News Online, 28 July 1999. Available at: http://news.bbc.co.uk/1/hi/uk/405716.stm (accessed 10 December 2017).
32  The *Guardian*, 7 January 2001.
33  The *Guardian*, 5 July 1999.
34  The *Guardian*, 20 May 2004.
35  The *Guardian*, 11 February 2004.
36  For example, *Police Diversity* (London: House of Commons Home Affairs Committee, HC 27, 2016).
37  C. Airey, 'Social and moral values' in R. Jowell and C. Airey (eds.) *British Social Attitudes: The 1984 Report* (Aldershot: Gower, 1984), p. 129.
38  Ibid, p. 123.
39  Ibid, p. 128.
40  N. Kelley, O. Khan and S. Sharrock, *Racial Prejudice in Britain Today* (London: NatCen/Runnymede Trust, September 2017), p. 10.
41  R. Ford, 'Is racial prejudice declining in Britain?' *British Journal of Sociology*, 59, 2008.
42  R. Ford and A. Heath, 'Immigration: A nation divided?' in A. Park, C. Bryson and J. Curtice (eds.) *British Social Attitudes: the 31st Report* (London: NatCen Social Research, 2014), available online at: www.bsa-31.natcen.ac.uk (accessed 12 December 2017), p. 81.
43  Kelley, Khan and Sharrock, *Racial Prejudice*, p. 6.
44  Ibid, p. 9.
45  K. Sian, I. Law and S. Sayid, 'The Media and Muslims in the UK' (Leeds, Centre for Ethnicity and Racism Studies, University of Leeds, 2012).
46  R. Ford, 'The decline of racial prejudice in Britain', Manchester Policy Blogs, August 21, 2014 available at: http://blog.policy.manchester.ac.uk/featured/2014/08/the-decline-of-racial-prejudice-in-britain/ (accessed on 10 December 2017).
47  Ford and Heath, 'Immigration', p. 79.
48  Extensive research on press representations of immigration since 2002 is summarised in J. Curran and J. Seaton, *Power Without Responsibility*, 8th edition (London: Routledge, 2018).
49  See Chapter 10.
50  Changing attitudes to other moral and social issues are summarised in R. Harding, 'Key Findings – Personal freedom: the continued rise of social liberalism' in Clery, Curtice and Harding (eds.) *British Social Attitudes 34*.
51  J. Curtice 'The vote to leave the EU: Litmus test or lightning rod' in Clery, Curtice and Harding (eds.) *British Social Attitudes 34*, p. 178.
52  Ibid, p. 163.
53  Ibid, p. 165.
54  Lord Ashcroft, 'How the United Kingdom voted on Thursday … and why', *Lord Ashcroft Polls*, 24 June 2016, p. 9. Available at: https://lordashcroftpolls.com/2016/06/how-the-united-kingdom-voted-and-why/ (accessed 10 December 2017).
55  Ford and Heath, 'Immigration', p. 81.
56  D. Goodhart, *The Road to Somewhere* (London: Hurst, 2017).
57  This is examined in an illuminating book: A. Barnett, *The Lure of Greatness* (London: Unbound, 2017).
58  'Let that lion roar: Johnson's speech in full', ConservativeHome, 3 October 2017. available at: https://www.conservativehome.com/parliament/2017/10/let-that-lion-roar-johnsons-speech-in-full.html (accessed 6 January 2017).

59 Curtice, 'The vote', p. 167.

60 Barnett, *Lure of Greatness*.

61 These stories are anatomised in two key sources: Euromyths: A-Z index of euro-myths 1992 to 2016 (European Commission). Available at: http://blogs.ec.europa.eu/ECintheUK/euromyths-a-z-index/ (accessed on June 12 2017); and 'Guide to the best euromyths', BBC 23 March 2007. Available at http://news.bbc.co.uk/1/hi/world/europe/6481969.stm (accessed on June 11 2017). Those cited here are only a few examples from a very large number of fake news stories.

62 D. Levy, B. Aslan and D. Biron, 'The press and referendum campaign', Reuters Institute for the Study of Journalism, University of Oxford, 2016. Available at: www.referendumanalysis.eu/eu-referendum-analysis-2016/section-3-news/the-press-and-the-referendum-campaign/ (accessed 8 June 2017).

63 Ibid.

64 The evidence supporting this conclusion is presented in Curran and Seaton, *Power Without Responsibility*, (8th edition), chapter 9.

65 W. Jennings and G. Stoker, 'For the UK public, politics is failing because of the flawed character of our political class', *Democratic Audit UK*, 2 August 2013. Available at: www.democraticaudit.com/2013/08/02/for-the-uk-public-politics-is-failing-because-of-the-flawed-character-of-our-political-class/ (accessed 12 December 2017). In this context, it should be noted that John Curtice ('The Vote', p. 168 ff.) argues that political disaffection was a weak influence on the referendum result. However, this is contradicted by other evidence. It may be that the broad measures that Curtice used – standardised political trust and efficacy questions deployed for years in comparative research – failed to capture the distinctive dynamic of resentment and fear in the British context.

66 K. Swales, 'Introduction' in *British Social Attitudes 33* (London: NatCen, 2016) Available at www.bsa.natcen.ac.uk/latest-report/british-social-attitudes-33/introduction.aspx (accessed 10 December 2017).

67 R. Johnston, K. Jones and D. Manley, 'Predicting the Brexit vote: getting the geography right (more or less)', LSE British Politics and Policy. Available at: http://blogs.lse.ac.uk/politicsandpolicy/the-brexit-vote-getting-the-geography-more-or-less-right/ (accessed 10 December 2017).

68 *Lord Ashcroft*, 'How the United Kingdom voted', p. 9.

69 Ibid, p. 10.

70 Curtice, 'The vote', p. 166.

71 *Ashcroft*, 'How the UK voted', p. 10.

# 13

# WHAT GOES AROUND COMES AROUND

*Ivor Gaber*

This chapter seeks to put the relationship between Labour's left and the media into the context of the major changes that have been taking place in Britain's political and media landscape. What started as a revolt against the Labour establishment by predominantly young, mainly urban and overwhelmingly left-wing party members, has virtually come full circle. The Labour leadership in the 1970s and 1980s saw as 'impossibilist' and electorally suicidal the demands of the 'loony left' which had gradually taken hold among Labour's grassroots (particularly at local government level). Following Tony Benn's failed attempt to win the deputy leadership of the Party in 1982, the left continued with their demands which were, for the most part, successfully repulsed by the party leadership. For the next ten years, arguably until the emergence of New Labour, this battle continued, although as we have indicated, some of the 'loony left' agenda – particularly with regard to equalities – was adopted by the leadership. But under New Labour, these 'left' policies were not given a prominent role in Labour's election campaigns in 1997, 2001 and 2005 because the leadership believed that they would be electorally unpopular.

However, in 2010, after thirteen years in the political wilderness, David Cameron's Conservative Party defeated Labour and in the process adopted some of the very policies identified with the left – including greater tolerance of differing sexualities – that had been regarded as outlandish and electorally damaging when they were promoted by Labour's left. Cameron took up these policies in an effort to 'disinfect' the Tories of the 'nasty party' germ identified by Theresa May back in 2002, although not without earning the undying enmity of the right-wing press in the process, notably the *Daily Mail*. This enmity was exemplified by headlines such as 'How Mr Cameron's Obsession with Gay Marriage is Killing the Tory Party'[1] or 'The Evidence that Blows Apart Mr Cameron's Claim that Gay Marriage Will Strengthen Families'.[2]

Under Ed Miliband's leadership, Labour flirted with a little more of the 'loony-left' agenda but never with great conviction; it wasn't until Jeremy Corbyn won the leadership in 2015 that Labour's policy wheel finally came full circle, with much of the left's agenda finding its way into the party's election manifesto in 2017 – and with many of the key personnel from the 1970s and 1980s identified with the 'loony left', (including Dianne Abbot, John McDonnell and Corbyn himself) – in leadership roles in the party. What goes around, comes around.

In the 1980s, Labour's hierarchy reacted to the press hostility engendered by the apparent (albeit short-lived) pre-eminence of left-wing policies, by offering some rebuttal of the criticisms of their policies in ways that, they hoped, would not amount to directly confronting the press, nor offending either of the party's increasingly antagonistic wings. But, as recounted elsewhere in this volume, Kinnock and Blair (or at least those surrounding them) came to see the press attacks on the left as, to some extent, important allies in their own intra-party battles. This involved not just failing to offer a wholehearted defence of these left policies, and personnel, that were under attack but, in some circumstances, actively colluding in such initiatives, with the aim of isolating and ridiculing the left, its policies and personalities. In 1995, for example, Margaret Hodge who had undergone a transformation from 'loony-left' leader of Islington Council to enthusiastic Blairite, distanced herself from her previous incarnation by saying: 'We thought we could change the world by passing resolutions'.[3] The attacks on the left came to a head when former GLC Leader, Ken Livingstone, sought the party's nomination as Mayor of London. As outlined in detail in Chapter 8, high profile Labour politicians launched a series of coordinated attacks on Livingstone and his policies. For example, former leader Neil Kinnock wrote: 'While he [Livingstone] led the Greater London Council the stories of high rates, public money for stunts, control by soft-headed hard left groups poured out of the press almost every day'.[4] As part of this offensive Blair and Brown, even though they were then Prime Minister and Chancellor of the Exchequer respectively, devoted time, energy and political capital to launching a series of vitriolic attacks against Livingstone. One marker of the closeness of the New Labour leadership to the right-wing press in this period was the fact that between 2000 and leaving office in 2007, Tony Blair had thirteen by-lined articles (mostly written by Alastair Campbell) published in the *Sun*.[5]

By the mid-1980s, the 'modernising' tendency within the Labour Party had gained the ascendancy at Westminster; it had secured acceptance – sometimes grudging – in the union and constituency wings of the labour movement. But it had failed to incorporate the social movement wing of the broad left – centred on questions of gender, ethnicity, sexuality, environmentalism and peace – that eventually coalesced around Corbyn. And it failed to develop policies that addressed the problems faced by a growing number of young people: soaring rents, precarious jobs and, in the case of former students, enormous debts. Large numbers of young people joined the Corbyn insurgency.[6] There was also a grassroots revolt, fuelled in part by electoral despair caused by Labour's losses in

Scotland to the SNP and the advance of UKIP in northern Labour strongholds. It found expression in the desire to fight for what activists believed in, rather than in a focus-group orientated party which was seen to be failing.

Conservative press attacks and internal party division, in the context of a continuing neo-liberal political ascendancy, at first seemed likely to bury the Corbyn revolt. But the results of the 2016 referendum on whether the UK should stay in the European Union, and the 2017 snap election, exemplified that many of the old political structures were breaking down. A survey by the global PR firm Edelman in 2017 found that general levels of trust in all institutions in the UK were at all-time lows. The research revealed that trust in the government (in general rather than the current one) which was already low at 36% in 2016 had fallen to 26% the following year. Trust in the media fell even more sharply – down from 36% to 24%. Trust in businesses fell from 46% to 33% and charities from 50% to 32%.[7] A European Broadcasting Union survey of trust in the media, reinforced these results. It found that in 2017, Britons' mistrust of their press was, by a significant margin, the highest in a survey of thirty-three European countries.[8]

It also needs to be stressed that although many of the ideas once associated with the 'loony left' are now widely shared, they are by no means universally accepted; papers such as the *Daily Mail* continue to wage a continuous, and highly vocal, war against them. But because these ideas are no longer seen as being the property solely of the left, the ideological target is now, equally, 'liberal opinion' and the 'metropolitan elite', and the intended audience is clearly those who feel left behind by the forces of globalisation and urban modernity – in other words, many of those who voted for the UK to withdraw from the EU in the 2016 referendum. These campaigns found the judiciary a particularly tempting target, exemplified by headlines such as 'Enemies of the People',[9] 'The Judges Versus the People'[10] and 'End Human Rights Lunacy'.[11] The very word 'Brussels' and the phrase 'political correctness gone mad' became familiar signifiers in the toxic, and profoundly illiberal, populist narrative which came to dominate the right-wing press. Thus, a battle once waged against the relatively easy target of the 'loony left' has now swelled into a much wider ideological crusade against a whole strand of contemporary thought and opinion.

In terms of the narrative about the relations between the Labour Party and the news media, there are vast changes in the media landscape between 1975 and 2018, that have to be taken into consideration. 1975 is as good a starting point as any – it is the year in which one of the first references to the 'loony left' can be found. It appeared in an article in *The Times* quoting the Labour MP Les Huckfield, 'warning' the Tribune Group of Labour MPs that its criticism of the then Prime Minister, Harold Wilson put them in danger of earning the title the 'loony left'.[12] Huckfield made this remark (mildly ironic since he himself went on to be seen as a key player in the 'loony left') at a time when national newspapers, the clear majority of which supported the Conservative Party, dominated the news media landscape. Once the *Sun,* which had grown out of the

Labour-supporting *Daily Herald*, had switched its support to the Tories in the 1974 General Election, only the *Daily Mirror* was left as an unwavering supporter of Labour, with the *Guardian,* and then the *Independent,* as sometime friends – a situation that was to remain unchanged up until the time of writing in 2018. There was a period when Rupert Murdoch switched the *Sun's* support from a flagging Conservative Party to Tony Blair's New Labour, but it was always clear that this support was contingent – for the man not the party – because Murdoch judged the Conservatives to be quite simply unelectable whilst at the same time viewed Blair as someone who would not be hostile to his media empire. Indeed, Blair was not just commercially supportive but politically as well, as he demonstrated when the two both supported the US/UK invasion of Iraq in 2003. The transparency of Murdoch's support for Blair, as opposed to Labour was made dramatically clear when Gordon Brown took over the Labour leadership in 2007 and the *Sun* simply switched back to its natural home as an enthusiastic, and largely uncritical, Conservative-supporting paper.

Apart from the right-wing dominated press, in 1975 there were just three TV channels available in the UK, with the more radical Channel Four still seven years away from its first transmission. There were commercial radio stations but, then as now, both radio and television news were dominated by the BBC. ITV did compete on the news front and more challenging current affairs programmes were produced by the commercial public service broadcasters, whilst the BBC's (now defunct) Community Programmes Unit was always prepared to challenge dominant narratives. Nonetheless, compared with the current media landscape this now looks like sparse fare.

There is, more or less the same line-up of newspapers[13] and political weeklies, but by 2018 the sources of news and current affairs (and of course entertainment, an important ingredient in creating and sustaining political norms) have mushroomed. There are hundreds of TV and radio channels plus countless digital sources of news, information and opinion (not all of it, by any means, trustworthy) available as websites, blogs and ubiquitous social media. We are comparing the horse-drawn buggy with the driverless car – there is no comparison.

In the early 1980s, at the height of the 'loony left' offensive by the Conservatives and the right-wing press, Labour's attitude to the using the media was, at best, ambivalent. Media experts who were advising and training the Party's back and frontbenchers reported having to sit through debates with those on the left arguing that they should have nothing to do with the 'capitalist media' and should rely instead on traditional methods of getting their message across, whilst those on the right saw no major problem with the media's characterisations of Labour; indeed, as discussed earlier, some saw the media as allies in their intra-party battles.[14]

The visceral nature of such divisions was symbolised for one informant when, in a triumph of hope over experience, the party decided to produce a party political broadcast devoted to 'puncturing the myth' that there was a division between the party's leadership and its left wing. The idea was to feature Roy

Hattersley, then a leading figure on the right of the Party, and Eric Heffer, from the left, chatting amiably in a TV studio how 'that which unites us is far greater than that which divides us'. The broadcast, if not a disaster, was far from a triumph. The fact that prior to transmission, neither would meet with the other to discuss the script played no small role in the distinct lack of on-air chemistry between the two politicians and hence the programme's lack of credibility. Another broadcast, featuring a politician seen as on the right, Labour's Shadow Chancellor, Peter Shore, had to be re-edited at the last moment at the insistence of left-wing members of the National Executive, in order to include a voiceover at the end of the broadcast saying: 'That was Labour's Shadow Chancellor outlining the Party's economic policies as devised by the National Executive and approved by the annual conference' – hardly the sort of catchy end to a broadcast likely to provoke a positive response from the uncommitted.[15]

In other words, the Labour Party's problems with the media in this early period were partially of its own making. Its media operation was underfunded, amateurish and constrained by the very real political divisions apparent throughout the Labour Party. The political divisions might have remained but the Party's response to the battering it was receiving, spearheaded by the right-wing press, was shortly to change when, in 1985, Neil Kinnock appointed a little-known television producer, Peter Mandelson, as the Party's Director of Communications. In short order, Mandelson set about transforming the Labour's media operation into a more robust and proactive machine. Mandelson, at the urgings of advertising executive Phillip Gould, created the Shadow Communications Agency, out of which, as Chapter 6 has outlined, the New Labour spin machine emerged – a machine, that many came to see as both facilitating and symbolising the New Labour project. But what the machine did not do, indeed was never meant to do, was to challenge the press's version of the 'loony left' and the supposed damage they were doing to Labour's prospects of coming to power.

The other side of the transaction that needs to be considered are the journalists at Westminster, known as the lobby. Back in 1975 the lobby ruled supreme. It was made up of the 'gentlemen of the press' and men they overwhelmingly were. Jeremy Tunstall's landmark study of the lobby[16] paints a vivid picture of this powerful group who played a key role in setting the national political news agenda. Tunstall's work, and the more recent study by Sparrow (2003)[17] reveals the essentially (small 'c') conservative nature of the lobby – with its almost masonic code of conduct. It does not require a great leap of imagination to consider just and how far from what they regarded as 'legitimate politics' the activists of the new municipal left must have appeared. Members of the lobby spent their working lives cocooned within the narrow confines of Westminster, being briefed by the Prime Minister's Press Secretary twice a day and, in between, lunching and dining with 'contacts' in Westminster's plush watering holes. They worked closely together so that although they were always searching for the journalists' fabled 'scoops', none wished to stray too far from the consensus in, for example, in trying to understand, and represent to the public, the political changes that were sweeping through the Labour Party.

Unlike today, the lobby had a virtual monopoly on political information. There were hardly any accessible alternative sources of news and hence the lobby journalists' interpretation of political events went virtually unchallenged. After Prime Minister's Questions, for example, correspondents would gather around the Prime Minister's and Leader of the Opposition's spin doctors seeking their interpretation of the day's encounter.[18] After being briefed, they would then form another pack, made up of the more senior members, who would then agree among themselves the 'top line' for the day. They did this partly because it was useful to exchange views as to the precise meaning of the spin' they had just heard, particularly when the spinner was someone as skilful at the game as Tony Blair's spokesman, Alastair Campbell, but also because it saved them from having to deal with their respective news desks later that evening demanding to know why a rival paper had a different lead. The pack nature of the lobby was memorably described by one of their most distinguished members, Anthony Bevins, whose journalistic experience included stints on the *Independent*, *The Times*, the *Mail*, *Express* and *Sun*. He wrote:

> it is daft to suggest that individuals can buck the system, ignore the pre-set 'taste' of their newspapers, use their own news-sense in reporting the truth of any event, and survive. Dissident reporters who do not deliver the goods suffer professional death. They are ridden by news desks and backbench executives, they have their stories spiked on a systematic basis, they face the worst form of newspaper punishment – by-line deprivation. Such a fate is not always a reflection on professional ability. Over the last 20 years, I have known fine journalists broken on that wheel; they lose faith in themselves, and are tempted to give up the unequal struggle. It is much easier to pander to what the editors want, and all too often that is a pulverised version of the truth – the lowest common denominator of news.[19]

But this monopoly of parliamentary and political news by the lobby has, in recent years, been somewhat reduced.[20] First, because the amount of parliamentary, as opposed to political, news carried by newspapers – and to a lesser extent by television and radio – has dramatically declined. In 1988, all five national broadsheet newspapers – *The Times*, *Guardian*, *Telegraph*, *Independent* and *Financial Times* – carried at least one page of parliamentary reports. Within ten years, none did.[21] Perhaps more importantly, since 1989 the lobby's monopoly of the chamber has been broken as a result of the televising of the House of Commons' proceedings. This has meant that when it came to the big parliamentary occasions such as the annual budget, major debates and the weekly Prime Minister's Questions – depending on what the main TV bulletins chose to show – viewers were now able to form their own judgements as to how the politicians had performed.

On the other hand, the decline in parliamentary reporting over the past three decades has changed the overall tenor of political coverage and not necessarily in a way that has ameliorated the essentially anti-left bias of the majority of the press. If anything, it has been accentuated. This is because, with roughly the same number of journalists in membership of the lobby, its members' focus has increasingly shifted from reporting parliament to reporting politics. This entails using their parliamentary base as a means of gaining inside knowledge about Westminster politics – much of which is based on solid information, but some of which is little more than rumour, scandal and gossip. Given the predominant bias of the lobby members towards the Westminster centre of political gravity, this has meant that politics and politicians outside this consensus, either geographically or ideologically, are poorly reported – either as a matter of editorial policy or journalistic oversight. In particular, there has been an expansion in the prominence given to the parliamentary sketch writers – political journalists whose prime function is to amuse – hence, given the domination of right-wing newspapers, this has inevitably entailed an increase in the mocking and deriding of left Labour politicians with greater frequency and venom than that devoted to their opposite numbers on the right of the Conservative side.

A related development in 1989 was the launch of Sky News, the UK's first 24-hour television news channel, marking the beginning of the 24-hour news cycle that has so impacted on the working day of politicians and political journalists alike. Prior to this, political journalists needed only to look for the main story of the day, either for their newspaper or radio or television bulletins; but in the world of 24-hour news that no longer sufficed. A constant stream of updates, blogs, tweets, posts etc. was now required, leaving precious little time for original research or reflection.[22]

So, have all these changes in the political media landscape changed how the Labour left has been reported? We would argue not, because despite the plethora of new media outlets, the agenda-setting power of the national press has, in essence, remained, despite the best efforts of the broadcasters to keep to the impartiality rules that their regulator requires. This ongoing agenda-setting power was encapsulated by Robert Peston, a senior broadcast journalist at the BBC and ITV, who – as quoted in Chapter 9 – said that his colleagues at BBC News were 'completely obsessed' by the agenda set by newspapers and that they followed the news leads of the *Daily Mail* and *Daily Telegraph* too frequently.[23] This obsession is reflected by the fact that most TV and radio news outlets still persist in featuring a daily press review (news websites were added in 2017) – which gives a prominence to the mainly right-wing news agenda of the press, out of all proportion to the declining sales of newspapers in the UK.

There is another factor at work that needs to be considered and that is that, in addition to the right-wing bias of much of the national press, political journalists are also biased, not specifically to the right but towards the consensus as defined within the so-called Westminster village they inhabit. This was highlighted by the lobby's later failings to anticipate, and report fairly, Corbyn's victory in the

first Labour leadership contest he faced in 2015. As noted in Chapter 9, Katy
Searle, Editor BBC Political News, told a BBC radio audience:

> I would say on that occasion we could have done more to find a Corbyn
> supporter. There is a large number of MPs that are against Corbyn and
> you can find yourself in a programme environment where the majority
> of the view in that room is leaning against Corbyn and that's something
> that shouldn't happen ... Traditionally our focus here at BBC Westminster
> has been across the road and that Jeremy's leadership has made us look
> beyond that.[24]

But perhaps the major reason why political reporting has changed so dramatically over the period under consideration is, quite simply, because of the impact
of the digital revolution. Its initial impact on how politics was reported appeared
to be minimal. For despite the fact that more and more people were receiving
their news online, their primary sources are still the mainstream media, with
the websites of the BBC and the newspapers far and away the largest sources of
news – still largely the case, although less so for younger people. The broadcasters' regulator Ofcom, in their 2016 survey, found that, in terms of news consumption, television was used by 69% of respondents whilst print newspapers
were used by 29%, radio by 33% and online sources by 48%. However, when
it came to the sixteen- to twenty-four-year-old group, the figures change dramatically with 49% quoting television as their main news source and just 14%
quoting newspapers, 20% quoted radio but 63% said they used online sources to
access news.[25] The annual Reuters Digital News Reports finds a similar trend,
reporting that more than four in ten adults over sixteen accessed news via their
social media feeds. The Report also notes a continuing fall in trust in the media
down from 50% to 43% between 2016 and 2017.[26] However, the two Labour
leadership elections that Jeremy Corbyn faced in 2015 and 2016, and the General
Election in 2017, may have set in motion a change in both the production and
consumption of political news that could be transformative.

Commentators have described the 2015 election as the first real social media
campaign[27]. The success of the Conservatives in that election that took the pollsters and commentators by surprise, has, in part, put down to their superior social
media campaign in which they spent more than £1 million with Facebook on
highly targeted advertising, reaching specific voters in specific constituencies.[28]
But in 2017, it was Labour's turn to dominate the social media campaign, very
much based on Jeremy Corbyn's two successful leadership campaigns in the previous two years, when his supporters used Facebook Groups such as Red Labour,
to garner support for him and, in particular, to mobilise people to turn up to the
nationwide rallies that were a central part of his campaign.[29] These rallies, which
were replicated during Labour's General Election campaign two years later,
might have seemed like throwbacks to the rallies that characterised many of the
'loony left' campaigns of the 1980s (with even with the same cast of politicians)

but there was something else going on as well. In a digital age, the rallies had the sort of visual impact that was particularly effective on television and social media platforms. Supporters shared the still and moving images of the huge rallies that created a sense of excitement and momentum (also, not coincidentally, the name adopted by Corbyn's support network).

In 2017, according to the social media commentator Alec Cannock, the Conservatives, and to an extent their supporters in the press, were 'overwhelmed by the sheer passion and virality of an online movement on the Left'.[30] That passion stemmed from the successful experience of the Corbyn campaigners in the two leadership elections he had faced and the success of Momentum in organising and mobilising his supporters and would-be supporters. By the time of the 2017 election, Momentum consisted of 150 local groups, 23,000 members and 200,000 supporters; this formed the backbone of Labour's successful online campaign of persuasion and mobilisation.[31] Newswhip is a social media consultancy that analysed the parties' social media activities in the 2017 General Election. They found that there were 4,360,000 engagements with Jeremy Corbyn's Facebook page in the four weeks of the campaign, compared with just 554,000 interactions with Theresa May's. And the Corbyn campaign posted 217 messages and videos compared with 57 by the Theresa May team. There was the same disparity found on the parties' official Facebook pages, with Labour's 450 posts attracting 2.56 million engagements, while the Conservative's 116 posts attracted less than half as many at 1.07 million.[32]

In terms of content, the Corbyn and Labour pages featured a much greater ratio of videos, which achieved far higher levels of shares compared with the Conservatives. As the Newswhip site observed: 'In this election, native video on Facebook was the message of choice for the political social media managers, and their reach far outstripped that of most other formats'.[33] Corbyn and Labour didn't just get the message across, they got out the vote, using social media to persuade young people to register, campaign and then vote. Connock observes: 'During the campaign, a record 1.05m 18 to 24-year-olds registered, including a quarter of a million – that's almost three per second – on deadline day alone'.[34] In the last three days of the campaign, Labour spent £100,000 on the social media platform Snapchat, much preferred to Facebook or Twitter by many of the younger demographic that Labour was keen to reach. An unnamed senior Labour official said: 'We targeted every single young person in the country irrespective of seat. We got 7.8 million young people to see our advert. A million people clicked the link to see where to vote in the final forty-eight hours. Nobody has ever spent £100,000 on Snapchat before in British politics'.[35] Labour's use of Snapchat was in marked contrast to its relative lack of interest in Twitter, the social media of choice of most journalists and politicians.[36] This lack of interest meant that much of the ferment taking place within public opinion, particularly among younger voters, went largely unobserved by Westminster-based journalists. This might well have been a factor in their failure to pick up the mood of voters which led to Labour's unpredicted net gain of seats in the 2017 election.

Labour's skilful exploitation of social media is perhaps best symbolised by the tactic that Jeremy Corbyn is reported to have adopted during the weekly Prime Ministers Questions confrontation with the Prime Minister. Traditionally, leaders of the opposition have sought to use their allotted six questions to discomfort the Prime Minister and thereby achieve a clip on the nightly news. Corbyn still aspires to this with most of his questioning, but one, and sometimes two, of his questions are designed to be used as Facebook clips with a message that his followers will like and share – reaching an audience that probably never watches the main television news bulletins.[37]

There was another factor at work that has increased the impact of a left Labour message – and that was that the mainstream media has now been joined by a growing number of hyper partisan left-wing news blogs – the Canary, Evolve Politics, Skwawkbox and Novara Media being the most prominent. Collectively known as the alt-left, as opposed to the alt-right which played such a key role in Trump's election in 2016, these sites carry news stories from an unashamedly left perspective. Kerry-Anne Mendoza, who edits The Canary says: 'We are absolutely biased .... We're biased in favour of social justice, equal rights – those are non-negotiable things .... Every press organisation has an editorial stance and we're certainly no different'.[38] During, and since, the 2017 election, the alt-left sites ran an almost unceasing critical commentary of the political coverage of the right-wing press and of the BBC (the other broadcasters seemed to have been more or less ignored). In particular, they shone a harsh spotlight on the reporting of the *Daily Mail* and the *Sun* and the BBC's Political Editor, Laura Kuenssberg. The Political Editor of the Buzzfeed news website, Jim Waterson, noted that this aspect of their coverage – in terms of hits and shares – was the most popular. Overall, using web-based data, Waterson demonstrated that the ability of these sites to get their stories initially clicked through, and then shared, was more than three times greater than that achieved by the mainstream media. The sites claimed readerships to rival that of some of the main news websites – Canary claim its articles regularly achieve 500,000 views and Another Angry Voice has claimed that one of its articles reached 1.5 million views.[39] These figures were largely substantiated by the independent Enders Analysis media consultancy, which noted that the alt-left sites were reaching larger Facebook audiences than most of the mainstream media brands.[40]

Waterson found that journalists who contributed to the alt left sites were, in the main, not interested in cultivating relations with mainstream politicians, in marked contrast with their colleagues in the established media. He reports the complaints of Labour party communications staff who told him they found it easier dealing with the right-wing press than the alt-left websites – which no doubt did not reflect the experience of their predecessors when they were briefing the media against the party's left, as described in earlier chapters. 'I think an awful lot of political journalists let themselves get far too close to the politicians they are supposed to be holding to account,' Tom Clark from Another Angry Voice told Waterson.[41]

All of which begs the question as to whether the affordances of digital media – news websites, alt-left blogs and the social media – have significantly undermined the power and influence of the right-wing press? Before seeking to answer this question, it is important to bear in mind that the alt left sites only began to make an impact during Corbyn's 2015 campaign. Their rise was, to some extent, a reaction against the success of some of the right-wing sites. It is worth noting that, according to Feedspot, a site that runs a weekly monitor of the metrics of political blogs, of the top ten most popular blogspots in the UK, of those sites that have an obvious party bias four are Conservative-supporting and two are Labour-supporting[42]. Two of the most prominent are the relatively mainstream Conservative Home (which claims an annual readership of three million)[43] and the unashamedly ultra-right, but highly successful, site 'Order-Order' – better known, as Guido Fawkes, the nom de plume of its founder, Paul Staines. The Guido site – which can be seen as at the cutting edge of Britain's alt-right – claims that in 2016 it had 42 million individual visits, compared with just under 20 million in 2010.[44] Staines has also forged a fruitful relationship with the *Sun*: he has a weekly column, he feeds the paper a string of exclusives and his most recent news editor, Harry Cole, joined the *Sun*'s political team. Other right-wing sites have equally useful relations with sections of the right-wing press so that a symbiotic relationship has developed between the two. This is in marked contrast with the alt-left sites that see the Labour-supporting press – the *Guardian* and *Mirror* – more as enemies than allies.[45]

But to conclude it is necessary return to the question of whether the power of the right-wing press has, in 2018, diminished in comparison to where it stood in 1975. If the answer is yes, or even 'possibly', then the new digital news environment is only half the story. The other half is the remorseless decline in newspaper sales that we have witnessed over the past two decades, as the economics of the media industries have been radically disrupted by the economic power of the major online players – primarily Google and Facebook. The challenge has been twofold and unremitting. First, the online news sites and social media platforms supply extensive news and feature content apparently for free (apparently because the price paid for access to most new sites is the users' personal data which becomes a valuable commodity in the hands of the online data consolidators – although this does not apply to the BBC which is one of the major online news providers). Second, because of this ostensibly free access, advertisers have found it far more cost-effective, in their search for their target audiences, to divert most of their advertising budgets to the online media. In 2017, internet-based advertising in the UK was £10.3billionn, up 13.6% on the previous year. By contrast, the spending on national print newspapers and magazines was just over £1billion, down 10% on the 2016 figure.[46]

This is not to suggest that the right-wing newspaper editors and proprietors have become toothless, penniless bulldogs. They still exercise great power through both their print and online publications if not as much through direct contact with their readers but, as referred to earlier in this chapter, through their influence on the news agendas of the BBC and other broadcasters. A YouGov poll after the 2017 election indicated that 32% of respondents said that it was newspapers that helped them choose who to vote for, compared to 16% who relied on social media sites. However, the poll also showed 51% of eighteen- to twenty-four-year-olds thought social media more influential, compared to just 28% who opted for newspapers; and 58% agreed that the 'advent of the digital age has diminished the influence of newspapers', but 48% said they still thought that newspapers have a 'significant impact on the outcome' of elections.[47]

The influence of newspapers is also, paradoxically, being assisted by the very online media that is causing them such problems and against which they inveigh daily. This assistance takes the form of two types of amplification of their news and views. First, because those news brands that have maintained free access online are still major media players – not just in the UK, but internationally as well. The *Mail Online* and the *Guardian* are in the world's top ten news sites – the *Mail* with 53 million monthly visitors and the *Guardian* with 42 million (in both cases, their largest readership is in the UK) and both have substantial followers on Twitter and Facebook.[48] The second way in which their content is amplified is via social media. Social media is now accessed by approximately two thirds of the over-sixteen population in the UK[49] and, although they might not see direct posts from the mainstream media, much of the general discussion derives from items that have first seen the light of day in the national press.

So, to try to answer the question posed earlier: the right-wing press is still perhaps the most important factor in making the weather in which politics is conducted (on and offline). However, Labour, and its left in particular, which in the past found itself being deluged by Tory-supporting newspapers, now can gain some protection from the inclement political weather by sheltering under their digital umbrellas. Whether this will provide them with sufficient protection over the long-term, remains to be seen.

## Notes

1  A. Pierce *Daily Mail* 26 July 2012.
2  P. Morgan *Daily Mail* 23 May 2013.
3  P. Routledge 'We got things wrong; profile; Margaret Hodge: the former Islington leader is finding it politic to eat humble pie' *Independent* May 28 1995.
4  N. Kinnock *People*, 21 November 1999.
5  Based on Nexis search results.
6  According to YouGov in the 2017 election among first time voters (those aged eighteen and nineteen), Labour was forty-seven percentage points ahead. 'How Britain Voted in the 2017 Election'. https://yougov.co.uk/news/2017/06/13/how-britain-voted-2017-general-election/.
7  Edelman Trust Barometer UK Findings. https://www.edelman.co.uk/magazine/posts/edelman-trust-barometer-2017-uk-findings/.
8  European Broadcasting Union (2017) 'Trust in the Media'. https://www.ebu.ch/news/2017/05/trust-gap-between-traditional-and-new-media-widening-across-europe.

9 Headline in an article in the *Daily Mail* 4 November 2016 attacking the Supreme Court ruling that the final decision on Britain leaving the UK had to be taken by Parliament.

10 *Daily Telegraph* headline 4 November 2016.

11 *Daily Express* headline 15 May 2006.

12 P. Symon 'Tribune group to discuss tactics after Wilson letter' *The Times* 17 June 1975.

13 Over this period of time the only daily to have ceased publication altogether is the short-lived *Today*, whilst the *News of the World* was forced to close as a result of the phone hacking scandal and the *Independent* has become an online-only newspaper. But the *daily I*, originally an off-shoot of the *Independent*, has established itself as a tabloid-size 'serious' paper. There has also been the establishment of the *Metro* freesheet which now distributes close to a million copies a day; it is published by the *Mail* group but seeks to be non-political in its coverage.

14 Information in this section is based on a series of informal private conversations with Labour media advisers; in particular the late Veronica Crichton – who, after a career as a Labour Party press officer and as Ken Livingstone's press officer, was a freelance party adviser and trainer.

15 Ibid.

16 Tunstall J. *Westminster Lobby Correspondents: A Sociological Study of National Political Journalism* (London: Routledge, 1970).

17 A. Sparrow *Obscure Scribblers: A History of Parliamentary Journalism* (London: Politicos, 2003).

18 See Gaber, I. 'The slow death of the Westminster lobby: the impact of the MPs' expenses scandal on political journalism' *British Politics* 4(4), 2009 pp. 478–497 for a fuller account of the workings of the lobby.

19 A. Bevins 'The crippling of the scribes' *British Journalism Review* 1(2), 1990 pp. 13–17.

20 Ibid.

21 J. Straw 'Democracy on the spike' *British Journalism Review* 4(4), 1993 pp. 45–54.

22 For more on this topic see I. Gaber 'The lobby in transition' *Media History* 19(1), 2013 pp. 45–58.

23 Quoted in the *Guardian* 'Robert Peston: BBC follows the *Daily Mail*'s lead too much' Maggie Brown and Jason Deans 6 June 2014.

24 Katy Searle speaking on Radio 4 *Feedback* 16 September 2016.

25 *News Consumption in the UK 2016* Ofcom June 2017. https://www.ofcom.org.uk/__ data/assets/pdf_file/0016/103570/news-consumption-uk-2016.pdf.

26 *Reuters Institute Digital News Report 2017*, (Oxford: Reuters Institute for the Study of Journalism). https://reutersinstitute.politics.ox.ac.uk/sites/default/files/Digital%20 News%20Report%202017%20web_0.pdf.

27 See 'The social media campaign: mobilisation and persuasion' D. Jackson and D. Lilleker in *Political Communication in Britain: polling campaigning and media 2015* Wring, Mortimore and Atkinson (Basingstoke: Palgrave Macmillan, 2017) pp. 293–314.

28 Ibid.

29 See R. Prince *Comrade Corbyn: A Very Unlikely Coup: How Jeremy Corbyn Stormed to the Labour Leadership* (London: Biteback Publishing, 2016).

30 Connock, A. 'Social death: how did millennial liberals lose the history's most digital elections?' in *Brexit, Trump and the Media* Mair et al. (eds) (Bury St Edmonds: Abramis, 2017) p. 386.

31 T. Shipman *Fall Out: A Year of Political Mayhem*, (London: HarperCollins Publishers, 2017).

32 Corcoran, L. (2017) How Labour and Jeremy Corbyn won the UK social media election, in three charts 13 June 2017 https://www.newswhip.com/2017/06/ labour-won-uks-social-media-election/.

33 Ibid.

34 Connock op cit, p. 388.
35 Quoted in T. Ross and T. McTague, *Betting the House: The Inside Story of the 2017 Election* (London: Biteback Publishing, 2017).
36 See J. Waterson 'The rise of the alt-left British media' *BuzzFeed* 6 May 2017. https://www.buzzfeed.com/jimwaterson/the-rise-of-the-alt-left?utm_term=.hsxBy80B2#.jce1lJA1X
37 See S. Bush 'Even as the Tories stumble, Labour is drifting, rather than marching, towards power' *New Statesman* 1 December 2017.
38 Ibid.
39 Ibid.
40 Connock op cit, p. 390.
41 Waterson op cit.
42 Top 25 UK Political Blogs & Websites on the Web Feedspot 16 December 2017. https://blog.feedspot.com/uk_political_blogs/.
43 *Conservative Home* – Advertise https://www.conservativehome.com/advertise.
44 *Order-Order* Review of 2016. https://order-order.com/2016/12/30/review-of-2016/.
45 Waterson op cit.
46 D. Ponsford 'UK advertising market grew to record £21.4bn in 2016 as Google and Facebook took the lion's share' *Press Gazette* 25 April 2017. www.pressgazette.co.uk/uk-advertising-market-grew-to-record-21-4bn-in-2016-as-google-and-facebook-took-the-lions-share/.
47 K. Schofield 'Newspapers more influential than social media during general election – poll *Politics Home* 26 July 2017. https://www.politicshome.com/news/uk/culture/news/87853/newspapers-more-influential-social-media-during-general-election-poll.
48 'Top 15 most popular news websites' *eBizMBA* website July 2017. www.ebizmba.com/articles/news-websites
49 *Adults' Media Use and Attitudes Report* Ofcom 2017. https://www.ofcom.org.uk/__data/assets/pdf_file/0020/102755/adults-media-use-attitudes-2017.pdf.

# INDEX

Sheep' 72–5; CRE (Commission
for Racial Equality) 190; education
82; immigration 187–8; institutional
racism 195, 197; Jews 187; Miliband,
Ralph 219–20; otherness, Ed Miliband
222–4; racism 191–2; Red Ed 220–1,
226–7; sex education 87–9; Winter of
Discontent (1978-9) 144
*Daily Telegraph* 65, 178; congestion charge
176, 244; CRE (Commission for Racial
Equality) 190; *Future of Multi-Ethnic
Britain* 201–3; institutional racism 195–6;
'race relations industry' 210; racism
192; reaction to report on racism 204;
Red Ken 176; sex education 94, 98;
targeting Labour 206–7
Dampier, Phil 63–4
Davies, Liz 174
decline in voters, Labour Party 126–9
delegitimating the new urban left 129–30
Democracy Day 48–9
Demos 183
Denning, Lord 42, 99
disturbances 27–8
diversity 182–3; anti-anti-racism 189–93;
*Future of Multi-Ethnic Britain* 201–4;
racism 198–201
divided parties, power of the press 121–6
"Dodgy dossier" 177
Doran, Anthony 72
Duffy, Gillian 179
Dyke, Greg 245
Dymond, Jonny 232

*East Anglian Daily Times* 65
*East London Advertiser* 186
Edgar, David 190
education: sex education *see* sex education
Education (No. 2) Act 1986 101
Education Bill 96–8
*Education for All* 192
effects research 118
Eggar, Timothy 65
elective dictatorship 16
Englishness 159
environmentalism 244–5
equality 159; gender equality 167–8,
242–4
ethnic diversity 182–3; *Future of
Multi-Ethnic Britain* 201–4
ethnic minorities 9–10
*Evening Star,* 'Baa Baa Black Sheep' 73
*Evolve Politics* 234
*Express and Star* 65
extreme spin 144

Facebook 234, 260–1
fake news 76–8
Falklands War 19
Farage, Nigel 225
Fawkes, Guido 263
fear 155, 158
feminism, 7, 10–11, 242–4
festivals, GLC (Greater London
Council) 46–9
Field, Frank 124
Fielding, Steven 155–6, 170–1
*Financial Times* 148–9; Wood, Deirdre 150
Finklestein, Daniel 235
Finlayson, Alan 142–3
Fitt, Lord 99
Fitzgerald, Julia 130
focus groups 169–70
folk devils 58
Foot, Michael 37, 140, 144–6, 235
Football Association 245
framing 118
Freedland, Jonathan 2, 222
Freedom Association 116n57
'Freedom Fighter of the Angry Suburbs'
88–91
future of multi-ethnic Britain 201–4
*Future of Multi-Ethnic Britain* 205, 210,
212, 213

Gale, George 18, 87
Gallagher, Noel 199
Gallagher, Paul 125
Gavron, Lady Kate 208–9
gay issue 111 *see also* homosexuality;
sex education
gay liberation 8, 11–12, 20, 32, 241–2
Gay Liberation Front 8
*Gay News* 83
gay rights 174
Gay Unity Group (Harrow) 32
gays 82–3; positive images 85–8
gender 20
gender equality 242–4; New Labour 167–8
general management committees
(GMCs) 157
generational war, Labour Party 17–21
GLC (Greater London Council) 9, 10,
28; abolition of 39, 119–20; advertising
campaigns 44–6; attitudes toward GLC
abolition 44–6; Coin Street project
13; community campaigning 46–9;
gay liberation 12; government's failure
to convince the people to abolish
49–52; grants 33–4; homosexuality
32; mirage of press power 119–21;